"In this visionary book, Professor Kolodziej brings to bear his lifelong formidable expertise in world politics to raise the alarm over the retreat of the liberal democratic model among nation states in the face of the rising challenge and growing influence of the competing authoritarian model, driven and promoted by China and Russia. The volume consists of an original analytic framework, referred to as OWL (Order, Welfare, and Legitimacy), which facilitates a comparative evaluation of the liberal democratic, Chinese, and Russian solutions to global governance. Reading the book will be highly rewarding to students and practitioners of international politics in pursuit of foresight and insight into the evolution and transformation of the international system, the great powers' competitive attempts at shaping it, and the resulting end-state of global governance."

Yaacov Vertzberger, Emeritus Professor of
International Relations, Hebrew University of
Jerusalem.

"A penetrating and provocative look at liberal-democratic and authoritarian approaches to the challenges of geo-political order, global economic systems and welfare, and contending claims of legitimacy. The author, who brings to bear his lifelong formidable expertise in world politics, comes down squarely on the side of liberal-democratic global governance. The book will be highly rewarding to students and practitioners of international politics."

Janice Gross Stein, Founding Director, Munk
School of Global Affairs and Public Policy,
Belzberg Professor of Conflict Management,
University of Toronto, Canada.

"Successful societies are based on order, welfare, and legitimacy. The liberal democratic model has been more successful than any other in meeting these criteria. In this tightly reasoned, compelling, and clearly written book, Kolodziej asks how the Westphalian system might be more effectively infused with democratic values in the face of challenges from a rising China and revanchist Russia."

Richard Ned Lebow, Professor of International
Political Theory, Department of War Studies,
King's College London, UK.

"In a post-pandemic world, our emerging global society cries out for governance — providing order, welfare, and legitimacy to the anarchic trends of the present. Steering between the current competition between democracy and autocracy, Kolodziej envisions new forms of democratic governance that rise above national interests to deal with worldwide crises. Thoughtful, stimulating, and future-oriented, this book will become even more relevant in the years to come."

Mark Juergensmeyer, Distinguished Professor of Sociology and Global Studies, Founding Director, Orfalea Center for Global and International Studies, University of California, Santa Barbara, USA.

"*Global Governance* has a very large virtue—it grounds the current Sino-American contest over approaches to international order in a comparative framework. All national and international systems face the needs to achieve order, welfare, and legitimacy. China and America have chosen different approaches to global governance and the contest between them will be a critical determinant of how the Twenty-First Century unfolds."

David M. Lampton, former Dean of Faculty and Professor and Director of China Studies Emeritus, Johns Hopkins School of Advanced International Studies (SAIS), USA. He currently is Senior Research Fellow at the SAIS Foreign Policy Institute, Washington, D. C.

GLOBAL GOVERNANCE

How do we prevent the next pandemic? Will governments successfully tackle climate change? Will they find ways to close the gap between the haves and have-nots and to eliminate poverty? Which solution – democratic or authoritarian – will determine the global governance of a flawed nation-state system?

This unique contribution to global studies advances a multidisciplinary theory that the governments of all human societies are the tenuous outcome of the competing solutions to the Imperatives of Order, Welfare, and Legitimacy (OWL). The OWL paradigm provides a common framework to evaluate the contrasting responses of the liberal democratic, Chinese, and Russian solutions to global governance. Underscored is the volume's contention that global governance is the overriding issue confronting nation-states and the diverse and divided peoples of what is now a global society for the first time in the evolution of the species.

The volume addresses a wide spectrum of audiences, united in their shared resolve that the democracies prevail in a projected century-long struggle between democratic and authoritarian regimes to determine global governance. Scholars, teachers, students, elected officials, policy analysts, media professionals, and engaged citizens who make self-government work will profit from this visionary and provocative study.

Edward A. Kolodziej is Emeritus Research Professor of Political Science and Founder and Director of the Center for Global Studies, University of Illinois Urbana-Champaign, USA.

GLOBAL GOVERNANCE

Evaluating the Liberal Democratic,
Chinese, and Russian Solutions

Edward A. Kolodziej

Routledge
Taylor & Francis Group

LONDON AND NEW YORK

Cover image: Matthew Kolodziej, Owl, 2021, acrylic on canvas, 56 x 65 inches

First published 2022
by Routledge
2 Park Square, Milton Park, Abingdon, Oxon OX14 4RN

and by Routledge
605 Third Avenue, New York, NY 10158

Routledge is an imprint of the Taylor & Francis Group, an informa business

British Library Cataloguing-in-Publication Data
A catalogue record for this book is available from the British Library

Library of Congress Cataloging-in-Publication Data
Names: Kolodziej, Edward A., author.
Title: Global governance: evaluating the liberal democratic, Chinese, and Russian solutions/Edward A. Kolodziej.
Description: Abingdon, Oxon; New York, NY: Routledge, 2022. | Includes bibliographical references and index. |
Identifiers: LCCN 2021032387 (print) | LCCN 2021032388 (ebook) | ISBN 9781032125442 (hardback) | ISBN 9781032159737 (paperback) | ISBN 9781003246572 (ebook)
Subjects: LCSH: International organization–Philosophy. | International cooperation–Philosophy. | Power (Social sciences) | Human security. | Legitimacy of governments.
Classification: LCC JZ1318.K6515 2022 (print) | LCC JZ1318 (ebook) | DDC 327.1/1–dc23
LC record available at https://lccn.loc.gov/2021032387
LC ebook record available at https://lccn.loc.gov/2021032388

ISBN: 978-1-032-12544-2 (hbk)
ISBN: 978-1-032-15973-7 (pbk)
ISBN: 978-1-003-24657-2 (ebk)

DOI: 10.4324/9781003246572

Typeset in Bembo
by Deanta Global Publishing Services, Chennai, India

To Three Muses
Late and Soon
Always in Tune

Anna, Alba, Antje

CONTENTS

PREFACE

The coronavirus pandemic has threatened every human being on earth. The piecemeal, uncoordinated, contradictory, and deeply flawed responses of state and non-state actors to this global crisis have exposed the profoundly debilitating absence of a universal government to address this scourge. The same dysfunction dogs other issues plaguing humans – mitigating global warming, protecting the world's ecology, sustaining economic growth, ameliorating poverty and gross inequality, preventing nuclear war as well as countless other issues.

This volume contends that the search for global governance is the primordial issue confronting humans, whether recognized by them or not. Absent governance no human society can survive, replicate itself, and thrive. This constraint is no less predicable of what is now, in ever-widening scope, rapidly accumulating thickness and depth, an increasingly connected and interdependent nation-state system, and the emergence of a global civil society for the first time in the evolution of the human species.[1]

The quandary confronting the states and peoples of the world is that they are too divided against themselves to become anytime soon, if ever, a tightly woven social fabric out of which an effective and legitimate government can be fashioned to collectively and constructively address their shared concerns. Humans are too disaffected by culture, religion, ideology, and language, split irreparably by clashing loyalties to tribe, ethnicity, and nations, and further rent by race, class, social status, gender, and sexual orientation.

There is no exit from their parlous plight. It is largely the unintended evolutionary product of the choices these tool-making, linguistically and conceptually endowed social animals have made. Over tens of thousands of years, they have repeatedly opted to take roads not taken before to create numberless new and oft times contending societies, marked by ceaseless wars over thousands of years. The contemporary anarchical, war-prone state system exacerbates and animates the profound mutual animosities informing the world's populations. Blocked are cooperative solutions to their inextricably entwined discontents.

What will pass for global governance in the foreseeable future will principally revolve around the conflict between two visions of global government within a nation-state system. The first is the liberal democratic model. It is currently under severe stress both internally and externally.[2] The failures of the liberal democracies to minister to the rights that accrue to the freedom and equality of their citizens gravely weaken their ability to create a Westphalian system with democratic characteristics.[3] In falling short of their promise they impair their capacity to meet the formidable challenges posed by authoritarian regimes to define global governance: an autocratic China under Chinese Communist Party (CCP) rule, tilting progressively toward totalitarianism, in tandem with the rise and infectious spread of illiberal, populist democracies, modeled on the Russian Federation and the regime of President Vladimir Putin.

President Joseph Biden's presentation to the 2021 Munich Security Conference echoes the central argument of this volume:

> We are in the middle of a fundamental debate about the future and direc-tion of our world. We're at an inflection point between those who argue that, given all the challenges we face — from the fourth industrial revolu-tion to a global pandemic — that autocracy is the best way forward … and those who understand that democracy is essential — essential to meeting these challenges.[4]

China and Russia want a Westphalian nation-state system with authoritarian characteristics. These regimes and their authoritarian counterparts cannot suffer liberal democracies. The Achilles heel that afflicts these regimes is their illegiti-macy when compared to the liberal democratic model. They do not rest on freely consented social contracts founded on majority rule and respect for civil liberties and human rights, possessed not only by the citizens of democratic states but by all humans as intrinsic rights.

Beijing and Moscow and other non-democratic regimes correctly conclude that their survival depends on disrupting and ensuring the failure of democratic governance, eroding the collective power of the liberal democracies, and extin-guishing the history of their achievements by vilifying their effectiveness and legitimacy. Liberal democratic regimes and the freedoms their citizens enjoy as well as their active engagement in how they will be ruled, however imperfectly, directly threaten their authoritarian rivals.

What is the value-added of this volume?

First, it globalizes Hannah Arendt's insight that "no cause is left but the most ancient of all, the one, in fact, that from the beginning of our history has determined the very existence of politics, the cause of freedom versus tyranny."[5] What Arendt was referring to, as the beginning of politics, was the fatal civil war between the allies of Athenian democracy versus those of authoritarian Sparta. That struggle has now been expanded to embrace all of the nation-states of the Westphalian system. No less engaged are all peoples today, whether free or oppressed.

Second, this volume advances a new way to think about governance within the constraints and vexing defects of the nation-state system. Any relevant theory of global government must begin with the flawed starting point of this war-prone system. Working within a nation-state system is one of the few points of agreement of most peoples whether under democratic or authoritarian rule.[6] Conversely, the emergence of a global society, comprising a nation-state system cleaving the world's populations into its national components, has blurred state boundaries and drawn populations and states closer together to reveal their interdependencies as never before. This volume meets a need to go beyond and enlarge mono-causal security,[7] economic,[8] sociopolitical,[9] cultural, or moral approaches[10] to explain how the global society is, or should be, governed. These discrete studies are necessary, but insufficient, to accurately portray either the multiple interrelated levels on which global governance, however currently impaired, functions or the causal interdependence of its central components.

Given the porousness of state boundaries, global politics is no longer just a struggle among nations for power, nor just what economic system will produce the most material wealth and equitably distribute that welfare among a population. Nor is the struggle just about who has a right to rule and who is obliged to obey. All three dimensions of governance – the geopolitical order, global economic systems, and contending claims of legitimacy – must be understood, as the moving, perpetually interactive, and mutually contingent parts out of which human societies fashion an effective and legitimate government.

Chapter 1 advances an interactive, multidisciplinary understanding of how the governments of all human societies are formed and sustained. I conjecture that governance can be provisionally defined as the capacity of humans, as social animals, to create working solutions, simultaneously, to three competing, fundamentally incompatible imperatives: Order, Welfare, and Legitimacy (OWL). The OWL framework is a "mental model."[11] Absent simplification of the complexity and causal interdependence of the principal components of governance, an understanding of the challenges and the dilemmas of governance cannot be fully understood. The governing regimes of human societies are both indispensable if a society is to survive, thrive, and replicate itself, and, paradoxically, responses to OWL imperatives are permanently unstable and vulnerable to collapse and implosion.

A singular focus on the discrete issues confronting the world's divided and distressed peoples obscures the necessity of governance as a prerequisite for their resolution. The OWL paradigm provides explanatory purchase in answering the question of why human societies arise and endure. The chapters below attempt to explain governance today at the level of the nation-state system and of the global civil society as a whole, encompassing all of the world's populations as a unit of analysis, to establish the premise of this discussion: that governance is the central challenge of this century.

Each OWL imperative is autonomous. Each possesses its own unique form of power, distinct process of decision-making to determine how its power will be used, and enabling actors who exercise the imperative's power to which they are consigned in pursuit of its end game objective, as if unconstrained by the countervailing power of competing imperatives. As Michael Mann suggests, each OWL imperative is "functionally promiscuous."[12] The holders of power of each imperative strive to occupy the governing spaces otherwise accorded its rivals. An effective and legitimate government is the evolving outcome of a pragmatic, oft times precarious, balance struck by the members of a society in responding to these ceaselessly contesting imperatives of power, inspiring and directing the behavior of states and peoples.

OWL power imperatives, braided tri-causal underpinnings of governance, are predicable of all human societies, since their first appearance in Africa. They are no less at work in the contemporary contentious pursuit of global governance. The power exercised by each of these autonomous but interdependent imperatives in shaping the government of human society is as variable and differentiated as human imagination allows, constrained principally by the environments in which this creative process unfolds.[13] The actual solutions developed by countless, discrete human societies in response to OWL imperatives are numberless in their architectural structures and in their substantive composition across human societies over time and space. To bring this interminable pursuit of governance up to date, the following chapters evaluate the contrasting responses of the liberal democratic, Chinese, and Russian models to OWL imperatives.

As the discussion proceeds, it is important to keep in mind what this volume is *not* about. I have eschewed casting the challenge of global governance within the contesting academic paradigms of current theories of international relations.[14] None fully services the broader purposes of this volume. The two most prominent schools – Realism and Liberal Institutionalism – capture some but scarcely all of the principal dynamic forces, which must be included, as interdependent moving parts, to explain the struggle for global governance. The limited paradigms of these two schools are incorporated into the OWL framework. The Imperative of Order draws on Realist theory through Thomas Hobbes; Liberal Institutionalism provides insights into the Imperative of Welfare through Adam Smith and to a lesser extent Karl Marx. Neither school adequately addresses the Imperative of Legitimacy. I rely on Jean Jacques Rousseau's understanding of legitimate rule and power to explicate and explain the response of states and peoples to the Imperative of Legitimacy as one of three central components of governance. Legitimate authority, invested by citizens in those who govern them, fundamentally distinguishes liberal democracies from their autocratic rivals. The Imperative of Legitimacy, an autonomous social power, assigns greater agency to individuals as well as to social groupings and movements to explain their governance than prevailing theories of international relations.[15]

Chapter 2 adopts a multidisciplinary approach to briefly review the responses of the liberal democratic states to OWL imperatives from the end of World War II to the implosion of the Soviet Union and the end of the Cold War in 1991. This period marks the ascendancy of the liberal democratic coalition and the magnetic attraction of the liberal model as a provisional solution to global governance. US Secretary of State Dean Acheson quite rightly observed that he and America's democratic allies, who erected the liberal democratic architecture for global governance after World War II, were *Present at the Creation.*[16]

For the Imperative of Order the liberal democracies accomplished two unprecedented achievements. By pooling their security interests in alliance, they relaxed the Hobbesian dilemma among themselves in which states in an anarchical system are induced to perpetually fear each other and to ceaselessly prepare for war to protect their security interests. By integrating their military resources they also magnified their collective power across OWL imperatives to contain the Soviet Union.

For the Imperative of Welfare the democracies created a global trade and financial market system, fueled by self-sustaining scientific discovery and technological innovation. It fostered unprecedented economic growth and provided ever-increasing material welfare for democratic populations as well as for those under authoritarian rule, notably China. The system promoted free and unfettered disposition of private and corporate assets across national boundaries. Beginning with the Marshall Plan to revive devastated European economies after World War II, the United States, initially at considerable expense to itself, underwrote the market system as a public good beneficial to all participants. In the long run it also benefited the American people as a return on investment.

The response of the liberal democracies to the Imperative of Legitimacy was their most significant achievement. Each national regime pledged its commitment to the moral ideal that every human was free and equal and that each national population had the inherent right to choose how it would be ruled and by whom. These ideals and the shared values on which they rested unified the democracies as the foundation for their claimed morally superior response to the Imperative of Legitimacy than that of their authoritarian adversaries.

Chapter 3 traces the fall of the liberal solution at the very time, ironically, that scholars and statesmen among the liberal democracies were predicting its inevitable ascendancy and expansion under the alleged hegemonic leadership of the United States.[17] From the perspective of this discussion, the process of erosion, which continues to the present, is rooted in the departures of the liberal democracies, principally the United States, from their postwar OWL solutions to global governance.

Chapters 4–6 apply the OWL template to China. Substantially contributing to the loss of power of the liberal democratic coalition has been the rise of a self-assured, economically and technologically advanced China on its way to military parity with the liberal democracies. Under the oppressive rule of the Chinese Communist Party (CCP), it challenges the current primacy of liberal democratic government. It offers its own model for other states and peoples to adopt as their solution to OWL imperatives.

Only one chapter, Chapter 7, is devoted to President Vladimir Putin's solutions to OWL imperatives. Russia's modest material power (California has a greater GDP) and Putin's crabbed vision of global governance warrant only a chapter. Whereas China has the leadership cadres, domestic regime control, resources, and resourcefulness to be considered a global power, Putin's Russia is consigned a subordinate spoiler's role in efforts to undermine the liberal design. Except as a model for illiberal populist rule, it has little else to offer other peoples. It is a disruptive regional power with outsized global pretentions, ruled by a corrupt, arcane, backward-looking autocrat, bent on restoring Russia again as a great power by tearing the liberal democracies down. From the perspective of game theory, the Russian model of global politics posits the interdependent exchanges of the states and peoples of the global society as implacably win-lose, zero-sum.

A concluding chapter suggests modest ways to strengthen a Westphalian system with liberal democratic characteristics. The liberal OWL model must not only be preserved but must also be substantially modified to meet the challenges of this century. Neither objective will be easy to achieve. This is not a short-run enterprise. A formidable China blocks the way to the future, aided by a reactionary Russia, obsessed with the past. There is, more importantly, the slide toward illiberal populist rule within former liberal democracies, exemplified most prominently by the since defeated American administration of President Donald J. Trump.

Even if the space accorded liberal democratic rule in global governance can be assured, by no means certain, there remains the resistance of populations around the globe to adopt the liberal model. Many are culturally and religiously opposed to Western values. Its moral principles and the heavy investments in civil engagement needed to make democracies work, as de Tocqueville recognized almost two centuries ago, have little appeal for many peoples.[18]

Strong resistance to liberal democratic rule does not diminish or denigrate this model's promise. The collective military, economic, technological, and scientific resources of the liberal democracies are a match for their principal rivals, China and Russia, and their fellow travelers. The liberal democracies hold the moral high ground that all humans are free and equal and have an inalienable right to choose those who will govern them. Only those governments are legitimate which are founded on these principles. The urgency of the moment, but the endeavor of this century, is to scale Abraham Lincoln's aspiration for the United States to the level of the global society: that government of, by, and for the people shall not perish from the earth. To paraphrase and widen the scope of Benjamin Franklin's prediction at the signing of the American Constitution: the democracies must hang together or, most assuredly, they will hang separately.

Edward A. Kolodziej
University of Illinois, Urbana-Champaign

Notes

1 Parag Khanna provides a detailed mapping of the material rise of a global society
  (Khanna, 2016); Linda Colley complements his depiction by tracing the global circu-
  lation of contending claims of legitimacy in the writing of constitutions since roughly
  the 18th century (Colley, 2021).
2 Diamond (2019); Ikenberry (2020); Kurlantzick (2013); Levitsky and Ziblatt (2018);
  Przeworski (2019).
3 As used in this volume, the Westphalian system refers to the accord of rival states that
  ended the Thirty Years War in 1648. Each state was recognized as a sovereign equal.
  Sovereignty also extended to the principle of non-interference in the internal affairs
  of the state, enshrined in Article 2 of the United Nations Charter. For a comprehensive historical review of the Westphalian system, consult the works of Paul Schroeder.
  See, for example, Schroeder (1994a, 1994b).
4 www.whitehouse.gov › 2021/02/19 › remarks-b...
  See also *The New York Times*, February 19, 2021, for another copy of the transcript
  as edited.
5 Arendt (1963, p. 11).
6 Hedley Bull, among the founders of the English school of international relations,
  provides a coherent explanation of the underlying global order of an otherwise anarchical state system. See Bull (1977).
7 Mearsheimer (2001); Waltz (1979). These self-proclaimed neorealists narrow realist
  theory to security. For a classical, balanced, and more nuanced understanding of realism, see Morgenthau (1985).
8 Hayek (1988); Rodrik (1998, 2012); Stiglitz (2006); Piketty (2014, p. 248).
9 Cerny (2010).
10 Lebow (2009); Singer (2011).
11 For a brief explanation and illustration of the utility of using mental models, see
  Richard Baldwin's historical review of the systemic changes in human trade from
  hunter and gatherer societies to the global market system of today (Baldwin, 2016,
  pp. 111ff).
12 Mann (1986, p. 17).
13 Jared Diamond develops how chance circumstance and differing environments help
  explain why some human societies have more power than others. See J. Diamond
  (1997).
14 I have elsewhere evaluated these and other contending schools of international relations in Kolodziej (2005).
15 A recent and excellent history of liberal institutionalism is Ikenberry (2020).
  Legitimacy does not play a central role in Ikenberry's narrative; the word itself does
  not appear in the index. Most of the key differences between realism and liberal
  institutionalism are presented in Robert O. Keohane's edited volume. See Keohane
  (1986). The liberal institutionalism approach is spelled out in R. O. a. J. S. N.
  Keohane (1989).
16 Acheson (1969).
17 Fukuyama (1992); Huntington (1991).
18 Marc Juergensmeyer's numerous and informed writings about religion and politics,
  caution against optimism that the liberal democratic model has much appeal to large
  segments of the world's populations. See Juergensmeyer (2003, 2008, 2005).

ACKNOWLEDGMENTS

This volume was inspired and informed by my experience as Founder and Director of the Center for Global Studies (CGS) at the University of Illinois from 2001 to 2016. Thanks to the distinguished faculty at the university and its world-class library, the largest state library in the United States, the Center was able to win four successive Department of Education-sponsored national competitions for funding and for being named a National Center for Global Studies.

Faculty across the campus, including the humanities, social sciences, information sciences, law, education, physical and biological sciences, engineering, and agriculture, launched new and exciting global studies courses at all levels in their disciplines. What clearly emerged was the reach of globalization into every field of knowledge. This fundamental transformation of the academy's teaching and research is scarcely unique to the University of Illinois. What CGS was able to do was fuse these otherwise siloed bodies of knowledge and research into a coherent, expanding global studies and degree program.

In important ways this is also a family affair. Antje, my wife of over 60 years, deployed her practiced editorial skills and sharp, critical eye to free the manuscript of countless spelling and grammar gaffs. I am responsible for any remaining rhetorical errors of omission or commission.

My son, Matthew, Professor of Art at the University of Akron, generously allowed me to use one of his arresting paintings for the cover. Going beyond filial obligation, he also permitted me to rename the triptych as OWL, reflecting the Imperatives of Order, Welfare, and Legitimacy, the conceptual tools used to compare and evaluate the liberal democratic, Chinese, and Russian solutions to global governance. I have so much confidence in the originality and creativity of Matthew's OWL painting that I welcome readers to initially judge the volume by its cover.

Appreciation extends to the two anonymous evaluators of the manuscript whose positive reviews advised publication. I am also indebted to the volume's endorsees, valued colleagues with whom I have had the pleasure to interact over the years. They are distinguished faculty at five eminent universities in four countries, adding an inadvertent global trope to the volume. Sincere thanks, too, to Anvitaa Bajaj, the editorial assistant, who expertly navigated this manuscript through the contract phase of the process. I am no less grateful to Mr. Narayanan Ramachandran and Anna Dolan and their staff for their professional handling of the editing and printing of the volume.

Edward A. Kolodziej
Champaign, Illinois

1

TOWARD A THEORY OF GOVERNANCE

Pursuit of Order, Welfare, and Legitimacy (OWL)

Let me stipulate at the outset what we all already know: with expanding reach and accumulating depth, humans are globally connected as never before in the evolution of the species.[1] They are entwined by multiple digital and media networks as well as interlocked by ground, sea, and air transportation systems. More entangling still is their unprecedented interdependence. What an individual, community, nation, or state may want depends on the cooperation of other actors, most of them anonymous. No need for additional examples than the coronavirus and global warming threats to all humans and the need for cooperation to cope with them, if not necessarily to fully resolve them.

We need not dwell on the obvious that globalization, as the product of connectedness and interdependence, is now profoundly embedded in the biological, psychological, social, political, and moral composition of all humans. Humans are now members of a global society of their own creation, whether they consciously acknowledge or deny this transformation of the human condition or whether they are merely observers and free riders on those engaged in its doings. Much hangs on whether humans, having constructed this society, an amalgam of deliberate choice and accident, will collectively make the necessary and difficult choices to affirm what they have wrought for their mutual benefit or whether they will allow their differences and disputes, deep and abiding, to plunge them unwittingly into a regressive spiral to their undoing. The decisions made by the world's populations and their social agents in addressing their shared and multiple and multiplying problems will determine to which endpoint they will be directing their common fate.

In positing what's real, namely the existence of a global society, it becomes readily apparent that, in light of the millennial experience of the species, no human society – and now a global society – can replicate itself over time, survive,

DOI: 10.4324/9781003246572-1

and thrive in the absence of a government.[2] What is tantamount to a tautological proposition raises the challenge posed by this volume. What we need is a provisional theory of governance that can conceivably be predicated of any human society beyond the particulars of time, place, and circumstance associated with each human society and epoch. What are, analytically, the common structures of power, decisional processes, and the actors executing the tasks and functions of governance and empowered to rule? Such a theoretical framework, however provisional, is needed to evaluate the current competing solutions for global government of the liberal democracies, China and Russia.

This chapter lays out a template within which to evaluate these competing models for the governance of globalization. It makes no pretense to being a theory of government. Its principal use is as a framework to assess the rival claims of these leading candidates to govern the interdependent transactions of the states and peoples of the world society.

The template rests on the conjecture that every human society must respond simultaneously to three competing imperatives in fashioning a government that works for that society: The Imperatives of Order, Welfare, and Legitimacy (OWL).[3] Solutions to these imperatives are innumerable over the evolution of the human species and over the countless societies, which humans have constructed. What is constant are these three competing underlying imperatives of governance. Each represents a distinct structure of power, incentives for rational decision-making to realize the endgame of each imperative, and in complex societies differentiated actors associated with each imperative.

These imperatives are not derived out of thin air. Their roots are embedded in the thinking and behavior of all human societies since the first creation of government among hunter-gatherer tribal groupings.[4] They are also revealed in the contributions of theorists who identified the relevance of a particular OWL imperative to a theory of government. I rely on Thomas Hobbes for Order, Karl Marx and Adam Smith for Welfare, and Jean-Jacques Rousseau for Legitimacy. Their thinking scarcely exhausts what remains to develop a tested theory of government through rigorous and comprehensive empirical and historical analysis. OWL imperatives are a starting point. They provide useful analytic tools to diagnose the governing health and ills of a global society.

The diversity of solutions to OWL imperatives across time, space, and circumstance does not demonstrate the absence of a universal structure to all human governments. Rather, it invites the search for such a structure. This discussion conceives OWL imperatives as the underlying elements and incentives for human choice in the construction of all governments. These analytic tools are helpful in comparing and evaluating the solutions to these imperatives launched by the United States and the liberal democracies after World War II and, more recently, by the Communist Party of China (CCP) and the Russian Federation under President Vladimir Putin as competing models for global governance.

Thomas Hobbes and the Imperative of Order

Let's begin with Thomas Hobbes. Breaking with Greek thought and Christian theology, focused on defining and creating an ideal polity on earth, Hobbes posited the Imperative of Order as one of the indispensable building blocks of the theory and practice of government. Hobbes's ordered society, a social construct of his creative intellect, is conceived to be outside of time and circumstance. That conceptual move permits him to fashion an analytic tool predicable of all societies — his own, most long gone, and still those yet to be constructed. In his imagined state of nature, before the formation of human society, humans are portrayed as in perpetual conflict with each other; all are at war with each other to get what they want and need from others. Left to their own devices, this is the underlying, inescapable nature of the human condition. To escape this fearsome predicament humans enter society to ensure their personal security, property, and freedom to pursue a myriad of other interests. Hobbes's description of this dismal and no-exit plight still remains telling:

> Whatsoever … is consequent to a time of Warre, where every man is Enemy of every man; the same is consequent to the time, wherein men live without other security, than what their own strength, and their own invention shall furnish them withal. In such condition, there is no place for Industry; because the fruit thereof is uncertain; and consequently no Culture of the Earth; no Navigation, nor use of the commodities that may be imported by Sea; no commodious Building; no Instruments of moving, and removing such things as require much force; no Knowledge of the face of the Earth; no account of Time; no Arts; no Letters; no Society; and which is worst of all, continuall feare, and danger of violent death; And the life of man, solitary, poore, nasty, brutish, and short.[5]

Only on entry into society can humans escape the unrelenting threat of violence besetting them. Only when humans fashion an order — a government — for a society can morality, norms, rules, and law come into existence. For these salutary benefits of social life to be realized, Hobbes contended that they had to enter into a social compact to consign overwhelming awesome power to a Leviathan. The Leviathan provides order as a prerequisite to realize the benefits sought by humans, which are endangered in a state of nature. He has awesome and overwhelming power to arbitrate differences and disputes between members of a society and to ensure that laws are observed. The tenure of the Leviathan's monopoly of power depends on furnishing an order for the society. Humans have the reciprocal right to expect order. Absent its provision, a new social contract would then have to be created for a reconstituted Leviathan undergoing a process of transformation likely to be no less violent than those which prevailed before humans entered into society.

There are several implications of Hobbes's theory of order that are relevant to a theory of government. First, all human societies are rooted in violence, both in escaping a ceaselessly threatening state of nature and in forming a government for society. Second, since force must necessarily be imposed on members of a society because the inclination to use force remains embedded in each person, then it stands to reason that the Leviathan, too, must be wary that its monopoly of power is always under the threat that it can be overthrown, This leads to the ironic conclusion that all solutions to the Imperative of Order are susceptible to dissolution. Each order that is established by force is exposed to being replaced by force again in a never-ending spiral as humans leave and return to a state of nature in each undoing of a seeming stable order.

What Hobbes's conception of order implies is that all solutions to the Imperative of Order are conventional, temporary, and temporal. In other words, a final solution to the challenge of order as a fundamental component of governance, while theoretically insoluble, is pragmatically attainable for a defined length of time. Much like Sisyphus humans are compelled to construct a time-bound order and government to forestall a downward spiral of perpetual conflict and the re-enactment of the tragedy of being human and prone to violence. The human condition of ever-threatening disruption and disarray can be relaxed and its adverse consequences tolerably lowered and contained, but never surmounted. The rise and fall of countless human societies and of their innumerable solutions to the Imperative of Order through history suggest that the specter of upheaval and dissolution accompanies all humanly devised governments, however creatively or cleverly they may have been fashioned.

A friendly amendment is necessary to Hobbes' conception of what it means to be human – ever under the threat of violence being visited on humans – and the assignation to a Leviathan with a monopoly of power to contain that threat. It is important to distinguish between Hobbes's revelation of the underlying violence of all governments and his then contemporary recommendation of a Leviathan. Hobbes conflates his pure theory of order with his belief that such an all-powerful entity is needed to quell the religious civil wars raging throughout England in the 17th century. From the perspective of a theory of government, the Imperative of Order depends on the choices made by humans as to which social entity they assign, or are compelled to assign, the monopoly of violence to rule them. The choice of a Leviathan admits to countless provisional solutions, whether in a king, chief, charismatic leader, junta, party, oligarchy, or elected representatives. What is inescapable is the response to the Imperative of Order in its pristine form. The "is" of the human condition should not be confused and obscured by the "ought" of what social entity should be accorded a monopoly of coercive power and the mantel of the Leviathan, however conceived, to surmount the underlying condition of a war of all against all.

Karl Marx and Adam Smith and the Imperative of Welfare

To found a theory of government solely on its origins out of force and violence does violence to the theory itself. Two theorists, Karl Marx and Adam Smith, introduce us to the Welfare Imperative. It is an essential element of the governance of all human societies. Responses to the Imperative of Welfare crystallize into an autonomous power structure, decisional-processes, and incentives for actor behavior. These characteristics of the power of the Imperative of Welfare are analytically distinguishable from the Imperative of Order. This distinction holds true even when these two imperatives are conflated, say among hunter-gatherer communities[6] or the feudal arrangements of premodern Europe or China.[7] The melding of Order and Welfare Imperatives can also be observed in the centralization of the power of these imperatives in the government of the Soviet Union, a solution to governance, which eventuated in the implosion of the regime.

According to Marx, the origins of the Welfare Imperative arise from the bio-sexual composition of humans as social animals:

> (M)ankind must first eat, drink, have shelter and clothing before it can pursue politics, science, religion … that therefore the production of the immediate means of subsistence and consequently the degree of economic development attained. … in a epoch form the foundation upon which state institutions, the legal conceptions, art, and even ideas of religion, of the people concerned have been evolved, and in the light of which they must, therefore, be explained and not vice versa.[8]

A century earlier, Adam Smith advanced a complementary starting point for the Welfare Imperative. He stipulated that the drive for human material betterment was endemic to humans as social animals. That precondition disposed humans to rely on each other to foster their shared need to "first eat, drink, have shelter and clothing." Smith explained that need as the inherent human "propensity to truck, barter, and exchange one thing for another."[9] The implication of this starting point of the Welfare Imperative is that humans can be expected to strive relentlessly to adopt best practices as their knowledge expanded of how to increase their material betterment.

On this score, Smith and Marx are in accord. Humans will seek and choose best practices for their individual and collective material advantage, if humans are not otherwise hindered or prevented by the power constraints arising from the Imperatives of Order or Legitimacy.

Several examples illustrate the frustration of best practices. The Soviet Union's centralized economy privileged the security of the Communist Party over the material benefits of participating in a global free market. For many Muslims, usury is rejected as contrary to their faith. Financing debt to promote economic growth is hampered as a result. Jared Diamond describes how the Norsemen sought to recreate their homeland's environment in Greenland rather than adopt the successful survival practices of Greenland's native population. That proved disastrous. Relying on their conditioned solutions to the Imperative of Legitimacy, drawn from their religious beliefs, their flawed responses to the Imperative of Welfare led to the eventual failure and dissolution of the settlement.[10]

While Smith and Marx converge on the human drive to material betterment, they radically departed in their contradictory conception of human freedom to effect this choice. For Smith freedom is the beginning point. Humans, equipped with unlimited tool-making capabilities as well as complementary cognitive and linguistic endowments, unlike brute animals, were able to use these unique animal resources to increasingly improve their material lot. In our epoch the fruits of these endowments and strivings to do better are the Industrial and Informational Revolutions and the global spread of their productive efficiencies through a progressively universal market system.

The road forward, as Smith intuitively grasped, but could not fully foresee, would be widespread social and political upheaval to bring about best practices. Before reaching this latest stage of material development, authoritarian regimes, feudal systems, plantation slavery, empires, guilds, and community mores, which restrained trade and economic development, would have to be destroyed. The very conception of wealth also had to be redefined as the accumulation of material goods by as many members of a society as possible rather than the amassing of gold and silver to fill the coffers of monarchs. Human values and moral constraints would have to be transformed into economic transactions and self-interested exchanges to facilitate the workings of the market.[11] What could not be predicted, when Smith penned the *Wealth of Nations,* were the tens of millions of deaths and destruction, which would result in the price of establishing a global market system. A free-market system was not a free good.

Adam Smith's stipulation that humans have an intrinsic "propensity to truck, barter, and exchange one thing for another"[12] disposed them to increase trade and investment on a global scale to sustain perpetual economic growth. Best economic, if not moral, practices would prevail over time, driven by human freedom and fueled by self-interest. Adam's classic portrayal of how these qualities work, if unleashed through global markets, would eventually replace less efficient and effective systems of economic production and exchange. His vision of a globally connected and interdependent market system aiding all humans remains the most compelling argument for its creation:

> In civilized society [man] stands at all times in need of the co-operation and assistance of great multitudes. ... It is in vain for him to expect it from their benevolence only. He will be more likely to prevail if he can interest their self-love in his favour, and shew them that it is from their own advantage to do for him what he requires of them ... It is not from the benevolence of the butcher, the brewer, or the baker, that we expect our dinner, but from their regard to their own interests. We address ourselves, not to their humanity but to their self-love, and never talk to them of our own necessities but of their advantages.[13]

Smith foresaw that the unexpected result of a selfish pursuit of wealth results, ironically, in the creation of multiplying public goods potentially available to all participants in a global market system. The self-interested economic actor, Smith explained,

> intends only his own gain, and he is in this, as in many other cases, led by an invisible hand to promote an end which was no part of his intention. Nor is it always the worse for the society that it was no part of it. By pursuing his own interest he frequently promotes that of the society more effectually than when he really intends to promote it.[14]

The unintended result is, in theory, the greatest amount of material plenty to the largest number.

Where, for Smith, human freedom is the starting point for best practices, it is Marx's utopian endpoint for humanity. Humans would be set free when capitalism was destroyed. As noted earlier, Marx concluded that capitalist markets, which Marx experienced in their early development, led to unequal and inequitable outcomes and to wretched lives for the millions drawn into its maw. Those who owned and controlled the means of production (best practices) enjoyed wealth well beyond what they contributed to the public good. They used their economic and technological monopoly and accumulated wealth to seize the coercive power of the state and oppress workers (the proletariat). Only the overthrow of a ruling capitalist class and the transfer of ownership of the means of production to the proletariat (the working class) could lead to human freedom and plenty.[15]

Under capitalism workers suffered because their social condition was determined for them. Marx insisted that "it is not the consciousness of men that determines their being, but on the contrary it is their social being that determines their consciousness."[16] Capitalism imprisoned them in social cages for the benefit of capitalists.[17] Once unshackled from the oppressive rule of the capitalist system and in control of the means of production, Marx's utopian endgame, the consciousness of workers would no longer be subject to their social being since they were now free and in possession of themselves. In a sense the history of oppressors and oppressed would end. Humans finally would be conscious of their freedom and their creativity.

Smith's and Marx's contrasting conceptions and evaluation of capitalist markets have important implications for the reach and impact of the Imperative of Order. The power structures of Order and Welfare are promiscuous.[18] While each is autonomous, their boundaries are permeable. There is a perpetual struggle for dominance of one over the other. For Marx that tension is embedded in the tendency of the capitalist system to oppress the working class.[19] The system also generates conflicts among capitalists and disposes them to war to gain ascendancy. For Smith, a market system has the opposite effect. It encourages cooperation to maximize human wealth and welfare for all of the participants.

That objective cannot be achieved under conditions of authoritarian rule, imperialism, and war.

Emmanuel Kant drew on Adam's expectation of peace through bartering and trucking:

> For *the spirit of commerce* sooner or later takes hold of every people, and it cannot exist side by side with war. Thus states find themselves compelled to promote the noble cause of peace, though not exactly from motives of morality. And wherever in the world there is a threat of war breaking out, they will try to prevent it by mediation, just as if they had entered into a permanent league for this purpose; for by the very nature of things, large military alliances can only rarely be formed, and will even more rarely be successful.[20]

Note that Kant expects self-interest rather than humanitarian idealism to promote peace. The state's monopoly of violence would be disciplined to facilitate commerce, protect private property, and regulate commercial exchange through the rule of law.

Conversely, Vladimir Lenin seized on Marx's portrayal of inherent social conflict, arising from the inequality and inequity of capitalist markets, notably finance capitalism, as the principal cause of World War I.[21] Capitalists not only oppressed a global working class but were also in conflict with each other. Lenin attributed World War I to the struggle among imperialist capitalists for hegemony. From an OWL perspective, Lenin portrayed the pursuit of the Imperative of Welfare in its capitalist form as the instrument by which to overwhelm the power claims of the Imperative of Order. Capitalists captured the state's monopoly of violent power to enforce their rule.

It is important not to get bogged down in the pros and cons of capitalism, whether viewed from the perspective of Adam Smith or Karl Marx. The aim of briefly sketching their ideas, however much they have been surpassed since their composition, is to reveal the analytic category of the Imperative of Welfare underlying both presentations of free markets. What is significant for a theory of governance is to identify the Welfare Imperative as independent of the Imperative of Order, each with its own claims on the other. Given the complexity of modern life, each has an autonomous structure of power with its own differentiated processes of decision-making and possessed of actors principally associated with its management and operation. In contrast, in the early life of humans when almost all were hunter-gatherers, these elements and their functions were melded in the governance of these relatively small communities. The distinction between the Imperative of Welfare and the Imperative of Order as well as the contrasting incentives for choice driving each component become clearer when the liberal democratic, Chinese, and Russian responses to these imperatives are developed in the following chapters.

Jean-Jacques Rousseau and the Imperative of Legitimacy

Rousseau introduces the Imperative of Legitimacy as coequal to the Imperative of Order and Welfare. The latter imperatives are vulnerable to power and dictation of the response of a society to the Imperative of Legitimacy – and vice versa. To better understand the contribution of Jean-Jacques Rousseau to the theory of governance, it is helpful to recall the centrality of human freedom for Rousseau, Hobbes, Smith, and Marx in responding to OWL imperatives. It is remarkable how all rely on human freedom to develop their contributions to OWL theory but reach radically different conclusions about its implications for human behavior.

All share the assumption that humans are free, but draw entirely different implications for the social consequences of their competing conceptions of freedom. Hobbes posits perpetual conflict as humans are in constant war with each other in a state of nature. For Smith, the opposite is the case; human drive to truck and barter encourages cooperation to realize the *Wealth of Nations*, to promote individual prosperity, and to result in the accumulation of private property. Marx condemns the capitalist system as impeding freedom. Humans strive for freedom but the capitalist system blocks their pursuit. Once overthrown and the factors of production are under the control of the proletariat (or all those who are oppressed), the resulting utopia sets humans free.

Rousseau takes issue with each contributor to the theory of government on his own terms. Like Hobbes he assumes a state of nature in which he conjectures that all humans are free and, therefore, are equal. Their existential being is neither material nor biological but fundamentally moral, immaterial, immanent, and subjective. Contra Hobbes, humans enter into a social contract with themselves to decide what form of government should rule them. Authoritative and legitimate rule comes from the bottom up, not from the top down through a Leviathan. The social contract creates the Leviathan and infuses that governing mandate with the authority and power to rule legitimately. Rousseau's conception of legitimacy on which liberal democracies rely to define legitimacy is fundamentally opposed to the conception of legitimacy of the Chinese Communist Party, as Chapter 6 delineates, or of populist majoritarian rule of Putin's Russia, the subject of Chapter 7. The people, not the Party, are the origin of legitimacy whose consensual content is defined not only by the constituent or institutional components of legitimate rule but also by the contextual or historical experience of a given population.

The opening pages of Rousseau's *Social Contract* summarize his case for legitimacy as intrinsic to governance:

> Man … is born free and everywhere he is in chains. One who believes himself the master of others is nonetheless a greater slave than they. How did this change occur? … What can make it legitimate? … If I were to consider only force and the effect it produces, I would say that as long as

a people is constrained to obey and does so, it does well; as soon as it can shake off the yoke and does so, it does even better. For in recovering its freedom by means of the same right used to steal it, either the people is justified in taking it back, or those who took it away were not justified in doing so. But the social order is a sacred right that serves as a basis for all the others. However, this right does not come from nature; it is, therefore, based on convention.[22]

Rousseau establishes the Imperative of Legitimacy as one of the three components of all governments. His solution to this Imperative, while of crucial importance for establishing the superiority of democratic rule, is tributary, first of all, to his contribution to a theory of governance. The Imperative of Legitimacy must be addressed in some form for a government to survive and for a society to thrive. Legitimacy also assumes an autonomous structure of power with unique processes of decision-making and incentives for the direction of human behavior in competition with those arising from the Imperatives of Order and Welfare. Reducing the Imperative of Legitimacy to Order, undergirded by coercive intimidation or pure force, as Hobbes would have it, or to Marxist insistence on economic determinism dismisses the indispensability of legitimacy as a determinant of the construction of human societies and their governance. Marx, in particular, has the causal arrows running in the wrong direction. Rousseau stipulates that the consciousness of men determines their being, not their social being which they are free to change at their bidding. These social chains into which humans are born are at the mercy of their freedom to achieve self-government.

Rousseau makes his case for the Imperative of Legitimacy by doing what Hobbes did before him. He reformulated the question animating the Greek hold on Western political philosophy and its value system. Like Hobbes, who departed from the Greek search to discover the ideal polity by substituting the question of order as the first question to be posed, so Rousseau also departed from the search for the constituents of an ideal polity, posed by Plato's *Republic* and *The Laws*.[23] Rather than attempt to answer a question that could not be answered, what is the ideal polity, the appropriate and answerable question to be posed was what social contract, based on human free choice, is the solution to legitimate rule for a particular people. The search for legitimacy in natural law was equally futile. The social contract was a human creation. Nor was the Greek and subsequent Western philosophical search for a just society in natural or theological exegesis any more pertinent. Legitimate rule, not justice or an ideal polity, was the imperative to be addressed. It is an imperative to which humans were equipped to respond as a derivative of their endowed capacity of free choice.[24]

Second, social contracts, arising from the freely expressed will of a people to govern their affairs, have the effect of informing not only the moral composition of each member of a society but also his or her very personal identity. Legitimacy empowers a people, not just those invested with the authority to govern. That power could then be relied upon to determine what solutions should be devised to respond to the Imperatives of Order and Welfare. As Rousseau observes, "the social order is a *sacred* right [italics added] that serves as a basis for all the others." Within the meaning of OWL imperatives, I take his characterization of the social order as the basis for all other orders, that is, for my purposes the Imperatives of Order and Welfare.

Whereas material tests can be submitted to assess the solutions to these latter two imperatives – who has the monopoly of power or what are best practices – legitimacy and legitimate rule are immaterial and subjective. They derive from the value systems humanly created and deeply held by a population and its leadership. Whereas pragmatic and workable solutions can be forged for members of society to accept a given order or welfare system, the same cannot be predicated of rival social contracts. Compromise is not readily achieved since the very moral composition of a society and the personal identity of those loyal to a particular social contract are being challenged.

Rousseau's conjecture helps explain the countless forms of social contracts fashioned by human societies since their appearance in the evolution of animal life on earth. In our own era, we readily witness this immense confusion of competing value systems and rival conceptions of legitimacy. Religious beliefs – Muslim, Christian, Buddhist – attract the allegiance of tens of millions. Secular ideologies – Fascism, Nazism, Communism, majoritarian populist, and liberal democracy – command the loyalty of still other millions. The dark side of this parlous condition is that conflict is generated as a function of divergent and irreconcilable principles of legitimacy.[25] The presumed peaceful solution to legitimacy of a particular human society translates into unremitting conflict between and among competing social contracts.

Against the background of this brief for OWL imperatives as the analytic and power components underlying all human governments, it is important to draw one final conclusion before reviewing and evaluating the three leading candidates for global governance. It should be readily apparent from even a casual reading of the history of government, from contemporary experience, and the pure logic and promiscuousness of each Imperative that no government, however well constructed and however well the balance struck among the competing claims of OWL imperatives, can ever reach a stable equilibrium. Which then of the three models to be evaluated is likely to change and institute reforms in governance to meet new challenges and exploit opportunities as they arise for the benefit of the citizens which these alternative models of a government are presumably expected to serve. The challenges of striking that balance are made infinitely more problematic under conditions of unremitting conflict between and among OWL solutions within an anarchical nation-state system.

This volume opts for restoration and strengthening of the liberal democratic coalition and model for global governance that emerged from the chaos of World War II. This is not just a plea for a return to a past that was also fraught and far from what the Greeks might have viewed as the realization of an ideal global polity. Nor is it a call for the return to OWL solutions that are now outdated to effectively surmount contemporary constraints or to exploit new opportunities for a better world. The return advocated here is to revalidate the coalition of liberal democratic regimes so that, collectively, they will have a significant, potentially even a dominant, say about what governance can be fashioned out of social conditions of a diverse and divided world population now confronting entirely new Order, Welfare, and Legitimacy challenges.

The following chapter outlines the responses of the democracies to OWL imperatives between the end of World War II and the rise of the liberal democratic model to ascendancy.

Notes

1 The most comprehensive presentation of the connectedness and interdependence of the world's peoples see the Preface, n. 1.
2 For support of this proposition, consult (Finer, 1999). For additional support, consult Fukuyama (2011), which provides additional support largely from the Imperative of Order perspective.
3 I have profited enormously from the magisterial work of Michael Mann. See Mann (1986, 1990). He deconstructs the social composition of all human societies into four competing sources of power: economic, ideological, military, and political. In drawing on his conception of social power, I decompose the governance of all human societies into three imperatives of power: Order, Welfare, and Legitimacy. OWL imperatives capture less of social power than Mann's conceptually more expansive lenses. For my purposes, a narrower focus has the virtue of making more precise the threefold imperatives of power underlying global governance, while affording me the conceptual tools to compare competing solutions to the elusive challenge of governing a global society both contemporaneously and through history.
4 Blainey (1976).
5 Hobbes (1997, p. 70). I have relied on the Flatman edition of the *Leviathan*, because it parallels my own view that Hobbes intended his conception of what makes humans human was meant to transcend his time and serve as a contribution to our knowledge of who we are, lamentable as that might be. A fictionalized version of Hobbes' endgame is William Golding's *Lord of the Flies* (Golding, 1954).
6 Blainey (1976).
7 Bloch (1961); Kirby (1954).
8 Quoted in Elliott (1981, p. 212).
9 Smith (1937, p. 13).
10 Diamond (2005).
11 Karl Polyani's philippic against the moral vacuity of market exchanges remains a classic critique (Polanyi, 1944). A contemporary, gentler criticism is Sandel (2012).
12 Smith (1937, p. 13).
13 Ibid., p. 14.
14 Ibid., p. 423.
15 Developing a critique of Marxism goes beyond the scope of this volume. Others, more equipped than me, have accomplished that critique. See, for example, Elster (1985) for an accomplished exegesis and criticism.
16 Marx (1970, pp. 3–4).
17 For a counter sociological critique in the mode of Max Weber, see Maryanski (1992).
18 The term is borrowed from Michael Mann (n. 3, above). Each OWL imperative, while autonomous, impinges on the viability of rival imperatives to shape and direct human behavior. The boundaries between one form of OWL power and another are permeable. Humans in control of one source of OWL power are drawn to inner-generated

incentives to overwhelm competitors for dominance in governing a human society. Hence each form of power is promiscuous.

19 Marx's representation of capitalism has little resemblance to its operation today. For a critique, see n.15.

20 Kant (1991, p. 114).

21 Lenin (1977). For a critique of Lenin's philippic against finance capitalism from a liberal economic perspective, see Schumpeter (1955, p. 612).

22 Rousseau (1978, p. 287, pp. 46–47).

23 Plato (2004).

24 The tension between claims of natural law and convention and their implications for a just and legitimately governed polity were problems introduced to me by Leo Strauss at the University of Chicago. I have reluctantly arrived at the disquieting conviction that Rousseau has the better of the argument. For Strauss' works raising the possibility of natural law, see Strauss (1953, 1963, 1979).

25 For a more expansive discussion of Rousseau's solution to domestic legitimacy and its failure to resolve the challenge of global legitimacy, see Hassner (1997); Hoffmann and Fidler (1991); Waltz (1959).

2

THE RISE OF THE LIBERAL DEMOCRATIC SOLUTION

The responses of the democracies to OWL imperatives after World War II fundamentally reformed the Westphalian nation-state system. In their response to the Imperative of Order, they partially democratized the nation-state system – a Westphalian subsystem with liberal democratic characteristics. Their responses qualified the expected behavior of states within a classical Westphalian system. The Atlantic Alliance stipulated that an attack on one member was an attack on all, and all were pledged to aid the stricken state. Member states also pooled their military resources. They created the North Atlantic Treaty Organization (NATO), the military arm of the Atlantic Alliance, to develop a joint strategy to contain Soviet expansion and to deter an attack on member states.

The mutual pledge of support relaxed, if not fully surmounted, the Hobbesian dilemma inherent in the traditional workings of the Westphalian system. Alliance partners had reason to fear the Soviet Union, but not each other. Their differentiated security interests and the military power of member states were integrated into NATO strategy as a collective responsibility.

In their response to the Imperative of Welfare, the democracies erected a global market system of free exchange to facilitate trade, investment, technological development, and scientific discovery for their mutual benefit. The system was open to all states, free or autocratic, if members accepted a rule-based economic system and its governing rules. States were expected to ensure the security of the market system, to support but not distort or suppress its processes of free decision-making in trade and investment to favor a state, to protect private property rights, and to enforce contracts by an independent judiciary guided by the rules of domestic and international law.

The response of the democracies to the Imperative of Legitimacy was the most significant departure from traditional state practices. Only democracies were invited to be members of the Atlantic Alliance and to participate in NATO

DOI: 10.4324/9781003246572-2

military strategic policies and military exercises. The melding of joint allied military power and security interests was tantamount to the creation of a collective Leviathan to provide for the security of alliance members, but a Leviathan disciplined to the constraints of liberal democratic rule. The alliance structure was designed to preserve and expand the space occupied by the democracies within an otherwise anarchical nation-state system.

The partial democratization of the interstate system and the promotion of civil liberties and human rights throughout the world society qualified and restrained the struggle for power among member states. Within the subset of the nation-state system of these cooperating states, democratic peoples temporarily freed themselves from the embalming fatality of a Hobbesian grip. Harnessing and disciplining the Hobbesian state to democratic principles of legitimacy had the ironic consequence of providing new sources of power to all allied states and peoples.[1] The confluence of the three power sources, arising from the collective response of the liberal democracies to OWL imperatives, conspired to limit the expansion of the Soviet Union and other Communist states. In the bargain, the democracies created the architecture for the liberal democratic model of governance of the global society.

This chapter briefly traces the responses of the liberal democratic states to OWL imperatives from the aftermath of World War II to the end of the Cold War in 1991. The partial democratization of international relations and global politics marked an unprecedented advance over the traditional war-prone Westphalian system. The democratically inspired OWL model also had the effect, however temporary, of enhancing the liberal democratic model's attractiveness as a model for global governance.

A cautionary note is advised in attempting to summarize a very complex history. In emphasizing those OWL choices that magnified the collective power of the democracies, I run the risk of overlooking or minimizing the weaknesses and contradictions that emerged in creating and implementing the liberal democratic model. Chapter 3, which focuses on the erosion of power of the democratic democracies and the fading attractiveness of the liberal model, corrects for that oversight.

The liberal democracies and the Imperative of Order

Hobbes on call and Hobbes at bay

In creating the United Nations, the liberal democratic states initially re-affirmed the nation-state system as their initial response to the Imperative of Order. They neither had the power nor the will to transform the system. The United Nations enshrines the nation-state into its Charter. Interference in the domestic affairs of member states is prohibited, a provision since rendered problematic by the connectedness and interdependence of the states and peoples of the global society.[2] National boundaries have never been more permeable. Each member state is accorded one vote in the General Assembly. In a major reform of the defunct

League of Nations, the Security Council is charged with the principal responsibility for addressing threats to regional and world security.

The Security Council was first composed of five Permanent Members, so-called big powers, with the material and moral wherewithal presumably to address threats to regional and global peace. Each Permanent Member – the United States, Soviet Union, China, United Kingdom, and France – was granted a veto over Council deliberations and decisions. The Security Council has since grown to 15 members, 10 of which rotate membership drawn from the General Assembly.

The UN's design to surmount the anarchy of the nation–state system and diminish the system's incentives for states to resort to force was dead on arrival. The rapid fall of the East European states and their absorption with East Germany and East Berlin under the control of the Soviet Union exposed the endemic impotence of the United Nations and its problematic utility as a solution to war. The Security Council was split throughout the Cold War between the democracies, led by the United States, and Communist states, led by the Soviet Union and, later, buttressed by the addition of Communist China in 1978.

A series of aggressive Soviet moves transformed global politics into a bipolar struggle between the liberal democracies and the Soviet Union. In a widely publicized speech in 1946, former British Prime Minister Winston Churchill proclaimed "from Stettin in the Baltic to Trieste in the Adriatic an iron curtain [had] descended across the continent."[3] The speech foreshadowed Soviet moves to solidify and expand its hold on Europe as the opening salvos of a global struggle with the democracies. Soviet transgressions in the half-decade after World War II convinced the United States and the Western democracies that the Soviet Union was prepared to use force to expand its influence in Europe and beyond.

The first manifestation of Soviet expansionist intentions crystallized in Moscow's pressures on Greece and Turkey in the immediate aftermath of World War II. The Soviet aim to control Eastern Europe and all of Germany then unfolded. East Berlin was blocked to Western entry in West Berlin, prompting an air rescue of the Western occupied portion of the city. Czechoslovakia next fell to Communist rule in 1948 in further consolidation of Moscow's hold on its East European satellites. The North Korean invasion of South Korea, purportedly sanctioned by Moscow, proved the decisive step to militarize the Cold War. Soviet transgressions in the half-decade after World War II convinced the United States and the Western democracies that the Soviet Union was prepared to use force to expand its influence in Europe and beyond.

The Truman Doctrine provided the rationale for American strategy to stem the expansion of the Soviet Union and to deter Moscow's use of force on a global scale. It was proclaimed to justify the Truman administration's request to Congress for US$400 million in assistance to Greece and Turkey. The aid was directed to defeat the Communist rebellion in Greece and to support Turkish resistance to Soviet demands on its territory and rights of passage through the Dardanelles. The sweeping scope of the Doctrine was reminiscent of Woodrow

Wilson's request to Congress to declare war on Germany, "to save the world for democracy."

President Truman declared

> that it must be the policy of the United States to support free peoples who are resisting attempted subjugation by armed minorities or by outside pressures. I believe that we must assist free people to work out their own destinies in their own way.[4]

In closing, President Truman went beyond the Wilsonian trope:

> The seeds of totalitarian regimes are nurtured by misery and want. They spread and grow in the evil soil of poverty and strife. They reach their full growth when the hope of a people for a better life has died. We must keep that hope alive. The free peoples of the world look to us for support in maintaining their freedoms. If we falter in our leadership, we may endanger the peace of the world — and we shall surely endanger the welfare of our own nation.[5]

The scale of the commitment, if taken literally, signified that global security, welfare, and democracy were nowhere unless everywhere. The Truman Doctrine mapped with the Imperatives Order, Welfare, and Legitimacy. It globalized the struggle against the Soviet Union and contested its Leninist ideological vision for the governance of a global society.

The actual strategy adopted by the Truman administration to address the Soviet threat was more circumspect. The global aspirations of the Truman Doctrine were lowered to what became the containment of the Soviet Union rather than the rollback of its conquests or the overthrow of the Communist regime. Truman assured the Republican Congress, chary about re-engaging the nation in foreign entanglements or war, that "our help should be primarily through economic and financial aid which is essential to economic stability and orderly political processes."[6] Three months after the proclamation of the Truman Doctrine, the Marshall Plan to restore West European economies, discussed below, was announced as the centerpiece of the administration's strategy to contain the Soviet Union and its surrogates.

The inspiration for containment drew from the so-called February 1947 long cable of George Kennan, the American *Chargé d'Affaires* in Moscow.[7] A summary of the cable was published shortly thereafter in *Foreign Affairs* in which Kennan explained the sources of Soviet conduct.[8] He described the leadership of the Soviet Communist Party as convinced of the Party's ultimate victory over the capitalist West. Much like the Chinese Communist Party's (CCP) conception of legitimacy,[9] Soviet leadership under Joseph Stalin believed it was infallible. That conviction was fused to the iron discipline of Party members to execute the Soviet vision. Kennan noted: "On the principle of infallibility there rests the iron discipline of the Communist Party. In fact, the two concepts are mutually self-supporting. Perfect discipline requires recognition of infallibility. Infallibility requires the observance of discipline."[10]

The implications of this absolutist stance were far-reaching. Truth had to be sacrificed to advance the Party's power. "This means that truth is not a constant but is actually created ... by the Soviet leaders themselves," observed Kennan.[11] Once a party line had been determined, the entire machinery of the Party, at home and abroad, is enlisted in promoting the new truth. Kennan described the process of power acquisition as long term and relentless. Only a strategy proportionate to the Soviet threat would suffice to preserve American democracy. The Soviet menace was posed in historic global proportions:

> [t]he thoughtful observer of Russian-American relations will find no cause for complaint in the Kremlin's challenge to American society. He will rather experience a certain gratitude to a Providence which ... has made their entire security as a nation dependent on their pulling themselves together and accepting the responsibilities of moral and political leadership that history plainly intended them to bear[12]

What strategy then was best suited to frustrate the Soviet threat? Kennan's recommendation, which the Truman administration adopted, was the containment of the Soviet Union:

> [I]t will be clearly seen that the Soviet pressure against the free institutions of the western world is something that can be contained by the adroit and vigilant application of counter-force as a series of constantly shifting geographical and political points, corresponding to the shift and maneuvers of Soviet policy, but which cannot be charmed or talked out of existence.[13]

United States containment strategy in the five years after the end of World War II was primarily economic and diplomatic, backed implicitly by its monopoly of nuclear weapons. Growing fears that the Soviet Union might use force to advance its global objectives prompted the Truman administration to seek allied assistance and to militarize the Cold War. The Truman administration concluded that the United States alone could neither contain nor deter Soviet expansion and aggression around the globe. A collective response of the democracies was needed.

The Soviet explosion of a nuclear device in 1949 and the North Korean invasion of South Korea a year later reinforced the decision of the United States and the European states to address the increased threat of war and to create a collective effort to deter Soviet aggression. In 1949 the United States and 11 European states signed the Atlantic Alliance. It was quickly followed by the construction of a multilateral force composed of the military of member states.[14]

The United States subsequently extended the NATO component to deter the Soviet Union and Communist aggression to democratic regimes in Asia and around the globe. Washington entered into over 40 bilateral and multilateral security pacts. Of particular importance were security alliances with Japan, South Korea, Australia, and New Zealand. This global security necklace, principally linked as its center to the United States, constituted the responses of the democratic states to the Imperative of Order.

From the perspective of the Imperative of Order, these security arrangements varied in the commitment of the United State to come to the aid of a treaty partner. The NATO commitment was deeper and entangling. NATO's military integration was tantamount to a collective Leviathan pledged to defend the democratic coalition and each of its members. More broadly, the democracies in Europe and Asia effectively erected a subsystem of democratic nation-states that magnified their collective power as greater than the sum of the individual state contributions. Of no less significance for the workings of an anarchic nation-state system was the profound change in the incentive structure of each member's security decision-making. Within the enclosure of the democratic alliance subsystem, each state was freed from the Hobbesian dilemma in their mutual security relations. Together, they could concentrate on deterring the Soviet Union and its surrogates and on managing and lowering the incentives for war with the Communist states.

The democracies built on these transformative responses to the Imperative of Order. Following the signature of the Alliance, the United States dispatched American troops to Europe as a guarantee of its commitment to European security. The Europeans also agreed to rearm and place their forces under joint NATO command, led by an American general. The European democracies, notably France, overcame their strong reservations about rearming Germany despite the still-fresh memory of having suffered from German aggression and occupation less than a decade earlier. In alliance with the United States, the European democracies, including West Germany, were counted on to deter Soviet aggression and to preserve an uneasy peace in the center of Europe. The massive concentration of Western military power in the center of Europe counterbalanced Soviet military power and its organization in 1955 of its East European satellites into the Warsaw Pact as a response to NATO's rearmament.

Of particular interest was how NATO fashioned a joint strategy among the diverse members of the Alliance to flesh out their response to the Imperative of Order. The solution was the so-called Grand Bargain, struck between the United States and the Western European states. The United States extended its nuclear guarantee to its European allies in return for their contribution of conventional forces to parry Soviet and Warsaw Pact armies. The stationing of 400,000 troops and their dependents provided a security deposit, so to speak, that the United States would use its nuclear weapons to create a credible deterrent against a Soviet attack. So large an American military and civilian presence was hostage to the American pledge to defend Europe.

The United States extended its nuclear umbrella to Europe on the condition that the Europeans would provide sufficiently large and modernized conventional forces to complement the stationing of American troops in Europe. The strengthened conventional military posture was designed to limit the initial outbreak of hostilities to non-nuclear levels, to control the escalation of the military confrontation, and bring the conflict to a swift conclusion favorable to NATO and European security without the use of nuclear weapons. To re-enforce its nuclear guarantee the United States installed approximately 150 nuclear weapons in five NATO countries (Germany, Belgium, Netherlands, Italy, and Turkey).[15] The Grand Bargain was, in the words of Lord Ismay, its first Secretary General, "to keep the Soviet Union out, the Americans in, and Germany down."[16]

This phase of the Grand Bargain was characterized as a posture of "Flexible Response" to address a wide spectrum of possible Soviet military aggressive moves short of a strategic nuclear exchange between the United States and the Soviet Union.[17] US Secretary of Defense Robert McNamara explained the rationale behind Flexible Response:

> Thus, we and our allies must maintain substantial conventional forces, fully capable of dealing with a wide spectrum of lesser forms of political and military aggression – a level of aggression against which the use of strategic nuclear forces would not be to our advantage … One cannot fashion a credible deterrent out of an incredible action. Therefore, security for the United States and its allies can only arise from the possessions of a whole range of graduated deterrents, each of them fully credible in its own context.[18]

The Grand Bargain accomplished two objectives. It contained Soviet military and political expansion in Europe. It also, and more significantly, demonstrated that the allies could in a sense create a collective Leviathan and discipline that entity to democratic rule and values. The Imperatives of Order and Legitimacy were fused to produce a new nation-state entity. A significant portion of the nation-state system would be under the rule of constitutionally elected regimes in the service of free peoples. This was no small achievement to collectively constrain the Hobbesian state, checked by the shared value systems of the democratic peoples. To put this achievement metaphorically, less than a decade after World War II, no one any longer expected Germany to attack France or vice versa.

This collective departure from classical Westphalian incentives and behavior has to be qualified by defection of the nuclear members of the Alliance. The United States, the United Kingdom, and France departed from the moorings of joint alliance decision-making in their creation of national nuclear forces. These remained under national control and were not placed under joint NATO command. The United States acted independently of the Alliance consensus on crucial nuclear issues. Until the efforts to reach nuclear arms control accords between Washington and Moscow in the 1970s bore fruit, both powers entered into an unregulated nuclear arms race. By the early 1960s Washington abandoned a minimum nuclear deterrent strategy in the wake of the Sputnik scare in October 1957. Sputnik demonstrated the ability of the Soviet Union to launch intercontinental ballistic missiles, armed with nuclear warheads and capable of reaching the United States. Influential strategists, like Albert Wohlstetter, cautioned that larger, invulnerable, quick action forces had to be developed to maintain the nuclear balance with the Soviet Union.[19]

This line of thinking gradually morphed into the Kennedy administration's strategy of "Mutual Assured Destruction (MAD)." Since both the United States and the Soviet possessed sufficient nuclear capabilities by the end of the 1960s to destroy each other in a first strike, Secretary of Defense Robert McNamara argued that deterrence could be maintained only on the condition that the United States could ride out an attack and still visit unacceptable damage on an enemy in a retaliatory second strike:

> The cornerstone of our strategic policy continues to be to deter deliberate nuclear attack upon the United States, or its allies, by maintaining a highly reliable ability to inflict an unacceptable degree of damage upon any single aggressor, or combination of aggressors, at any time during the course of a strategic nuclear exchange — even after our absorbing a surprise first strike.[20]

In the late 1960s, the United States deployed a nuclear force of 2,200 nuclear weapons averaging more than one megaton of explosive power each. Only a fraction of this force – 400 one-megaton weapons – was needed to survive to launch a second strike capable of destroying "one-third of the [Soviet] population and one-half of [its] industry."[21] The triad of strategic nuclear delivery vehicles dedicated to delivering the second strike comprised 1,000 Minuteman launchers, 41 Polaris submarines carrying 656 missile launchers, and 600 long-range bombers.[22]

Secretary McNamara conceded that the deployed nuclear force exceeded the requirements of a reliable second strike. The driving force behind the deployment of overkill nuclear forces, as Secretary McNamara explained, was "this action-reaction phenomenon that fuels an arms race."[23] McNamara anticipated that this action-reaction would continue after his tenure if the two sides were unable to reach an agreement on a lower level of nuclear capability to ensure mutual assured destruction. By the end of the 1980s, the nuclear weapons stockpiles on both sides had increased multiple times. At their peak the United States disposed 35,000 strategic and tactical nuclear warheads; the Soviet Union, 37,000.[24]

Strategists on both sides were locked into the mentality of the mutually assured destruction strategy. Both sides believed that unless each met the latest material increase in nuclear forces of their rival their commitment to a credible deterrence posture would be perceived as diminished. This perceived loss in deterrence credibility purportedly afforded a determined opponent incentive to launch a first strike, however much that fateful decision would annihilate the homelands and populations of both the United States and the Soviet Union. An alleged delicate balance of terror increasingly assumed the form of a mutual suicide pact.[25] The action-reaction process described by McNamara increasingly assumed more the form of a psychologically driven arms race in which actual nuclear capabilities assumed a symbolic significance ostensibly signaling a rival's willingness to use nuclear weapons – an unfolding virtual nuclear war.

The fear grew on both sides that the nuclear arms race might get out of hand as a consequence of accident or miscalculation. To lower the risk of nuclear war, Moscow and the United States entered into arms control agreements to begin a process of reducing the number of intercontinental delivery vehicles and the number of nuclear warheads on each side. [26] They also limited the number of vectors, which could be MIRVed (Multiple Independently Re-Entry Vehicles). Upsetting these stabilizing initiatives, the Reagan administration's proposal to build a defense against nuclear attacks – the so-called Star Wars initiative – sparked a new arms race, prompting mass demonstrations in the West opposed to the reheating of the nuclear confrontation. The program to develop a defensive nuclear shield was later downsized, partly because it became clear, through testing, that a nuclear aggressor, even a small nuclear state like North Korea, could defeat a defense system and partly because the Soviet Union's collapse temporarily lowered the risk of a nuclear war.

The United States also became the most prominent nuclear arms proliferator during the Cold War. Washington provided the missile and submarine technology for the survival of the British nuclear deterrent, while Britain provided the nuclear warheads, assisted by US technology. It also afforded Britain naval facilities in the United States to refurbish the British nuclear fleet.[27] While the United States officially opposed the development of an independent French nuclear force, the porousness of American controls over the transfer of nuclear technology substantially aided France's development of a nuclear *force de frappe*.[28] These lapses in nuclear policy had the effect of creating a two-tier system within the Atlantic Alliance between nuclear and nonnuclear states. The three nuclear powers had greater leverage in determining NATO's operational nuclear strategy than their nonnuclear allies. How these states might come to the aid of a nonnuclear state or how they might pursue a national strategy that might be adverse to the security interests of a nonnuclear ally was never fully addressed.

Both Britain and France took out insurance policies by acquiring nuclear weapons as a vehicle to influence US nuclear policy and strategy. In light of the special relationship between the United States and Britain, London put a positive face on its nuclear initiative. It rationalized its construction of nuclear forces, not as a threat to the United States, but as an addition to the alliance deterrent to Soviet aggression. Its possession of nuclear weapons would ostensibly compel Soviet strategists to take seriously the threat that the British might use their nuclear weapons to stop a Soviet military attack on the West if the Soviets were persuaded that the United States would not come to the aid of its European allies.

The strategy underlying the French *force de frappe* was more straightforward in the strategic aim of its nuclear forces. It was pointedly directed as much at the United States as the Soviet Union. In the event of the failure of the United States to use its nuclear forces to deter a Soviet attack, the French nuclear forces were expected to fill what was posited as a gap in the Western deterrent. France's possession of nuclear weapons and their possible use would act as a trigger on the US deterrent against Soviet aggression.

British and French nuclear forces under national control moves served to dilute the commitment underlying NATO's collective security guarantee. France under President Charles de Gaulle made that point explicit when he withdrew France from NATO command and ordered all American troops out of the country, while keeping France within the Alliance to gain access, however, weakened by its own actions, to the Alliance's collective security guarantee. The upshot of the British and French nuclear deterrents was to place them in parallel with NATO strategy in their principal mission to deter a Soviet attack, but outside the boundaries of NATO strategy in the leverage they exercised over American nuclear strategy and practice.

The most glaring departure from the liberal democratic model and a repeated reversion to the incentives of the unconstrained Hobbesian state system revolve around repeated and largely failed US military interventions in the developing world to counter real or perceived Soviet and Communist influence. Only a brief *tour d'horizon* can be attempted here to substantiate the continued independence of the United States in deploying its military forces outside of the Atlantic Alliance, but the use of which had serious implications for the security of Alliance members. The Central Intelligence Agency aided a coup of the elected regime of Mohammad Mosaddegh in Iran in 1953 and continued to support the authoritarian rule of Shah Mohammad Reza Pahlavi until it was overthrown in 1979. In 1954 the American Central Intelligence Agency (CIA) also successfully engineered the removal from office of President Jacobo Arbenz Guzman in Guatemala and installed a military junta. During the administration of President Ronald Reagan the United States covertly supported the Contras, right-wing rebel groups, in apposition to the Marxist Sandinista regime in Nicaragua. Throughout this period, beginning even before the outbreak of World War II, the United States had allied with the religiously conservative, antidemocratic Wahhabi regime of Saudi Arabia, an alignment continuing until today.

The costly US intervention in Vietnam, begun under the Eisenhower administration, to support successive non-democratic regimes persisted until the fall of South Vietnam in 1975.[29] Even when it became abundantly clear by the late 1960s that North Vietnam would defeat the United States and the South Vietnamese regimes it supported, the Nixon administration and his Secretary of State, Henry Kissinger, continued to pursue the war in a vain effort to show resolve in the Cold War struggle with the Soviet Union. That enhanced military commitment did not preclude the loss of South Vietnam and the forced departure of American forces in 1975. In retrospect, there appears to be no causal relation between what proved to be a fabricated show of resolve in Vietnam and the eventual outcome of the Cold War – a dumb show that resulted in additional loss of lives and casualties which might have otherwise been avoided.

Africa was not spared. The United States intervened in the Congo crisis in 1960 to prevent a perceived Communist takeover. The CIA conspired with local factions to assassinate the Congo's Prime Minister Patrice Lumumba, who was perceived to favor Communist and Russian interests. Support for apartheid in South Africa was a mainstay of successive American administrations. American CIA influence was also at work in 1973 in overthrowing the duly elected regime of President Salvador Allende in Chile and conspiring in his assassination. In combatting real or perceived Communist penetration of Latin America, the United States tolerated military regimes in Argentina, Brazil, and Chile. The promotion and protection of open, free societies, democratically elected regimes, civil liberties, and human rights were sacrificed to fears of Soviet and local Communist expansion. One scholarly report found that the United States had intervened in 81 foreign elections between 1945 and 2000.[30] American arms transfers to non-democratic governments which violated human rights continued throughout the Cold War and thereafter.[31] The liberal model of legitimacy was subordinated to the dictates of the Imperative of Order.

These glaring deviations from the code of liberal democratic rule, while sapping its moral appeal in the developing world, did not forestall its eventual ascendancy in the Cold War. The damage done to the Western alliance and, notably to US power and prestige in its failed interventions in the Third World, did not have a decisive outcome on the Cold War, the tarnishing of American and Western moral stature to the contrary notwithstanding. A fuller explanation for the implosion of the Soviet Union and the end of the Cold War and the impact of the democratic liberal model on these outcomes will be summarized at the end of this discussion after examining the responses of the democracies to the Imperatives of Welfare and Legitimacy in more detail. These elements of the democratic model are significant to explain the ascendancy of the democratic model at the end of the 1990s.

The liberal democracies and the Imperative of Welfare

After World War II, the Western democratic coalition created a global market system in which they committed their individual prosperity to the collective wealth of its members. The US Marshall Plan grant of US$12 billion (US$120 billion in 2020 dollars) jump-started European economic reconstruction.[32] It was a key part of the Truman Doctrine's containment strategy. Aid was made available on the condition that these war-torn states, including West Germany, would not only develop plans to promote their national recoveries but they would also cooperate in cross-border economic projects to advance their economic interdependence.

A second and equally significant motivation for the Marshall Plan was to bolster the electoral prospects of democratic political parties, notably in Italy and France, to defeat their powerful Communist rivals. Economic recovery led by non-Communist democratic parties was understood as a prerequisite for the preservation of liberal democratic rule among the West European states. The resulting coalition of democracies, fostered by the United States, to stop Soviet expansion and frustrate Communist Party influence in European politics was a central element of overall Western strategy. The Marshall Plan, an economic and geopolitical initiative, marked a key starting point of the Cold War. The Marshall Plan, the Atlantic Alliance, and the creation of NATO military forces and strategy were integral parts of the Truman Doctrine to contain the Soviet Union.[33] From the perspective of this volume these responses, however much flawed by defections from the model, notably by the United States, still constituted responses to OWL imperatives that laid the foundations of the liberal democratic model for global governance.

In the long run, the creation of a global market was among the decisive initiatives that contributed significantly to the eventual ascendancy of the democratic states in the Cold War. With the United States pledged to underwrite the market system, the democracies erected the International Monetary Fund, the World Bank, and the Organization of Economic Co-Operation and Development (OECD) to facilitate its operations. Mutually beneficial reciprocal economic agreements facilitated trade and investment. To stabilize economic growth and to create greater stability the United States underwrote the financial stability of the democratic coalition by tying the currencies of the West European states to the dollar at a fixed amount of gold. This US paper currency system survived into the late 1960s. By then the West European states were well on the way to recovery.

The consequence of these mutually supportive economic moves, led by the United States, allowed the liberal democracies not only to assist each other in expanding economic growth for all members but also to develop welfare plans that suited the unique political and socioeconomic conditions of each state. Their response to the Imperative of Welfare had, collectively, both a positive economic transatlantic impact on the members of the democratic coalition and a stabilizing political effect on the regimes of each member state.

The increasing wealth of the liberal democratic states afforded them the resources to expand the welfare state in each of the democratic states to unprecedented levels. The democratic global state, epitomized by the United States, became the market, competitive, and entrepreneurial state; the scientific research and technological developmental state; the safety net state for the young, poor, old, unemployed, and medically impaired; and the health, education, leisure, and recreational state. These expanded functions supplied a host of new and innovative public goods. The sum total of this vast assumption of welfare functions had the countervailing effect of essentially eliminating incentives to use force in the governmental and in civil societal relations of the democratic states. Peaceful and mutually supportive economic and technological exchanges provided the basis for ever-greater amounts of public goods to enhance the welfare of their populations. In responding to the Imperative of Welfare the democracies muted and restrained the war-prone proclivities of the Hobbesian state among themselves.

Going further in responding to the Welfare Imperative and the emerging governance of the democratic coalition, the United States also actively supported European initiatives to foster Western Europe's economic and political integration. The first step was the creation of the European Coal and Steel Community (ECSC) in the early 1950s engaging six European states,[34] including France, West Germany, Italy, Belgium, the Netherlands, and Luxembourg. The security interest underlying the ECSC was member control of Germany's steel and coal policies, key resources in rebuilding the German army. German rearmament required allied consent to preclude the reemergence of German aggression. The ECSC promoted greater European economic and political integration as well as sustained economic growth. The pooled sovereignty of the ECSC's member states in these policy areas marked the first step toward the eventual construction of the European Union.

The United States pressed for greater European economic integration than the ECSC. ECSC members next chose to form the European Economic Union (EEC). Its long-term, ambitious aim, yet to be realized, was to proceed to political union through economic integration. The initial passel of the ECC's six members eventually expanded over the next decades to twenty-eight states before the United Kingdom's withdrawal from the EU in 2020. What is particularly striking about this evolution is the sustained support issuing from successive American administrations for European Union. The United States was willing to accept the creation of a closed economic system if it would eventually lead to political union. The prospect of finally ending Europe's civil wars since the 15th century compensated for whatever might be lost in economic competitiveness or damage to American interests. Peace would later prove to be an economic multiplier for all of the democracies.

The cooperative responses of the United States and its European allies to the Imperative of Welfare not only increased their collective economic power but also spurred their technological development to their mutual benefit. The success of these cooperative moves had the effect of strengthening the Welfare Imperative of the liberal democratic model. Their shared responses to the Imperative of Legitimacy over the course of the Cold War added additional power to the liberal democratic model. The combination of the three power sources flowing from the democracies' responses to OWL imperatives proved decisive in establishing the liberal democratic model by the end of the century as ascendant in the competition to define global governance.

The liberal democracies and the Imperative of Legitimacy

The liberal democracies reconciled two potentially antagonistic notions of legitimacy, one national, the other universal. The intrinsic value and integrity of each state's historical, linguistic, religious, and cultural differences were affirmed; national diversity was enlisted to strengthen the coalition. States concerned that their national identities might be submerged in the Atlantic Alliance or by a European Union were reassured that they had a voice and stake in the two associations. President Charles de Gaulle's decision to order all American troops from France and his reliance on the *force de frappe* asserted an extreme form of national identity, but not to the extent that Gaullist France severed its commitment either to the Atlantic Alliance or to the European Union. Indeed, France's qualified membership in both organizations had the effect of dampening Cold War tensions without putting the Alliance itself in jeopardy.[35]

All liberal democratic states also committed themselves to apply universal principles of liberal rule. Robert Dahl's *Democracy and Its Critics* delineates the central components of the constituents of liberal democratic rule:[36] that all humans are free and equal; one person, one vote to undergird majoritarian rule; recognition and protection of minority rights; the protection and promotion of civil liberties and human rights at home and abroad; press and media freedom; right of peaceful assembly and petition; and equality before the rule of law, administered by an independent judiciary.

Parallel to their mutual security commitments to aid each other under attack, the democracies also supported the preservation of democratic government in states under siege. Member states recognized and supported the French Fifth Republic to preclude a military *coup d'etat* and a military takeover of the Fourth Republic as a consequence of the Algerian crisis.[37] They also put sufficient pressure on the Greek military junta in Greece to induce it to relinquish power and return the country to democratic rule.

The depth of the commitment of the democracies went beyond formal application of constituent rules and procedures to include contextual elements. Both constituent and contextual elements of democratic rule are central to the unique social contracts fashioned in each democratic state. In each country, actual democratic practices included those uniquely historically forged norms and values, which castellated around these institutional and constitutional constraints in the governance of a member state. American democracy depends on a written constitution as well as the workings of a two-party system, which does not appear in the Constitution. Britain, without a written constitution, depends on a political culture whose norms are the product of centuries of consensual practices dating from the 13th century and the Magna Carta.

The statesmen who designed the Atlantic Alliance and the European Union had a capacious conception of democratic legitimacy. They meshed both the constituent and contextual elements of legitimacy in such a way that they melded these indispensable elements of democratic legitimacy to suit the political culture of each member state. In a sense they pragmatically reconciled the contrasting conceptions of legitimacy of Edmund Burke and of American and French Revolutionaries. In attacking the upheaval of the French Revolution, Burke grounded legitimacy in the history, culture, and norms of the British people.

Legitimate rule was infused organically in the formation of each citizen. These *contextual* components of legitimacy complemented written constitutions, i.e., *constituent* practices, which were favored by the French and American revolutionaries, who cast their lot with universal values.

Burke's insistence on contextual restrains on the power and authority of governments is indispensable, as Steven Levitsky and Daniel Ziblatt argue,[38] to buttress formal constituent limitations on democratic governance. They refer to widely shared political cultural values whose absence in practice explains *How Democracies Die*, the title of their volume. They cite two practices that appear to them to be crucial: that opponents in a democracy view each other as legitimate and that once in power the ruling majority will exercise "institutional forbearance" and not use its electoral success to gain an unfair advantage or, worse, to retain power permanently. As the drift toward populism in Poland and Hungary, as well as the United States, indicates these contextual constraints are fundamental to prevent majority authoritarian rule through the ballot box.

The pressures mounted by the democratic states to complete the dissolution of Europe's empires after World War II were also a significant outcome of the partial democratization of interstate and global politics. While the collapse of the European imperial system did not always lead to the democratization of an independent state, the end of European imperialism did set in motion a trend in that direction. The independence of Algeria in 1963 completed the dissolution of the French empire. Similarly, Portugal's hold on its African colonies ended in the 1970s. Continued democratic pressures on the apartheid system in South Africa led finally to the dismantling of the apartheid system and the introduction of democracy, however shaky, into South Africa.

The belated military intervention of NATO in the Balkan Wars in the 1990s and the attraction of membership in the European Union also set in motion democratic forces, a work in process by no means assured across these states. It is also important to keep uppermost in mind, to preclude attributing too much to the power and attractiveness of the democratic model, that many of the states, which gained interdependence, still show few signs of any interest in joining the democracies. The democracies are also in the process of squandering their gains, the subject of Chapter 3.

The rise of the democratic model

Before we turn to the erosion of the democratic model, it is important to step back for a moment to assess its contribution to the implosion of the Soviet Union and the end of the Cold War. The rise of the liberal democratic model, resting on a confluence of three power sources arising from responses to OWL imperatives, is a necessary, if not fully sufficient, explanation for these seismic shifts in international relations and in global politics. The success of the democracies in containing and defeating the Soviet Union falsified doubters who believed that they could not indefinitely sustain a costly containment strategy. Walter

Lippmann's critique of the containment strategy summarized the attacks on the Truman Doctrine.[39] Critics contended that democratic populations would grow weary of supporting a strategy stretching decades, as Kennan's diagnosis of the Soviet threat indicated. A global containment strategy was also expected to dissipate the power and resources of the democracies in endless local armed conflicts around the globe. Lippmann averred that the democracies did not possess the strength, will, and resourcefulness to sustain a Truman Doctrine of seemingly limitless involvement in foreign enterprises.

Lippmann's views enjoyed purchase in policy circles throughout the long half-century struggle with the Soviet Union. There was sustained popular resistance to foreign involvements, reaching a high point with the Vietnam War. That did not dissuade three successive administrations from continuing the Cold War struggle: Jimmy Carter brokered Egypt's and Jordan's recognition of the Israeli state; Ronald Reagan pressured the Soviet Union to end its control of Berlin and, implicitly, Eastern Europe and launched an increase in defense expenditures that put increasing pressure on the Soviet Union's limited economic and technological resources; and George Bush organized a coalition of democratic and Arab states to repel the Iraqi invasion of Kuwait. In different ways, these initiatives demonstrated the will and resilience of the American people to support an active and costly security and foreign policy.

Within the conceptual framework of this discussion, realist and neorealist theorists explain the implosion of the Soviet Union largely to the response of the democracies, principally the United States, to the Imperative of Order. Power sources arising from democratic state responses to the Imperatives of Welfare or Legitimacy are given less weight as determinative for the end of the Cold War on terms favorable to the West. The Soviet Union's inability to keep pace with the military buildup and technological sophistication of the United States and its allies are identified as the decisive factors for the Western victory. Vastly increased defense spending and advances in military technology overshadowed Soviet efforts to compete with the United States and its Western allies. The Reagan administration's launch of a nuclear defense program – the Star Wars initiative – putatively revealed to the Soviet leadership that it could not compete with the West unless it underwent profound economic and political reform.

The realist explanation for the Soviet implosion has some explanatory purchase.[40] It still falls short of the broader explanatory power of the triad of power sources supplied by the West's responses to OWL imperatives. At the level of the Imperative of Order or organized violence, the Soviet Union was still a match for the United States and its Western allies. Its vast conventional army in central Europe and the Warsaw Pact balanced the resources of the West at this level of confrontation. Its tactical and strategic nuclear arsenal was also as powerful and potentially capable of destruction as the Western counterpart. The police and secret services of the regime maintained firm control of the Soviet population and those of the Soviet Union's satellites. An OWL framework introduces other indispensable factors into the mix of converging forces that led to the breakup of the Soviet Union.

The contrasting responses of the Soviet and Western blocs to the Imperatives of Welfare and Legitimacy provide a more persuasive explanation for the Soviet demise. The significance of sustained Western economic, scientific, and techno-logical development placed enormous pressures on the Soviet Union and exposed the endemic failure of a centralized economy, insulated from market competi-tion, either to provide for the material betterment of the Soviet people or of the populations of Soviet satellites. It could not even compete with the smaller Asian Tigers[41] or Communist China.[42]

The rate of growth of the Soviet economy steadily declined as a percentage of global GDP between 1950 and 1980. In 1960 the Soviet Union and the Warsaw Pact states accounted for 14 percent of the world's GNP, while the Western states reached 61 percent. Thirty years later the proportion of world GNP of the Western states rose to 75 percent, while the European Communist states' percent fell to half the 1960 level.[43] Absent the restoration of a market economy and its integration into the global market system, reforms that the Chinese Communist Party successfully navigated,[44] the Soviet Union would inevitably fall further and further behind its Western rivals and Communist China.

Soviet reform of the state's centralized political and economic institutions had the unintended result of unraveling Communist Party control of the Soviet regime and dismantling the state. The combined effect of *Glasnost* or political opening, *Perestroika* or economic liberalization, and failed and futile experiments in democratization had the combined effect of a perfect storm that overwhelmed Communist Party rule and the Soviet state.[45] The Soviets' haphazard and ill-informed application of market reforms not only undermined Party control of the Soviet state and its East European satellites but also failed to stimulate economic growth. The Chinese Communist Party never made that mistake in cracking down on demonstrations for political liberalization in the Tiananmen Square massacre.

The flawed response of the Soviet Union to the Imperative of Legitimacy was the *coup de grâce* of its undoing. The ideology of the Soviet Union envisioned the creation of the "Soviet man." The Party's illegitimacy in the eyes of most peoples of the Soviet republics, including Russians themselves, was fatal to Communist rule. Lurking not far below the surface of the Soviet economic upheavals was the intractable nationalities' problem. The Soviet Union was never able to create a new Soviet citizen – the "Soviet man" – to which all of its diverse subjects could declare their paramount loyalty and into which they would dissolve their discrete national, cultural, and religious identities.

Despite the Communist Party's monopoly of violence and its possession of millions of personnel in the military, police, and secret services, it failed to manage the nationalities problem as it attempted to liberalize its economy and governing institutions.[46] The national, cultural, and religious divisions within Soviet society across 15 Soviet Republics and the East European satellites overwhelmed the Party. In December 1991 the Soviet Union was dissolved into 15 predominantly national component parts. The Russian Federation, the largest of the Soviet republics, arose from this dismemberment. For the first time in the history of the Russian people, they elected a President in what proved in short order to be a failed attempt to adapt their rule to a democratic model. Never having experienced liberal democratic rule, history was not on their side.

Russians were also increasingly unwilling to bear the cost and burdens of controlling unruly satellites in East Europe. They were even less keen to sustain Moscow's global engagements around the world. Nor were Moscow's satellites willing any longer to acquiesce to its coercive rule. Unlike the Atlantic Alliance and the European Union, which embraced national diversity as a strength, the diverse and clashing identities of the Soviet Union and the Warsaw Pact could not be reduced to the fictitious union of a universal Soviet man. Western unity did not depend on effacing national identities. It universalized those identities in ascribing to all of these diverse groups the moral equivalence embodied in the freedom and equality of all humans.

Obviously, there is more to the story of why the Cold War is now history and the Soviet Union has been consigned to the ashbin of history. I have used the failed Soviet experiment to highlight the importance of approaching the connectedness and interdependence of the peoples and states of the global society from an OWL perspective of governance. It makes no claims to a comprehensive theory. It does insist that to understand globalization and the challenge of global governance the three structures of OWL power have to be simultaneously relied upon to account for the behavior of states and regimes. In their responses to OWL imperatives, the leadership of the Western states forged a model for global governance that proved to be the undoing of the Soviet Union. In their failed responses to OWL imperatives, Communist Party leadership destroyed the Party and the Soviet state.

We now turn to the erosion of the democratic model commencing at the very time of its ascendancy.

Notes

1 Eric Jones makes this point in demonstrating how a more liberal (but still autocratic) Britain and Netherlands were able to acquire greater power than their monarchical rivals in the contest for ascendancy in Europe (Jones, 1987, 1988).
2 Note that in UN Secretary General Kofi Annan's acceptance speech of the Nobel Peace Prize for 2001 on behalf of the United Nations, he stated that "the sovereignty of States must no longer be used as a shield for gross violations of human rights" – an implicit amendment of the UN Charter.
  www.nobelprize.org/prizes/peace/2001/annan/lecture/
3 www.history.com/this-day-in-history/churchill-delivers-iron-curtain-speech
4 https://alphahistory.com/coldwar/truman-doctrine-congress-speech-1047.
5 Ibid.
6 Ibid.
7 https://nsarchive2.gwu.edu/coldwar/documents/episode-1/kennan.htm
8 Kennan (1947).

9 See Chapter 6, China and the Imperative of Legitimacy
10 Kennan (1947, p. 573).
11 Ibid.
12 Kennan., p. 582.
13 Ibid., p. 576.
14 For an in-depth discussion of the NATO Alliance and US security alliances, see Osgood (1962, 1968).
15 www.nti.org › analysis › reports › nuclear-disarmament
The United States also stationed nuclear weapons in South Korea, the Philippines, and the Western Pacific.
16 css.ethz.ch › digital-library › articles › article.html
17 Flexible Response as a strategy is discussed in detail in Kolodziej (1966), pp. 326–364.
18 Presentation to Congress of Robert McNamara on September 19, 1967, on assured destruction 2006/01/30:CIA-RDP70B00338R000300100105-8
19 Wohlstetter (1959).
20 2006/01/30:CIA-RDP70B00338R000300100105-8
21 Ibid.
22 Idem.
23 2006/01/30:CIA-RDP70B00338R000300100105-8
24 Norris and Kistensen (2010).
25 For the history of the nuclear arms race, see Kaplan (1983, 2020) and Freedman (1989). See also Craig (1986) for a technical discussion of nuclear weapons and the targeting requirements of mutually assured destruction.
26 For background to these nuclear arms control negotiations, alternately titled SALT I and II and START, see Talbott (1979, p. 108); Talbott (1984, p. 147).
27 Gowing (1974).
28 I extensively cover the French acquisition of nuclear forces and the French theory of deterrence to trigger US nuclear forces and to deter Soviet aggression in Europe: (Kolodziej, 1974, 1987), *passim*.
29 Defense (1971); FitzGerald (1973); Halberstam (1972).
30 Levin (2016).
31 Blanton (2005).
32 The history of the European Union is covered in Dinan (2010).
33 Capaccio (2018); Jones and Talbott (2017); Stell (2018).
34 Capaccio (2018); Stell (2018).
35 See Kolodziej (1974) for an evaluation of Gaullist Cold War policy, which sought to lower the likelihood of war.
36 I have relied extensively on Robert Dahl's defense of the superiority of democratic rule over its authoritarian rivals, developed appropriately enough in the form of a Greek dialogue (Dahl, 1989). His capacious grasp of democratic theory breaks out of the straightjacket of the nation-state. His thinking parallels that of other global-oriented democratic theorists. Nobio Bobbio, like Dahl and Hannah Arendt, poses the principal struggle of this century as the contest for ascendancy between liberal democracy and its authoritarian rivals. See Bobbio (1987). Jan-Werner Müller cogently elaborates on the central elements of democratic rule, developed by Dahl and Bobbio, and affirms democracy's moral superiority, based on freedom and equality, and identifies the central institutions required to put these principles to work. Müller (2021).
37 Jackson (2018, pp. 509–563).
38 Levitsky and Ziblatt (2018).
39 Lippmann (1947).
40 See Wohlforth (1994) for a discussion of the purported importance of realist theory to explain the Soviet collapse. Among realist theorists, Kenneth Waltz is least persuasive (Waltz, 1964, 1986). Waltz's reliance on a unipolar explanation of state behavior discounted the formidable forces unleashed by responses of states and peoples to

the Imperatives of Welfare and Legitimacy. His constrained realist paradigm was ill equipped to anticipate the economic and political reforms both of the Soviet Union and of Communist China. For a critique of the realist and neorealist explanations for the end of the Cold War, consult (Lebow, 1994; Lebow, 1995). See also Kolodziej (2005), especially pp. 77–126, for an evaluation of the leading schools of international relations and their conflicting explanations for the end of the Cold War.

41 Taiwan, Singapore, South Korea, and Malaysia. The shortcomings of the Soviet Union's centralized economic system are extensively covered in the scholarly literature. See, for example, Ericson (1987); R. E. Ericson (2013); Kornai (1992).

42 The decision of the Chinese Communist Party to enter the global capitalist market system is covered in Chapter 5.

43 These data are covered in Kolodziej (2005, pp. 107–109).

44 See Chapter 5, China and the Imperative of Welfare.

45 Chapter 7 develops this theme.

46 Carrère d'Encausse (1993).

3

THE FALL OF THE LIBERAL DEMOCRATIC SOLUTION

The erosion of the Imperative of Order

The liberal democratic coalition failed its first test in the wake of the implosion of the Soviet Union and the end of the Cold War.[1] The liberal democracies had the opportunity to turn a formerly implacable adversary into a partner to strengthen European and global security. They squandered that historically unprecedented opening. No Marshall Plan was launched to assist the Russian Federation's transition to a market economy and to an open, democratic political system. A Russian people and elite, with no experience in democratic government or little understanding, much less appreciation, of the heavy burdens of broad civic engagement to make it work, were left on their own.[2] In contrast the democracies welcomed a defeated Germany, which had visited upon them far more death and devastation than the Soviet Union, into the democratic coalition.

Liberal democracy failed to take root in the transition from the Soviet Union to the Russian Federation.[3] The economic chaos of a too rapid and badly prepared transition to a capitalist economy and the absence of foreign assistance led to the immiseration of the Russian people. Nor could the seeds of liberal democratic rule flourish in what proved to be a dysfunctional experiment in democratic rule, exacerbated by the rapacious theft of state assets by a small elite of enterprising entrepreneurs.[4] The experience of that ill-starred experiment soured the Russian people on liberal democratic rule. Abruptly exposed to foreign competition, they were poorly equipped to compete in a global market system. It is not surprising that they would turn to Vladimir Putin, who offered them a life preserver in the form of a populist regime to restore public order and to arrest the downward slide to economic ruin. President Putin quickly consolidated his power, assisted by oligarchs under his control who commanded the principal sectors of the

DOI: 10.4324/9781003246572-3

Russian economy. The small window available to the democracies to draw the Russian Federation into their orbit was slammed shut.

In a global society, increasingly uncongenial to democratic rule, it is essential that the democracies provide other peoples, disposed to adopt the liberal model, aid to widen the governing space accorded to democratic regimes. In failing to make the democratic promise available to the Russian people, they acted against their own self-interests in the struggle to establish democratic rule as the principal form of governmental rule of the nation-state system and the global society. Exacerbating the West's unconcern for Russia's political and economic plight was its indifference to the perceived negative impact of NATO's expansion into Eastern Europe and the Balkans on Russian security interests. These systemic acts of omissions and commission foreshadowed the fading attractiveness of the liberal democratic model for Putin's Russia. We will never know whether substantial Western economic assistance and security assurances might have prevented the rise of an illiberal Russian regime. What is certain is that the Western states did not try to obviate these unfortunate outcomes.[5]

We now turn briefly to identify the principal defections of the liberal democracies from their positive responses to Order, Welfare, and Legitimacy (OWL) imperatives in the postwar World War II era. Identifying the significant departures of the liberal democracies from their adherence to successful OWL imperatives, the product of their cooperation, is important. These are markers for what has to be done if the liberal democracies are to regain their footing to meet the challenges to global governance: to relax the Hobbesian dilemma in their mutual security relations and those of other states; to maintain a well-regulated rule-based market system that precludes its implosion; to provide increasing welfare for their populations, notably those adversely affected by globalization, mobile capital, and technological innovation; to assist developing states to improve their material lots and to provide the resources and know-how to cope with climate change and epidemics, like COVID-19; and to adhere to the constituent and contextual, civic norms of democratic governance while promoting the spread of democratic regimes, civil liberties, and human rights. All this is a tall order, but indispensable if the liberal democracies are to preclude China's totalitarian regime and Russia's illiberal majoritarian model from populating the Westphalian nation-state system with autocratic regimes and dominating the spaces devoted to the governance of the world's contentious peoples.

On the heels of President Putin's installation of a populist regime, the United States took a fateful step to pursue its own interests at the expense of Atlantic Alliance unity. Earlier, the Alliance's intervention, led by the United States, to repel Iraq's seizure of Kuwait in 1991 confirmed a key principle of the nation-state system: the sanctity of state boundaries and their insulation from revision through force. In contrast to the 2003 invasion of Iraq to overthrow the Saddam Hussein regime, the first armed encounter with Iraq in 1991 reinforced international law. In nullifying Iraq's attempt to control Kuwait's oil resources, the Atlantic Alliance affirmed the United Nations Charter, nation-state sovereignty, and, more generally, the integrity of the nation-state system. The speed and effectiveness with which the democratic coalition mounted their counteroffensive to the Iraqi territorial grab of Kuwait demonstrated the collective power of the democracies to preserve the principle of self-determination, one of the few universally acknowledged principles of a fragile Westphalian system.[6]

Approximately a decade later, the United States violated the principle of national sovereignty with damaging effects on the cohesion of the Atlantic Alliance and on the mutual trust shared by Alliance members, based on the assurance that alliance members would respect the specific security interests of all allies. On March 19, 2003, the United States attacked Iraq, joined by what the Bush administration announced was a "coalition of the willing," including the United Kingdom, Poland, and Australia. They charged that Baghdad had failed to comply with several Security Council resolutions requiring the Saddam Hussein regime to permit the entry of UN inspectors to ensure that Iraq was not developing nuclear weapons. Colin Powell, the United States Secretary of State, presented to the UN Security Council what later was exposed as a false claim that Iraq was developing weapons of mass destruction. Against this backdrop, the Bush administration proclaimed that diplomacy had failed to gain Iraq's compliance with UN resolutions, notably Resolution 1441, and that a *casus belli* existed justifying war. The Bush administration bolstered its justification for war by also accusing the Hussein regime, also falsely, of collusion with Al Qaeda terrorists.

The UN Security Council never authorized the Iraq war. French Prime Minister Jacques Chirac explicitly declared on March 10, a little more than a week before the US-led invasion, that France, a key ally, would veto any UN resolution, which would automatically lead to war. The split in the Alliance did not dissuade either Washington or its expedient allies of the moment to launch an attack to eliminate a non-existent Iraqi nuclear weapons program and to overthrow the Hussein regime for aiding and abetting terrorism – allegations without foundation.

The United States cited three criteria, purportedly drawn from international law, to justify war. First, every state has a right to protect its national interests when its security is threatened. American-fabricated nuclear and terrorist threats to the United States and its allies met the first criterion for war. Second, if the international community could or would not disarm a state's nuclear weapons programs in violation of international sanctions, then the United States was obliged to assume that responsibility. Going further, third, the Bush administration declared that, if conditions were propitious to overthrow the Hussein regime and to install a democratic government to protect and promote human rights, it would be obliged to avail itself of that opportunity.

Both France and Germany opposed the Iraq war, splitting the Atlantic Alliance. To blunt their opposition, the Bush administration divided Europe into old and new Europe. France and Germany represented old Europe, presumptuously characterized as outdated and unable to address new threats to the Alliance and international security. New Europe, cobbled together as the "coalition of the willing," was primed to meet the Iraqi threat. Members supporting military intervention included Britain, Netherlands, Denmark (but not Belgium), the southern states of Portugal, Italy, and Spain (but not Greece), and Eastern Europe states newly incorporated into the Alliance.

Robert Kagan characterized the Washington-induced split in cosmological terms in which "Americans are from Mars and Europeans are from Venus. … [W]hen it comes to setting national priorities, determining threats, defining challenges, and fashioning and implementing foreign and defense policies, the United States and Europe have parted ways."[7] Kagan accurately foretold that the rupture would progressively grow wider and deeper over the next generation. That foreshadowing culminated in the election of Donald J. Trump in 2016.

Basing national security policies on temporal, conjectural, and shifting coalitions of the willing rather than on long-term Alliance consent and member cohesion started the United States down the path of return to the pre-World War I international system as a Hobbesian struggle for power. In pressing American security interests by circumventing Alliance accord, the Bush Doctrine ignored the overall security interests of its foremost European allies. The Doctrine disaggregated the Alliance into individual states and sorted them out, depending on whether a member state supported or opposed the American use of military power, whether against Iraq or other state and non-state actors. In a larger sense, the Doctrine was applied to all states. International organizations, whether the United Nations, the European Union, or the Atlantic Alliance, were similarly reduced to policy options that advanced or impeded US strategic moves, not as international institutions supporting a collective liberal democratic solution to global governance.

The Bush Doctrine's reliance on coalitions of the willing also implicitly undermined Article 5 of the Atlantic Alliance treaty that specified that an attack on one Alliance member was an attack on all. This commitment extends to the obligation that allies take into account the national security interests of all members when one or more of its partners was preparing to use force or launch a deliberate war. Allies are expected to weigh the impact that their unilateral actions might have on the security interests of their partners and on the international community. Relaxing the Hobbesian dilemma went beyond the assurance that member states would not attack each other. It also covered – or most assuredly it would have to cover – the expectation that the pooled sovereignty of the Alliance required regard by each alliance member of the security interests of each of its partners before acting unilaterally in defense of its real or perceived particular security interests.

Contrast the American departure from its alliance obligations in the second Iraq intervention with the extraordinary gesture of alliance unity, which *Le Monde* proclaimed on September 12, 2001: *Nous sommes tous Americains* (We are all Americans). This was the sole instance that Article 5 of the Atlantic Alliance was invoked to demonstrate alliance solidarity with a member state in the wake of the terrorist attack on the United States. One is also reminded of the decision of the Kennedy administration to consult with French President Charles de Gaulle about its decision to "quarantine" (i.e., to blockade) Cuban ports to prevent Soviet ships from delivering missiles to Havana. It demonstrated the administration's sensitivity to its obligation to take into account the security interests of its allies as it embarked on a dangerous strategic move that threatened a nuclear war and the outbreak of World War III.[8]

At the time of the 2003 Iraq invasion the democracies enjoyed, collectively, predominant but scarcely overwhelming power within the nation-state system and across the global society. Their geopolitical reach and military strength were largely uncontested; their economic and technological prowess, unmatched; and the moral superiority of their legitimate rule, based on the consent of the governed, unassailable. Their converging, postwar responses to OWL imperatives achieved this high point in the contest for global governance. Characterizing the United States as a hegemon – even a liberal hegemon – capable of dictating the behavior of other states, is misleading and unwittingly attributes more power to the United States to have its way with other states or even non-state actors.

The full breadth of American power and its effectiveness depends on its allies. Alone, the United States is not a Leviathan of the international system in the Hobbesian sense, possessed of awesome, compelling power.[9] The notion that the United States could get the world it wanted, unilaterally, as a would-be hegemon is an inflated portrayal of its power as an alleged superpower. The evident American failure in Vietnam against a vastly weaker opponent or its impotence, displayed in its inability to free the American legation held hostage by Iran for over a year, are scarcely the stuff of a hegemon. If American interests and those of the liberal democracies are to be advanced, American power must necessarily be magnified by the collective power and support of its allies. That is, unquestionably, the lesson to be learned from the Cold War experience.

Acting together, the liberal democracies demonstrated that they could successfully contest the geopolitical power, economic prowess, and moral legitimacy of the Soviet Union, a formidable opponent. They were also able to expand the democratic space of governance to other states to enhance their global power.[10] Note that neither China nor Russia has allies. They pointedly eschew them as the succeeding chapters recount. Alliance cohesion and cooperation is an indispensable asset in combating the lure of the Chinese and Russian solutions for global governance. In dissipating alliance power the United States and the members of the coalition of the willing exposed their vulnerability and those of other members. Division within the democratic coalition gravely weakens the attractiveness of the liberal democratic model. Absent unified cooperation among the democracies in crafting joint policies to address global issues, they will be unable to determine the global agenda to address these challenges and to contain Chinese and Russian power and their global aspirations.

By enfeebling Alliance cohesion the second Iraq war struck a blow at the trust on which member states were willing to pool their security interests. The unprecedented act of mutual assurance of the first Iraq war, as Chapter 2 described, relaxed the Hobbesian dilemma among Alliance members. The ironic outcome of the 2003 Iraq war, justified to advance the space accorded democratic regimes, fostered instead a Westphalian system more akin to the Chinese and Russian models for governance rather than to the democratic ideal. Chaos and the emergence of the Islamic State of Iraq and Syria (ISIS) rather than the spread of democratic governance in the Middle East were the unintended outcomes of the Iraq invasion by an ill-conceived and necessarily transient "coalition of the willing."

Democratic rule under conditions of connectedness and interdependence evolved along two intertwined parallels: domestic and global. In the postwar world, the United States had fused these two lines of democratic rule and power by leading its Alliance partners to respond collectively to OWL imperatives. It is difficult to exaggerate the significance of this achievement. The democracies reduced the Hobbesian incentives for conflict and war among them. They also erected a market system promoting their collective material progress. Their commitment to liberal democratic rule enlarged the space accorded to legitimate rule, the product of the consent of the governed through free and unfettered elections in which the civil and human rights of minorities were also protected. In going it alone with whatever coalition of the willing it could muster, the United States began to fracture the solidarity of OWL imperatives on which the collective power of the democracies depended to underwrite their solution to global governance.

The strategic doctrine of the Bush administration, which was the rationale for the invasion of Iraq and the overthrow of the Saddam Hussein regime, had the unintended but predictable result of eroding alliance power and severely damaging the trust that held alliance members together. First, the Doctrine stipulated that the United States possessed uncontested military power. America's alleged military superiority negated attempts, whether by foes or friends, to challenge its status. The second element asserted that the United States could act preemptively to use force in any part of the globe against any adversary at a time and place of its choosing without having to consult alliance partners or the United Nations Security Council. It was assumed that overwhelming American coercive power would be victorious.

Third, the Bush Doctrine assigned the United States the role of an arbiter of the moral behavior of other states and non-state actors and licensed Washington to deter and forcefully roll back defections from right conduct. The Bush Doctrine echoed President Woodrow Wilson's speech to Congress requesting a declaration of war against Germany to advance the "rights of mankind" and to make the world "safe for democracy"[11] – universal objectives presumptively defined by the United States alone.

President Bush's address to the West Point graduating class of 2002 reaffirmed the first component of uncontested American military power:

> Competition between great nations is inevitable, but armed conflict in our world is not. More and more civilized nations find ourselves on the

same side — united by common dangers of terrorist violence and chaos. America has, and intends to keep, military strengths beyond challenge ... thereby making the destabilizing arms races of other eras pointless, and limiting rivalries to trade and other pursuits of peace.[12]

President Bush effectively pledged American military might as a public good to pacify the Hobbesian struggle for power among states by asserting an inflated and flawed claim to true Leviathan status.

The publication of the *National Security Strategy of the United States* in 2002 announced the limitless scope of American military intervention even when "uncertainty remains as to the time and place of the enemy's attack."[13] The document declared

> the United States has long maintained the option of preemptive actions to counter a sufficient threat to its national security. ... To forestall or prevent such hostile acts by our adversaries, the United States will, if necessary, act preemptively.[14]

Published in September 2002, the Bush administration's strategic doctrine signaled the US military intervention in Iraq six months later.

The third component of the Bush Doctrine moved beyond military force to establish the United States as the final judge of global morality. In his West Point speech, President Bush underscored this American responsibility:

> Some worry that it is somehow undiplomatic or impolite to speak the language of right and wrong. I disagree. ... There can be no neutrality between justice and cruelty, between the innocent and the guilty. We are in conflict between good and evil, and we do not create a problem, we reveal a problem. And we will lead the world in opposing it [sic.][15]

The assertion that the United States would lead the world in combating evil and making the world safe for democracy, with force if necessary, recalled the presidential campaign slogan of Barry Goldwater in 1964: "Extremism in the defense of liberty is no vice."[16] As if taking his cue from Goldwater, President Bush identified Iran, Iraq, and North Korea as the "axis of evil" in his 2003 State of the Union Address.[17] A Westphalian system with liberal democratic characteristics, ostensibly resting on the consent of the governed, would be paradoxically created by force, if necessary, the risk of falling into a limitless Hobbesian rabbit hole of incessant state conflict notwithstanding.

President Trump down the rabbit hole

President Donald J. Trump deepened the paradox underlying the Bush Doctrine. Whereas Bush still clung to the need for the United States to have some allied support in the form of coalitions of the willing to legitimate its use of force and spread democracy by force, the Trump administration repudiated the Doctrine. The United States had little need for alliances to "Make America Great Again."[18] They were portrayed as burdens and barriers to the realization of President Trump's campaign slogan in the presidential election of 2016, a bumper sticker posing as national strategy. The administration reverted to a classical form of realist theory, rooted in the pre-World War I system of perpetual struggle between and among states, each fearful and distrustful of each other. American military capabilities were not a public good. They were solely at the disposition of the United States.

The Trump administration reduced the Atlantic Alliance to contingent market transactions. Members were viewed as a gaggle of disreputable petitioners greedily seeking American financial and military support. They were not seen as allies united in the common purpose of ensuring the united power of the liberal democracies, a key element of their collective strategy to expand democratic rule around the globe. Trump repeatedly voiced his preference to withdraw the United States from the Atlantic Alliance and "go it alone," if each European state did not meet its financial pledge of spending two percent of their GDP for defense.[19]

In July 2020 President Trump partially made good on his intention to weaken the US commitment to NATO on these grounds. He authorized the withdrawal of 12,000 US troops from Germany without consulting either Berlin or other alliance partners. He explained American troop presence in Germany as too costly because Germany had failed to meet the two percent of GDP target for defense spending set for Alliance members:

> We're reducing the force, because they're [sic] not paying their bills. It's very simple. They're delinquent ... We spend a lot of money on Germany, they take advantage of us on trade and they take advantage on the military, so we're reducing the force.[20]

American troops, ostensibly dedicated to Alliance security, were transformed into mercenaries. For those who remember Britain's hiring Hessian troops to crush the American Revolution, American NATO forces in Europe had become the new Hessians.[21]

The Trump understanding of the market system as a network of specific bilateral relations between contending states replicated his geopolitical approach to interstate relations. Each set of transactions with a specific state was evaluated on the basis of how it advanced either American economic or geopolitical interests. Unlike the Bush Doctrine, President Trump saw no need for coalitions of the willing, nor did he recognize an obligation to adhere to a rule-based market system, whether conceived in strategic or economic terms.

To this anarchic calculus the President personalized the strategic and foreign policy of the United States. The touchstone whether a state was valuable or not depended on its contribution to the President's financial and political interests. This trope flows throughout informed commentary about Trump's understanding and use of American power.[22] Mary Lee Trump, President Trump's niece and a practicing psychologist, diagnosed the president not only as psychologically impaired but also as a threat to the national security of the United States.[23]

Evidence for her diagnosis is found in the president's use of Congressionally approved arms to Ukraine to induce the newly elected Ukrainian president to find proof that former Vice-President Joe Biden had lobbied to foster the interests of the Burisma Holding company, a major gas producer, which had hired Hunter Biden, Joe Biden's son, as a consultant.[24] The disclosure of the President's politically self-interested behavior, whose allegations proved to be false, provoked his first impeachment by the House of Representatives for seeking the assistance of a foreign power to bolster his reelection campaign.

The direction toward which President Trump's economic and geopolitical relations were leading the United States, incrementally, as much deliberately as mindlessly, was toward American support for a flawed anarchical interstate system without liberal democratic characteristics. Allies and foes, real or perceived, were disaggregated into isolated state-to-state relations. Once the administration stripped all states of any privileged status as an enduring ally, it followed logically that allies could be – and were – criticized more than autocrat regimes. President Trump repeatedly expressed admiration for their unquestioned rule, denied him by the Constitution and by still politically viable civic normative constraints.

Threatening allies with trade sanctions or with decreasing American military assistance and American commitment to NATO fostered Russian strategic objectives to weaken the democratic alliance. At a July 2018 meeting in Helsinki, President Trump accepted President Putin's denial that Russia had interfered in the presidential election of 2016. The president's certification of Putin's denial directly contradicted the unanimous consensus to the contrary of all US intelligence agencies, the exhaustive findings of the Mueller Report,[25] and a thousand-page report of the Senate Foreign Relations Committee, issued in August 2020.[26] Despite Congressional sanctions on Russian oligarchs and bipartisan support for NATO to deter Russian aggression, the President favored normalizing the Russian takeover of Crimea and its military intervention in eastern Ukraine. He sought unsuccessfully to convince the other members of the Group of Seven to return Russia as a member, what he characterized as a matter of common sense.

The list of favored authoritarian leaders extended beyond Russia. Over the four years of Trump's administration, President Trump praised the authoritarian leaders of North Korea, China, the Philippines, Hungary, Poland, and Turkey. Despite the vilification of China for its failure to meet Trump's trade demands and for ostensibly creating the coronavirus pandemic, President Trump referred to President Xi Jinping on several occasions as a friend.[27] At a G-20 meeting in Osaka, Japan, in June 2019, the president declared President Xi as "the greatest leader in Chinese history"[28] in seeming efforts to flatter his way to increase the

US bargaining position in stalled trade negotiations. John Bolton also reported the president's approval of President Xi's internment of over a million Uighurs in concentration camps.[29] At the same meeting, he also pressed Xi to have China purchase more American soybeans and wheat to help the President with farmers, hurt by his tariffs on China, in order to bolster his bid for reelection in 2020.[30]

Kim Jong-un received similar praise for his dictatorial rule over North Korea. On August 1, 2019, President Trump tweeted that Chairman Kim "has a great and beautiful vision for his country, and only the United States, with me as President, can make that vision come true."[31] At a rally the next month in West Virginia the President went further: "He [Kim] wrote me beautiful letters, and they were great letters. We fell in love."[32] John Bolton concluded that the president's personalization of his relation with Chairman Kim "was our North Korea policy,"[33] the North Korean nuclear threat notwithstanding.

Other authoritarian rulers also enjoyed President Trump's approval. He praised Philippine President Duarte's crackdown on the drug trade, resulting in thousands of vigilante deaths. He sided with President Recep Tayyip Erdogan over America's Kurdish allies in exposing them to Turkish force by abruptly withdrawing American troops from the Turkish border.[34] An extensive report of the failure of the president to pay taxes for several years despite hundreds of millions in reported profits (purportedly offset by losses) revealed that he had received payments from Turkey, creating a conflict of interest with potentially adverse implications for US security interests.[35] Poland's growing illiberal populist majoritarian democracy was also given the president's blessing by the visit of the Polish president just before his narrow reelection in 2020. Hungary's illiberal democracy was also accorded a presidential boost during the visit of Prime Minister Victor Orban to Washington in 2019.[36]

Weakening alliance cohesion and cooperation with Europe paralleled similar moves in Asia on two fronts. In an apparent attempt to ingratiate himself with Kim Jong-un and against the advice of his Secretary of Defense, President Trump canceled joint military exercises between US and South Korean forces without consulting South Korea. The United States also dealt directly with Pyongyang in lieu of presenting a united allied position in bargaining with Kim Jong-un. Japan and South Korea, America's principal Asian allies, were sidelined in what proved to be a futile effort to reach a nuclear agreement with North Korea, whose nuclear missiles targeted both Japan and South Korea.

US strategic responses to China's expansive claims in the South China Sea[37] were also diluted as a consequence of the administration's reluctance to raise this issue while trying to extract trade concessions from China to advance his electability. Rather than develop a united front with the states confronting China in the South China Sea, the Trump administration decided to go it alone. Its bargaining position and that of allies and interested states in the regions were accordingly weakened on several fronts: in negotiations over trade with Beijing; in containing Chinese power in the South China Sea; in deterring Chinese aggression against Taiwan; in protecting threatened international sea lanes; and in preserving the right and access of China's neighbors to the vast resources of the area.

An American-led collective response was not initiated to include all of the states bordering on the South and East Asian Seas with significant interest in their resources and in the continued internationalization of these waters. In the absence of pushback, the American lapse in strategic resolve, as well as the missed opportunity to harness support of allies and interested Asian states to contain Chinese expansion and aggression in the region, strengthened President Xi's determination to advance China's claims, bolstered by threatening shows of force against Taiwan and Beijing's progressive militarization of the South China Sea, the subject of the next chapters.

In retrospect, beginning with the decision of the Bush administration to overthrow the Hussein regime in 2003, the United States has been principally responsible for the erosion of the power of the liberal democracies in their response to the Imperative of Order. Going beyond the Bush administration, President Trump further diluted the collective power of the liberal democratic states and deepened the mutual distrust of alliance members. That his implied approval of the Chinese and Russian solutions to the Imperative of Order has not been fully implemented in US strategy owes much to the countervailing resistance marshaled within the United States, particularly in Congress, and among America's allies in Europe and Asia.

President Trump's first Secretary of Defense, General James Mattis, echoed these concerns in resigning from his post. In his departing letter to the President, Mattis expressed the same understanding, stated here, of the magnification of American power as a consequence of the collective power of the democracies:

> [O]ur strength as a nation is inextricably linked to the strength of our unique and comprehensive system of alliances and partnerships. While the US remains the indispensable nation in a free world, we cannot protect our interests or serve that role effectively without maintaining strong alliance and showing respect to those allies.[38]

The damage to American security interests and power will not be easily reversed. Even if future American administrations return to geopolitical, economic, and diplomatic strategies to restore collective democratic power, as the Biden administration insists are top priorities, the memory of US defection from alliance solidarity will not be erased. It is important to remember that even in his 2020 defeat, President Trump received more votes than any other Republican president in history. Support for his go-it-alone "Make America Great Again" strategy has deep roots within American public opinion. Once trust among allies in matters of national security is gravely undermined, it is not easily repaired nor ever fully restored. The betrayal of a friendship or infidelity in marriage may be forgiven but neither can ever be forgotten.[39] In President Biden's first foreign policy pronouncement at the Munich Conference on Security in February

2021 proclaimed that his administration was re-committing the United States to its alliances.[40] The real question was whether he could deliver American voters to underwrite that assurance.

Thanks to wavering US loyalty and commitments to alliance solidarity, its alliance systems in the West and in Asia are in tatters. Only a return to the responses of the OWL imperatives of the postwar era can resolve the crisis. Only alliance solidarity can contain the Chinese power and staunch the infectious spread of the Russian majoritarian populist model.

The crisis of the liberal democratic model is not simply its geopolitical erosion. The responses of the liberal democracies, and notably the lapses of the United States from previously positive responses to the Imperatives of Welfare and Legitimacy, further impair the democracies in their efforts to preserve and extend their power to determine how the endemic and inescapable interdependencies of the states and the populations of a global society are to be governed.

Erosion of the Imperative of Welfare

Given space constraints, I will restrict myself to one issue to which the liberal democracies, notably the United States, departed from previous positive responses to the Imperative of Welfare: the growing inequality within the liberal democracies, outpaced by the United States, over the past half-century until now. This issue is systemic across the liberal democracies, resulting in the structural and growing disparity in incomes and material wealth between an increasingly smaller number of haves and a growing number of have-nots as well as the unequal distribution of welfare benefits across these states.[41]

This brief case study both illustrates and highlights other relevant issues that additionally underscore the breakdown of democratic responses to the Imperative of Welfare. The United States has been especially at fault in contributing to these self-defeating lapses. These include the near collapse of the global financial system in 2007–2008;[42] disarray in the West's confrontation of the COVID-19 pandemic and the temporary withdrawal of the United States from the World Health Organization (WHO) in the midst of the epidemic; the Trump administration's rejection of the Paris Accord to cope with global warning; tariff wars, the fragmentation of the global trading system, and the weakening of the World Trade Organization; and the breakdown in the United States and European Union cooperation in collectively confronting China's state-directed capitalist challenge to the Western, rule-based global market system. There is also the relinquishing of democratic leadership in assisting the economic growth of developing states to create incentives for their adoption of the liberal democratic model. The democracies lack a coordinated plan to counter China's Belt and Road Initiative to dominate the world economy, covered extensively in the next chapter.

All of these issues relate to the response of the democracies to the Imperative of Welfare, but their full discussion here would deflect attention from my major concern: to focus on the challenge of global governance and on the flagging power of the liberal democracies to make their case for global governance in a conflict-prone nation-state system, inherently susceptible to armed conflict and global war.

Growing inequality among the liberal democracies

While economists and policy analysts disagree on what methods and data should be used to measure inequality across the liberal democracies, there is general consensus that labor has been the clear loser between the haves and have-nots over the past 40 years.[43] The burden to spur economic growth has fallen on low and semi-skilled labor in the response of the liberal states to three still ongoing trends: economic globalization; technological innovations, including the substitution of capital for labor; and political policies pursued by the democracies, notably the United States and the EU,[44] which are adverse to those whose incomes place them at the bottom quadrants of the population. Not surprisingly, economists also differ on which of these three trends explains the increasing inequality with respect to income, accumulated wealth, and nonwage forms of compensation,[45] including health, education, family support and child care, disability and unemployment insurance, and retirement contributions.

During the heyday of labor wage growth from the end of World War II to the 1970s, American and European Union markets were essentially autarchic, largely insulated from international competition. The production of goods and services was concentrated within the boundaries of the nation-state.[46] The pressure to seek international markets and to cut the cost of production drove multinational corporations to develop and expand to global markets. This period led to several fundamental changes in the world economy adversely affecting high-wage labor in the democracies. Offshore investment skyrocketed to take advantage of large pools of foreign, low-wage unskilled labor in the production of textiles, furniture, electronics, and other labor-intensive areas. The production of goods and services was increasingly de-nationalized.

As the next chapter details, national factories were also de-constructed into the multiplication of discrete supply chains across global markets states to cut corporate costs. On the plus side, increased competition led to lower consumer prices and improved and more reliable products than could be achieved by an autarchic system. Detroit automakers learned this hard lesson as they lost market shares to foreign producers, notably Japan and Germany.[47] Conversely, while consumer gains were diffused throughout national populations, the damage to labor of increased competitiveness fell hardest on previously high-wage earners. Among the liberal democracies, offshore investment in low-wage developing states resulted in millions of job losses; shorter worker hours; average wage income decline; and higher worker turnover. The convergence of these "perfect storm" outcomes enlarged and accelerated inequality in income and welfare across the democracies.

Not surprisingly, labor bargaining power across the democracies also substantially eroded.[48] A report of the Organization for Economic Co-Operation and Development (OECD) noted a steep decline in union membership. With 1980 as 100 percent for the index of union density, membership fell to 60 percent in 2016 with the trend line pointing downward. Labor protection also declined. An OECD index registered a drop from 100 percent in 1980 to 75 percent in 2006.[49]

In 1956, approximately 28 percent of all workers in the United States were union members. By 2016 that number shrank to five percent. The losses were particularly acute in the private sector. Corporations facing union demands for increased compensation or better working conditions undercut the bargaining power of labor by threatening to relocate elsewhere, as often as not to a developing country, if labor refused to accept its take-it-or-leave-it proposals. Shattered was the social contract between capital and labor of the postwar period. Enhanced and stiffened corporate bargaining power, aided by supportive local, state, and federal legislation, further weakened labor's bargaining power and deepened its plight. The proliferation of right-to-work laws, noncompetitive labor contracts, arbitration procedures favoring corporations over labor, no-poaching and collusion agreements, and resistance to increases of the minimum wage disciplined labor to corporate demands.[50]

The largest gainers from offshore investment were the developing states, principally China, India, Mexico, and Brazil as well as a lesser number of states in Central and Latin America and East and South Asia. China, as the next chapter develops, was the largest gainer. Western investment played a significant role in China's success to have lifted hundreds of millions of Chinese from poverty in a generation. A mutually beneficial bargain was struck between multinational corporations and China. The Western multinationals exploited China's enormous pool of unskilled, low-wage labor at the expense of Western labor and significantly underwrote China's ability to lift hundreds of millions out of poverty. As a byproduct of Western investment and the transfer of industrial know-how, China also became the hub for the creation of the supply chains that currently undergird the global production of goods and services.

President Xi Jinping's presentation to the World Economic Forum in Davos in January, 2021, underscored the crucial importance of China's retention of its dominant position. He censured efforts both to re-nationalize global supply chains and to sanction China for its system of state-directed capitalism:

> [T]o willfully impose decoupling, supply disruption or sanctions, and to create isolation or estrangement will only push the world into division and confusion. …We should … keep the global industrial and supply chains stable and open. …. It serves no one's interest to use the pandemic as an excuse to reverse globalization and go for seclusion and decoupling.[51]

The dependency of the United States and other democratic states on Chinese supply of emergency medical equipment to cope with the COVID-19 epidemic exposed their vulnerability to supply chains not under their control. Xi was right that a return to an autarchic world economic system would be disastrous for all states, but mindless submission to the corporate and national interests driving supply chains was no longer a feasible strategy for the protection of national security.

Technological innovation and the major shift of multinational corporations to invest more in capital than in labor represent the second important driver of global inequality. The share of national income received by workers fell 64.5 percent in the third quarter of 1974 to 56.8 percent in the second quarter of 2017.[52] This drop is directly related to the greater portion of productivity gains going to capital, corporate management and CEO compensation, and holders of stock and other income-generating instruments than to labor. The Brookings Institution's Hamilton Project reported that between 1947 and 2017, real labor productivity increased more than 400 percent, but compensation to labor increased only 300 percent.[53] During the recovery from the Great Recession in 2007–2008,

> growth in capital intensity (the ratio of capital services to labor hours) has fallen far short of historical norms, even contracting in 2011 and 2012. This means that workers have less capital to work with, which impairs their productivity and wages.[54]

The biggest losers in the digital revolution, begun in the 1970s and 1980s, were unskilled and semi-skilled labor in the democracies. They are likely to be further adversely impacted by the emerging next industrial revolution, driven by rapid advances in Artificial Intelligence. This trend will further automate the repetitive labor of unskilled and semi-skilled workers, extending to clerical staff and, progressively, to the professions of accounting, finance, medical diagnosis, and mid-level management. Powerful incentives of cost savings and of increased efficiencies in production and service industries, afforded by AI, are inducing corporations to accelerate the choice of AI over labor.

MIT economist, Doran Acemoglu, captures the damage to labor and family households if the AI trend is not balanced with resources being devoted to assist workers to adapt to this emerging revolution:

> While in the four decades after World War II automation and new tasks contributing to labor demand went hand-in-hand, a very different technological tableau began in the 1980s — along **more automation** and lot less of everything else. Automation acted as the handmaiden of inequality. New technologies primarily **automated** the more routine tasks in clerical occupations and on factory floors. This meant the demand and wages of workers specializing in blue-collar jobs and some clerical functions declined.[55]

Labor unions correctly concluded that increased investment abroad would create more jobs in other countries, principally in the developing world, than at home.[56] The transfer of job-creating technological innovations abroad would be lost to domestic labor. The resulting increased demand for college-educated and higher skilled workers further diminished the demand for low and semi-skilled labor. In 1979 holders of bachelor's degrees could expect to earn 134 percent more than those with only a high school education and those with advanced degrees 154 percent more. By 2016 those ratios shifted upward. Those with a Bachelor's degree and an advanced degree could expect a rise, respectively, of 168 and 213 percent.[57] These gaps would be deepened as demand for professionals in managerial, engineering, finance, consulting, and design occupations increased in response to the revolution in automation.[58]

The impact of globalization, mobile capital, and technological innovation on accelerating and deepening inequality among the liberal democracies can be seen across a broad spectrum. Widening inequality is measured by the Gini coefficient for each state in which the higher Gini number for a country indicates the greater income inequality for that country. A study by the OECD found that the Gini coefficient rose in 17 of 22 countries. It rose by four points in the United States in the mid-1980s. Twenty years later, the United States registered the highest Gini coefficient among OECD states. The United States is the clear outlier among advanced Western states, measured by its high Gini coefficient of 41.4 in 2018.[59]

In the United States, inflation-adjusted wages were only 10 percent higher in 2017 than in 1973. Annual real wage growth was just below 0.2 percent.[60] Hourly wage earnings in 2016 dollars grew very slowly between 1973 and 2017.[61] The largest gain between 1991 and 2017 saw an increase of 15 percent in real wages and 36.33 percent in material benefits, like health and unemployment insurance.[62] Since the 1980s to the first decade of the 21st century, in the majority of cases covering the liberal democracies the richest ten percent grew faster than the bottom ten percent. For the United States, the top ten percent grew at a ratio of 14 to 1 relative to the bottom ten percent.

The public policies of neglect among the liberal democracies, notably in the United States, in their failure to assist workers to adapt to the new world economy was a significant cause of increasing inequality. The failure was one more of omission than commission.[63] Thanks to the minority rule of Congress, outlined in the next section on the Imperative of Legitimacy, legislation to increase the federal minimum wage was stuck at US$7.25 an hour for decades. Inflation ineluctably reduced the real wages of workers.[64] Little was also done to assist the families of the working poor by increasing the Child Tax Credit or the Earned Income Tax. Unemployment insurance was made available, but for a restricted period of time to encourage work, even if jobs for low-skilled labor were not available.

A more relevant policy to help labor than time-limited unemployment insurance would have been to provide funding for job training to position workers to meet the demand for higher skilled labor in the digital era of increased global competition. Little funding was devoted to worker retraining and what was available often proved ineffective and wasteful.[65] There was little funding for effective training programs or community colleges where successful programs for skilled occupation had been developed. While capital had no difficulty moving in and out of the country, workers were not provided moving expenses to go where jobs were in demand. Corporate and professional moves were largely covered in the private sector, but no equivalent support was available to workers seeking employment in the private or public sectors. The rate of worker mobility in the search for higher paying jobs also declined since the 1990s for workers of all ages, education levels, and states of residence.[66]

Multinational corporations, competing in foreign competition, enjoyed privileged access to state and federal funding and material support throughout the long period of wage stagnation since the 1970s. The federal government underwrote corporate research and development across a wide spectrum from AI to pharmaceuticals, communications, and electronics. Multiple forms of tax breaks were available to corporations. Subsidies aided oil and gas. Tariffs protected sugar, tobacco, cotton, and ethanol production from foreign competition. Corporations also escaped taxation on earners abroad if they did not repatriate those profits. One estimate reports that corporations hold US$2 trillion in foreign accounts.[67]

Taxing corporate offshore assets, if repatriated, would underwrite public infrastructure programs and domestic investment with the salutary effect of increasing labor employment and of raising wages. Tax laws, however, encouraged foreign over domestic investment. More jobs were created abroad than at home. From 1990 to 2011 employment surged in US overseas multinational affiliates, doubling over these two decades. During this period, the share of employment by multinationals in the United States declined from 79 to 66 percent. In effect, multinational companies were creating foreign jobs at a greater rate than in the United States.[68] Apple, for example, has about 50,000 employees in the United States but employs hundreds of thousands of workers in China, Taiwan, and elsewhere.

The richest Americans also escaped taxation on a grand scale. The narrow definition of income rooted in the US Tax Code shields billionaires from taxation. Most of their accumulated wealth is in the form of unrealized gains in the form of stock and property. They pay taxes on their wealth only when they sell these assets. In June 2021 *ProPublica* published leaked tax filings of 25 of the richest people in the United States.[69] These billionaires saw their wealth grow, collectively, from 2014 to 2018 by US$401 billion. They paid a total of US$13.4 billion in federal income taxes over this five-year period, a tax rate of 3.4 percent.

Equity firm CEOs were especially adroit in gaming the Tax Code to escape taxation. A key loophole permitted them to transform high management fees into capital gains rather than to declare them as income. The capital gains tax rate is 20 percent vs. a federal income tax rate of 37 percent for high-income individuals. It is estimated that this feat of tax legerdemain costs the federal government $130 billion over a decade.[70]

Focusing on the richest of the top rich earners – Warren Buffett, Jeff Bezos, Michael Bloomberg, and Elon Musk – further dramatizes the inequity, which is embedded in the US Tax Code. In the 2014 to 2018 period, their wealth grew, respectively, by US$24.3 billion, US$99.08 billion, US$22.5. billion, and US$13.9 billion. They paid, respectively, US$23.7 million (0.10%), US$973 million (0.98%), US$292 million (1.30%), and US$455 million (3.27%).[71] Meanwhile, in this period households saw their wealth increase by US$65,000, largely through home ownership, but they were taxed US$62,000, pretty much wiping out their net gains. Put another way, the personal tax bill for the wealthiest persons was US$1.9 billion, while wage earners, according to *ProPublica* sources, paid US$143 billion.[72]

It is important to recognize that variations in inequality across the democracies are not just the inexorable workings of free markets. This fluctuating condition of inequality is also in no small part the result of the public choices that a people and its leadership make. Gross inequality, where the super-rich extract from the market income and assets that exceed the value that they contribute to the proper functioning of markets, rests on policy choices. The wealth of billionaires, described above, exemplifies public policy which is legalized and institutionalizes inequality on a vast scale in the United States. Conversely, Scandinavian countries chose to diminish inequality as a choice, while actively supporting a free market system. These differences in the responses of the democracies to the Imperative of Welfare also reveal, *ipso facto*, their contesting notions of legitimacy and social justice.[73]

Hidden below the surface of widening income and welfare inequality is the scourge of widespread urban social dislocation as the result of job losses. In many ways the disappearance of work, both unemployment and fewer hours of work, have a more devastating effect on the urban poor than low wages and income stagnation. William Julius Wilson's research compared the difference in social decay between neighborhoods where the poor had jobs or did not. In the latter instance, Wilson found that many of today's problems in the inner-city ghetto neighborhoods – crime, drug use, family dissolution, high divorce rates, increased child poverty, low levels of social organization, etc. – are fundamentally a consequence of the disappearance of work. These socially disruptive impacts fell unequally on Blacks and other disadvantaged groups who were structurally unemployed.[74]

The ethics of labor-corporate relations was also transformed to justify the destruction of the postwar social contract. Milton Friedman, a world-celebrated Nobel Laureate in Economics and founder of the Chicago School of Economics, implicitly justified the breakup as essential for the protection of free markets and for the preservation and extension of political freedom.[75] In a celebrated article in *The New York Times Magazine*,[76] Friedman portrayed the notion of corporate social responsibility as a vestigial relic of the notion that CEOs and businessmen had communal obligations other than making money. Their sole loyalty was to their employers – stockholders and their material wealth. Friedman argued that

> in a free-enterprise, private-property system, a corporate executive is an employee of the owners of the business. He has direct responsibility to his employers. That responsibility is to conduct the business in accordance with their desires, which generally will be to make as much money as possible.[77]

The chasm between capital and labor and the antagonism between corporations and workers could not have been more pointedly drawn. Labor was reduced in this rendering of corporate responsibility to a commodity to be purchased at least cost to increase profits.

US tax reform strengthened laws already encouraging investment abroad to escape taxation. Decreased federal revenue hobbled Washington to address the welfare needs of an aging population, education, or the rehabilitation of a decaying national infrastructure as a drag on economic competitiveness. The gap between the haves and have-nots was further cratered by raising the ceiling on nontaxable inheritance. A brief word about these shifts of income from the four bottom quadrants, especially the bottom fifth, to the top quadrant highlights the blow to inequality.

The US 2017 tax reform bill deepened further the downward trend toward inequality. The bulk of tax benefits went to the top 10 percent of households and individuals, with much of this increase allotted to those earners at the one per-cent of the population, with even a greater share going to those at the one-tenth of one percent level of earnings. Under the law, the top fifth, one percent, and one-tenth of one percent receive tax cuts, respectively, of US$7,000, US$61,000, and US$215,000. The lowest fifth, second, and third were accorded tax cuts, respectively, of US$70, US$390, and US$901.

The already great disparity in wealth held by a small number of households was widened in raising the ceiling of what could be transferred to beneficiaries. The top fifth of the US population possesses approximately 85 percent of the nation's wealth. Between 1982 and 2012 the richest one percent of the popula-tion doubled their share of national income from 10 to 20 percent. The 16,000 households in the top .01 percent quadrupled their share from one percent to five whose annual incomes were US$24 million.[78] A democracy based on one person, one vote and equality before the law slipped further into an oligarchical regime controlling the nation's wealth and possessed of a corresponding preponderant political voice to protect and to increase their wealth through legislation. The richest of the rich do not have to cheat on their taxes. They can rely on laws of their own making to pay little or no taxes and yet meet what the law providen-tially requires to underwrite their lavish lifestyles.

Corporate tax rates were also cut from 38 to 21 percent. This brought US tax-ing of corporations in line with the trend among other countries to cut corporate rates. Between 2000 and 2018, 76 countries cut their corporate tax rates. In 2000, more than 55 countries had corporate tax rates at about 30 percent, in 2018 that number fell to 20. The International Monetary Fund characterized the harmful effects to states involved in the competition to cut corporate tax rates: "When one jurisdiction crafts a new tax loop hole or secrecy facility that successfully attracts mobile money, others copy or outdo it in a race to the bottom."[79]

The corporate tax cut was designed to promote investment but led instead to corporate buy-backs of corporate stock, enhanced CEO and management compensation, and increased distribution of dividends and capital gains to stockholders, most of who are in the ranks of top earners. Past legislation, providing for decreased tax exposure if corporations moved all or part of their operations abroad and earned profits through these foreign affiliates, was enlarged through the 2017 tax reform. Decreased revenue from trillions of dollars in tax cuts spelled decreased revenue available to meet the increasing costs of Medicare, Medicaid, and Social Security, education, and infrastructure, while raising through circular political logic the charge that spending for these public goods had to be slashed for lack of funds.

Erosion of the Imperative of Legitimacy

A critical determinant of a regime's legitimacy is its capacity to provide for the material welfare of its whole population, certainly not to favor the most advantaged economically and politically. The case study covered above – rising income and material welfare inequality – reveals the failure of the liberal democracies to address the plight of lower income earners and their vulnerability to global competition, mobile capital, and technological innovation. Among the liberal democracies the United States is the leading offender. The tax reform bill of 2017 compounded these failures of omission and commission. Inequality has not only grown but also shows few signs of diminishing any time soon either through market or governmental reforms.

Shortcomings in providing for the welfare of the populace have been reinforced by the defection of liberal democratic regimes from the institutional rules and civic norms that are foundation stones of liberal democratic rule. The rise of populism across the liberal democracies is the most prominent challenge to liberal democratic government. The United States has not been spared this threat. It arrived at the precipice of taking that plunge on January 6, 2021, when a mob, inspired by President Trump's repeated lie that his electoral defeat was rigged, assaulted the US Capital, Congress, and the Constitution to stop the count of electoral votes investing Joe Biden as president.

Unlike majoritarian populism in Poland, Hungary, and Turkey, as Anne Applebaum reminds us,[80] American populism is lodged in a minority comprised of otherwise fragmented elements which have coalesced into an anti-democratic movement within a minority Republican Party under the thrall of former President Trump. The very institutions and rules designed to protect minorities from what James Madison termed majority factions are now among the key vehicles by which a populist minority, paradoxically, can seize power legally under the Constitution by violating liberal democratic rules of fair play, resting on free and unfettered elections in which access to voting is available equally to all citizens. The conundrum confronting popular (not populist) government in the United States is the overshadowing threat of rule by a minority governing legally, but illegitimately. Before probing the elements of the American conundrum some context is needed to understand the attraction of populism as a global movement and the particular form that it has assumed in American politics and governance.

A principal threat to liberal democratic rule arises from within the liberal democracies. Pogo's lament captures the paradox: "We have met the enemy and they are us."[81] The emergence and infectious spread of populist, majoritarian regimes out of previously liberal democratic states poses an inherent existential threat to liberal rule. Russia provides a vivid example of the descent, much abroad today, toward autocratic populism. The roots of populism, like weeds, arise simultaneously along with those nurturing democratic rule. James Madison warned in No. 10 of the *Federalist Papers* about the vulnerability of the American republic to populism. Alexis de Tocqueville also cautioned about the possibility of the tyranny of the majority.[82]

Populism in the guise of a majority-imposed authoritarian rule lies always just below the surface of liberal democratic governance. It has a long history of periodic outbursts that break through to strangle democracy.[83] It currently enjoys widespread popular support. Anne Applebaum captures the declining attraction of liberal governance in the subtitle of her volume, *The Twilight of Democracy*, as *The Seductive Lure of Authoritarianism*.[84] That allure does not assume a single form, predicable of all populist regimes. Each populist regime emerges primarily from within the special socioeconomic and political conditions of a liberal democracy. Each defection from liberal democracy is in a sense *sui generis*, shaped largely from the particular domestic circumstances as well as the regional and global setting in which the populist infection thrives. Like an uncontrolled virus, populist regimes spread the infection to other liberal regimes. Viewed globally, as populist regimes corrupt democratic government, they occupy, cumulatively, more and more of those spaces of global governance that would otherwise accrue to the liberal democracies. Their expansion encourages their replication elsewhere.

Why do populations choose authoritarian populist regimes? Why do they prefer to follow a populist leader, often prejudicing their own self-interests and material welfare? Why do they vote for authoritarian rule rather than the freedom of self-government? While the sources for the choice of populations to abandon liberal government are in dispute, the fact of abandonment is not. No clear, unproblematic answer is possible to explain the subversion of democratic rule.[85] One can speculate that the failures of liberal democracies to live up to the promise of effective governance can explain their repudiation. That is tantamount to a tautology. A review of the scholarly literature suggests that the reasons for the breakdown range over a wide spectrum of factors. Deep political polarization, the demonization of opponents, and chronic and bitter struggles for power between rival groups, which sap the effectiveness of government, sour a population on democratic politics. The brief and bitter experience of the Russian people with democracy in the first decade of the Russian Federation, covered in Chapter 7, illustrates how quickly a people can turn to populist rule in a vain attempt to escape their quandary and discontents.[86]

There is one thread in various colorations that runs through all populist regimes. They assert that they alone represent all of the people in contrast to the fractured, pluralist representation associated with liberal democracies. Only a populist regime and its leader can purportedly represent all of the people and thereby surmount the confusion and under-representation of the people as a whole, produced by countless groups engaged in an interminable struggle for power that divides people. Only the populist party and its leader can truly embody the people as a whole. As Nadia Urbinati observes, "Populism is … internal to and a challenge to representative democracy; it competes with it on the meaning and practice of representation."[87]

It is important not to equate populism with fascism. Unlike fascist leaders who repudiate elections as the test of legitimacy, populism relies on elections for the sanction of legitimacy. While both fascism and populism assign supreme authority to a leader, they achieve that objective through different means. Carl Schmitt's defense of fascism provides a rationale for the underlying paradoxical claim of populist regimes that they can at once represent all of the people – the claim of the fascist leader – while excluding their critics and opponents from political participation and influence through a rigged electoral process.

Populism draws inspiration from Schmitt's conception of representation as the "will of the people." The people's "will," ostensibly a palpable entity, transcends individual citizens to comprise the nation as a whole, which the populist regime alone represents. Schmitt reconciled the contradictions underlying the fascist conception of the people in this mysterious way:

> The unanimous opinion of a hundred million private persons is neither the will of the people nor public opinion. … [D]emocracy is something other than a registration system for secret ballots. Compared to a democracy that is direct, not only in the technical sense but also in a vital sense, parliament appears [to be] an artificial machinery, produced by liberal reasoning, while dictatorial and Caesaristic methods not only can produce the acclamation of the people but can also be a direct expression of democratic substance and power.[88]

By stipulating the existence of the "direct expression of democratic substance and power" to which only the populist leader and party are privy, the populist regime appeals to divergent groups who are marshaled into a ruling electoral majority. Across populist regimes, the divergent groups comprising the populist majority share a sense of identity loss within a liberal democratic regime. They hold both uncompromising grievances against a liberal regime and deep suspicion and hatred of its supporters. They feel locked out of representation or underrepresented. Their voices are not heard and their concerns are dismissed or assailed. This emotionally charged social movement sets the stage for the emergence of populist rule. The real or perceived denigration of majorities or of significant minorities of their identities in liberal democracies, whether variously expressed in social, class, cultural, or religious denotations, fuels the spread of populist regimes.

To preclude attacks on populist regimes as fascist, populist regimes, as Federico Finchelstein explains,[89] modified Schmitt's Caesaristic notion of legitimacy. They retain elections as the touchstone of populist rule. In this way populist regimes, like Juan Peron's in Argentina and those which spread to other states in its wake, could both reject fascism and still claim to be more democratic than the liberal democracies. Populist-directed elections – some free, most rigged, and manipulated – promote the myth of a singularly integrated moral community over and above and superior to the individual citizen. Rejected by populist rule is the inevitably fractured composition of the population, which is morally held together by the Rousseaunian principles that all humans are free and equal. The divergent identities and interests jostling for power within the politics of a liberal democracy are expected to accede to these unifying principles and to the equality of all citizens and elected officials before the rule of law. All populist regimes reject Rousseanian principles.

Those supporting a populist regime are equal as a consequence of the exclusion of their opponents. To paraphrase George Orwell's insight in *Animal Farm*, all citizens are equal, but some are more equal than others. Stipulated privileged citizenship will differ from one populist regime to another. In the American context, white supremacists and many within the Christian community assert an inherent right – even an obligation – to impose their values and norms on the nation as a whole. They identify citizenship not as an idea of one person, one vote, but as a selective attribute of being white and Christian. These qualities are stipulated to be the foundation stones of the American nation and Constitution. Those possessing these redeeming properties have an inalienable right to determine who should vote and to govern a regime. The repudiation of equality before the law was the *cris de coeur* of those who attacked the US Capitol on January 6, 2021. However much they may have had differences in their ranks, they were united in the cry "to take back America" – their America – and to "Make America Great Again," rallying tropes of the Trump presidency to ensure that the power and legitimacy to rule lies exclusively with a white, Christian population.

The histories of India and the United States illustrate this tension between an inclusive and exclusive conception of citizenship underlying populist rule. From the inception of independence and the creation of the Indian state, Indian society has been profoundly split over its identity. The problem of defining who is truly Indian resolved itself into two opposed solutions. At issue, as Scott Hibbard defined the dilemma,

> is whether that national community ought to be defined inclusively — with membership extended to all members of the population — or whether full membership should be reserved for those of the dominant community. In other words, should the nation be defined along religious or secular lines.[90]

In the three-quarters of a century since independence, the Indian peoples have oscillated between these two endpoints in defining legitimate rule and Indian citizenship.[91]

The Bharatiya Janata Party (BJP), the dominant party in India since 2014, would transform India and its ruling part into a Hindu majoritarian populist regime. Excluded would be India's 200 million Muslim minority, representing approximately 18 percent of the population in contrast to approximately one billion Hindus, who comprise 80 percent. The Hindu nationalists propose to invest all Indian citizens with *Hindutva* or "Hinduness," whether they wished to be incorporated into that metaphysical group or not.[92] Carl Schmidt's "will of the people" become all those who are informed by "Hindutva." This cultural move transforms India from a secular into a Hindu state.

Since the introduction of slavery in 1619, the United States has been plagued by a similar struggle to define who is a citizen. The Constitution defined Negro slaves as three-fifths persons with no right to vote. Native Americans were not included in the Preamble of the Constitution of "We the People." The Civil War, which ended slavery, was then carried forward until now as a struggle for white supremacy, centered but not exclusively practiced in the South. Jim Crow institutionalized white supremacy through segregation under the euphemism of separate but equal. Class divisions between rich and poor whites were muted and submerged in the commitment to suppress Negroes.

In his classic work on *Southern Politics in State and Nation*, V.O. Key identified the primary system as the principal vehicle used in the south to ensure white supremacy. Various means were used to suppress voting – poll taxes, the ability to read, intimidation, and even lynching to dissuade participation in elections, all the products of Jim Crow. Negroes were excluded from the primaries. Whites then would choose a candidate who invariably won public office in the general election.[93] That system held until the 1960s when voting rights bills opened the way for Blacks to vote and to be eligible for public office in the south. President Richard Nixon subsequently exploited widespread opposition to Black voting in his "southern strategy."[94] That strategy, which implicitly endorsed white supremacy and racism, shifted a majority of voters in the south from their traditional support of the Democratic to the Republican Party. The realignment of the parties preserved white supremacy now embodied in many voters loyal to the Republican Party.

President Trump went beyond so-called "dog whistles," silently signaling Republican sufferance of white supremacy. His takeover of the Republican Party openly mainstreamed white supremacy, adding anti-Semitism and anti-immigrant sentiment for good measure. He embedded these "anti's" into national politics and as articles of faith within the Republican Party. The unquestioning support of a majority of Republicans for former President Trump, many of who accept his claim, rejected by 60 courts, that he was cheated from reelection, has revamped the Party as a populist party, increasingly possessed of anti-democratic features.

The attack on the Capital, Congress, and the Constitution by his supporters has had a transformational impact on American politics. The party struggle for power can no longer be portrayed simply as a traditional competition between liberals and conservatives, both of who accept a shared understanding of the Constitution and civic norms. For the foreseeable future, as long as Trumpism can be sustained, party competition is more accurately characterized as a struggle between liberals and anti-liberals, that is, between those who believe in one person, one vote and those who privilege only those voters who support the party's leader, populism in its raw form.

Other populist or aspiring populist regimes also promote identity politics over adherence to the constituent and contextual civic norms of liberal democratic rule, protecting the freedom and equality of all citizens. The Polish Law and Order Party of Jaroslaw Kaczynski and the Fidesz Party of Victor Orban proclaim both regimes as Christian and anti-immigrant. Both oppose the European Union's policy of admitting Muslims into Europe from other countries fraught with civil war and crushing poverty. Both strive to undermine secularism in Poland and Hungary and establish traditional religions as the foundation of legitimate rule.

Similarly, but from an opposed religious perspective, Prime Minister Recep Tayyip Erdogan has effectively transformed Turkey from a secular to a Muslim state. From yet a different quarter, Nicolas Maduro continues the lead of his deceased predecessor, Hugo Chavez, to rule on the basis of class division. Supporters of the regime, many from the poorest classes of the nation, are the "real people" of Venezuela. Russia, also a secular state, uses elections to marginalize opponents. Those who remain intransigent are harassed, convicted of violations of the law, or simply exiled, imprisoned, or assassinated.[95]

What all of these populist regimes and wannabe populist regimes, like the Trump presidency, have in common is that large portions of voters, a majority in most instances, are willing to pledge unwavering support both for their chosen restrictively defined group and allegiance to the group leader over the moral community of all citizens who are free and equal, the foundational principle underlying a liberal democratic regime. Under populism the constituent and contextual norms of a liberal democracy are made hostage to autocratic rule.

A review of the principal strategies and policy tools as well as coercive and persuasive instruments relied upon by populist leaders and parties to acquire and hold onto power exposes the vulnerabilities of liberal governance and the mounting obstacles that must be surmounted before the liberal model can be re-established where it has been usurped. This is a collective enterprise existentially imposed on all democracies, if each, independently, is to remain a liberal democracy. That cooperative effort is also merged with the larger challenge of ensuring that the space accorded liberal governance across the nation-state system is not diminished further and that the pooled power of the democracies is progressively enlarged to keep the competing non-democratic models in check.

Populist regimes also share two additional characteristics. First, in basing their legitimacy on elections, they reject both the constituent and contextual civic norms which constrain the use of power in liberal democracies.[96] These consist of checks and balances or the separation of powers as well as historically observed civic limits to preclude the illegitimate use of power.[97] An elected leader, embodying the will of the people, as Carl Schmidt contends, is not bound by the rules of a liberal democracy. Pluralistic liberal societies, inherently polarized and divided, are perpetually engulfed in incessant conflicts. Checks and balances, separation of powers, and traditional norms frustrate the self-proclaimed populist leader to represent the people as a whole as he defines them. Only he can solve the nation's problems if freed from what are portrayed as outdated traditional practices as well as constitutional and normative straitjackets.[98]

Second, populist regimes display no inhibition in violating the multiple civil norms that have evolved over time which surround and support constitutional governance. These buffers refer, *inter alia*, to the preservation of the basic trust in the institutions of government and the press, tolerance of diverse and opposing viewpoints, truth-telling, shared notions of basic facts as the basis for evaluating governmental policies and their outcomes, the acceptance of a common good above the narrow interests of each citizen, and a willingness of citizens to sacrifice to advance the nation's common good.

Criticisms or continued opposition of the leader are portrayed as tantamount to an attack on the people whom he alone represents.

Divine qualities and omniscience are often attributed to the leader. Eva Peron proclaimed "Peron is a God for all of us, to the extent that we do not conceive of the sky without Peron. Peron is our sun, Peron is the water. Peron is the life of our country and the Argentine people."[99] Many Evangelical Christians, who are among President Trump's staunchest supporters, believe he is sent from God.[100] Rick Perry, President Trump's former Secretary of Energy, stated that he is God's "Chosen One."[101] By President Trump's own account, he is also an uncommon genius and smarter than anyone else – a *Very Stable Genius*.[102] He contended that his knowledge extended over a wide range of expert areas, from predicting the trajectory of hurricanes to advising best medical practices to control of the COVID-19 pandemic, including the inappropriate use of medicines dedicated to other illnesses and the disparagement of protective masks and social distancing.[103]

Attacks on liberal democracy are launched simultaneously on several fronts. The courts are among the first targets of populist rule. Unfavorable rulings are vilified as biased. Judges perceived as opponents are retired or dismissed to provide opportunities for loyalists to take their places. The scope of authority of the courts to constrain the populist regime is narrowed or nullified. Critics and rivals are harassed, punished, and jailed for alleged infractions of the law. Rule by law gradually replaces the rule of law before which all are equal. The notion of a neutral judiciary is reduced to an oxymoron.

Parallel assaults are against a free press. Written and broadcast journalism as well as social media platforms and the internet are brought under state control. News at odds with populist regime priorities and its narrative are dismissed as fake news. Alternate facts are substituted for factual, empirically verified reporting. In a TV interview, Kellyanne Conway, an adviser to President Trump, affirmed Trump's disproved assertion that the crowd size of his inauguration was greater than that of President Obama, by defending the use of "alternate facts" in a TV interview: "Think about what you just said to your viewers [about] crowd size at the inauguration. That's why we feel compelled to … put alternative facts out there."[104] Journalists are also hampered in carrying out their work. They and their media outlets are branded as enemies of the people. Along with China, Saudi Arabia, and Egypt, Turkey has imprisoned the most journalists. As of December 30, 2018, the Erdogan regime had arrested 165 journalists, convicted 75, and sought an additional 148.[105] Threats and duress father self-censorship.

Facing the criticisms and attacks of a free press and media outlets, populist regimes invariably create their own systems of communicating directly with the population. The aim is to dominate the news cycle and to allow only its narrative to reach the public. Only its interpretations of regime policies are permitted to be aired. What remaining non-governmental sources of information that may still be operating are co-opted by the regime either by using the coercive techniques noted earlier or by offering the blandishments of bribery or access to power. During his presidency, President Trump's Twitter feed counted viewers in the tens of millions and enjoyed wide support from conservative talk radio and Fox News.[106]

Muzzling or enlisting the intellectual class is also an important priority of the populist regime. Victor Orban closed Central European University because it was perceived as a threat to the Orban regime. George Soros, a Hungarian émigré who helped create and finance the university, sought to educate college students in liberal values. Anne Applebaum traces the defection of former advocates of liberal governance in Poland, Hungary, and the United States – respectively, Jacek Kurski, Maria Schmidt, and Laura Ingraham. She presents them as representatives of a much larger segment of the intelligentsia who abandoned liberal values across these states to champion the populist regime. These sophistic enablers recall those who, once liberal supporters of the Weimer Republic, swiftly switched their allegiance to Hitler's Nazi regime when the winds of power changed.[107] Czeslaw Milosz recounts the same turnabout in postwar Poland.[108] Former critics and opponents of Communist rule abruptly became collaborators and propagandists for the Communist regime installed by the Soviet Union.

As critics are silenced and former opponents are co-opted in the consolidation of populist power, it comes as no surprise that all opinions other than those flowing from official sources, notably the populist leader, will crowd out dissenting views. Scientific knowledge and facts are subordinated to political power. Expertise at odds with a regime's political priorities is dismissed as self-interested, ill-informed, and corrupt or, worse, as an attack on the leader, his party, and *ipso facto*, on the people who he alone represents. All populist regimes also assault the bureaucracy to bring it in tow. There is no space for a nonpolitical and nonpartisan opinion. Under populism, there can be no space accorded to a neutral bureaucracy and professional expertise independent of political opinion. The Polish, Hungarian, Turkish, and Trump regimes made a point of replacing public servants with loyalists.

The Trump presidency: minority populism serving minority rule

American populism has a long history, dating from 19th nativism and anti-immigration to Huey Long, George Wallace, and President Trump. The Trump brand of populism is too complex to be fully developed here. How and why American politics has moved toward populism requires far more discussion than can be attempted here. I have concentrated on key flaws in the design of the Constitution and the erosion of traditional norms in the conduct of American politics as enabling Trumpian populism to emerge and prosper. A large minority of voters is now aligned in opposition to liberal democratic rule. They form a wide-ranging anti-democratic coalition still loyal at this writing to former President Donald Trump. The Republican Party under the sway of Trump has become the funnel through which the complex elements of the populist coalition find expression.

William Barr's conception of the unitary executive is a good place to begin to expose the roots of Trumpian populism. Barr, President Trump's Attorney General, provided a patina of legitimacy to President Trump's disregard of constitutional and traditional norms constraining his exercise of unchecked power. Traditionally, the Attorney General is expected to be loyal to the Constitution, not to the President. The conventional norm, recognized by previous presidents in greater or lesser but still to a discernible degree, is that the Attorney General is not the President's legal counsel. Barr largely abandoned that norm in servicing the Trump presidency.

Barr's strained interpretation of the unitary executive frees the President from Congressional and court oversight or restraint. In a memorandum describing his notion of the unitary executive, Barr stipulated that

> the Constitution ... places no limit on the President's authority to act on matters which concern him or his own conduct. ... While the President has subordinates — the Attorney General ... — who exercise

prosecutorial discretion on his behalf, they are merely "his hand," ...
[T]he discretion they exercise is the President's discretion, and their decisions are legitimate precisely because they remain under his supervision.
... Nor does any statute purport to restrict the President's authority over
matters in which he has an interest. ... [The Department of Justice] concluded that the conflict-of-interest laws cannot be construed as applying
to the President.[109]

The Courts, including the Supreme Court, are also barred from enquiring "how
the executive, or executive officers, perform their duties in which they have
discretion. Questions, in their nature political, or which are, by the constitution and laws, submitted to the executive, can never be made in the courts."[110]
During a president's tenure in office, the separation of powers is essentially sus-
pended. State laws, legislatures, and the courts are no less constrained from limiting the power of the president even in cases involving his personal interest since
those are transformed and absorbed by his office. So much for federalism and the
Courts as limits on the president's exercise of power.

Through legal and constitutional legerdemain, William Barr reconciled the
tension between the Attorney General's obligation to uphold the Constitution
and his advocacy of the almost unlimited authority purportedly invested in the
president by the Constitution.[111] The doctrine of the unitary executive allows the
president to fire Inspector Generals across all of the federal departments if they
report wrongdoings by the President or his administration. According to Barr,
the President can without impunity end the careers of civil servants and military
officers who revealed presidential improprieties. Only an onerous, emotional
and partisan process of impeachment by the House of Representatives and Senate
conviction can check the president. He can presumably pardon himself under the
doctrine of the unitary executive and the Leviathan-like authority accorded the
President every four years. The institutionalized anti-majority prescriptions for
voting in the Constitution conspire with a wide range of ingenious manipula-
tions of electoral processes by the Trump-dominated Republican Party to suppress the votes of opponents at the federal and state levels to facilitate minority
populist rule.

The Framers of the Constitution worried about an inherent defect of democratic rule. A majority faction could seize the government's coercive powers
through election and impose its will on a majority. What the Founders could not
foresee is that a determined minority could also be able to impose both its ideological, religious, and racial beliefs as well as its self-interested economic interests
on a majority. The Electoral College, gerrymandering, and multiple forms of
voter suppression work in tandem to favor minority control of the presidency,
the Senate, the federal judiciary, and Supreme Court as well as federal and state
legislative bodies. These political barriers preclude the extension of statehood
and the addition of two Senators from the District of Columbia and Puerto Rico,
both of which have larger populations than many states.

The Electoral College inflates the electoral votes of states with small over those with large populations. They have a greater say in electing the president and Senate majorities despite garnering a minority of votes. In the presidential elections of 2000 and 2016, a Republican presidential candidate received a minority of votes cast but won the presidency with a majority of electoral votes. The discrepancy between nationally aggregated votes for Democratic and Republican Senators is particularly conspicuous. North Dakota and California with populations of 762,000 and 42,000,000, respectively, have two Senators. In the 2016 and 2018 elections for the Senate, the 45 Democratic and two independent Senators who represented more people than Republican Senators won only 47 seats versus 53 for the Republicans. Minority control of the presidency and the Senate empowers a Republican minority to place like-minded judges on the federal bench. For the first time in American history a president who lost the popular vote appointed three judges to the Supreme Court.

Gerrymandering further enhances minority rule at Congressional and state legislative levels. Drawing partisan legislative districts allows legislators to choose their constituents rather than the reverse. In 2018 state elections in three presidential battleground states – Pennsylvania, Michigan, and North Carolina – Democratic legislators garnered more votes than their Republican opponents, but had to cede control of these state legislatures to a Republic minority thanks to gerrymandering.[112] Democrats whose electoral base is in urban areas over less populated rural areas dominated by the Republicans must win super majorities to win control of Congressional and state legislatures.

Multiple forms of voter suppression, especially of minorities – Blacks, Latinos, low-income groups, and college students – reinforce minority rule promoted by the Electoral College and gerrymandering. Some pertinent examples illustrate but scarcely exhaust the scope and creativity of these suppression efforts. These include onerous voter ID requirements, impediments to voter registration, large-scale clearing of election registers, ending same-day registration and early voting, limiting voting stations in minority communities, restricting the number of drop boxes to receive mail-in votes, and slowing the delivery of mail-in ballots past the date of election. According to the Brennan Center for Justice, as of March, 2021, legislators in 47 states introduced 361 restrictive voting provisions.[113] Iowa, Georgia, and Florida had already passed voter suppression legislation and Texas followed suit in September 2021. These restrictions were also designed to increase voter lines to the disadvantage of Black and minority voters, dramatized by the Georgia law which made it a crime to provide water for voters waiting to vote.

The Supreme Court gave wind to these suppression movements. In *Shelby v. Holder* it lifted the provision of the Voting Rights Act of the 1960s requiring federal oversight of voting discrimination. This ruling immediately prompted Republican legislatures in Texas, North Carolina, and Wisconsin to pass restrictive voting measures to make voting more difficult for groups, notably minorities, favoring the Democratic Party. The Court also opened the floodgates to unlimited campaign spending in *Citizens United v. FEC*. It ruled that money is free speech, a decision that favors individuals and corporations with deep pockets over most voters. Political inequality compounded economic inequality, the "Gold Dust Twins" of electoral politics. In sum, gerrymandering permitted representatives to choose their voters, not the reverse; the combination of large donors with a heavy thumb on voting scales and voter suppression underwrote a strategy to cobble together a 270 Electoral College majority for a favored presidential candidate despite his losing the popular vote; and if this strategy failed, then, *faute de mieux*, there was always the default to the charge that opponents stole the election – a conjuncture of moves to undermine democracy; and to preclude reliance on a default strategy, Republican legislatures in Georgia, Arizona, and Texas empower state legislatures to authorize an election, not experienced election officials, opening the way to voter count manipulation.[114]

The capstone of minority rule in the United States is the Senate filibuster. On all issues, other than budgetary and spending bills, 60 votes are needed to override a filibuster, that is, calling the question to vote on bills. Finding 41 Senators to filibuster poses little difficulty. The election of this blocking coalition is the product of a host of divergent groups coalescing as an anti-democratic coalition[115] As Adam Jentleson explains, "Because of the way the modern Senate has evolved, combined with the trends of polarization and negative partisanship that have shaped America, this faction is able to wield power far out of proportion to its numbers."[116] This anti-democratic minority is nestled within the Republican Party under the thrall of former President Donald Trump. It is not an exaggeration to affirm William Howell and Terry Moe's conclusion of the extensive review of Trumpian populism that "the GOP has become the organized means for populism's attack on American democracy."[117]

If a minority Republican Party can win federal and state elections by exploiting institutional electoral rules and by hampering and blocking the votes of opponents, there is then no incentive to broaden the Party's appeal to fashion a ruling majority coalition. Minority populist rule hollows out the workings of a liberal democratic regime. President Trump did not so much create these impediments to majority rule as he exploited and expanded their availability to win an election. His defeat in 2020 will not eliminate the populist threat to democratic rule. Only broad reform of electoral rules and practices as well as a restoration of the norms of political restraint by both parties can return the United States to a fully functioning liberal democracy. That is a counsel of virtue since preserving the principles of one person, one vote and the rule of the majority must pass through the formidable barriers erected by the minority to retain power and to defeat efforts for electoral reform. One is reminded of Edmund Burke's warning that "a state without the means of some change is without the means of its conservation. Without such means it might even risk the loss of that part of the constitution to which it wished the most religiously to preserve."[118] Nothing less is at stake than the loss of majority government, the integrity of elections, and the affirmation of one person, one vote under the rule of law.[119]

Whither governing globalization?

It is a stunning irony that at the very ascendancy of the liberal democracies to dominance of the Westphalian system the seeds of its eroding power were already deeply planted. As the Soviet Union imploded, Francis Fukuyama was heralding the inevitable adoption by the world's populations of the liberal democratic solution for global governance.[120] Other Western scholars joined the chorus, proclaiming the inevitability of world government with liberal democratic characteristics.[121] Overlooked was the cautionary observation of informed scholars that most peoples of the globe rejected liberal democratic values.[122] Many, like the Russian people in the wake of the Soviet Union's collapse, who were disposed to adopt a democratic solution, were ill-prepared, without assistance, to assume the burdens of democratic rule. The triumphant democracies forgot or unwittingly dismissed De Tocqueville's insight that a liberal democracy not only required the active civic engagement of its population in self-government but also help from other democracies, too.

Even as repugnant triumphalism spread across the democracies, reaching its highest expression in the Bush Doctrine, the V-Dem Institute of Gotherburg University was collecting data tracking the erosion of democratic rule across the globe. The "third wave of autocratization," as the V-Dem report of 2020 notes, had already begun in the 1990s.[123] The United States was among the leaders of this downward spiral. It finds that the United States declined substantially on the V-Dem Liberal Democratic Index from 2010 to 2020, slipping from 0.83 in 2010 to 0.73 a decade later.[124] The V-Dem attributes this slippage "as a consequence of President Trump's repeated attacks on the media, opposition politicians, and the substantial weakening of the legislature's *de facto* checks and balances on executive power."[125] Who could have predicted that Congress, notably the Senate, would actually be in collusion with the president to undermine democracy in America? So much for the protection of the separation of powers.

The erosion of the liberal democratic solution for governing globalization can be directly traced to the individual and collective defections of the democracies, principally the United States, from the OWL imperatives of the postwar period. Donald Trump's presidency accelerated that demise. It corrupted and polarized American politics and forfeited alliance leadership of the democracies by favoring authoritarian rule abroad. President Trump's go-it-alone quest to Make America Great Again abandoned the previously and mutually productive and constructive responses to OWL imperatives which underwrote the power and attraction of the liberal democratic model. The shared solutions of the democracies to OWL imperatives fostered the ascendancy of the liberal model at the end of the 20th century. The pooling of their security interests and the subsequent maximization of allied power in their pledge to defend each other relaxed the Hobbesian dilemma in their relations with each other and provided the bulwark against Soviet expansion in Europe.

The joint efforts of the democracies also erected a market system that promoted economic growth and technological development to unprecedented levels for the benefit of the largest number of the world's populations. All regimes, free or autocratic, which were willing to play by market rules, were invited to join the global market system. Chapter 5, which details the dramatic and unprecedented growth of China's economy and its rapid technological development, would have been impossible if it had not chosen to be integrated into the Western-created market system.

The commitment of the democracies to the constituent and contextual, civic rigors of democratic governance also demonstrated that regimes dedicated to the freedom of their populations could also produce effective government in response to the Imperatives of Order and Welfare.

Absent a concerted effort by the democracies to address their shared culpability in allowing – indeed accelerating – their self-inflicted demise, the Chinese and Russian solutions will increasingly become the norm. Their autocratic solutions – totalitarian in Chinese dress, populist in Russian garb – will gradually dominate the spaces devoted to governing the nation-state system and the billions of its contentious inhabitants. They, not a fractured and fragmented democratic coalition, will decide and determine the responses of the world society to OWL imperatives. The world will then revert to the dangerous rivalries that brought peoples everywhere the wholesale loss of life and incalculable material devastation of two world wars, now under a threatening cloud of possible nuclear annihilation.

Against this grim setting, we now turn in the following chapters to evaluate the Chinese and Russian solutions for global governance and the threats they pose to free, transparent, accountable, and legitimate governance, world peace, economic prosperity, and progress toward the equitable distribution of wealth and welfare to the world's populations.

Notes

1 Consult Stephen F. Cohen for an informed critique of the Western failure (Cohen, 2000, 2009).
2 Cohen observes in the frontispiece of his 2000 volume that the flawed reforms of the Yeltsin presidency left "70 percent of Russians living below or barely above the official poverty line while depriving them of their life savings, welfare subsidies, health care provisions, and job security."
3 Chapter 7 details the political upheaval and rapacious theft of state assets that plunged Russia into political and economic disarray.
4 Consult, especially, Belton (2020); Dawisha (2015).
5 See Chapter 7 for a more detailed analysis. See also Loftus and Kanet (2019).
6 Hedley Bull makes the best, if overly optimistic, case for global order of an inherently anarchical system (Bull, 1977). Ceaseless interstate conflict and the unrelieved threat of war are scarcely eliminated in an anarchical state system as two world wars in the 20th century confirm.
7 Kagan (2003, p. 2).
8 Jackson (2018, pp. 561, 590, 674). See also Kolodziej (1974), *passim.* for an extensive discussion of the French case.

9 Ikenberry (2011). John Ikenberry uses the term *Leviathan* to characterize the indispensability of American leadership to ensure the power of the liberal democracies, a position that this volume affirms. However, Hobbes used the term to refer to the overwhelming power of a monarch – or any regime – to command those subject to its rule. Using Leviathan as a term to characterize American power misguidedly invests the United States with an attribute that it has never possessed. As the discussion below develops, this misleading attribution infected strategic thinking within the second Bush administration to justify the invasion of Iraq in 2003 to democratize Iraq by force and to ostensibly spark a dynamic to produce a democratic Middle East more to the administration's liking.

10 Huntington (1991). Unfortunately, the democracies failed to build on their success in their flawed responses to the distress of the Russian Federation and to the rising threat of China.

11 www.firstworldwar.com/source/usawardeclaration.htm
   See Ikenberry (2020, pp. 100–140), expertly covers Wilsonian internationalism, which proposed to use war to make the world safe for democracy and to end all wars. The second Bush administration embraced a muscular form of Wilson's universalist vision of America's role in global politics to justify the use of American military power to shape the state system with democratic characteristics.

12 https://georgewbush-whitehouse.archives.gov/news/releases/2002/06/20020601 -3.html

13 georgewbush-whitehouse.archives.gov/nsc/nss/2002/

14 Ibid.

15 Ibid.

16 For citation to the claim and commentary, see www.niskanencenter.org/on-the -saying-that-extremism-in-defense-of-liberty-is..

17 www.washingtonpost.com/news/the-fix/wp/

18 This generalization pervades John Bolton's experience as National Security Adviser to President Trump (Bolton, 2020, pp. 139–140) and *passim*. See also Rucker and Leonnig (2020, p. 270).

19 Bob Woodward cites the president's repeated disparagement of NATO allies, especially Germany, and his view that they are more a burden on the US treasury than an asset. See Woodward (2020, pp. 1–3, 81, 131–132, 140–142, 186; for NATO, pp. 26, 29, 200, 205, 235, 276, 335; and for Germany, p. 391).

20 https://abcnews.go.com/Politics/us-withdraw-12000-troops-germany/story?id =72051446

21 See Atkinson (2019), *passim.*, for his discussion of the British hiring of Hessian troops to fight in the American Revolution.

22 See, for example, Bolton (2020); Rucker and Leonnig (2020); Wolff (2018); Woodward (2018, 2020).

23 Trump (2020).

24 Bolton (2020), *passim.*

25 Mueller (2019).

26 *The New York Times*, August 8, 2020.

27 For example, Bolton (2020, p. 304).

28 *The Wall Street Journal*, June 17, 2020, reports excerpts from Bolton's book. Interestingly enough, the copy of Bolton's book, which I purchased, does not refer to the President's request for Xi's help.

29 Ibid., p. 312.

30 *The Wall Street Journal*, *The Washington Post*, and the English newspaper, *The Independent*, reported Bolton's revelation on July 17, 2020.

31 Ibid., p. 361.

32 *The Washington Post*, February 25, 2019.

33 Bolton (2020, p. 361).

34 Ibid., pp. 192ff.

35 *The New York Times,* September 29, 2020.
36 Bolton (2020, p. 304).
37 China's South China Sea strategy is discussed at greater length in Chapter 4.
38 Quoted in Woodward (2020, p. 141).
39 There is more to be said about US defections from the Imperative of Order of the postwar period than can be developed here. Excluded here, but relevant to that larger discussion, is the renewed nuclear arms race with Russia, the rejection of the Iranian nuclear accord by the Trump administration to forestall Tehran's acquisition of nuclear weapons, the renunciation of the Intermediate-Range Missile treaty, and the insistence that China join in nuclear arms talks with the US and Russia, a move that might have the perverse effect of encouraging China to increase its long-range nuclear forces to keep pace with its rivals and to abandon its minimum nuclear deterrent strategy. See Chapter 4 where this issue is treated.
40 See www.whitehouse.gov › 2021/02/19 › remarks-b...
41 There is a large and growing scholarly literature that covers the income inequality spreading across market states, including China. Central to this research area are the publications of Thomas Piketty and his associates. See Piketty (2014); Piketty et al. (2017). For data on specific countries, consult *World Inequality Report, 2018*: wir2018.wid.world › files › wir2018-summary-english
For the United States, with a discussion of the politics of income inequality, see Reich (2020); Saez and Zucman (2019).
42 I have dealt extensively with this issue. See Kolodziej (2016), especially Chapters 5 and 6, pp. 153–226.
43 See Elsby et al. (2013) and Karabarbounis and Neiman (2014). The data and graphs of the Hamilton Project of the Brookings Institution are an extremely valuable source. In succinct and accessible form they summarize relevant measures of labor stagnation in the United States since 1980. Cited sources are helpful (Shambaugh, 2017).
44 Space limitations preclude an extensive discussion of inequality within the European Union. Jonathan Hopkins covers the harsh conditions imposed on Greece, Spain, Portugal, and Ireland by the European Central Bank, the European Commission and the International Monetary Fund in bailing them out in the midst of these crises. See Hopkins (2002), especially, pp. 153ff; for GINI coefficients of most states, see the World Bank listing, which cite t\heir GINI status, variably, over a 20-year period. https://data.worldbank.org/indicator/SI.POV.GINI?view=map
Piketty (2014) is also a foundation source.
45 For the stress on globalization as the driver of inequality, consult Haskel (2012); for technology, Autor (2008) and Goldin and Katz (2010); for political policy, Piketty (2014); Piketty et al. (2017); Saez and Zucman (2019).
46 Edward Alden makes this point as a jumping off to the globalization of markets and the loss suffered by high-wage, low-skilled labor among the Western states Alden (2017, pp. 1–10).
47 Halberstam (1972).
48 Edward Alden extensively develops the loss of power of American labor through his discussion. See Alden (2017), *passim.*
49 See three reports of the Organization for Economic Co-Operation and Development (OECD): OECD (2008, 2011, 2015).
50 For additional data about the loss of labor power, see Shambaugh (2017, p. 6) and Autor (2016).
51 https://news.cgtn.com/news/2021-01-25/Full-text-Xi-Jinping-s-speech-at-the-virtual... Xi's presentation is especially significant for Chapters 4 and 6 with regard to China's responses to the Imperatives of Order and Legitimacy. XI's endorsement of democracy, freedom, and international law is hollow in light of the Chinese Communist Party's oppressive rule over 1.4 billion Chinese citizens.
52 Shambaugh (2017, p. 1).
53 Ibid., p. iii.

54 Ibid., p. ll.
55 See the article by Daron Acemoglu, "AI's Future Doesn't Have to be Dystopian," at http://bostonreview.net/science-nature/faron-acemoglu-redesigning-al (bold original). See also his larger study, *Redesigning AI: Work, Democracy and Justice in the Age of Automation.* Acemoglu (2021).
56 Alden (2017, pp. 89f).
57 Shambaugh (2017, p. 3).
58 See n. 55.
59 See n. 44 for World Bank GINI coefficient listings.
60 Shambaugh (2017, p. i).
61 Ibid., p. ii.
62 Ibid., p. iv.
63 This thesis is exhaustively developed by Edward Alden in Alden (2017).
64 Autor (2016).
65 Alden (2017, pp. 107ff).
66 Davis and Haltiwanger (2014); also Shambaugh (2017, p. 7).
67 A Tax Institute study of the University of California, Berkeley, estimates that 10 percent of multinational corporation earnings abroad are shifted to tax havens. http://gabriel-zucman.eu/missingprofits/. A later study in April 2021, by Professors Ammanuel Saez and Gabriel Zucmac, economists at the University of California, Berkeley, who have published extensively on income inequality in the democracies, found that US billionaires now own $4.25 Trillion in capital assets, "out of which $2.7 Trillion are gains that they haven't paid tax upon yet." https://eml.berkeley.edu/~saez/SZ21-billionaire-tax.pdf
68 Thomas Anderson, "Summary Estimates for Multinational Companies: Employment, Sales, and Capital Expenditures for 2011," Bureau of Economic Analysis, April 18, 2013, www.bea.gov/newsreleases/international/mnc/2013/_pdf/mnc2011 .pdf. Also Alden (2017, p. 84).
69 www.propublica.org/article/the-secret-irs-files-trove-of-never-before-seen. *ProPublica* has not disclosed the source of these released tax data, which are protected under penalty of law from being made public.
70 Lengthy *New York Times* evaluation, June 12, 2021.
71 *n. 69, ProPublica* estimate., pp. 3–4.
72 Ibid., p. 8.
73 Poverty, defined by those living at or below subsistence, can also be viewed as a nation's public policy and choice. Ezra Klein extends a country's choice of inequality to poverty. See *New York Times*, June 13, 2021. I deal extensively with the issue of poverty as a public choice in Kolodziej (2016, pp. 208–220).
74 Wilson (1999). See also McFate (1995).
75 Nancy MacLean places Friedman's call for the narrowing of corporate responsibility to making money in the broader movement of the rising anti-democratic movement to install permanent minority rule in the United States in the name, ironically, of personal freedom. See MacLean (2017), *passim.*
76 See Milton Friedman, "The Social Responsibility of Business Is to Increase Its Profits," *The New York Times Magazine*, September 13, 1970.
77 Ibid.
78 Kolodziej (2016) and citations noted, pp. 195–196.
79 Quoted in Jeff Stein, "Yellen Pushes Global Minimum Tax as White House Eyes New Spending Plan," *The New York Times*, March 15, 2021. A detailed analysis of the competition to the bottom is found in the OECD study, Tax Statistics, Second Edition. www.oecd.org › tax › tax-policy › corporate-tax-st...
80 Applebaum (2020),
81 Pogo is of course the cartoon creation of Walt Kelly.
82 See Horwitz (1966).
83 See Finchelstein (2019), which frames populism historically and globally.

84 Applebaum (2020).
85 I have relied on a wide range of sources in developing this section on legitimacy and the challenge of populism. Four have been especially helpful: Applebaum (2020); Finchelstein (2019); Müller (2016, 2021). Applebaum focuses on the defection of former liberal intellectuals and their support of populism; Finchelstein frames the various forms of populist regimes and populist socio-political movements in a historical setting as a global process; Müller brilliantly dissects the many complex features of populism as assaults on the democratic process. The incisive scholarship of Nadia Urbinati (Urbinati, 2014) provides useful insights.
86 Chapter 7, "The Russian OWL Model for Global Governance," develops this point.
87 Urbinati (2013, p. 17).
88 Quoted in Müller (2016, p. 52).
89 Ibid., (2016).
90 Hibbard (2010, p. 116).
91 Hibbard provides a brief, trenchant history of this struggle from Indian independence to the first decade of the 21st century, Ibid., pp. 115–176.
92 Recent laws passed by the BJP to privilege the Hindu religion and to undermine the Indian secular state are develop in my chapter, "Defining Legitimacy and Citizenship in the People's Republic of China and India," in *Enduring and Emerging Security Issues in South Asia*, Washington, DC, Brookings, Forthcoming.
93 Key (1949). Isabel Wilkerson, who won a Pulitzer prize, incisively characterizes voter suppression as a caste system, borrowing from the Indian experience Wilkerson (2020).
94 William Howell and Terry Moe trace Nixon's southern strategy to its crystallization in President Trump's mainstreaming of white supremacy (Howell and Moe, 2020, pp. 21–112).
95 See Belton (2020), *passim*. She details the depredations of the Russian secret service.
96 To a greater or lesser degree the works cited in n. 85 elaborate on identity politics under populist regimes and its challenge to liberal democracy. For a brief review of recent scholarship with respect to the United States, see Thomas E. Edsell's "I Fear That We Are Witnessing the End of American Democracy." *The New York Times*, August 26, 2020.
97 These constituent and contextual constraints on power are covered in Chapter 2, The "Rise of the Liberal Democratic Solution to Global Governance."
98 As we will see in Chapter 6, the Chinese Communist Party goes further than populist regimes. It invests itself with the exclusive awesome power to squash all dissent to ensure its rule.
99 Cited in Finchelstein (2019, p. 251).
100 *Washington Post*, December 18, 2019.
101 Ibid., November 25, 2019.
102 The President's self-identification of himself as a genius with knowledge surpassing experts across a broad spectrum of issues is explored in Rucker and Leonnig (2020).
103 President Trump strongly insisted that COVID-19 patients use hydroxychoroquine, a malaria drug, which was proven to be ineffective and potentially harmful to combat COVID-19.
104 www.cnn.com/2017/01/22/.../kellyanne-conway-alternative-facts/index.html
105 en.wikipedia.org/wiki/List_of_arrested_journalists_in_Turkey; and
www.forbes.com/sites/niallmccarthy/2018/12/13/where-the-most-journalists-a
106 www.npr.org/2019/03/07/701052337/the-white-house-and-its-shadow-cabinet-President Trump described his use of Twitter as his megaphone to the world: "This is my megaphone. This is the way that I speak directly to the people without any filter. Cut through the noise, Cut through the fake news. That's the only way I have to communicate. I have tens of millions of followers. That is bigger than cable news.

I go out and give a speech and it's covered by CNN and nobody's watching, nobody cares. I tweet something and it's my megaphone to the world." Quoted in Müller (2021, p. 92).

107 Fritzsche (2020); Heberle (1945) recount this sudden change in allegiances of the German population and elites.

108 Milosz (1953).

109 For the full text of the 19-page memorandum, check www.vox.com/policy-and -politics/2018/12/20/18150165/mueller-barr-memo.

110 Ibid., page numbers are not provided in the memorandum.

111 This trope runs throughout the volumes by Bob Woodward and John Bolton (Bolton, 2020; Woodward, 2020).

112 https://madison.com/wsj/news/local/govt-and-politics/republicans-keep -majorities-

113 Brenan Center for Justice, "State Voting Bills Tracker 2021" www.brennancenter. org/our-work/research-reports/state-voting-bills-tracker-2021

114 The threat of voter manipulation and the corruption of the electoral process are outlined in essays, respectively, by Richard Hansen and Thomas Friedman in *The New York Times*, April 23, 2021, and May 11, 2021.

115 American populism is too complex and still evolving to be fully treated here. The following works are helpful in differentiating its numerous features: William Howell and Terry Moe, on the rise of American populism (Howell and Moe, 2020, especially pp. 1–112); Alan Abramowitz, Adam Jentleson, and Ezra Klein, on the rise of polarization, the electoral benefits of negative partisanship, and the politics of division (Abramowitz, 2018; Jentleson, 2021; Klein, 2020); Norris Pippa and Ronald Inglehard and John Sides et al., on the political backlash of those fearful of losing their jobs, income, social status, and identity, particularly acute among white voters and a neglected working population (Pippa and Inglehart, 2019; Sides, 2018); Daniel Williams, on the rise of the Christian Right as a political force Williams (2010) and Robert P. Jones, specifically, on the support of American Christianity for White Supremacy (Jones, 2017, 2020); William Spitzer, on the politics of gun control (Spitzer, 2018); and Larry Bartels, on income inequality and, implicitly, the support of Trumpism and populist politics by many in the moneyed class (Bartels, 2016).

116 Jentleson (2021, p. 133). Spending and budgetary bills can pass by majority vote in the two houses through a process of reconciliation. Both the Republican-sponsored tax reform of 2017 and the Democratic-sponsored COVID-19 stimulus bill of 2021 passed through reconciliation. However, all other important legislation – protect- ing voter rights, regulations controlling climate change, and the like – must pass through the filibuster.

117 Howell and Moe (2020), p. 81. The process of transforming the Republican Party into an anti-democratic party can be traced earlier, before Donald Trump's capture of the party. See Mann and Ornstein (2012).

118 Burke (2019, p. 6).

119 There is already a large and growing body of scholarly and public interest publica- tions detailing the erosion of Constitutional government and liberal democratic rule in the United States. Besides the citations noted throughout this volume, see Huq and Ginsburg (2018); Mounk (2021).

120 Fukuyama (1992).

121 Wendt (2003).

122 See Juergensmeyer (2008).

123 See the report of the Varieties of Democratic Institute, Democracy Report 2021, Autocratization Turns Viral. www.v-dem.net › publications › democracy-rep...

124 Ibid., p. 19. The V-Dem Index is an impressive measure of democratic practices. It is more complex than the Freedom House annual reports, which also reveal

the erosion of liberal democratic rule. See Freedom House, *Freedom in the World 2021: Democracy under Siege* https://freedomhouse.org/report/freedom-world/2021/democracy-under-siege

125 V-Dem Report for 2020, p. 19.

4

CHINA AND THE
IMPERATIVE OF ORDER

In broad strokes this chapter identifies the Chinese Communist Party's (and China's) principal responses to the Imperative of Order as a key element of its solutions to OWL imperatives for global governance.[1] The CCP pursues a long-term strategy to foster a Westphalian self-help, multipolar system of nation-states, stamped with Chinese characteristics. This CCP quest precedes President Xi's rise to power in 2012.[2] President Xi Jinping has given new and accelerated impetus to this CCP objective, moribund during the presidency of his predecessor, Hu Jintao.

This China-centered anarchical system is expected to eventually surpass the Western democratic coalition for ascendancy in determining OWL imperatives. The CCP believes that two historic trends favor the long-term realization of this vision. The first is the CCP's stipulated superiority of the Chinese model; and, second, the expected complementary demise of global liberal democratic power, the consequence of the endemic, interminable group conflict fostered by the pluralistic politics of these regimes. The absence of domestic order, which the CCP-inspired model purports to ensure, saps the capacity of liberal states to provide for effective government. The January 6, 2021, assault on the US Capitol by domestic terrorists, incited by a seditious American president, a would-be populist autocrat, provides purchase for CCP assurance of Chinese superiority. The CCP foresees that authoritarian regimes, mirroring the CCP model for China, will gradually replace not only the space occupied by the liberal democratic democracies within the nation-state system but they will no less decisively shape the global civil society to their liking.

The precondition for the realization of this long-range objective is avoiding a cataclysmic nuclear exchange between China and the United States. China's nuclear deterrent, based on a strategy of mutual assured destruction (MAD) and no first use of nuclear weapons, is expected to preclude this catastrophic

DOI: 10.4324/9781003246572-4

event, while providing the bedrock for a security system within which to employ China's enlarging and increasingly sophisticated non-nuclear military forces and multiple non-coercive tools of power to propel and sustain its global rise.[3]

At serious odds with its announced no-nuclear-war posture is China's regional buildup of nuclear and conventional military capabilities to gain strategic superiority in the South and East Asian Seas and in Asia more generally. China claims this vast area as its sphere of interest. Whereas its global military strategy currently remains defensive, its posture in asserting its sovereignty over the seas surrounding its exposed borders is of late progressively more assertive and aggressive.[4]

Military parity with the West, notably the United States, and regional military superiority in Asia and, specifically, in the South and East China Seas, are not ends in themselves. They are the prerequisites for the success of the Belt and Road Initiative (BRI). The Peoples Liberation Army (PLA) provides an expanding security framework within which the BRI is nested and within which it is expected to function. Cast and working within this framework, the BRI is China's vehicle to reconcile competing and conflicting security postures.[5] It is the principal component of China's global strategy to realize its version of the Westphalian system, while precluding the eruption of a global nuclear war to which that system is susceptible.

In lieu of Western and, specifically, US security alliances to ensure a world order favorable to the values and interests of the liberal democracies, China has embarked on a long-term enterprise to create a complex network of geo-economic partnerships with countries around the globe, principally in the developing world. Created would be an elaborate, intricate, and self-sustaining latticework of infrastructure, transportation, and communications projects. This security architecture is projected to place China at the center of these regional and global economic and political alignments with states around the globe, including Western democracies. Its implementation is designed to weaken and potentially unravel the Western security system, as states would be drawn into the Chinese orbit. Implanted, too, would be a market system under Chinese leadership and, where feasible, control. The BRI, as *The Economist* observes, "represents the prototype for an emerging geopolitical bloc at a time when the rules-based [liberal democratic] order is under shaky American leadership."[6]

The expanding web of these partnerships, with China at its center and its primary financial underwriter, would be an alternative to Western-style security alliances. These economic alignments have the added advantage of melding the specific economic interests and policies of partner states with those of China. In its pursuit of a welfare imperative, developed in the next chapter, China's BRI complements and bolsters a China-centered security system and its preferred multipolar world order. President Xi, joined by a chorus of CCP and governmental officials, tirelessly insists that BRI is a win-win relation between China and its partners in contrast to what they allege are win-lose alliance systems threatening to allied states and world peace.

With references to the pursuit of a theory of global governance, outlined in Chapter 1, the significance of the CCP's response to the Imperative of Order turns Kant and Hobbes on their heads.[7] Kant's solution to perpetual peace, resting on a world of liberal republican regimes and trading states, is implicitly, if not deliberately, invoked to justify China's objective to create a multipolar global anarchical system of nation-states populated by authoritarian governments. The BRI, the design for a new territorial and maritime silk road, is relied upon to relax, if not fully surmount, the Hobbesian dilemma. Force and the ever-present possibility of global and regional war remain uppermost in Chinese security thinking, in tribute to Hobbesian expectations, but reliance on armed coercion, real or threatened, to assert Chinese preferences, when necessary, in their relations with other states is tempered by the priority assigned to economic and technological development as the favored approach to achieve sustained economic growth and ensure China's global leadership.

The following chapters extend the significance of the BRI initiative for the CCP's response to the Imperatives of Welfare and Legitimacy. Among the formidable obstacles to the Chinese model ascendancy is China itself. The Xi regime's aggressive assertion that the South and East China Seas are within China's exclusive sphere of influence, and its expanding military buildup of the region to underwrite its claims threatens the global security system which it is attempting to construct.

Military parity with the West to preclude global war

Mao Zedong's aphorism about the sources of political power still animates the CCP's solution to the Imperative of Order, domestic, and global: "Political power grows out of the barrel of a gun. Our principle is that the Party commands the gun, and the gun must never be allowed to command the Party."[8]

There are two important dimensions to Mao's precept. The first is that CCP rule over the Chinese state and population is born out of violence and is sustained by it. As Kerry Brown observes, "It is audacious for Xi's Party, with its roots in terror, illegality, and revolution, to present itself as the bastion of stability and justice six decades after coming to power by force of arms, insurrection and war."[9] Sheer material power, the ultimate and limiting form of which is violence, encapsulates and extinguishes any notion or hint of a Rousseaunian conception of legitimacy underpinning CCP governance. The distinction between power and legitimacy, as Chapter 6 delineates, is a distinction without a difference. CCP rule is legitimate because it exercises a monopoly of power.

The second dimension of Mao's aphorism is that the PLA is an arm of the Party.[10] The PLA is the CCP's gun. In serving the Party first, the security of China and the Chinese people are necessarily ensured, according to Party beliefs crystallized into strategic doctrine. The PLA, in tandem with the CCP's extensive internal security forces, fosters the Party's survival, welfare, and evolving interests. What is good for the Party is, *ipso facto*, good for the Chinese state and people. When Deng Xiaoping ordered the PLA to squash the Tiananmen Square student uprising in 1989, he reminded wavering Party leaders of the Maoist principle that "the Party commands the gun." Chinese citizens are expected to submit to the Party's military muscle and domestic police power or otherwise forfeit their freedom – even their lives.[11]

Since the CCP's rule derives from its monopoly of power, that power serves the Party first and then, in the order of priority, the Chinese state and people. The logic of this circular reasoning is that the CCP, like Putin's Russia, embraces interstate multipolarity as its solution to the Imperative of Order for global governance. That anarchical condition is viewed as best suited to advance the Party's interests at home and abroad. Each state is expected to depend on its own capabilities and on its varying and mutating alignments with other states and non-state actors, depending on changing circumstances, to realize its contingent and long-range interests. Western-like alliances are ruled out. They are viewed as a threat to Chinese security and regional power. President Xi Jinping's presentation to the 2014 Conference on Interaction and Confidence Building Measures stated that "it is disadvantageous to the common security of the [Asian] region if military alliances with third parties are strengthened."[12] If China's Asian neighbors are bereft of access to alliance support – notably to US naval and air power – China's overwhelming military power has free reign to dictate regional security.

China's creation of the Shanghai Cooperation Organization (SCO) exemplifies its efforts to organize Asian states under its leadership without formally committing China to their security. China's 2019 Defense White Paper observes that the SCO seeks a "constructive partnership of *non-alliance* (*ital.* added) and non-confrontation that targets no third party, expanding security and defense cooperation and creating a new model for regional security cooperation."[13] A self-help multipolar system is viewed as best suited to advance Chinese security interests. As early as the first decade of the 21st century, strategic thinking in Chinese circles argued that "a relatively democratic and multipolar world with mutual checks and balances would be beneficial for its [China's] security, stability, and development. A trend toward multipolarization would provide China peaceful development with even more strategic opportunities and room to maneuver."[14] That systemic framework within which to project Chinese power regionally and globally has since been adopted and accelerated by President Xi Jinping to guide strategic thinking and the modernization of the PLA, the CCP's coercive arm.

A Westphalian multipolar system with Chinese characteristics translates into a decided CCP and Chinese advantage if coercion has to be used to impose Party and state values and interests on other, weaker states, especially those in Asia. Chinese air, ground, sea, and space capabilities are greater than any other regional state.[15] The gap in military power between China and its neighbors is projected to expand, not contract, in the immediate future and thereafter as China strives to assert its hegemony over East Asia, while progressively achieving global parity with the military capabilities of the United States and the Western states.[16]

The alignment between two authoritarian states – CCP's China and Putin's Russia – is a temporal convergence of interest to undermine the security alliances of the democratic states and the Western global order. Both share the goal of expanding the number of authoritarian regimes that reflect their own oppressive rule. The greater the number of anti-democratic regimes and the larger the number of democratic states in internal disarray the more supportive is the international environment for Moscow and Beijing to exercise their power for their relative advantage and to anchor their shared objective of a multipolar system.

Given their power disparities and their competing regional and global objectives, their current alignment against the West has little likelihood of leading to a security alliance between them. Nor should lingering remembrances of past military clashes between Moscow and Beijing be overlooked as dampening incentives for striking such an accord. The 1969 seven-week border war between the Soviet Union and China comes readily to mind. China's need for access to Russian oil, gas, and resources draws the two states together. China's voracious appetite for energy subordinates potential tensions over arms sales and competition for influence in Central Asia, Africa, the Middle East, and other regions that push them apart.[17] In principle Chinese and Russian strategic thinking share an anathema to alliances, like NATO, or mutual security commitments between the United States and Asian states (Japan, South Korea, Australia, New Zealand).

Both Moscow and Beijing accurately assess the Western democratic solution to OWL governance as a threat to their authoritarian rule. A strong security alliance of liberal democratic states is a formidable obstacle to their promotion of an international system of authoritarian states. What they could not have expected is that the Trump administration's anti-alliance "America First" strategic posture and Britain's break with the European Union would providentially advance their Westphalian global order. The return of the Biden administration to alliance commitments does not fully offset the confidence of allies in the United States since over 74 million Americans or 47 percent of the electorate voted to retain Trump in office. The self-weakening of the Western alliance, military and economic, *ipso facto* fosters a self-help world order in which China's global power is enhanced and Russia, with fewer resources, is strengthened as a regional power with global pretensions.

Russia and China trust that an enlarging number of authoritarian states will bolster their nation's security, weaken democratic coalitional power, and strengthen their oppressive domestic rule. In contrast to the notion of collective security of the Western states, Russian power is not a public good pledged to guarantee the security of the states falling within its sphere of influence, including those states and peoples ruled formerly by the Russian empire and, subsequently, by the Soviet Union. Russian military force is a policy tool to control the foreign policy alignments of weaker states – Ukraine, Georgia, Moldova. No less in importance is Moscow's use of its limited military capabilities to forcefully reintegrate Crimea, to divide the West states by intimidating eastern members of the NATO alliance in Europe, to incite civil war in Ukraine to preclude its entry into the EU or NATO, to block similarly any movement by Georgia or Moldova to align with the West, and to intervene militarily in the Middle East and Africa to support client states and non-state actors opposed to the United States and to Western influence. The principal exception to Russian cooperation with the Western states is its membership in the treaty to preclude Iran's development of nuclear weapons.

With vastly more and progressively larger military, economic, and techno-logical resources at its disposal, China has greater power than Russia to promote a multipolar system with Chinese characteristics. In the long run, CCP leaders project China as the dominant power first in Asia and, over time, as ascendant in the international system, overtaking the United States, the European Union, and any other cluster of states. Like Russia, China prizes its privileged status as a Permanent Member of the UN Security Council. It enjoys the status of a global power with a say in all matters important to China. The current and projected expansion of its military capabilities is expected to match its UN status.

The PLA is not designed as a public good in the form of security guaran-tees to other states at a level of commitment of the NATO treaty in which an attack on one state is an attack on all. Chinese military power is keyed to par-ticular Chinese security and foreign policy interests. There is no contradiction between this self-interested posture and ad hoc engagements with democratic states for mutual advantage to protect oil lanes in the Persian Gulf from pirates or for the dispatch of Chinese troops to support UN peacekeeping operations in failed states or to provide for humanitarian relief. These initiatives, along with its signature to the agreement with Iran to preclude its development of a nuclear weapon, are consistent with its big power objectives and status as a Permanent Member of the UN Security Council.

China, like Russia, relies on a broad spectrum of military and non-military resources to pursue its interests. China's greater capabilities also afford it more choices in using its multiple power resources. This provides CCP leadership with a greater probability of success than Russia in balancing cost-risk-benefit out-comes to the Party's advantage at each junction point in its transactions with other state and non-state actors. Nor does Beijing have to rely so heavily as Moscow on asymmetric warfare in combating the West. While there is ample evidence of Chinese success in stealing Western military and technological secrets and in violating commercial, trade, and property rights, China stops short of large-scale Russian-like interference in the electoral processes of the United States and the Western democracies.[18] To do so would undermine Beijing's insistence that other states refrain from intervening in the domestic affairs of other states and that they refrain from attacking the CCP's legitimacy and its violation of civil liberties and human rights.

Beijing's multipolar strategy does not rest primarily on its expanding coercive power to exert its influence over its neighbors. China's military expansion sup-ports but does not dictate the choice of the Party's non-coercive policy tools. As Mao insisted and as his successors also affirmed, "the Party commands the gun, and the gun must never be allowed to command the Party." President Xi's ambi-tion to eventually create a Chinese military that can fight and win wars is quali-fied and sobered by his recognition that a global nuclear war would be disastrous for the Party and China.[19] China is not building a force to win an unwinnable war. In contrast to its more aggressive regional strategic posture, notably in the South and East China Seas, Beijing's global strategic stance is presently defensive, an observation at odds with the opinion held in some Western circles of Chinese hegemonic aspirations through military might.[20]

An appraisal of Chinese military capabilities and their long-term composition suggests that, as Anthony Cordesman argues, China's expanding military power does not have to lead to armed conflict with the United States.[21] This guardedly optimistic view of intense competition and febrile co-existence between two powerful rivals is echoed in an op-ed presumably placed by the CCP in *The New York Times*.[22] The CCP's decision to reach Chinese military parity with the United States can be viewed as a coercive framework within which to deploy China's formidable non-coercive powers to promote China as a model for other authoritarian states,[23] to leverage its influence in its relations with other states, and to establish its credentials as a global power.

CCP leadership proposes to compete with the United States and the West on China's own terms by eventually surpassing them economically and tech-nologically. That is the announced intent of its industrial policy for 2030 to overtake the West in the production of artificial intelligence.[24] A Defense Department report to Congress on China's military capabilities and strategy confirms this assessment. While expanding its economic and technological prowess, China has also demonstrated considerable skill in diplomatically mak-ing headway with other states and in launching effective "influence operations against media, cultural, business, academic and policy communities" in the United States and the West.[25] China's power toolbox includes soft power to influence the hearts and minds of friends and adversaries to voluntarily do its bidding,[26] cyber-crime to bolster the competitive position of its private and state-owned corporations in global markets, and theft of commercial, tech-nological, and military know-how from other states by the Chinese state and corporations.

China's strategic nuclear forces, those capable of reaching US cities, are con-figured to stabilize the nuclear balance between Beijing and Washington. They are designed to lower the likelihood of a nuclear war between China and the United States. At a global level CCP leadership has resisted reducing its differ-ences with the United States to a purely coercive or, to use game theory, to a zero-sum relationship, since it relies largely on a more complex and nuanced non-coercive strategy, like BRI, to weaken the West. The exception, as devel-oped below, concerns China's militarization of the East and South China Seas and the Taiwan Straits.[27] The CCP is playing the long game in mounting its challenge on the Western system. An evaluation of its strategic nuclear doctrine and weapons arsenal as well as its long-range delivery systems reveal a restraint and prudence not matched either by the United or the Soviet Union and its Russian Federation successor.

There are several noteworthy features of the Chinese nuclear forces that contrast with US and Russian nuclear forces and the strategies guiding their use and objectives. Both the United States and Russia have vastly larger nuclear arsenals. Whereas both Russia and the United States have nuclear arsenals in excess of 6,000 nuclear weapons, China has an estimated arsenal of 280 to 290 nuclear weapons, about as many as France.[28] Both former Cold War rivals still strive for an elusive counterforce superiority that, purportedly, could disarm their opponent's nuclear forces in a first-strike attack. Recent reports of their development of long-range hypersonic velocity missiles, configured with Multiple Independently Targeted Reentry Vehicles (MIRVs), are consistent with the evolution of their nuclear competition, extending from the Cold War until now.[29]

From the start of its nuclear program in the 1960s, Beijing adopted a mutual nuclear deterrent strategy. The aim was, and still is, to develop a sufficiently large invulnerable nuclear force to ride out a first-strike nuclear attack and, in turn, have sufficient remaining nuclear forces to inflict unacceptable human and material damage on an aggressor. The Chinese rationale for a nuclear posture of mutual assured destruction echoes US Secretary of Defense Robert McNamara's presentation of MAD to Congress during the Kennedy administration.[30]

Currently, China's counter-value force depends (1) on land-based, largely mobile, ballistic missiles to deliver approximately 218 nuclear warheads, (2) on four Submarine-Launched Ballistic Missiles (SLBMs) launching 48 warheads, and (3) on aircraft to carry gravity bombs to target. What is especially noteworthy about these delivery systems is that most are medium and intermediate range. Many of these nuclear forces are more suited for use in the South and East China Seas against US naval forces and bases in the region than as weapons configured to reach the continental United States.

These limitations are being addressed. China's mutual assured destruction posture will be significantly upgraded with the entry of new hypersonic long-range missiles in the 2020s. The Dongfeng-41 will be able to travel at 25 times the speed of sound and to reach targets more than 9,000 miles away. They have several unique features when compared to China's existing strategic nuclear ballistic missiles that weaken the stability of the nuclear environment. They also combine both greater speed and accuracy with maneuverability to more effectively penetrate advanced missile-defense systems and destroy missile launchers.[31]

Despite the projected upgrade in China's strategic long-range nuclear strike capability, its MAD posture probably will not fundamentally change. The Dongfeng-41 does not signal a move toward a counterforce nuclear posture and engage the United States and Russia in a competitive nuclear arms race. As long as China confines its strategic nuclear force to a MAD posture, however enhanced in the future, there is credibility in Beijing's announcement of a no-first-use policy and its corollary insistence that it will not use nuclear weapons against a non-nuclear state or in nuclear free zones. A Chinese Ministry of Foreign Affairs states the Chinese nuclear policy clearly and succinctly:

> China has always pursued the policy of no first use of nuclear weapons and adhered to a self-defensive nuclear strategy that is defensive in nature. China will unconditionally not use or threaten to use nuclear weapons against non-nuclear weapon states or in nuclear weapon-free zones, and will never enter into a nuclear arms race with any other country. China has always kept its nuclear capabilities at the minimum level required for maintaining its nation's security.[32]

Thus far, improvement in the precision, reliability, range, invulnerability, MIRVing, quick reaction solid-fuel capability, and the development of hypersonic missiles are designed to strengthen, not abandon, China's MAD strategy. Beijing has preferred to adapt to both nuclear giants at a lower level of nuclear readiness than its principal nuclear adversaries. China's long-range nuclear modernization program follows the same formula. Since its acquisition of nuclear weapons in the 1960s, Beijing relies on its less costly, second-strike posture to ensure its counter-value strategy. Trusting to deterrence over the inherent, trigger-prone instability of a first-strike counterforce strategy, CCP leaders are acutely aware that a nuclear war would be tantamount to national self-immolation and the destruction of the CCP. What progress the CCP has made in making China a global power and in lifting hundreds of millions from poverty over a century since the founding of the Party would be undone overnight.

Moscow and Washington make the avoidance of a nuclear war, an estimable objective, progressively more difficulty to achieve. The enlarging size, capability, and acceleration of the US–Russian nuclear arms race threaten the viability of China's MAD strategy. Restraint may not be possible in the future. The development of the road-mobile Dongfeng-41 ICBM, a new long-range bomber, and the modernization of its submarine fleet, armed with improved Sea Launched Ballistic Missiles (SLMBs), will diminish the vulnerability of China's nuclear forces. Their entry into the Chinese nuclear arsenal may sustain the confidence of Chinese military planners that an upgraded MAD strategy can still deter the nuclear forces of its adversaries. What remains disquieting to Chinese military planners is that the trillions of dollars being spent by Washington and Russia on new and more menacing first-strike nuclear weapons over the next decade, like supersonic missiles, may drag China into an arms race that it has successfully resisted until now.[33]

East and South China Seas: China's Monroe Doctrine

China's increasingly aggressive behavior in the South China Sea is at cross purposes with its announced global defensive military posture and reliance principally on non-coercive means to foster a stable multipolar system of authoritarian states.

China's militarization of the islands of the South China Sea and its regional military buildup of conventional and advanced nuclear-armed supersonic and cruise missiles, as well as anti-access/anti-denial missiles, contradicts its announced preference for a self-help multipolar system through non-coercive competition with the United States and the West.

CCP leadership conceives the East and South China Seas as China's exclusive sphere of influence and falls within China's sovereign control. Herein lies the seeds of a possible military clash between the United States and Chinese forces that could rapidly escalate from a regional to a global war which neither rival wants.[34] Repeated governmental pronouncements assert that China will be "resolute in defending its sovereignty" in the South China Sea and that it "would take necessary measures" to protect its interests.[35] The Chinese Defense White Paper of 2019 echoed this declaration:

> China resolutely safeguards its national sovereignty and territorial integrity. The South China Sea Islands and Diaoyu Islands are inalienable parts of the Chinese territory. China exercises its national sovereignty to build infrastructure and deploy necessary defensive capabilities on the islands and reefs in the South China Sea, and to conduct patrols in the waters of Diaoyu Islands in the East China Sea.[36]

Unpacking China's expansive assertion of sovereignty over most of the South China Sea reveals the significance that the CCP attaches to the region.[37] It goes far to explain the Chinese military buildup and strategy in the region. Chinese maps regularly display a so-called "nine-dash line" that covers most of the South China Sea as Chinese sovereign territory.[38] Beijing rejects both the sovereign claims of its neighbors with respect to the islands, rocks, sandbars, coral reefs, or shoals of this area and their jurisdictional access to the extensive living and non-living resources of the South China Sea that conflict with Chinese interests.

China's exclusionary stance over territorial and jurisdictional rights in the South China Sea as well as its efforts to regulate the marine navigation and over-flights encompassing its "nine-dash line" are tantamount to a Beijing declaration of the Monroe Doctrine for the South China Sea. China's reach is currently beyond its grasp. The complexity of the issues surrounding the South China Sea, the multiple states and non-state actors pushing back against China in the region to press their own counter sovereign claims and resource interests, and the presence of American military forces in the region are factors and forces that currently limit China's ability to get its way. Closing the gap between reach and grasp has assumed a long-term CCP work in progress, a permanent and ingrained aspiration and inspiration of China's foreign and international policies.

China is ready to go it alone. It is prepared to violate international laws, treaties, and established norms that block its assertion of sovereignty over the South China Sea. In 2013 the Philippines brought a suit against China to establish its sovereignty and jurisdictional access to waters of the South China Sea.

Three years later an Arbitral Tribunal, citing key articles of the United Nations Convention on the Law of the Sea (UNCLOS),[39] held that China's signature to the UNCLOS "extinguished" its historic claims "to resources within the nine-dash line."[40] China was also denied its Exclusive Economic Zone (EEZ) and continental shelf claims in the disputed area. These were awarded to the Philippines. These included Philippine sovereignty over Mischief Reef and Second Thomas and Scarborough Shoals.[41] China was also charged with having infringed upon Philippine sovereign rights to explore for oil in its Exclusive Economic Zone and to protect Philippine fishermen in the area.

The Tribunal also found that China's land reclamations around the Spratly Islands failed to preserve the marine environment protected by UNCLOS. The Tribunal held that China's dredging, artificial-building, and reconstruction activities inflicted permanent damage to the disputed area under Philippine sovereign rule, while "permanently destroying evidence of the natural condition of multiple insular features [of the environment] through such activities."[42]

The Philippines' so-called "Scarborough Shoal" case established the primacy of UNCLOS as an important basis for determining the rights of the Southeast Asian states to the South China Sea as well as the commercial and military navigation and over-flight controls of the region. In asserting the South China Sea as its sphere of influence, China ignores its obligations under UNCLOS. It pits itself against both its neighbors and those of the international community,[43] which depend on the free use of the South China Sea as well as unfettered access to its living and non-living resources. China rejected the Tribunal's decision favoring the Philippines' sovereign claims. It also continues to violate not only the fishing rights of the Philippines but also those of Indonesia and Vietnam.[44] China continues to challenge the Philippines' "exclusive economic zone." In May, 2021, Chinese military vessels, masquerading as fishing trawlers, transgressed Whitsun reef in the Spratly Islands, which is three times closer to the Philippines than China.[45]

The South China Sea is of central importance not only for the states of Southeast Asia but also for all states of the international system. It is a crucial sea-lane of communications connecting the east-west route between the Indian and Pacific Oceans and the north-south route between Australia and New Zealand to Northeast Asia. Over half of the top ten container ports are located in or around the South China Sea. Keeping these commercial arteries open is a major concern of the entire international community. In 2016 US$3.37 trillion of trade and 40 percent of global liquefied natural gas transited through the South China Sea.[46] Ninety percent of Japan's oil passes through the area. Estimates of oil and gas deposits near the disputed Spratly Islands range from 105 to 214 billion barrels of oil and 266 trillion cubic feet of gas reserves. Living and non-living resources also bulk large. The area contains one of the largest resources for fish, providing 25 percent of the protein to 500 million people and 80 percent of the Philippine diet. Mineral resources in phosphorous, tin, manganese, copper, cobalt, and nickel are also estimated as abundant.[47]

However significant the living and non-living resources of the South China Sea may be, they are subordinate in salience to China's security concerns. Whoever controls the navigation and over-flight of the South China Sea directly impacts China's core security interests.[48] That overriding priority is evidenced in China's increasing militarization of its waters both through its buildup of forces and through land reclamation in the Spratly Islands to establish military aircraft landing, logistical, surveillance, ship docking, and weapons emplacement facilities. Beijing has also developed the Yulin Naval Base on Hainan Island to enable rapid access of its warships to the Pacific Ocean and the South China Sea. Yulin houses several naval warships, China's nuclear submarine forces, and a fleet of diesel-electric submarines capable of attacking enemy ships, notably those of the United States and its allies, Australia, New Zealand, Japan, South Korea, and Taiwan.

There is an unresolved tension between China's efforts to control the East and South China Seas and the insistence of other states to free use of the Seas as well as over-flight and maritime navigation in pursuit of their commercial and security interests. The conflict is particularly vexing for the United States. It relies on the freedom of the seas for the operation of its naval fleets and military forces in the region. The South China Sea connects American bases to Asia, the Indian Ocean, and the Persian Gulf. Their vulnerability to Chinese warships and conventional submarines as well as surface-to-surface, air-to-surface, and cruise missiles threaten US bases as well as America's military assets in the area.

China confronts a dilemma of its own creation. On the one hand, except for the Korean War when Western armies at China's border threatened the CCP's rule over China, CCP leaders have sought to avoid a global war with the United States. China's mutual nuclear deterrent posture; its no first use of nuclear weapons; its reluctance to engage in a nuclear arms race with Washington and Moscow; its support for non-proliferation accords and its signature of the nuclear accord with Iran – these policies underwrite a "no-war" commitment. On the other hand, the Chinese militarization of the South China Sea to assert its sovereign claims and to seek eventually a hegemonic position in the South and East China Seas undermines its "no war" stance. Its military forces are expected to "build a stable, peaceful Asian security environment in which China plays a leading role and other countries lack the ability or motivation to militarily challenge China over its 'core' interests."[49] This strategy raises the possibility of an armed confrontation between the United States and China, precisely the scenario, which CCP leadership wishes to avoid.

It is difficult to reconcile a "no war" posture with China's reliance on military force and coercive threats to preserve and promote its interests in its sphere of interest. China has developed military capabilities, including new regionally positioned nuclear weapons, designed to provide strong-armed muscle to establish its regional hegemony. The PLA's modernization in the East and South China Seas is counted upon to deter an armed clash; manage a crisis if it arises; and, if an armed exchange should erupt with an adversary (i.e., the United States), to control escalation and rapidly end the exchange on terms favorable to China.

This is a risky strategy, suffused with multiple uncertainties. What China may consider a defensive move in a crisis may be interpreted, as a consequence of misperception, miscalculation, or accident, as an aggressive act by American policymakers. It is no mean challenge to calibrate the limited use of force to match whatever stake is at issue in a conflict and avoid an unwanted escalation beyond the control of the adversaries to their mutual disadvantage. The burden for effective crisis management is not only China's challenge but also that of the United States. The Chinese and American military buildup in the East and South China Seas revive the Cold War image of two tense scorpions in a bottle.

The number of possible untoward armed incidents increases with the United States and other states as Chinese security, investment, and economic interests enlarge beyond East Asia. These are both substantive and territorial. A Rand Corporation study identified 11 fields, which China has defined as an area of national security interest, ranging from political, military, and economic to technological, informational, and ecological.[50] Territorially, security extends from the Chinese mainland and its coastal EEZ to encompass its claimed sphere of influence in the South and East China Seas and then outward to cover the trade routes on which it depends for unrestricted access to energy and needed industrial resources and for the unimpeded transport of its goods to foreign ports.[51]

The Belt and Road Initiative (BRI) – a New Silk Road – extending from China to Africa, the Middle East, and Europe – and progressively beyond – enlarges the scope of Chinese security interests. The BRI generates a dynamic that expands China's security interests and the PLA's obligation to defend the corporations, professional cadres, and thousands of Chinese workers enlisted in building the New Silk Road. There is the ever-present danger then that BRI projects will become ensnared in local conflicts, threatening Chinese citizens and economic interests, necessitating Chinese military intervention to protect them. In a self-help interstate system, which China favors and promotes, non-coercive power goes just so far.

The modernization and buildup of Chinese military forces in the South China Sea is impressive over the course of a generation.[52] There are several significant features to the expansion of Chinese military power in the area. Two aircraft carriers, and a third under construction, provide a platform for aircraft, anti-ship missiles, and drones to threaten American forces or to assume anti-pirate and humanitarian missions under UN auspices. Added to these capabilities are increasing numbers of warships, like the REMHAI-guided-missile cruiser, to form key components of the PLANavy's carrier strike group. These naval assets are complemented by the entry into service of DF-26 Intermediate-Range Ballistic Missile (IRBM) capable of reaching American bases in Guam and beyond to a range of 4,000 kilometers.[53] Most threatening to the US–Pacific fleet is the entry into service in 2019 of medium-range hypersonic missiles with a range of approximately 2,000 km. They can be armed with nuclear or conventional arms for precision targeting of US naval forces and bases. According to Pentagon sources, there is no defense against these weapons.[54]

The nuclear submarine fleet is also being modernized to provide additional deterrence capability for China's nuclear mutual assured destruction strategy. Construction is expected to begin in the early 2020s on China's third-generation Type 096 nuclear-powered Ballistic Missile Submarine (SSBN), armed with JL-3 Sea-Launched Ballistic Missiles (SLBM). Its nuclear and non-nuclear-powered submarines are capable of targeting US overseas bases (e.g., Guam) and the naval and ground-based deployments of Western forces. China already has the largest naval force in terms of ship numbers.

New stealth aircraft carrying short- and long-range missiles hold US naval forces at bay. These will be carried by J-20 stealth fighters, which entered into service in 2017, and H-6 bombers with a range of 3,300 kilometers.[55] Plans are to develop more advanced follow-ons in the near future. China is also improving its space-based systems for electronic warfare and cyber capabilities to degrade the war-fighting capabilities of its rivals. Within the scope of Chinese strategic thinking, the emphasis remains on avoiding an armed clash with the United States or its allies in the region and on bringing hostilities, should they erupt, quickly to end on terms favorable to Chinese forces and interests.[56]

Within its claimed sphere of influence in East Asia and, specifically, in the East and South China Seas, China has adopted an "active defense." It is designed around a rapid-response strategy that coordinates and directs joint sea-air-ground military capabilities to dominate the region. On that score, the Pentagon has concluded that except for US forces China dominates all other countries in East and Southeast Asia. Its militarization of the South China Sea and its creation of military bases in the area, principally within the Spratly Islands, provide China with the capability to prevail in any military exchange with its neighbors.

The US Defense Department now concedes China's military ascendancy within its sphere of influence. In his presentation to the Senate Armed Services Committee in 2018, Admiral Philip S. Davidson observed that once the islands being created by China are fully occupied,

> China will be able to extend its influence thousands of miles to the south and project power deep into Oceania. The PLA will be able to use these bases to challenge U.S. presence in the region, and any forces deployed to the islands would easily overwhelm the military forces of any other South China Sea-claimants. In short, China is now capable of controlling the South China Sea in all scenarios short of war with the United States.[57]

This sobering assessment assumes an even more ominous challenge to US naval forces in light of US Naval War College projections that envision a PLANavy with more than 430 ships and 100 submarines by 2030, double the size of the US fleet.[58] The Chinese plan is to gain superiority on the strength of its conventional naval and air capabilities to diminish incentives for opponents to employ nuclear weapons. This expectation underestimates American nuclear strategy that does not affirm a no-first-use doctrine.[59]

The Belt and Road Initiative (BRI)

The BRI is central to the realization of President Xi's dream for China.[60] It is a dream grounded in China's responses to OWL imperatives. From the perspective of the Imperative of Order, the BRI is woven into the PLA's modernization. The increasing geographic reach of the PLA and its progressively improving military and technological prowess provides the security framework within which Chinese economic, financial, and technological capabilities are protected and projected around the globe, while ensuring the CCP's monopoly of power over the Chinese population. The BRI is as much an elemental component of China's national security as it is central to China's rise, in the not too distant future, as the world's largest economy, fully capable of competing technologically with the Western democracies, and even outdistancing them in selected but key areas, including, *inter alia.* communications, green energy industries, robotics, and artificial intelligence.[61] The BRI cannot be disentangled from the PLA. Akin to a DNA molecule, they are wound together into a double helix as China's response to the Imperative of Global Order.

The BRI is no less the central feature of China's response to the Imperative of Welfare. As Sarwar Kashmeri observes, the BRI is "far more than merely an infrastructure investment, the Belt and Road Initiative is a masterful grand strategy to create nothing less than a new world order based on the Chinese model of government and its financial institutions."[62] Bruno Maçães doubles in brass, titling his study of BRI accordingly as *Belt and Road: A Chinese World Order:*[63] The BRI "initiative," he concludes, "is a project of economic and technological development, culminating in a new global political and economic order."[64]

Capping these responses to Order and Welfare Imperatives is President Xi's dream of a New Silk Road, which is more than a complex collection of economic and technological infrastructure contracts between China and BRI partners. It is envisioned as the creation of a subsystem of the nation–nation system under Chinese tutelage. Within this web the lure of the Chinese authoritarian model is expected to gain ascendancy over the liberal democratic alternative. The legitimacy of the CCP, as power, progressively assumes the norm for the governance of the BRI states and, *ipso facto*, for the governance of the global society. Xi's CCP is relying on the BRI to reshape global governance more to its liking across OWL imperatives.[65]

The Belt and Road Initiative, an unprecedented program projected to take decades to complete, dwarfs the Marshall Plan for Western Europe. It is the CCP's principal strategic vehicle to implant a multipolar global order with Chinese characteristics. The significance of the BRI can neither be dismissed nor ignored. Nor can its challenge to the Western liberal system arising out of World War II be exaggerated. Through China's military parity with the West, dominance of its Asian sphere of influence, and the BRI, the CCP intends to fundamentally reshape the global security order, to inflect free markets to accommodate China's state capitalism, to dissuade states from adopting the liberal democratic model, and to populate the global society with authoritarian states. Against the backdrop of President Xi's dream for China, endorsed by a submissive CCP, the BRI is at the epicenter of China's responses to OWL imperatives. The importance that the CCP attaches to the BRI is underscored by its incorporation into the Chinese constitution as an "objective of the state" in November 2017.[66]

Can Xi's dream become a reality? Or is Xi's dream for China simply that, like previous visions of other states, as aspiring hegemons, striving to shape an anarchical nation-state system in their own images. The discussion below traces the scope of BRI. It also evaluates its prospects and delineates serious flaws in its design and execution. The balanced assessment prompts a cautious expectation that the liberal democratic solution remains a strong option for other states to adopt.

Components of the BRI

President Xi Jinping announced the Belt and Road Initiative in two visits, respectively, to Central Asia in September 2013 and, subsequently, to Southeast Asia the following month. He pledged one trillion dollars, later eight, for the unprecedented initiation of multiple infrastructure, transportation, communications, and cyber network projects to spur economic growth in the developing world. (Leandro, 2018).[67] The BRI applies China's successful experiment in economic growth to the developing world.[68] Initially radiated from China through Central Asia, BRI now extends at this writing to 139 states on all continents in seven brief years.[69]

The BRI comprises both a territorial and a maritime component. Its territorial elements breathtakingly range over roads, railways, dams, bridges, tunnels, air links, internet connectivity, schools, hospitals, energy grids, power generating equipment, and telecommunications. The maritime or Road segment of BRI focuses on opening sea lanes and creating a chain of ports to provide access for China from its coastline through the East and South China Seas and unto the Indian Ocean and therefrom to the Persian Gulf and the Suez Canal, spilling finally into the Mediterranean and reaching Europe through Greece and Italy.

The ports and resources associated with this vast maritime Road complement the BRI's Belt projects. Chinese firms operate 93 ports across the globe which they either partially or fully own. This necklace of ports provides China with several commercial advantages. As parts of the BRI program, these ports furnish Chinese companies leverage to win contracts with host states, reward local supporters, and more easily access host resources. There are also the geopolitical security dimensions of facilitating intelligence gathering and of possibly manipulating trade flows to gain leverage over host policies. Some of these ports are concentrated near maritime chokepoints and key sea lines of communications. There is no immediate cause for alarm of expanding Chinese port controls. According to Chinese military strategists, these ports are not capable of sustaining major military operations. They are also a long way from being transformed into military bases for wartime use.[70]

Given BRI's global reach and complexity, an exhaustive description of each project goes well beyond the scope of this volume. An overview and selected illustrations of BRI projects capture their enlarging impact on global governance without undue and confusing detail. The territorial component can be reduced to an integral set of so-called economic corridors.[71] The first is the China–Mongolian–Russian corridor extending to Lithuania and the Latvian port cities on the Baltic. Both Baltic states receive financing under BRI. The second connects the Chinese heartland from Xingjian to Kazakhstan, Russia, Belarus, Central Europe, and the Northern Mediterranean.

The third corridor links Kazakhstan, Kyrgyzstan, Tajikistan, Turkmenistan, and Uzbekistan to Iran, Turkey, the Persian Gulf, and the Mediterranean Sea. All these states are BRI recipients. The fourth corridor is linked exclusively to Pakistan, which is the largest recipient of BRI funding. The reported US$65 billion, 15-year project is projected to modernize Pakistan's road, rail, air, energy, and transportation systems. The goal of the China–Pakistan Economic Corridor (CPEC) is to link the Pakistani Port of Gwadar to China's Xinjiang Province and beyond to other corridors.[72]

The fifth corridor sweeps southward to Bangladesh, India, and Myanmar and extends to the sixth corridor connecting Kumming and Nanking in China to Laos, Vietnam, Cambodia, Thailand, Malaysia, and Singapore. All are BRI partners. The Singapore partnership is different from the others in Southeast Asia in that it is a two-way street in which both states invest in each other.

Building on these corridors are BRI platforms that invest Chinese funds into Eastern Europe, the Middle East, Latin America, and Africa. The Chinese–African connection is particularly significant. Chinese interest in exploiting Africa well precedes BRI's launching.[73] The BRI builds on already sunk Chinese investments. Primary targets include ten states, extending from Tunisia and Algeria in North Africa to Kenya, and South Africa. As increasing labor costs make Chinese supply chains costly, China is developing Africa as the next global workshop under Chinese entrepreneurial direction and control.[74] There are approximately 1,500 Chinese firms engaged in manufacturing in Africa. FAW, a state-owned Chinese firm, produces trucks for the African market. Chinese carmakers, construction materials producers, and light manufacturers of consumer products have established enterprises in Nigeria. Chinese Lesotho garment factories produce yoga pants for Kohl stores, jeans for Levi Strauss, and sporting equipment for Reebok.[75] From the Chinese perspective, Africa is not "defined by poverty; it is characterized by promise and optimism, with eight of the ten fastest-growing economies in the world over the next decade projected to be on the continent."[76]

Africa also plays a central role in the development of the maritime segments of the BRI. The Djibouti port of Doraleh provides China's access to the Mediterranean and Europe through the Red Sea and the Suez Canal. China established its first military base in Djibouti. Its location on the Horn of Africa, astride a narrow strait, endows Djibouti with unique strategic importance. It is the key junction between the West and East of the Chinese maritime Silk Road. The BRI design is to connect Djibouti with a string of ports linking Kyaukpyu in Myanmar to Hamnabtota in Sri Lanka, and then to Gwadar in Pakistan.[77] The sweep is ambitious, connecting the South China Sea to the Indian Ocean that leads to Djibouti and then onward through the Suez Canal onto the Mediterranean, leading to the states of North Africa, the Middle East, and Europe.[78] The endpoint of this maritime Road segment of the BRI is the Greek Port of Piraeus. The Chinese state-owned shipping group, COSCO, invested US$9 billion to buy a controlling share in the port. From Piraeus the maritime BRI is projected to meet up with the territorial Belt of BRI coming from the north corridor through Russia, East and Central Europe, the Balkans, and southern Europe.

To secure passage through the Suez Canal, Egypt has become a prime recipient of Chinese and BRI investments. BRI finances the Suez Canal Economic Zone to upgrade Egyptian ports and improve infrastructure and transportation projects for economic development. Dozens of Chinese companies are also encamped in Egypt to implement BRI objectives and to underwrite Egypt's export industries. Notable among these is Egypt's emergence as a leading exporter of fiberglass.[79]

Overarching these BRI territorial and maritime sites is China's launching of a Digital Silk Road (DSR). It is envisioned as a global network connecting all of the continents. The spearhead for the digital DSR is the multinational communications giant Huawei, working in conjunction with a host of smaller national champions.[80] By 2020 Huawei signed more 5G contracts than any other telecom company, half of which are in Europe. It has shipped 70,000, 5G base stations globally. Huawei has also built 70 percent of the fourth-generation networks (4G) in Africa and is positioned to lead in 5G contracts. Across the globe, Huawei's success has enabled six thousand Chinese internet companies and more than a thousand Chinese technology products to enter foreign markets.

BRI cannot succeed simply as an investment strategy. It requires the creation of an elaborate political framework within which to make BRI work to facilitate economic growth and development, to relieve poverty, and, most importantly, to expand China's (and the CCP's) power and influence. BRI applies Deng Xiaoping's cautionary advice to the BRI, viz., that politics and economics must march in lockstep if a multipolar world order led by Communist China is to be realized:

> We maintain that the safeguarding of political independence is the first prerequisite for a Third World country to develop its economy. ... The consolidation of political independence is necessarily a process of repeated struggles. In the final analysis, political independence and economic independence are inseparable. Without political independence, it is impossible

to achieve economic independence; without economic independence, a country's independence is incomplete and insecure[81]

The CCP has implemented Deng's theory of political and economic development advice along a number of interdependent and mutually reinforcing fronts, while under Xi Jinping departing fundamentally from his later prudent counsel that China eschew an aggressive foreign policy.[82]

Ninety percent of BRI financing is in the form of interest-bearing loans in contrast with the Marshall Plan, which aided European states with direct grants. Loans are largely made by major Chinese state-owned banks – the Export-Import Bank of China and the China Development Bank (CDB).[83] In contrast to Western practices, including those of the IMF and the World Bank, BRI loans have been largely unconditional, earning Beijing a positive reputation as a provider of aid and investments.[84] While BRI loans are substantial, they remain a small portion of Chinese bank lending. CDB and China EXIM committed only 2.9 percent and 3.1 percent of their assets, respectively, to BRI as of the end of 2018.[85]

China has also created a number of multilateral investment banks to attract state and private funding for BRI. These include the Silk Road Development Fund (SDF), the Shanghai Cooperative Organization (SCO), the New Development Bank (NDB), and the Asian Infrastructure Investment Bank (AIIB). By June 2018, membership in the AIIB, had grown to over 100 countries. Included were Western democracies, like Britain, which joined over the objections and non-participation of the United States.[86] While these ventures are promising as tools to fund development, they have not replaced Chinese state banks as the principal source of BRI funding.[87] China's creation of several multilateral developmental banks, the Asian Infrastructure Investment Bank prominently among them,[88] have not attracted substantial state or private funding for BRI projects, many of which were evaluated as commercially unprofitable.[89]

The BRI's political reach extends to a series of strategic partnership agreements with states across the world. Between 1994 and 2014, China signed strategic partnerships with 52 states.[90] China has a comprehensive strategic partnership with the European Union and with African states. Multiple bilateral accords beyond those not covered by strategic partnerships deepen and strengthen interdependencies between Chinese and partner economic interests. Forums provide for periodic meetings between regional partners and China. Examples are the 16 + 1 Forum bringing together East European states with China,[91] the Forum on China–Africa Cooperation, and China and the Community of Latin American and Caribbean States Forum.

By 2017, 19 regional states signed agreements with the BRI. Joint communiqués are occasions to affirm Chinese BRI objectives.[92] Individual BRI projects are viewed in Chinese planning as building blocks of regional and global integration under Chinese sponsorship, not as separate and stand-alone from each other. That integration process is further advanced by a Cyberspace Silk Road linked to communication satellites and to a growing number of fiber optic cables in the Asia-Pacific region, which carry 98 percent of emails, telephone calls, and internet traffic.[93]

Evaluating the BRI and the Imperative of Order

The BRI's jerry-built and sprawling structure and its piecemeal enlargement furnish a somewhat shaky scaffolding for Chinese and BRI partners within which to engage in sustained negotiation, bargaining, restructuring, and provisional accords to regulate trade and investments as well as the how and wherefore of executing BRI projects, their control, and ownership. From these disparate BRI projects and their discrete realization, new, pragmatic, scenario-specific norms and rule-making are arising to regulate BRI Chinese-partner relations. It is still too early to determine whether BRI as a Chinese-centered global economic and political project will eventually overwhelm what is now a tattered Western trading system in disarray. The Trump administration's war of tariffs on China and allies raises a serious question whether the quest to develop globally defined rules within the framework of the World Trade Organization will continue to guide economic and financial transactions and to ground these transactions in firm rule-based legal and uniform protocols applicable to all global traders and investors.[94]

In assessing the global implications of the BRI, it is important to acknowledge that there are several positive public goods dimensions to this ambitious developmental scheme. First, from the perspective of the Hobbesian dilemma, the BRI shifts the competition between an authoritarian state and its aligned coalition of dictatorial regimes vs. the Western democracies to an economic rivalry for preeminence to define the Welfare imperative and, *ipso facto*, to place a Chinese stamp on the global order. At a theoretical level of analysis covered in Chapter 1, the CCP has Hobbes negotiating with Adam Smith and Immanuel Kant to define the governing Imperatives of Global Order and Welfare. In redirecting a deadly rivalry between authoritarian and democratic regimes to non-violent, but still intensely competitive battlefields, the BRI relaxes the incentives of the Hobbesian dilemma, without fully relieving their pressures on decision-makers. These contradictions are visible and at the heart of the tension between the CCP's pursuit of an aggressive South China Sea strategy in zero-sum terms and its continual harassment of Taiwan, while presenting BRI, misleadingly, as win-win for all participants. The authoritarian-democratic economic rivalry to determine a key element of global governance is still less susceptible to an unwanted and unwitting armed clash between China and the United States than the unrevealed fear of war and full exposure to the "Thucydides' Trap."

Second, China also provides more foreign state assistance to combat global poverty and to spur economic growth in the developing world than any other state or group of states. It has assumed a leading role in furnishing these critical public goods to advance global welfare, filling a gap left by Western states.

Western financial corporations, like Western states, show little interest in loaning funds that require long lead times before they can be profitable, if at all. BRI loans dwarf the assistance of the IMF, the World Bank, and, collectively, all Western states. As banker for the developing world, China holds more debt than all other government creditors combined. By 2018 the amount owed to China by the entire world is estimated at US$5 trillion, 6 percent of global GNP.[95]

Third, and paradoxically for a proclaimed socialist state, China has been a staunch proponent of free and open global markets, a position critically evaluated in the next chapter. This posture contrasts with the Trump administration's reversion to tariff wars and subsidies for American industries, notably agriculture. China's Belt and Road Initiative is portrayed as complementary and supportive of the Western market system, however much its actual policies and behavior may belie its announced commitment.

While the BRI creates norms and rules that run counter to the Western ideal of a uniform rule-based market system (often recognized more in the breach than in the observance by the West), China's deviation has not strayed so far from these eroding constraints as to constitute a rupture, much less a replacement of Western domination. Not surprisingly, the fracturing of the Western trade system and disposition of democratic states, with the United States in the lead, to depart from once prevailing norms and rules for economic exchange has given voice to what was until recently a farfetched view that China may "resurrect a liberal international order."[96]

China has inserted codicils into its strategic partnerships with BRI recipients and bilateral agreements to affirm free trade zones and unfettered global markets. Chinese investments have also positioned some BRI partners to industrialize and successfully compete in global markets, as the Egyptian and Lesotho examples suggest. Industrial startups in Africa in the service of exploiting Africa's low labor costs to become conceivably the world's next workshop and an alternate supply chain hub to China further the competitive market theme in BRI development.[97] Through these moves, China supplies significant, if qualified, public goods to sustain an open market system, albeit deployed to favor Chinese national interests.

Fourth, and at odds with the Trump administration, China has assumed a leading role in championing the causes of controlling climate change and of protecting the ecology of the planet. Codicils affirming China's commitment to these objectives are inserted in bilateral accords and in its strategic partnerships with other states. These obligations are affirmed, for example, in the 2017 Joint Communiqué of the Leaders of the Roundtable of the Belt and Road Forum for International Cooperation:

> We are determined to protect the planet from degradation, including through taking urgent action on climate change and encouraging all parties which have ratified it to fully implement the Paris Agreement, managing the natural resources in an equitable and sustainable manner, conserving

and sustainably using oceans and seas, freshwater resources, as well as forests, mountains and dry lands, protecting biodiversity, ecosystems and wildlife, combating desertification and land degradation so as to achieve sustainable development in its three dimensions in a balanced and integrated manner.[98]

This commitment, signed by 30 states and the director of the IMF, might well have been composed by the Environmental Defense Fund, the Sierra Club, or Greenpeace. With the return of the United States under the Biden administration to the Paris climate change accord, Beijing and Washington have at least one area where cooperation is possible, dramatized by President Xi's participation in the zoom meeting organized by the Biden administration to affirm the US commitment to the reduction of greenhouse gasses.

Important Chinese national interests are just below the surface of these public goods commitments. BRI projects, like those with Pakistan, are expected to open China's western interior to development. Energy and resource security to motor the Chinese economy is strengthened. The territorial and maritime corridors of BRI diminish the risks run by China in relying too heavily on the narrow passage of the Straits of Malacca to supply needed energy and material resources and to reach global markets. Eighty percent of China's energy imports pass through the Straits. Access to Russian oil, gas, and minerals serve a trifecta of economic and political interests of Moscow and Beijing: supplies are insulated from American or Western sanctions and impediments; payments are in local currencies, including the use of the Renminbi; and the Chinese–Russian goal of a multipolar world is advanced. Other economic objectives are of equal national importance: full employment by exporting surplus Chinese labor and expertise; the award of valuable construction and industrial contracts to increase the profits and viability of Chinese companies, notably state-owned corporations; the continuation of these BRI projects in the form of upgrades and repairs; and to close these virtuous circles, a seemingly endless stream of royalties and licensing fees.

The expected long-term benefits of BRI overshadow these particular, significant economic gains. If successful, the BRI would integrate Chinese and BRI client state economic and industrial policies. Complex economic geographies, drawing advantage of both specialization and connectivity, would facilitate efficient production outcomes. The BRI is not predominantly about infrastructure but about integration. Individual nodules would be linked into networks of global supply chains under BRI organizational direction. National borders would be increasingly blurred. Through its access to the economic policies of other states, China would be able to organize production across these supply chains.

Bruno Mações summary of Richard Baldwin's depiction of the new globalization captures BRI's ambitious scope:

> [T]he offshoring of production tasks shifts the effective geographic boundaries of competition. The units facing each other in the global market

are no longer nations but value chains. … Thus when China develops a policy toward important commodity producers, it is less interested in security access to commodity markets than in building highly efficient value chains where one can occupy the top segment. It knows that its competitive advantage results from this organizing role.[99]

Put another way, in an increasingly integrated and interdependent world, the BRI's "most distinctive trait," as Maçães observes, "is the incessant competition between different ideas of how worldwide networks should be organized."[100] Chinese control over these value chain networks positions it to determine both global industrial and technological standards.[101]

The downsides of the BRI

In assessing the public goods provided by the BRI and its promotion of Chinese interests, one might well recall a George Bernard Shaw character who exclaimed: "Too good to be true." In many ways China's BRI is "too good to be true."

The BRI extends the CCP's authoritarian model of rules to the developing world. Internet sovereignty, a cardinal CCP principle, is fostered through the dissemination of Chinese communications technology through corporations, like Huawei, which are technically private, but which operate under CCP control. Through BRI developing states receive Chinese know-how about how they, too, can control the information available to their populations, block criticism and dissent, and provide a state-controlled narrative to favorably frame public policies and their results.

The BRI's Digital Silk Road is an effective vehicle to transfer Chinese technology to authoritarian regimes to maintain their monopoly of power. China is the largest exporter of surveillance systems to over 50 countries. Authoritarian regimes are particularly interested in acquiring these tools of population control. Edwin Ngonyani, Tanzanian Deputy Minister of Communications, voiced the interest of authoritarian regimes in these tools of population control. He praised the effectiveness of CCP censorship, a view shared by authoritarian regimes and illiberal democracies: "Our Chinese friends have managed to block such media in their country and replaced them with homegrown sites that are safe, constructive and popular."[102]

China's export of its governing model may not be as seamless as the quote of the Tanzanian Minister suggests. BRI projects entangle China in the complexities and contradictions of conflicting religious, cultural, social, economic, and political divisions within each partner state. CCP leadership and BRI planners present BRI projects largely as physical and engineering problems to be solved. These are the easy part of these projects. "Exaggerated attention to the physical and economic infrastructure," as Robert Bianchi observes, "overshadow the greater importance of the social and cultural networks they are supposed to sustain."[103] Each project ensnares China in these tightly woven webs over which it has limited power to control and in which CCP leadership evidences slim understanding of the adverse implications of these entanglements. Somewhat unwittingly, China is now enmeshed in the particular social dynamics and internal power struggles of each BRI state. President Xi's characterization of these projects as win-win outcomes are narrowly measured by economic and physical outcomes. Their real human significance is in the social and political currency of each partner state.[104] Win-win loses its luster in the win-lose struggles into which BRI intrudes between local rivals. Win-win fades further from realization as Chinese investments are dissipated by the infirmities of fragile states. Sapping their impact are regional and global flows of narcotics and other substance abuse materials with which Chinese officials must cope in implementing BRI projects.

What has not been sufficiently understood by CCP leadership is that fierce Chinese nationalism and regime self-regard also animate BRI partner regimes and foreign populations.[105] No less than the CCP, they demand respect and acknowledgment of their interests in developing BRI projects. If national leaders neglect their responsibilities to bargain hard with their Chinese BRI counterparts or are exposed for taking bribes, they confront publics who resist Chinese dictation. As Robert Bianchi concludes in his valuable study of *China and Islam*: "Time after time, citizens and provincial leaders pressure national government to rethink and renegotiate Chinese-sponsored projects — not merely to fine-tune their execution, but to redistribute their burdens and advantages."[106]

This conclusion is especially relevant to China's relations with Muslim states. Tensions suffuse China's BRI negotiations with Pakistan, Turkey, Indonesia, Iran, Nigeria, and Egypt. All of these states have illustrious histories and view themselves as current and future leaders in their regions with a global reach and importance. They, like China, jealously protect their autonomy. They insist that they have their own spheres of influence.[107] For these states, the BRI is not in the service of Chinese interests, but those of the receiving state. In renegotiating a substantial reduction of its BRI contract with China, Malaysia decried the corruption associated with the project and criticized the loans as a new version of colonialism. Echoing these sentiments, the former president of the Maldives charged that BRI investments were a land grab under the guise of development.[108]

China's internment of over one million Uighurs, Kazakhs, and Kyrgyzs also weakens the appeal of Chinese investments in Muslim countries. Rising militant Islam throughout Asia and the Middle East pose obstacles to Chinese BRI ambitions.[109] Religious concerns reinforce fears of Chinese domination. Bianchi notes that "citizens of Muslim countries will reject any appearance of tutelage from China just as vigorously as they resisted earlier efforts of domination by the United States, Europe, Russia, or Japan."[110] China has attempted to pre-empt Muslim concerns by buying off key Muslim states. Beijing signed a US$400 billion agreement to invest in Iran in return for oil. Pakistan is also the largest Asian recipient of BRI funding.[111] These economic ties have served to blunt their criticism of Chinese violations of human rights in Xinjiang.

Overlooked initially in BRI planning have been the negative impacts of BRI on partner states, on China's interests, on CCP rule and power, and on BRI's effectiveness. BRI officials have had to renegotiate national projects in response to partner pressures. Compromises include reductions in contracts as too costly or ridden with corruption as well as concessions to use local labor over imported Chinese workers and to enlarge the input of partner states in project decision-making. These factors are at work in projects with Kazakhstan, Pakistan, Myanmar, Malaysia, and Sri Lanka.[112]

Pragmatic, ad hoc rules and norms to fit each national project opens the CCP and President Xi Jinping, in particular, to domestic criticism that CCP leadership makes significant concessions to partner states, while increasingly imposing totalitarian rule over its own population. Rifts are cleaved between the CCP and the Chinese people and, potentially, within the Party itself. The BRI ignites contradictions between external flexibility and the internal rigidity of CCP's rule at home. BRI is certainly shaping globalization and global order, but, unintentionally, it has also set in motion potentially powerful forces within China, questioning both the BRI and, implicitly, Xi's leadership of the CCP. Critics, like Sun Wenguang, a physicist, and Zu Zhangrun, a law professor, suggest that there is dissent within the CCP about the priority assigned to the BRI over widespread and urgent domestic needs. Viewing the BRI as a form of "vanity politics," Zu portrays the BRI as a serious impediment to internal economic development and the elimination of poverty:

> Rural destitution is a widespread and crushing reality; greater support through public policy initiatives is essential. Without major changes, half of China will remain in what is basically a pre-modern economic state. That will mean that the hope to create a modern China will remain unfulfilled, if not half-hearted.[113]

China's BRI still falls short of what the developing world needs. The infrastructure, transportation, and communication requirements of developing states exceed the resources of any state. China itself is a developing state. The Asian Development Bank estimates that US$26 trillion would be needed between 2016 and 2030 to close the infrastructure deficit in Asia alone, quite apart from other continents.[114] The Asian region, led by Chinese investment, annually invests approximately US$880 billion in infrastructure, while investment needs are estimated to total two to three trillion dollars each year. China obviously cannot fill this gap.

In its attempt to fill that gap through the BRI, both China and its partners have embraced a risky strategy that threatens their financial stability. While BRI funding represents only a small share of Chinese bank loans, default of BRI projects could have a damaging ripple effect on the banking systems as a whole. In less than 20 years total assets in the Chinese financial system grew from US$1.7 trillion to US$38.4 trillion. These totals vastly surpassed the asset value of American commercial banks of US$17.4 trillion.[115] Defaults on BRI loans and the loss of expected interest on them further weakens the Chinese banking system. Much depends on the economic viability of BRI projects. The evidence so far suggests that many BRI states are not keeping up their end of these projects. Their governmental institutions are weak; corruption is rampant; and they do not possess the level of expertise to complete BRI projects and maintain them. Lowered projections of Chinese economic growth, exacerbated by the coronavirus pandemic, and the currently poor return on BRI investments limit China's capacity to sustain the level of investments in BRI projects that it was able to maintain since its inception.

Many BRI partners are ensnared in a strangling debt trap. A 2019 World Bank report concluded that forecasts of economic growth of BRI projects evaluated by the Bank were exaggerated. The report found "that, over the medium term, debt vulnerability is ... expected to worsen in 12 of the 43 examined recipient countries."[116] Even if BRI forecasts of economic growth were achieved, 11 recipient states were expected to experience severe indebtedness. The report concluded that "it is questionable, therefore, that the BRI's promised inclusive economic growth will deliver sufficient benefits to offset pronounced debt vulnerabilities that have emerged in some of the world's poorest countries."[117]

Another study by the Center for Global Development evaluated the investment grade of states within BRI's orbit of then 68 states. The list was pared to 23 states, which were rated by the IMF and World Bank as below investment grade. Of these, eight were singled out as particularly vulnerable: Djibouti, Pakistan, Maldives, Laos, Montenegro, Mongolia, Tajikistan, and Kyrgyzstan. What these studies were unable to take into account are the massive losses in global GDP and, specifically, in Chinese economic growth due to the coronavirus epidemic. It will take some time to fully assess the damage the 2020 epidemic has inflicted on the BRI.

The implications of the debt trap for Djibouti and Sri Lanka are of particular interest to global security. Both states were included in the first cut of 23 states of the report of the Center for Global Development.[118] The experience of these states with Chinese loans raises the specter of a return of colonialism in Chinese garb. In defaulting on its Chinese loans, Sri Lanka had to compensate China with the lease of its port at Hambantota for 99 years and control of the port's surrounding territory. Sri Lanka's partial surrender of sovereignty is reminiscent of the unequal treaties of foreign extra-territorial control imposed on China by the Western imperial powers in the nineteenth century.

Sri Lanka's fate confronts Djibouti. Its external debt increased from 50 to 85 percent thanks to Chinese loans, the highest of the eight states at risk. By 2016 China will have provided US$1.4 billion in BRI funding. If Djibouti also defaults on its loans to China, it may have to cede its port to Chinese leasing and even ownership. Threatened then are the military bases and personnel of the United States and the other Western states and Japan in Djibouti. A financial breakdown could then slide unwittingly into a military clash between China and its Western rivals.

In a nutshell, these debt traps pose a dilemma for the CCP. If China assumes all or most of these national defaults, it risks the viability of the BRI and damage to the Chinese economy. If it pushes these debts on weak and failing states, it earns not only their ire but it also soils its reputation as a responsible global banker and supplier of public goods.

Two other claims made for the BRI require serious qualification, namely, that the BRI supports all efforts to combat climate change and that it champions free and unfettered free markets. Despite China's merited efforts to meet its obligations under the Paris Accord and its leadership in developing renewal energy, it remains the world's biggest emitter of greenhouse gas emissions. China consumes more coal than the rest of the world. Dozens of coal-fired plants are added annually to China's electrical grid. These plants, according to a Columbia University report, account for ten percent of the world's CO_2 emissions. Through BRI China is also the leading financier of coal-fired power plants in dozens of countries around the world.[119]

China's commitment to free and unfettered markets, championed by President Xi Jinping,[120] parallels the contradictions embedded in its economic behavior. As the next chapter on China's response to the Imperative of Welfare delineates, its economic policies belie that commitment. Its brand of state capitalism relies heavily on state-owned companies – characterized by some as *Crony Capitalism*.[121] Added to these anti-free-market practices is continued Chinese state and corporate theft of foreign technology and compromise of property rights, sanctioned by a court system under tight CCP rule.

State-owned corporations pose particular problems for the maintenance of a free market system. The SOEs act as a lobby within the CCP's BRI decision-making. They receive favored loans from state-run banks, subsidies, tariff assistance, and governmental regulation of foreign corporations that enhance their market competitiveness. Seventy percent of BRI's total contract value is in centrally controlled SOE accounts. Since SOEs are viewed not only as economic champions in global markets by the Xi regime but also as integral parts of China's national security and the CCP's control of the Chinese population, there is every likelihood that SOEs will continue to enjoy a disproportionate share of BRI contracts despite their inefficiencies and susceptibility to corruption, evidenced in criticisms made by BRI recipients. "Given the prominent role of SOEs in the BRI," notes an International Institute of Strategic Studies study,

> genuine efforts to enhance SOE competitiveness in the initiative would lead to the SOEs bearing the financial costs of failed projects. However, should Beijing continue to prioritize political incentives over productivity and efficiency, SOEs will continue to be primarily employed as instruments to advance state-driven mandates at the expense of domestic financial prudence.[122]

The Digital Silk Road also confronts a rocky future. China has yet to master the design and manufacture of the most advanced microprocessors and logic and memory chips. This technology is essential for the continued development of artificial intelligence, machine learning, high-performance computing, electric vehicles, and telecommunications. In this area, the western democracies have maintained their lead. Since the incentives of globalization are moving all states toward increasing reliance on a digital economy, this is one area in which the West can potentially preserve a competitive edge. A qualification has to be added to this optimistic appraisal. Taiwan, not the United States or the European democracies, is the global leader in microprocessors. Its success actually increases the CCP's incentive to put pressure on Taiwan to fall under Beijing control, much like Hong Kong today.

Conclusions

The CCP's solution to the Imperative of Order of a multipolar system is itself a danger to China and to the world's populations. The Westphalian system, with or without Chinese characteristics, is fundamentally unstable. The Hobbesian incentive, embedded in a nation–state system, of states seeking hegemonic dominance over other states, particularly much abroad among great powers, is both compelling and illusory, evidenced by two world wars and the precariously balanced nuclear arms race between the United States and the Soviet Union. China is a big player in its preferred multipolar order, but it does not, nor can any other state, control that system. China's aggressive moves in the South China Sea exacerbate the instability of the system. Nationalism, the handmaiden of the nation–state and a key control over the Chinese population, eggs the system to its self-destruction.

The Belt and Road Initiative, wittingly or not, is a right move to sidestep, if not fully escape, the "Thucydides' Trap." It is a right, if cautious, step to deflect attention and resources from war to economic competition. Whether, alone, the BRI can substitute for mutual security guarantees between states and verifiable arms control accords is problematic. It is certainly less reliable than the alliance guarantees of the Western democracies with each other during the Cold War, however much the reliance on these assurances has now eroded with the rise of authoritarian movements, illiberal democracies, and nationalism within the Western camp. Security guarantees, when solid, trustworthy, and grounded on shared values, are profoundly more reassuring than the pragmatic and often provisional economic transactional relations of the BRI. As BRI projects sour, there is evidence of an increasing assertion of a zero-sum nationalistic assertion of Chinese interests in bargaining with BRI partners. So much for the unvarnished claims of win-win. The economic interdependence of the European imperial powers before World War I did not preclude a global conflagration. It was no barrier to war, as many erroneously believed.[123] The CCP's solution to the Imperative of Order for global government is itself the problem to be resolved.

Notes

1 Throughout Chapters 4–6, I will use China, as a state, and the Chinese Communist Party (CCP) interchangeably. While the functions of the Party and the state can certainly be differentiated, I have adopted the Party's characterization of itself. According to Party doctrine, the Party *is* China in the sense that what China is today is the result, exclusively, of the Party's leadership as a Leninist Party. Consequently, the security of the Party is ipso facto the security of China.

2 Deng and Moore (2004).

3 Other observers of CCP behavior share my evaluation of Chinese strategy. See Cordesman (2019); Wright (2017) for supportive data. For a more narrowly focused appraisal of Chinese strategy, foreseeing a military clash with the United States, see Allison (2017, February 2020), who coined the metaphor of the "Thucydides's' Trap."

4 If one traces numerous newspaper accounts from President Xi Jinping's assumption as the head of the CCP in 2012 to the present, there are numerous reports of Chinese military shows of force to establish Chinese sovereignty in the South and East China Seas. See, for example, *The New York Times*, March 19, 2021, and the China Power Project, viewing China's military-diplomatic relations.
https://chinapower.csis.org/china-military-diplomacy/
See also the website of the Asia Maritime Transparency Initiative (AMTI) for detailed coverage of Chinese militarization of the South China Sea, covered below.
https://amti.csos.org/

5 I will be using BRI throughout, namely China's Belt and Road Initiative, in lieu of a "new silk road" or OBOR, namely, One Belt One Road, however BRI otherwise appears in the citations below.

6 The *Economist Special Report: China's Belt and Road*, February 8, 2020, p. 2.

7 See Chapter 1, p. 6.

8 See Mao Zedong, *Problems of War and Strategy*
M Zedong – *Selected Works of Mao Zedong*, 1938. This is a compilation of Mao Zedong's thinking about war and strategy. The quote above is found in his address to the Sixth Plenary Session of the Chinese Communist Party on November 6, 1938. The Defense Intelligence Agency, *Chinese Military Power 2019* cites Mao's doctrine as informing current Chinese strategic thinking. Affirmation of Mao's principles of war and strategy is found in
htthps://www.dia.mil › China_Military_Power_FINAL_5MB_20190103.

9 Brown (2017b), p. 20.

10 That the PLA serves the CCP rather than the Chinese state and people is a view that may initially be difficult to accept when compared to the relation between military forces and democratic states in which civilian rule is paramount. The CCP controls the state and the PLA. This view is also echoed in a survey of CCP's modernization of the PLA. See also ns. 16 and 17 below.
www.cfr.org/backgrounder/china-modernizing-military. I share Kerry Brown's view that the CCP resembles the Curia of the Catholic Church, which embodies the body politic of all Catholics living and deceased since the founding of the Church and those future adherents who will be baptized in this Holy Body. Brown (2017a, 2017b), *passim*.

11 Deng Xiaoping dismissed Communist Party Secretary Zhao Ziyang from office for resisting the use of the PLA to smash the student uprising in Tiananmen Square.

12 Quoted in Heath et al. (2016), p. 14. Xi is referring to the security ties between the United States, Japan, South Korea, Australia, and New Zealand as well as, implicitly, US military aid to Taiwan.

13 Full Text of 2019 Chinese White Paper: *China's National Defense in the New Era*: https://www.csis.org/analysis/chinas-new-2019-defense-white-paper

Members of the SCO include India, Pakistan, China, Kazakhstan, Kyrgyzstan, Russia, Tajikistan, and Uzbekistan.

14 Quoted in Heath et al. (2016), p. 11. The views are those of Ge Dongsheng, a military officer and an alternate member of the 15th CCP Central Committee. Here democratic refers to the power and influence of each state within a multipolar system. It has no relation to what is conveyed by the notion of a liberal democratic regime.

15 See the Defense Intelligence Agency study of Chinese military power www.xinhuanet.com › english › 2019-07 and Defense Intelligence Agency: *China Military Power 2019*
www.dia.mil › China_Military_Power_FINAL_5MB_20190103A

16 These Chinese objectives are discussed at length in reports, respectively, of the Department of Defense and the Rand Corporation. See Heginbotham (2015). For a briefer report on Chinese military objectives, see Maizland (2020).

17 See also Lian (2018).

18 Instances of Chinese success in stealing military and commercial secrets and violating property rights through hacking are reviewed by Keith Bradsher in *The New York Times*, January 15, 2020. In February, 2020, a federal indictment was issued for four Chinese military officers for hacking into Equifax, stealing trade secrets and the personal data of 145 million Americans. See also the report of Katie Benner, *The New York Times*, February 10, 2020.

19 Both the Chinese White Paper on Defense for 2019 and the Defense Intelligence Agency's assessment of Chinese military strategy converge on the aversion of the Communist Party to a global war. See *Chinese National Defense in the New Era*
www.xinhuanet.com › english › 2019-07 and Defense Intelligence Agency: *China Military Power 2019*
www.dia.mil › China_Military_Power_FINAL_5MB_20190103A
See n. 3 for additional sources.

20 See Zakaria (2020), who critiques policy analysts alarmed by the growth of China's military power and its expansionist aspirations. Except for aggressive Chinese moves in the South Asia Sea, this analysis shares Zakaria's portrayal of China as a formidable opponent but not as an imminent military threat to the United States. For a more pessimistic evaluation of Chinese military capabilities and intent, see, *inter alia.*, (Fanell, 2018).

21 Additional support for the proposition that Chinese military policy is subordinated to the use of non–military policy tools to advance Chinese interests is found in Anthony H. Cordesman's evaluation of the 2009 Chinese *White Paper on Defense*. www.dia.mil › China_Military_Power_FINAL_5MB_20190103

22 See the views of Zhou Bo, a senior colonel in the PLA and an alternate member of the 19th CCP Central Committee. It is highly unlikely that Zhou Bo's views were personally his own, but those vetted by CCP authorities. *The New York Times*, February 3, 2020.

23 Additional support for the view that Xi Jinping seeks to export the Chinese authoritarian model is found in Elizabeth Economy's NY Council on Foreign Relations blog: "Yes, Virginia, China Is Exporting Its Model," December 11, 2019. The discussion of China's Belt and Road Initiative below supports Economy's position.

24 Check the report that Beijing Wants AI to Be Made in China by 2030
www.nytime.com/2017/07/20/business/china-artificial-intelligence.html

25 https://media.defense.gov/2018/Aug/16/2001955282/-1/-1/1/2018-CHINA-MILITARY-POWER-REPORT.PDF, p. i.

26 Glaser and Murphy (2009); Kurlantzick (2007); McGiffert (2009).

27 A 2015 Rand Corporation Report tracks the evolution of Chinese capabilities in these areas. Heginbotham (2015), pp. 285–310.

28 I have relied on several sources, which, in turn, cite other relevant sources in developing their estimates of Chinese nuclear strategic thinking, nuclear capabilities,

delivery systems, and projected modernization programs. Works include (Cordesman, September 2018) and a briefer but no less authoritative report to the American Federation of Scientists and published in the *Bulletin of Atomic Scientists* (Kristensen and Korda, 2019). For an overview of the nuclear capabilities of the nine nuclear powers, see (Kristensen and Norris, June 2019). Finally, two articles in *International Security* by Fiona Cunningham and M. Taylor Fravel are valuable as sources, based on original Chinese sources and interviews. The first in 2015 affirms the credibility of Chinese no-first use; the second in 2019, while affirming the no-first doctrine, is skeptical about Chinese confidence that nuclear weapons will not be introduced into a conventional conflict with the United States because escalation could not be controlled. Cunningham and Fravel (2015, 2019).

29 *The New York Times*, January 2, 2020, p. 1.

30 See Chapter 2 for Defense Secretary McNamara's presentation of MAD.

31 For a description and evaluation of Chinese ICBMs and shorter-range hypersonic missile carriers, see International Institute of Strategic Studies, *Hypersonic Weapons and Strategic Stability*, March, 2020.
www.iiss.org/publications/strategic-comments/2020/hypersonic-weapons-and-strategic-stability

32 Quoted in Kristensen and Korda (2019), p. 173. This statement of Chinese nuclear policy is restated in China's New 2019 Defense White Paper www.csis.org/analysis/chinas-new-2019-defense-white-paper
The Pentagon affirms Chinese second-strike doctrine.
See the Statement of Admiral Philip Davidson before the Senate Armed Services Committee on April 17, 2018, p. 9:
www.armed-services.senate.gov/hearings/18-04-17-nominations_--davidson...
Note that United States nuclear strategic doctrine still declares first-use of nuclear weapons in a nuclear clash. See Freedman (1989); Kaplan (1983, 2020) for the history of the survival of this doctrine whose logic is underwritten by U.S. adoption of a counterforce strategy.

33 Anthony Cordesman stresses this point (Cordesman, September 2018).

34 Brendan Taylor identifies four flash points of a possible military clash between China and the United States and its Western allies. All are in East Asia: Taiwan, South Korea, East China Sea, and South China Sea. (Taylor, 2018). See, especially, pp. 97–132. For supporting confirmation, consult (Miller, 2018), pp. 239ff.

35 Quoted by Zhang, p. 149.

36 www.csis.org/analysis/chinas-new-2019-defense-white-paper
The islands referred to in the defense paper are the Spratly and Paracel Islands. Diaoyu Island is the Chinese name for the Japanese name of the island as Senkaku.

37 There is a rich and growing scholarly and public policy literature covering the multiple state conflicts centered on the South China Sea. Only those features of these conflicts that bear directly on the challenge of global governance are developed here. Works that were helpful in providing the background for this discussion include (Diokno et al., 2019; Dittmer, 2018; Dittmer and Bing, 2017; Dutton, 2011; Fanell, 2018; Hayton, 2014; Miller, 2018; Roy, 2013; Roy, 2016; Taylor, 2018).

38 See Dutton (2011), p. 46, for a map of the U-shaped line, which is also referred to as the "nine-dash line." It should be noted that the Chinese interpretation of the nine-dash line has not been consistent when viewed from the conflicting statements of relevant Chinese bureaucracies. See Hayton (2014), pp. 250–252, 265–269.

39 The Court's citations are found at www.un.org/Depts/los/convention_agreements/texts/unclos/unclos_e.pdf

40 Schofield (December 2016, p. 340). Schofield summarizes the Tribunal's decisions. For a more complete discussion, consult (Vitug, 2018). Pertinent explanations of the implications of China's defeat are found in (Hong, December 2016).

41 Schofield (December 2016, p. 342).

42 Ibid. pp. 343–44. See p. 345 for a map of the South China Sea and the Spratly Island reefs and shoals covered by the Tribunal's award to the Philippines.

43 For an evaluation of EU interests in the South China Sea, see the extensive SPIRI study (Ghiasy, 2017).

44 *New York Times*, "China Chases Indonesia's Fishing Fleets, Staking Claim to Sea's Riches," March 31, 2020. This incident, one of a continuing stream, confirms China's refusal to recognize the Arbitral Tribune's adverse ruling in the Philippine case and its rejection of the claims of its other South China Sea neighbors, Vietnam, Malaysia, Indonesia, Brunei, and Taiwan, the latter a special case.

45 Economist, May 29, 2021, p. 35.

46 For data, see the Global Conflict Tracker page of the Council on Foreign Relations www.cfr.org/interactive/global-conflict-tracker/conflict/territorial-disputes -south-china-sea

47 See N. Roy (2016), pp. 11–22 for data.

48 Consult (Roy, 2013, 2016), *passim.* for the Chinese military buildup in the South China Sea. More authoritative is Admiral Philip Davidson's assessment before the Senate Armed Services Committee. See n. 54 below.

49 Heath et al. (2016), p. 9.

50 Ibid., p. 10.

51 Cole (2016).

52 Given space limitations, this discussion focuses on the impressive professional and strategic planning of Chinese military modernization to support its posture in East Asia and, especially, in the South China Sea. For a more comprehensive treatment of the increasing power projection capability of the PLA, consult the following: Defense Intelligence Agency: *China Military Power 2019* www.dia.mil › China_Military_Power_FINAL_5MB_20190103A; the Defense Department Annual Report on Military and Security Developments in China 2019 https://media.defense.gov/2018/Aug/16/2001955282/-1/-1/1/2018-CHINA -MILITARY-POWER-REPORT.PDF; and Chinese White Papers on Security and Defense. For example, consult the 2019 Paper: *Chinese National Defense in the New Era.* www.xinhuanet.com › english › 2019-07
A salient priority of Chinese military modernization is the development of a blue ocean navy. As Chinese economic interests expand so also do its political and strategic interests and for naval power to protect them. Studies of Chinese efforts to expand its naval power are Erickson (2016) and Heginbotham (2015).

53 *Economist,* March 13, 2021, p. 35.

54 I have relied principally on the testimony of the Commander of the Indo-Pacific Fleet to the Senate Armed Services Committee. His lengthy statements in 2018 and 2019 provide the most current Pentagon assessment of Chinese military capabilities in East Asia and, specifically, how these forces are positioned for deterrence and combat missions in East and South China Sea. For 2018 and 2019 statements, respectively, see:
www.armed-services.senate.gov/hearings/18-04-17-nominations_--davidson...
https://armedservices.house.gov/_cache/files/6/2/62797eeb-3fa2-425d-8e20 -2d6d72a83862/

55 *The Economist*, March 13, 2021, p. 35.

56 Ibid., pp. 5ff.

57 www.armed-services.senate.gov/hearings/18-04-17-nominations_--davidson... See p. 18.

58 Cited by John Power, *South China Morning Post*, February 17, 2020.

59 Cunningham and Fravel (2019) stress this point.

60 Xi Jinping's dream of Chinese renewal and global power is a prominent trope throughout his views about governing China. They go well beyond China's borders, as configured in the BRI (Jinping, 2014). Elizabeth Economy traces Xi's vision for

China through his speeches and public presentations, providing a larger portrait of Xi's dream than his treatise on the Chinese government. See Economy (2018).

61 Leandro (2018) develops the geopolitical dimensions of the BRI, closely parallel-ing my view that the BRI is embedded in the CCP's security policy objective to advance a multipolar system.

62 The quote is from the packet cover of Sarwar A. Kashmeri's study of the BRI (Kashmeri, 2019). I share his view with the important proviso that the BRI be viewed as an instrument of China's solution to global order; hence the BRI should be viewed as nested working within a PLA security framework.

63 Maçães (2018), p. xi.

64 Ibid. This view of BRI as an instrument of CCP global security strategy is shared by John Bolton, National Security Advisory to President Trump, and Philip Davidson, Commander of the Indo-Pacific Command, n. 54. See also Lew and Roughhead (2021), pp. 329–330. The latter study restricts BRI to an economic strategy, and not as an element of a larger OWL strategy as presented here.

65 The *Economist's Special Report on China's Belt and Road Initiative,* February 8, 2020, pp. 3–4, essentially reaches the same conclusion as this discussion, though in more restricted terms than presented here, which relies on the template of OWL imperatives.

66 The growing literature about BRI is too large to review here. Four recent works on which I have extensively relied are: Chaisse and Gorski (2018); Kashmeri (2019); Leandro (2018); Lew and Roughhead (2021). The latter citation views BRI as an economic program, contrasting with my evaluation. From the perspective of President Xi's geopolitical and economic designs and his Dream for China, it seems sensible to integrate PLA modernization with the BRI as complementary and mutually supportive elements of Xi's and the CCP's collective vision to govern globalization.

67 Three official Chinese documents provide an authoritative description of the scope of the BRI and are indispensable for understanding the program. See (1) Chinese State Council, For Text of the Vision for Maritime Cooperation under the Belt and Road Initiative, June 20, 2017, www.beltandroadforum.org/english/n100 /2017/0410/c22-45.html; (2) Joint Communiqué of the Leaders Roundtable of the Belt and Road Forum for International Cooperation, May 5, 2017. www.fmprc.gov.cn/mfa_eng/wjdt_655385/2649_665393/t1462012/shtml; and (3) Ministry of Foreign Affairs and Ministry of Commerce of the People's Republic of China, Vision and Actions on Jointly Building Silk Road Economic Belt and 21st-Century Maritime Silk Road http://en.ndrc.gov.cn/newsrelease/201503/t20150330_669367.html

68 China's economic growth through massive investments in infrastructure, transpor-tation, and communications is developed in Chapter 5.

69 Gordon et al. (2020), p. 4.

70 Lew and Roughhead (2021), pp. 61–65.

71 Maxillian Meyer and Xin Zhang view these corridors as key vehicles to extend Chinese influence and power. They conclude that China's corridor complex forms a pattern in which "not the nation or the region but the corridor" is the principal unit of analysis to track Chinese power. See 10.1080/09692290.2020.1741424

72 Notes 4–5 of (Lew and Roughhead, 2021) reports 139 BRI projects with states around the globe, including European Union members, notably Italy and Greece.

73 See Brautigam (2009).

74 Kashmeri (2019); Sun (2017).

75 Ibid., p. 7.

76 Ibid., p. 6. See also Sun (2017) and Center for International Development at Harvard University, "Growth Projections based on 2014 Global Trade Data" *The Atlas of Economic Complexity,* http://atlas.cid.harvard.edu/rankings/growth-predictions-list/

77 Gordon et al. (2020, p. 5).

78 Lewis and Moise (2018, pp. 40–43).

79 Kashmeri (2019, pp. 79–80).

80 Lew and Roughhead (2021, p. 70ff) cite ZTE, China Mobile, China Telecom, Alibaba, Tencent, Baidu, and JD as government-directed corporations, which have been enlisted into the Digital Silk Road.

81 Speech by Chairman of the Delegation of the People's Republic of China, Deng Xiaoping, at the Special Session of the U.N. General Assembly, April 10, 1974. https://marxists.org/reference/archive/deng-xiaoping/1974/04/10.htm

82 Kerry Brown quotes Deng accordingly: "Observe calmly; secure our position; cope with affairs calmly; hide our capacities and bide our time; be good at maintaining a low profile; and never claim leadership (Brown, 2017a), p. 19. President Xi has clearly abandoned Deng's prudent advice, not unlike Teddy Roosevelt's cautionary counsel for the United States to "Walk softly but carry a big stick." Xi prefers a big stick, but no longer believes China should walk softly. He repeatedly asserts the CCP's determination to replace the Western model and China's sovereignty over the South China Sea and Asia as China's sphere of influence.

83 Gordon et al. (2020, p. 7).

84 Carrai (2018); Copper (2016).

85 Lew and Roughhead (2021, n. 101).

86 Chaisse and Gorski (2018, pp. 22) and *passim*. The AIIB and the other Chinese investment banks are discussed through this edited volume. Carrai (2018) focuses specifically on these institutions and compares them favorably to Western investment instruments.

87 Gordon et al. (2020, pp. 19–26).

88 Carrai (2018), especially pp. 117ff.

89 Gordon et al. (2020, pp. 19–26).

90 Lewis and Moise (2018, p. 102).

91 Gorski (2018).

92 Communiqué of the Leaders Roundtable of the Belt and Road Forum for International Cooperation, May 5, 2017. www.fmprc.gov.cn/mfa_eng/wjdt_655385/2649_665393/t1462012/shtml, item 12 of the Communiqué.

93 Leandro (2018, pp. 99–101). See also Eli Huang, "China's Cable Strategy: Exploring Global Undersea Dominance," *The Strategist*, December 4, 2017 www.realcleardefense.com/2017/12/04/china039s_cable_strategy_exploring_ undersea_dominance_298700.html

94 This is one of the principal generalizations that can be drawn from the comprehensive 28-chapter edited volume of Chaisse and Gorski (2018).

95 Gordon et al. (2020, p. 11). These statistics are drawn from a Kiel Institute Working Paper of June, 2019: www.ifw-kiel.de/fileadmin/Dateiverwaltung/IFW -Publications/Christoph_Trebesch/KWP_2132.pdf

96 Vines (2016). See also Carrai (2018); Nathan (2016). These articles present the case that China conforms to conventional trade and investment norms, while noting deviations, which they contend are not tantamount to an overthrow of Western-developed norms and rules.

97 Sun (2017).

98 Communiqué of the Leaders Roundtable of the Belt and Road Forum for International Cooperation, May 5, 2017. www.fmprc.gov.cn/mfa_eng/wjdt_655385/2649_665393/t1462012/shtml, item 12 of the Communiqué.

99 Maçães (2018, pp. 80–81). Richard Baldwin's *tour de force* is indispensable for any discussion of the Imperative of Welfare and, specifically, of Chinese economic and technological development (Baldwin, 2016). The entire volume should be read to more fully grasp the factors which explain the Chinese miracle and the central importance of BRI to China's response to the Imperative of Welfare. See

also Baldwin's subsequent volume (Baldwin, 2019) on the revolutionary impact of Artificial Intelligence (AI) on global labor and on AI's adverse effects on the socio-economic and political stability of national societies and, by extension, of the nation-state system. Similarly, Daron Acemogul warns of these upheavals (Acemoglu, 2021)

100 Maçães (2018, p. 185).

101 Ibid., pp. xiii ff.

102 Economy (December 11, 2019). Her report is found at www.cfr.org/blog/yes-virginia-china-exporting-its-model

103 Bianchi (2019).

104 Even a casual reading of the voluminous work on world religions and cultures destroys any notion of a final endgame to the search for global governance. See Juergensmeyer (2003, 2008, 2005). In light of this readily available scholarship, it is baffling that anyone would contend that the liberal solution to global governance would ever be universally accepted as a solution to OWL imperatives. See Fukuyama (1992) for a triumphalist view of liberal democracy. What can be reasonably expected is that the liberal democracies will return to the OWL solutions of the postwar period and through appropriate reforms to meet new post-Cold War circumstances, they will re-create a sustainable, powerful liberal democratic subsystem within the nation-states system to contest China and Russia and other authoritarian states.

105 See Bianchi (2019) for an excellent in-depth survey of six Muslim countries with BRI projects and the complexity of the negotiations between them and China about their design and execution. Also helpful for African states are French (2014); Sun (2017). Two other works cite instances, here and there, of the many difficulties and challenges confronting Chinese officials in implementing the BRI. Chaisse and Gorski (2018); Kashmeri (2019); Sun (2017). Newspaper accounts, NGO centers, like the Institute for Security and Development Policy, the Council on Foreign Relations, the Carnegie Foundation for International Peace, and the Center for American Progress, *inter alia*, have experts on China which publish reports and podcasts about the difficulties faced by China. The citations here are designed to illustrate, not exhaust, this dimension of BRI. The most comprehensive source for ongoing scholarly work on BRI is provided by Professor Richard T. Griffiths of Leiden University working in cooperation with the International Institute for Asian Studies. Consult his "Belt and Road Initiative: electronic Library (Version 4.0 October 2019)
     at https://iias.asia/research/newresilkroad-contact

106 Ibid., p. 151.

107 Bianchi (2019) does an especially excellent job in describing China's BRI problems with these states.

108 Testimony of Admiral Philip Davidson before the Senate Armed Services Committee, February 12, 2019https://armedservices.house.gov/_cache/files/6/2/62797eeb-3fa2-425d-8e20-2d6d72a83862/ p. 8.

109 Small (2015).

110 Idem, p. 3.

111 *New York Times*, March 29, 2021. See also Lew and Roughhead (2021), ns. 122-23 of the report.

112 For references to these pushbacks, see Gordon et al. (2020); Kashmeri (2019).

113 Quoted by Maçães (2018, pp. 164–165). This critique is supported by a recent evaluation of rural poor in China and the low level of education of millions of children who are entering a global work force requiring increased technological training. See Rozelle and Hell (2020). Also relevant to keep in mind is the extreme complexity of China's people and leadership as well as China's economic diversity. Tony Saich observes that the diversity of Chinese society "explains the CCP's obsession with 'unity of thought' and the building of conformity." He notes that he "has met party members more conservative than the former British prime minister Margaret

Thatcher, and yet others who describe themselves as social democrats or as belonging [to] the the democratic faction within the party. Some are among the richest folk in the land, some are true believers, and some are simply trying to advanced their own careers." (Saich, 2021, p. 2).

114 Cited in Carrai (2018, p. 111). Asian Development Bank, Meeting Asia's Infrastructure Needs," 2017.
www.abd.org/defalt/files/publication/227496/special-report-infrastructure.pdf

115 Gordon et al. (2020, p. 16).

116 Ibid.

117 Ibid.

118 I have relied principally on Hurley (2016) in covering the debt problems of partner states associated with BRI. His data draw on the report of the Center for Global Development.
See also the Kiel report on China's risky loan strategy, n. 95; Gordon et al. (2020, pp. 11–15); Lew and Roughhead (2021); and the World Bank report on China
http://documents.worldban.org/curated/en/72367156082662349/pdf/A-Framework-to-Assess-Debt-Sustainability-and-Fiscal-Risks-under-the-Belt-and-Road-Initiative.pdf

119 Barry Sandalow is responsible for a 2019 Columbia University report and podcast, which provide a comprehensive evaluation of China's energy policy. It accents the many positive initiatives taken by China to combat climate change, but also cites the countervailing domestic pressures that drive China to continue unabatedly to construct coal-fired power plants. See the full report at
https://energypolicy.columbia.edu/research/report/2019-guide-chinese-climate-policy
On September 7, 2021, President Xi announced that China will not build new coal-fired power projects abroad under BRI. However, he did not say either that existing contracts with developing states to build coal-fired projects would be cancelled or that China would stop building these units at home. New York Times, September 9. 2021.

120 See President Xi's address to the World Economic Forum, January 17, 2017
www.china.org.cn/node_7247529/content_40569136.htm. Also the collected speeches of President Xi Jinping (Jinping, 2014). See, for example, pp. 128 ff. and *passim*.

121 Pei (2016).

122 Gordon et al. (2020, p. 18).

123 Angell (1909).

5
CHINA AND THE IMPERATIVE OF WELFARE

Imagine a world in which the Chinese Communist Party (CCP) had not initiated broad and deep economic reforms in the late 1970s. What if China had continued along the disastrous path of the Mao Zedong era, characterized by low and negative economic growth? Adding to China's economic despair, Mao's Great Leap Forward (1958–61) and the resulting famine took the lives of an estimated 36 million Chinese.[1] Mao's Cultural Revolution, launched shortly thereafter, plunged the Chinese economy further into an unrelenting crisis.[2] What if Mao's autarchic system and his promulgation of an anti-market ideology had prevailed to become a model for other developing states? The world economy, as we know it now, would never have emerged. It is not an exaggeration, as William Overholt contends, that Chinese reformers, led by Deng Xiaoping,[3] "ensured that the entire global economy became a global economy."[4] Beijing had help. Doubling down on Overholt, Thomas Friedman observes, "America accommodated and effectively facilitated the rise of the world's next largest superpower, China. And together the Chinese made globalization more pervasive and the world more prosperous."[5]

The West, notably the United States, welcomed China into the Western market system and membership in the World Trade Organization (WTO), motivated in no small part by the illusion that the CCP would gradually complement its adaptation to free markets by adopting a liberal democratic regime. The Tiananmen massacre, crushing student-led demands for democracy and a check on corruption, should have ended any hope that the Party would relinquish control, even at the expense of decreased economic development. The expectation of liberal democratic change still lingered in Western capitals throughout the first decade of the 2000s. Policymakers in the administration of President Barack Obama harbored this view until the end of the Hu Jintao regime.[6] President Xi Jinping's installation of rigid authoritarian rule in 2013, combined with China's

DOI: 10.4324/9781003246572-5

defections from market rules, voided the likelihood of regime change in the foreseeable future.

The CCP has a formidable case to make for the Chinese solution to the Imperative of Welfare. Over 30 years, thanks to the slow, deliberate, punctuated, and selective exposure of progressively significant elements of the Chinese economy to domestic marketization and Western market discipline, hundreds of millions of Chinese were raised from poverty, a historically unprecedented achievement. Enormous Western investment over a generation, encouraged and facilitated by the CCP, and the substantial transfer of Western technology and industrial know-how were indispensable in realizing this transformational reform of the Chinese economy. Throughout this transition, the Chinese Communist Party continued to rule China with an iron hand, while gradually adapting the Chinese economy to the Western market system despite undergoing large-scale internally contested Party reforms and upheaval.[7]

The ascendancy of Xi Jinping to power in 2013, for what promises to be a lifetime stay as Secretary of the Communist Party, President, and Commander-in-Chief of the Peoples Liberation Army, abruptly revealed the vacuity of the self-deceptive projection of a democratic West onto the Chinese regime.[8] Worse still for the West is President Xi's boast that the Chinese authoritarian regime is a superior model for economic development than the Western solution to global welfare, tethered to liberal, democratic rule. Xi's "Made in China 2025" modernization plan and his equally ambitious Belt and Road Initiative (BRI) to tie all of the continents to the Chinese economy are designed to enhance China's status as the world's largest manufacturer and the developing states' principal banker and financier. Xi's China now seeks to have its cake and eat it, too: retain sole and undisputed control of the 1.4 billion Chinese, bend the Western free-exchange system to China's advantage, and indelibly stamp the Westphalian system with Chinese characteristics.

The impressive results of the Chinese experiment lend credence to the CCP's insistence that China, not the West and certainly not the United States, will be the model for economic growth for developing states. China's example of rapid economic growth and technological progress as well as its ambitious BRI enterprise are offered as evidence of China's ascendancy and the attractiveness of the authoritarian model for global governance. Between 1978 and 2005, the Chinese economy annually grew about 9.5 percent. Productivity increased from .5 to 3.8 percent, with productivity contributing 40 percent during the reform period and only 11.4 percent before. Trade as a ratio of GDP jumped from 10 percent before reform to 70 percent by 2005. Chinese output was 38.2 percent of Japan's in 1978. It grew to 219.2 percent by 2004. The private sector's contribution to GDP, with agriculture still collectivized, was zero in 1978. It climbed to 59.2 percent by 2003. It has steadily advanced since then. The number of Chinese living in abject poverty, measured as per capita income of less than $1.25 a day, precipitously declined from 840 to 84 million between 1981 and 2011, a record unmatched by any Western state over so short a period of time.[9]

While the manufacturing capacities of Japan, Germany, Britain, and the United States have declined between 2000 and 2018, China's has grown from 8 percent of world production to 25 percent.[10] By 2018 the value of China's manufacturing complex exceeded the combined value of the United States, Germany, and South Korea.[11] The West's deindustrialization paralleled China's rise as the world's workshop. In 2014 China alone produced approximately 12 billion shoes, enough to provide two pairs of shoes and one or two toys to every member of the human race.[12] Beijing also dominates the world's supply chains on which most Western states are now dependent.[13] China's more than 14 trillion dollar economy is the second largest after the United States. It is projected to surpass the American economy in the very near future.

The evolving globalization of the Chinese economy[14]

How did a Leninist Party accomplish these feats? Over little more than a generation how did China gradually grow out of a command economy over a generation into a largely, if still conspicuously imperfect, market system? How was it able to adapt to global trade and financial competition and enter the World Trade Organization in 2001? China's transition commenced very shortly after the death of Mao Zedong in 1976, which can be dated with Deng Xiaoping's address to the Communist Party's Central Committee on December 18, 1978. Deng rejected Mao's implacable ideological conviction of perpetual global class struggle. He proposed instead a narrower, pragmatic objective: development of the China's economy while, paradoxically, strengthening Party rule through the decentralization of economic decision-making.[15]

The CCP's decision under Deng's leadership to open the Chinese economy to the Western global markets and to introduce large-scale market practices into China had profound impacts on the Chinese *and* the world economy. The reforms unleashed incentives to increase production, notably in agriculture, and private enterprise competition in low technological industrial areas. Of more consequence was the CCP's decision over the resistance of the remaining Maoist wing within the Party to elicit and welcome Western investment, technology, and industrial know-how into China. Spurred was unprecedented economic growth, setting China on an upward curve of sustained economic growth and technological development to rival today its Western benefactors.

This radical relaxation of suffocating Party and governmental dictation of the economy commenced fortuitously at the very time of what Richard Baldwin characterizes as a revolutionary "unbundling" of global trade, the production of goods and services, the flow of capital, technology, and industrial know-how from the economically advanced North to the poor and underdeveloped South.[16] China profited most from this systemic shift,[17] largely enabled by multinational corporations. The Chinese economic miracle cannot be fully understood unless the reform of its economy is set within the larger transformation of the global economy's evolving market architecture.

The backdrop for these transformational economic moves harkens back to the industrialization and the modernization of Western states and societies. Breakthroughs in land, sea, and air transportation accelerated the speedy transfer of primary materials and consumer goods, essential to the growth of global markets and the unprecedented creation of material wealth, largely concentrated in Western states of the North, principally the United States and the West European states. The production of goods and services was largely nationally based. Richard Baldwin describes the period from the end of the Napoleonic Wars to the 1990s, as the "bundling" of the productive industrial and technological resources of the world in the West. Western states and their enterprising, skilled, and creative populations controlled a monopoly of the world's advanced technology and industrial capabilities. The factory system, driving global markets, was enclosed within the boundaries of the nation-states in which its productive parts were concentrated. The North monopolized the advanced technological means of productive capital and labor. Production, trade, and capital movements were still grounded in the Ricardian principles of national comparative advantage. The developing world was largely excluded from this phase of economic globalization except for their roles as providers of the primary resources needed for production and as consumers.[18]

Launched roughly at the end of the 20th century, the "unbundling" of this largely Northern sequestered system of production, trade, investment, and technological know-how shattered the "building" phase of economic globalization. The revolution in transportation that motored the first stage of economic globalization was bolstered and spurred forward by the socioeconomic and political impact of a revolution in communication and transportation in the second half of the 20th century. The constraints on ideas and technology flowing across state borders were dissolved as knowledge about how to make goods and services more efficient, cheaper, abundant, and profitable were now globally dispersed as never before.

Global communication networks also made possible the efficient and effective coordination of the fractionating of global manufacturing into thousands of global value supply chains. They surmounted the barriers posed by national boundaries in the "bundling" phase of globalization. Unbundling has the paradoxical effect of bundling the North and South together into a progressively interdependent and integrated global economic system. Value supply chains denationalized factories. They now flowed over state boundaries. Some multinational corporations no longer operated factories. Thanks to improved modes of transportation and communication, sports equipment companies, like Reebok and Nike, reverted to firms, which coordinated the work of foreign enterprises and low-wage labor to produce the goods they designed and marketed around the globe. Northern labor was also denationalized, forced to compete with lower wage labor in the developing world. Millions of high-paying jobs were offshored to the developing world. The implicit social contract between corporations and the holders of capital and labor after World War II was shredded. Generated were large-scale socioeconomic and political upheavals, which still plague Western economies. In a turnabout, developing countries, like China and India, now compete on an equal plane with their former suppliers of know-how; in some areas, like wind power, they are besting them. The principle of comparative advantage has less purchase since any enterprise or state capable of entering the second wave of globalization can compete on an equal footing.

China was the principal beneficiary of the second phase of globalization. The Deng reforms exploited these profound changes in the global economy. His control of the CCP and Chinese economic policy moved reforms along three fronts. First, agricultural communes were abolished. Responsibility for the production of food reverted to family farming. While the Communist Party and the state retained ownership of the land, a legacy of socialist ideology, farmers were granted rights to work plots as their own and retain whatever profits they might earn after meeting Party-state defined levels of production. Farmers had confidence that in meeting production levels they could retain the profits from producing more. This profound shift toward personal and family self-interest and away from the disincentives of communal farming resulted rapidly in vastly increased agricultural production. The reform gave farmers, who represented the largest economic group, a stake in Party rule. Access to home-ownership also increased, providing further support for Deng's reform program and bolstering Party authority and power among homeowners. Home-ownership in China now exceeds even that of the United States.[19]

Additional market incentives were then directed to local governments to spur rural industrialization. Townships and villages were authorized to create Township and Village Enterprises (TVEs). They assumed several different forms of ownership, whether as collectives, joint venture enterprises with a local owner, private ownership, or household businesses. Of the 12 million which were formed, ten were privately owned.[20] Given the enormous unused labor supply in the countryside, priority was initially assigned to labor-intensive production, covering small-scale consumer and industrial goods – toys, tennis shoes, housewares, automobile and bicycle accessories, etc.

In a very short period, TVEs grew exponentially and assumed an increasingly important role in the economy. Over a generation between 1980 and the middle 2000s, the contribution of TVEs to Chinese GDP grew from 6 to 30 percent. TVE owners relied on governmental and CCP promises that their property rights and profits would be respected as a consequence of the institutionalization of reform rules. TVEs' share of rural employment during this period rose from 9 to 27 percent. One informed observer credits TVEs with having created more than jobs.[21] In tandem with this growth, the percentage of rural household net income from wages and nonagricultural sideline businesses rose from 26 to 47 percent.[22] It was in this early period of reform that hundreds of millions of Chinese were raised out of poverty.[23]

What was particularly striking about the development of TVEs is their impact on leadership and career incentives within the Communist Party. Under a command economy, ideological loyalty and patronage networks tended to determine movement up the ladder of power within the Party. With the creation of TVEs and the encouragement of enterprise and private profit-taking, the incentive system for Party promotion fundamentally changed. Since the Party controlled appointments of local Party and state officials, the shift in reform priorities to economic growth put a premium on the economic performance of local leadership. As William Overholt observes, "In China, a mayor seeking promotion will be judged by whether he has met specific goals such as increasing a city's GDP, investment, foreign investment, educational performance, and employment."[24] The accent on performance, begun modestly with TVEs, would eventuate in educated and experienced cadres fully capable of managing a modern economy and competing on a global scale. Like the beneficiaries of rural reforms, these managers, too, had a stake both in reform and in allegiance to Party rule.

The most controversial element of this early reform package was Deng's proposal for Special Economic Zones (SEZs). Over the strong resistance of conservatives, Deng created several SEZs throughout China to attract foreign investment, a striking — and risky — departure from the Japanese, Taiwanese, and South Korean strategies for economic development, favoring domestic over foreign investment. SEZs were designed to achieve the twin aims of increasing Chinese exports and of importing Western technology. In achieving both objectives, Deng and his supporters marginalized critics who characterized SEZs as an abandonment of Marxism and class warfare only to return to the era of the economic zones imposed on China by Western imperial powers in the nineteenth century.

The outright repudiation of ideological purity had several important consequences for China's rise as an economic power. Exports boomed. Even today, foreign firms produce about half of all exports and three-quarters of high-tech exports.[25] As a condition for entry into the Chinese economy, a foreign firm is often obliged to collaborate with its Chinese counterpart and to transfer its technology and know-how. Chinese firms have been increasingly able to turn the tables on their foreign partners and compete against them in communications, cell phone production, and automobiles. As exports expanded, China carefully favored its own firms through financial and regulatory support as well as through high tariffs on imports. The explosion of Chinese industrial capacity placed China at the center of multiplying global value supply chains, tying China and foreign firms into production networks across a broad spectrum of industrial and consumer products. Complementing these moves was the Party's decision to encourage thousands of Chinese students to study abroad. A virtuous circle was set in motion: China's best students would learn Western best practices, ranging over scientific research and protocols, engineering, and industrial production, and then return to China to incorporate these innovations into the workings of the Chinese economy, thus spurring economic growth and affording the Chinese economy a competitive edge.

The ruling consensus within the Party, headed by Deng, decentralized Party governance without losing Party control in sanctioning local decision-making to marketize the domestic economy and to allow China to gradually escape from its Maoist command straightjacket. Heretofore, monopoly profits and rents were accorded Party members for their loyalty to the Party. Deng's reforms transformed the incentive structure for Party members. Rewards were now to be allocated on the basis of their economic performance. Party entrepreneurs, bureaucratic elites, and corporations were expected to address the Party's priority for economic growth and for a reliable and more predictable system of meeting the revenue needs of the central government. In meeting Party revenue targets, their reward was retention of some of the income and profits of their enterprise and enhanced social and economic status within the Party hierarchy.

To ensure that revenue was turned into Beijing's coffers, millions of family farms, hundreds of thousands of state enterprises, hundreds of foreign corporations, and all 30 of China's provinces signed contracts with their bureaucratic superiors to meet central governmental revenue targets. Decentralization had the seemingly paradoxical effects of centralizing Party and government revenues while expanding private incomes and wealth. Loosened Party oversight, increased emphasis on market-driven decisions, and decreased governmental interference in deciding the allocation of resources enlarged and sustained national economic growth without loss, ultimately, of Party rule.

The Party's violent suppression of the Tiananmen Square student uprising in June 1989 temporarily disrupted the continuation and expansion of economic reforms. Once the Party had re-established its control and foreign criticism had subsided by the early 1990s, the very success of the reforms propelled the economy forward. Increased spending on roads, bridges, railroads, and airports provided a modern infrastructure to support Deng's export strategy. It also attracted foreign investment, like the development of the Pudong district in Shanghai, a model extended to other regions of China.[26] Several formidable challenges to strengthen the Party's power were next overcome: the centralization of taxes, banking, and capital markets, and, most critical of all, the diminution of conservative and labor opposition to downsizing and streamlining. To some degree rent-seeking by inefficient state-owned enterprises, while never eliminated, was also reduced, only to re-emerge again under the Xi Jinping regime. [27]

The key to meeting these challenges was Deng's appointment of Zhu Rongji as Premier. Zhu moved first to rationalize and centralize China's fiscal and financial systems – taxes, banks, and capital markets. The central government was initially starved for funds as a consequence of the decentralization and fragmentation of tax revenue collection. In 1993 local revenues increased by 35 percent, while those of the central government shrank by 6.3 percent. Leveraging his authority over the Chinese economy, Zhu revised the system of revenue sharing by streaming revenues first to the central government, which in turn would return a portion to local units.

Zhu next centralized the banking system. He appointed himself as governor of the People's Bank of China. With the power to appoint and remove the heads of the People's Bank branches, he gained increased control of the Chinese credit system while ensuring adequate credit for enterprises and infrastructure programs supporting reform efforts and cutting back on dubious lending practices at the local level. The dissolution of thirty-two provincial branches of the People's Bank and their re-emergence in nine regional branches completed this phase of Zhu's centralization campaign. Local officials seeking credit now had to seek approval from the People's Bank firmly under Party control.[28]

Entering into a joint venture with Morgan Stanley, Zhu also created the first modern Chinese investment bank to handle China's initial public offerings of stock in large state-owned firms. Stocks in China Telecom, Petro-China, Industrial and Commercial Bank of China, and Agricultural Bank of China were placed on global financial markets. Non-performing enterprises, like Guangdong International Trust and Investment Corporation, drowning in $4 billion of debts, were liquidated.[29] Increased Party-state control of banking, finance, monetary policy, and capital flows furnished the tools to weather the 1997 Asian financial crisis and the much more destructive world financial meltdown of 2008, triggered by the collapse of Lehman Brothers.

State-owned enterprises (SOEs) were more difficult to reform. Managerial and labor groups strongly opposed their dismantling. The trick was to modernize them by exposing them to the competition of the private sector without losing Party control over the transition or the demise of the SOE system as an instrument of Party rule. Millions of workers relied on the "iron rice bowl" of cradle-to-grave employment, a benefit to the workers but a drag on the economy. Managers expected to retain their positions permanently despite incompetence and as a reward for corruption, cloaked as loyalty to the Party. Rongji's reforms cut SOEs from 127,600 to 34,280 by 2003. He also bet that the millions of workers thrown out of work would find jobs in the growing private sector. The strategy worked, blunting criticism of this painful shift keyed to fostering greater efficiency and competitiveness.

These market reforms persuaded a willing West to admit China into the World Trade Organization in 2001. The West expected China to accept the WTO's "rules of the game." China did actually conform to many of these expectations while pursuing a long-range strategy, designed eventually to bend the WTO and the world economy to China's preferred rules and interests. In joining the WTO, China skillfully avoided either the privatization of state enterprises as a condition for entry or the Party's relinquishment of the Party's control over non-state enterprises.[30] The West's unwitting complicity in facilitating an ever tighter Party–state–corporate–civil nexus of authoritarian rule would loom, progressively, as a formidable challenge to Western economies. Huawei, China's national champion in the global competition to dominate G5 communications systems, exemplifies China's increasing capacity to shape the global economic system to its advantage, once it had become a member of the Western market system. No longer resigned to producing and exporting cheap consumer and generic industrial products to the West, China now supports high-tech initiatives to steal a march on the West in robotics, electronics, green technologies, AI, and cellular panels – with more fields yet to be tapped.

From state-capitalism[31] to crony capitalism[32]

The centralized, Party-directed Chinese model for economic growth continues as the touchstone for governmental policy. The decentralization of Party authority and oversight of the 1980s – what Yasheng Huang calls "directed liberalism" – gradually gave way to the re-centralization of economic and political policies and decision-making. The near-disastrous experience of the Tiananmen uprising spurred this trend. The Chinese economy reverted increasingly to state- over market-driven growth, capped now as the privileged mode of the Xi Jinping regime. Market-driven growth has been rebalanced to favor SOEs, which facilitate Party control of the economy, Chinese corporations, and the Chinese people. State capitalism is now in the ascendancy.

To gain some sense of the current Chinese political economy it is useful to compare the reforms initiated by Deng Xiaoping with changes introduced by President Xi Jinping. Deng's reforms integrated several re-enforcing components of the economy to produce unprecedented GDP growth. The movement of large worker populations from the rural to urban areas created an enormous pool of cheap labor to propel exports and earn foreign currency. Foreign capital was attracted to meet global demand for Chinese goods at the expense of Western domestic labor, denominated in millions of jobs lost to Chinese low wages. Advanced technology and know-how accompanied foreign capital as an expected condition for doing business in China. In the Deng era, Chinese domestic investment prioritized expenditures in fixed assets, the rapid and expansive development of infrastructure to support an export and foreign investment strategy, and the development of technically skilled cadres to run the economy. Slavish loyalty to the Party was not sufficient to insulate Party members from sanctions if it were not accompanied by economic performance. The aim was to create a meritocracy within the scope of Party loyalty to strengthen CCP rule.[33]

As China gradually grew out of the Maoist command economy,[34] private businesses assumed an increasing share of economic activity and production. The re-organization and significant downsizing of State-Owned Enterprises (SOEs) in the 1990s, greater liberalization of finance, and the influx of billions in foreign capital bolstered the movement toward a capitalist economy, with the proviso that these reforms remained under uncompromising Party-state control. The liberalization of finance, capital, monetary, and credit policies was not fully exposed to market discipline. Nor were the Western centrality of private ownership and the right of individual and corporate ownership to dispose their assets and investment largely free from Party and state controls. State ownership of the means of production was particularly strong in rural areas. Farmers were granted rights to use land for economic production and personal gain, but not to own the property or to freely dispose of their assets as they might wish.

Whatever the shortcomings of China's evolving model of economic growth, it was able to weather the near total breakdown of the global financial system of the 2007–08 crisis. In contrast to the slow and deficient responses of the Western states – notably the United States, which shared much of the blame for the crisis – Chinese Party-state controls of the economy prevented a meltdown. Central decision-making facilitated the rapid deployment of a large recovery package to staunch the financial hemorrhaging.

The global financial collapse reinforced Chinese elite opinion that Western free-market practices had to be substantially regulated by the state. There is now a consensus, domestic critics to the contrary notwithstanding, that a fully liberalized economy is not in the interests of the Party, the state, or the Chinese people. Capitalism with Chinese socialist characteristics – state-driven capitalism – was the way to go for China. It was also Beijing's message to the developing world, carried forward by Xi Jinping's Belt and Road Initiative, discussed in the preceding chapter, that leadership of the world economy and globalization would pass from the West to East, with China in the vanguard of this shift in the center of gravity of the world economy.

Constraints besetting continued economic growth

For over a generation the evolving Chinese model of economic growth, whether in its early decentralized and, later, in its more centralized form, served the Chinese people and the Communist Party well. By the end of the first decade of the 2000s, however, the Chinese economy confronted multiple and re-enforcing challenges, some inherent in the mix of its history, ideology, Party governance and leadership, and, most importantly, the CCP's fusion of power with its self-declared legitimacy. These limitations weaken China's claim as a model for other states, whether advanced or developing. First, China's very success is a major contributing factor. As per capita income increases – eight times by one estimate between 1978 and 2015[35] – it is harder for a country's economy to grow than when per capita income was low.[36] There is less room for expansion. Rapid and sustained GDP growth launched by the reforms of the early 1980s was beginning to plateau by the end of the first decade of the 2000s. As China enters the first half of the 21st century, its maturing economy is expected to grow at annual rates well below those of its rapid growth era even as the demands of the economy increase.

Other factors hindering growth include the diminishing returns on prioritizing exports to drive the economy, the diminishing returns of infrastructure investments, and the increasing costs of labor.[37] The initial investment in real estate that propelled growth is running its course, while also resulting in heavy debt and banking exposure. The reliance on state-owned corporations for economic growth, global competitiveness, and governance results in inefficiencies in investment and management. Economic policies are then driven more by Party loyalty, especially to CCP leadership, and to political clout than market exigencies. Ceaseless public pressures to increase growth and raise per capita income generate demand for more and more energy. The result is significant damage to the environment and to the health of the Chinese people. An aging population requires more spending on welfare nets, notably health, as traditional family care becomes less readily available in an advanced, modernized economy based on transactional exchanges, and not on shared community values and familial affection.[38] As economic growth slows, there are fewer resources not only to address rising pressures to strengthen China's welfare nets, those for health, education, and pensions but also to support ambitious foreign and strategic designs, like the BRI. President Xi Jinping's dream of raising the material wealth of hundreds of millions, notably those in agriculture, remains a reach beyond his grasp.

Adding to these constraining economic factors are two especially significant and seemingly intractable factors: inequality and corruption. Deng Xiaoping's avuncular counsel that it was alright to get rich has morphed into widening inequality in the distribution of income, accumulated wealth, and opportunities for advancement. Increasing inequality also damages the Party's ideological commitment to an egalitarian society. Inequality in its many economic and financial forms undermines the Party's legitimacy in failing to achieve or at least advance toward that socialist vision, frustrated and fundamentally foreclosed by the creation of a quasi-capitalist economy and widespread crony capitalist practices.[39]

At the end of the Maoist era, China was among the world's most egalitarian societies. Its Gini Coefficient, measuring inequality stood at .3, with 1.0 as perfect inequality. The downsides of Maoist equality were economic autarchy, repudiation of the Western market system, and China's insulation from foreign trade and access to technological innovation. These policies condemned hundreds of millions of Chinese to grinding poverty. The upsides of reforms were rising GDP and per capita income, accompanied inexorably by increasing inequality, measured not only by the elements already noted but also by the increased power and rent-seeking of SOEs and private corporations. While estimates of China's Gini Coefficient vary among economists, ranging from .41 to .5, there is agreement that there has been a progressive rise in China's Gini Coefficient since the initiation of economic reforms.[40] With most analysts expecting inequality to continue to expand, absent large-scale governmental intervention to arrest and reverse this trend. There is little evidence that inequality will be reversed any time soon despite slogans committing the CCP to "common prosperity."

Between 1978 and 2015 the top ten percent share of income rose from 27 percent to 41 percent (106 million Chinese). The bottom 50 percent (532 million Chinese) declined from 27 percent to 15 percent.[41] In this period, the share of income of the top 1 percent rose from 6 to 14 percent. Another indicator of the significance of political connections and income inequality is the reported wealth of members of China's legislature. Their combined wealth is estimated to exceed one trillion dollars.[42]

In a race to the bottom of states where inequality is prevalent, China and the United States are neck and neck, with the United States outstripping China in the period between 1978 and 2015. In the United States, the share of income of the top 1 percent rose from 11 percent to 20 percent. The bottom 50 percent in the United States shared only 12 percent of national income, below China's 15 percent. With an urban population twice as large as the United States, China is just only slightly less unequal in income distribution than the United States.[43]

What is particularly remarkable is the shift from public to private wealth. In 1978 public wealth stood at 70 percent; private, at 30 percent. By 2014 the percentages were reversed with private wealth accumulation (housing, domestic capital, financial assets, etc.) at 70 percent and public wealth at 30 percent.[44] The share of accumulated wealth of the top 10 percent rose from 40 percent in 1995 to 67.4 percent in 2015, while the bottom 50 percent held only 6.4 percent of private wealth.[45] The middle 40 percent fell from 44 percent in 1995 to 26 percent in 2015.[46]

The rural–urban split is no less dramatic. Between 1978 and 2015 the urban population grew from 100 to 600 million. The rural population increased more slowly from 400 to 500 million. The ratio of urban to rural income also shifted in favor of urbanites. The ratio stood at 195 percent in 1978. It then shifted upward to favor urban dwellers to 350 percent.[47] Since farmers rent, but do not own the land they farm, these rights can be sold from underneath them for the profit of local governments and private developers. Millions who moved to urban areas for jobs and improved economic conditions are deprived of access to basic welfare resources, like health, housing, and education, which are afforded urban Hukou populations.[48] The cost of economic growth was then laid upon the shoulders of rural populations and vulnerable urban labor. [49]

Because of the success of Chinese economic reforms, increasing inequality notwithstanding, public confidence in the Party and government's ability to sustain economic growth currently remains stable.[50] The Chinese population appears to accept that, while inequality of income and wealth is glaring, the actual material condition of each Chinese and family has substantially improved since the Maoist era, when income and wealth were distributed more equally.

What gross statistics about inequality mask is the fact that "all boats rose," thanks to market reforms. As Pikkety and associates conclude:

> The key difference between China and the United States is that in China the bottom 50% also benefited enormously from growth: the average income of the bottom 50% was multiplied by more than 5 in real terms between 1978 and 2015, which is less than macro growth and top income growth, but still very substantial. Presumably this increase can make rising inequality much more acceptable, especially for a country starting from very low living conditions — at least until a certain point. In contrast, bottom 50% income growth has been negative in the United States (-1%).[51]

China's middle class, though less fortunate than the top ten percent of the population, has also profited substantially from the Deng reforms and their later more qualified implementation. Whether a rising generation, facing the prospect of unemployment and underemployment, supported by weak and unreliable welfare nets to protect them, will accept inequality is problematic.[52]

In Xi's estimation, more threatening to Party control and legitimacy is the corruption deep and pervasive throughout China's economic and political system. Combating corruption and increasing the Party's indictment of malefactors have been central themes of Xi's public pronouncements and priorities since his rise to power in 2012.[53] "We must tirelessly combat corruption, and always remain vigilant against it. We should keep it in mind that 'Many worms will disintegrate wood, and a big enough crack will lead to the collapse of a wall'"[54] The Communist Party, Xi's wall as a metaphor of Party rule, risks collapse unless corruption is brought under control to ensure the trust and confidence of the Chinese in the Communist Party. "Failing to tackle corruption," Xi emphasizes, … "will inevitably lead to the downfall of the party and the state. …"[55] Checking corruption, much less eliminating it, won't be easy, since this cancer in its many forms infects every level of Party and state governance.[56]

Xi's preoccupation with corruption is justified. As a leading institute which provides comparative data and measures of corruption and the integrity of governance of 180 states observes:

> Corruption is especially worrying for Chinese political leaders because the legitimacy of the party and of the political system in general is not based on elections, as in democracy, but on a political meritocracy that selects and promotes leaders with superior ability and virtue. … Hence, in China, the level of corruption is indicative of the level of meritocracy, and therefore of legitimacy of the political class.[57]

Recall that ending corruption was a key demand of the students in Tiananmen Square. The Party implicitly acknowledged widespread corruption in having to use force to suppress the student uprising in 1989 and to drive awareness of its existence underground, but not necessarily extinguishing public consciousness of how deeply corruption is woven in the Chinese government at all levels.

If the corruption indexes of Transparency International (TI) and the World Bank are reliable, Xi's corruption campaign, while more extensive than those of his predecessors, does not appear to have made as much progress in combating corruption as he maintains. Transparency International Global Corruption Barometer (GCB) reports that 73 percent of respondents in China actually believed that corruption had increased under Xi. China's corruption is at the top of countries in the Asian-Pacific in 2017. The TI's Corruption Perception Index (CPI), which collects data on how corrupt the public sector of a country is seen by business and country experts, reports a slight improvement between 2014 and 2017. In 2017 China was 77th out of 180 countries. Its CPI improved from 36 to 41.[58] The World Bank's Control of Corruption Index also notes some marginal improvement, but not a break from the pervasive corruption, endemic to Party-state governance. "In the last five years, China moved from a score of 0.44 on a scale from − 2.5 (weak) to 2.5 (strong governance performance) to a score of −0.25 in 2016."[59]

President Xi's anti-corruption campaign is aimed at all levels of the Communist Party and beyond. Xi insists, "We should continue to catch 'tigers' as well as 'flies, when dealing with … misconduct and corruption problems that directly affect the people's livelihood. All are equal before the law and Party discipline; whoever is involved in a corruption case must be thoroughly and impartially investigated."[60] Between 2012 and 2013, for example, more than 180,000 officials were punished for disciplinary issues, compared with 160,000 in 2012 and 140,000 in 2011.[61] The large number of corruption indictments and convictions, which Xi's regime has produced, has still not significantly inflected China's high corruption scores.

Most of the 180,000 cases were "flies" by President Xi's measure. He also moved against "tigers." In quick order he convicted his rival, Bo Xilai, the former party chief of Chongqing, of corruption and dismantled his patronage network, a threat to Xi's power.[62] Other "tigers" were also punished or dismissed from office. The Commission for Discipline Inspection (CCDI), a central anti-corruption unit,[63] announced in December 2012 that 285 high-level officials were brought under investigation.[64] Among these were Zhou Yongkang, a former member of the Politburo Standing Committee and Li Chuncheng, a former deputy secretary of the Sichuan Provincial Party Committee.[65] It is important to remember that the CCDI is answerable only to the Chinese Communist Party, not to the Chinese judiciary, which is also under Party control. The CCDI's central importance in the anti-corruption campaign contradicts Xi's claim that all are "equal before the law." Only Xi determines whether the rule of law is being applied or whether the law as rule should prevail.

What explains the intractability of corruption in China and, paradoxically, China's ability under Communist Party rule to have corruption and economic growth, too? Economic growth has actually increased corruption. As Chinese specialists have pointed out, the massive wealth produced by reforms generated compelling incentives for political officials and business professionals at all levels of the Party and government to skim off these gains without staunching economic growth in the process.[66] Add, too, the special role assigned to State-Owned Enterprises by the Party. That policy invites large-scale rent-seeking. Data consistently show that private enterprises are more efficient, more profitable, and contribute more to the economy than SOEs.[67]

An important part of the explanation for why China can have its cake and eat it, too − corruption and increasing economic growth − is simply the size of the Chinese economy.[68] It can tolerate and absorb enormous corruption slush without fatally crippling economic growth. China can currently function under the burden of corruption, albeit at productive levels below what would be possible under the discipline of market competition. The same cannot be confidently predicated of the Russian economy. Russia's Kleptocracy would appear doomed to internal collapse unless President Putin and his oligarch cronies abandon their avaricious practices and address the precarious system of welfare supporting the Russian population. Whatever may be said of the Chinese economy, it is not a Kleptocracy. Oligarchs do not command the heights. The gains from corruption are real and palpable and reach large segments of the Chinese population. In contrast to the Putin Kleptocracy, China under Xi's nuanced brand of corruption reaches large segments of the Chinese population. As long as the flow of corrupt wealth remains widely distributed, the Party can very likely count on the beneficiaries of corruption.[69] The CCP's control of information reaching the public also provides the Party with a large measure of insulation from criticism or examination of governmental corruption.

Widespread incentives for graft are only part of the answer for the weaving of corruption into the fabric of Chinese government from the village and township to the cities and into the Party and governmental system. Corruption assumes an institutional role in governance. Graft is not just an individual transgression against the interests of the Chinese people and the Communist Party. It assumes a collective form. As Ting Gong argues:

> As the economy grew ... corruption shifted from a largely individualized form of power abuse into ... "collective corruption," which allowed corrupt officials and their confederates outside the party state to pursue greater illegal gains and to reduce the risk of exposure by forming protective networks — known as "protective umbrellas."[70]

Minxin Pei reaches much the same conclusion. Corruption and crony capitalism in China arise from what Pei terms the "collusion of elites."[71] These networks include Party leaders and apparatchiks, governmental officials, private entrepreneurs, and criminals. They form clusters of corruption throughout the governmental system and economy.[72] Millions in official positions have a stake in these clusters. Graft keeps greedy officials loyal to the Party. Conversely, their participation in corruption provides something to hold over their heads should they oppose Party rule.

Corruption, crony capitalism, rent-seeking enterprises, and Chinese criminal networks are endemic flaws of the Chinese system. They are particularly apparent in State-Owned Enterprises. Reform of SOEs, announced early in Xi Jinping's presidency, has largely not materialized. As Elizabeth Economy's detailed study of SOE notes:

> In each of the five core areas of SOE policy reform — the role of the SOE in the Chinese political system, SOE management, SOE efficiency and competitiveness, the role of privatization, and the tolerance for SOE

failure … the picture of reform suggests marginal rather than transformational change.[73]

Xi has repeatedly emphasized the significance of SOEs for Party governance. In
2016 Xi asserted "Party leadership and building the role of the party are the root
and soul for state-owned enterprises. … The party's leadership in state-owned
enterprises is a major political principle, and that principle must be insisted on."[74]
SOEs are essentially agents of the state. Large formally privatized firms, like the
communications giant, Huawei, also depend on governmental support and insulation from domestic competition posed by foreign corporations. Xi Jinping and
the Party have designated these enterprises as national champions whose missions
are to dominate key sectors of the global economy.

What else explains the toleration of large-scale corruption, but short of arresting economic growth and global competitiveness? Part of the explanation for
resolving this paradox derives from the mixed incentives to which colluding
elites are responding. They have an overriding, shared interest in concentrat-
ing their corruption on graft in all of its multiple forms rather than engaging
in policy-defeating corruption. To a large degree their material wealth, status,
career opportunities, family well-being, and power depend not only on fun-
neling some of China's economic growth to their personal accounts but also on
their performance as agents of the state and Party.[75] These latter constraints –
really incentives – further China's economic growth and global power. They also
serve to check how much corruption the system can take. Corruption falls short
of undermining policies that furnish the economic growth on which corruption
depends to be beneficial to Party members and the CCP.

How then should we interpret Xi's anti-corruption campaign? There is little statistical data, noted earlier, to indicate that Xi's campaign has made much
progress in denting system-wide corruption. This supports Andrew Wedeman's
contention that successive Party corruption campaigns act more like a governor
on an automobile, keeping the car from going beyond a set speed. These anti-
corruption campaigns of which Xi's is only the latest check excesses that might
well get out of hand and threaten Party rule and legitimacy.

The most significant outcome of Xi's anti-corruption campaign would appear
to be his elimination or marginalization of his rivals and, concomitantly, his
installation of his own ruling coalition of the Party. Xi's anti-corruption efforts
can be viewed as tantamount to rebuilding the Party in his image. Partial evidence for this conclusion lies in his use of Party mechanism to expose and punish malefactors rather than the courts.[76] Although the courts are under Party
control, they are not as efficient and swift-reacting as Party mechanisms under
Xi's direction to rid him of rivals. Minxin Pei makes the pertinent point that "an
opportunistic strongman … can vanquish his political opponents through tac-
tics disguised as anti-corruption efforts."[77] President Xi is evidently well aware
of this power tool. This view is shared by other China scholars who view Xi's

arbitrating power over corruption as designed not only to limit corruption to protect Party rule but also to eliminate competitors and to silence dissenters to his rule.[78]

Whether Xi's rise in personal power serves the Party's interests and its collective power is problematic. Corruption as a power tool saps Party member morale and undermines the integrity of governing institutions. It prompts elite disunity and incipient power struggles. The Party may well appear strong on the surface under the leadership of a strong man, but below, at the level of Party membership and at all levels of government, it may be vulnerable to decay and disunity. Centralized power also breeds insecurity and indecision at all levels of Party and governmental control. These dilemmas confront President Xi and any Chinese dictator.

Is the China model a solution to the Welfare Imperative?

The Deng reforms, as William Overholt observes, contributed significantly to the creation of a global market economy. During the first generation of reforms leading to China's entry into the World Trade Organization, China acceded to a rule-based solution to market governance. Within the chrysalis of an organized and relatively stable and predictable global economic order, Chinese enterprise and state support gained increasing control of the shift from national industrial production to the control of global value chains and the deconstruction of the nationally based factory system into transnational networks of supply chains. The launching of BRI also provides China with additional leverage to influence the industrial policies of client states to favor Chinese interests.

The next test of the Chinese model and its response to the Imperative of Welfare is the competition to determine what digital platforms will become globally dominant. These technologies provide the platforms for the creation of other technologies, which will shape business, government, and the ordinary, daily lives of billions around the globe. These platforms promise to surpass the value of global supply chains. American firms are in the lead. In order of capitalization, Apple is the largest (US\$2.03 trillion), followed by Microsoft (US\$1.62 trillion), Amazon (US\$1.57 trillion), and Google's Alphabet (US\$1.2 trillion). China trails with Tencent (US\$719 billion) and Alibaba (US\$695 billion).[79]

From the perspective of global governance, the contest over platform dominance boils down to a sharp divide between Western democracies and China. China presses national digital sovereignty as the standard to be adopted by all states. Applied universally, each state would then be able to control what information its populations would be allowed to access. That capacity is especially important for autocratic regimes. It is crucial for the CCP. Digital sovereignty justifies the CCP's internet firewall, detailed in the next chapter, which monitors and restricts the flow of information available to the Chinese peoples. Digital sovereignty also permits China to access the global platforms of the democracies to acquire the knowledge, know-how, and information required for sustained economic growth and technological development on which the survival of the CCP depends for its survival.

The interest and values of the democracies lie with an open global digital system. Application of that principle underlies the success of American and European multilateral corporations to corner the platform domain. The absence of cooperation among them hampers them in keeping ahead of China. The United States and the European states compete not only against China but also against each other. The United States and the European Union also clash over whether and at what level to tax these platform tech giants and to what extent should they be regulated to protect corporate and personal privacy.

An *Economist* report joins the issue between China and the democracies over global platform competition:

> [I]f the democratic countries cannot agree on common rules in the digital realm, China could end up setting the rules for large swathes of the world. The result would be a technosphere engineered for the comfort and support of autocracies.[80]

China possesses significant assets in the race of the swift. While the democracies compete among themselves and China, the CCP does not have to compete with itself. Xi's CCP speaks with one voice to ensure its power at home and abroad. It puts all of the state's resources behind those platforms and their corporate creators, which are designated as China's champions. The BRI's rapid expansion to all regions of the globe steals a march on a divided West. It is too early to know what the endgame of digital platform competition will be. What is certain is that the eventual balance that will eventuate between free and authoritarian states will have a significant, potentially decisive impact on whether democratic or Chinese characteristics will prevail in global governance.

Once a solution, China is now a formidable obstacle to continuing progress in creating a universally extensive global economic system in which states play by agreed-upon rules and on a level playing field. Xi's CCP, while proclaiming to support an equipoised system for all participants, reject what Thomas Friedman characterized precipitously as the rise of a "Flat World" in which China would play by Western rules.[81] For China to assume a leadership global role, the Chinese Communist Party would be obliged to launch fundamental economic and political reforms. China's economic model, notably Xi Jinping's state-directed version, serves his and the Party's interests and survival. Liberating China's economy and regime threatens both. Party, governmental, and national interests preclude any return to the market system that existed before China's entry at the turn of the century.

In falling short of free-market expectations and departing from market discipline, Xi's China, joined now by the equally disruptive market practices of President Trump's America, plunges the world's states and peoples, interconnected and interdependent as never before, into permanent turmoil. Deng era reforms propelled both the growth of the Chinese and the global economy. Not only did China make economic globalization possible, but for the first time in Chinese history it also raised hundreds of millions of Chinese out of poverty and created a thriving, educated middle class. Millions more around the world also experienced increased incomes and accumulated wealth as a consequence of the global market system. An economic war between the United States and China would threaten the welfare of all parties. The seeming impossibility of a hot war moves toward a probability.[82] The Imperative of Welfare yields ground to the Imperative of Order.

China's deviation from market rules is multiple and mutually reinforcing. Although the second-largest economy, China still uses high tariffs to favor domestic industries, especially its national champions. Chinese controls, restricting access of foreign firms to financial services and credit, hobble them in competing with Chinese companies. Corruption and kickbacks mar the approval process for the authorization of a business to enter the Chinese market. Both domestic and foreign firms must run this costly and corrupt bureaucratic gauntlet. The World Bank's indicator of ease of starting a business in China ranks China at 151, next to the Congo, in a list of approximately 200 countries.[83] Overholt report that "there are extraordinarily few privately owned companies in China that can survive without giving shares, jobs, or power or well-compensated board seats to government and Party officials."[84]

The government's control of the inflow and outflow of capital hinders but does not preclude hundreds of millions of dollars in capital flight. The Party's control of the judicial and court system at all levels provides dubious assurance for domestic and especially foreign companies that their property rights will be respected under law. While working through formal legal channels to transfer capital out of China is bureaucratically difficult, capital flight through illegal avenues continues to rise, amounting to hundreds of billions of dollars annually. Many wealthy Chinese, risking indictment for corruption, prefer to put their assets in foreign countries, notably Western states, rather than trust the Chinese banking system or the Party and government to keep its promises to protect their personal wealth. There is no reliable rule of law in China. The Party is the law. Party decisions are neither transparent nor is the Party accountable to an independent legislature or judiciary other than itself, much less to the scrutiny of a free press and media and the Chinese people.

An overlooked measure of a drag on the economy is the massive capital flight in the period between 1984 and 2014. Frank Gunther presents data to show that

> the accumulated capital flight of the last thirty years is $3.2 trillion. ... Capital controls ... have little effect on the volume of such flight. [The] likely causes of recent capital flight are corruption, income inequality, transaction costs, and desire to migrate.[85]

Since 2005, capital flight has accelerated, reaching $425 billion (plus or minus $60 billion) in 2014 versus $332 billion in 2012. Half of the $3.2 trillion in capital flight occurred six years before 2014. The $435 billion flight of capital in 2014 represented 17 percent of China's total exports of goods and services and 195 percent of the country's current account. In that same year the ratio of capital flight to foreign direct investment was 165 percent, that is, outward capital flight was greater than direct foreign investment for every year in the decade 2004–14. The total capital flight between 1984 and 2014 at $3.2 trillion was 80 percent of the country's international reserves of $3.9 trillion.[86] Capital flight also hampers China's ability to control its enlarging central and local debt, estimated at 266 percent of China's GDP in 2017, rising from 162 percent in 2008.[87] This level of corruption dwarfs the amount of capital flight attributed to President Putin and his oligarchs covered in Chapter 7. With so enormous a loss of Chinese capital through flight, the prospect of financing Xi's ambitious BRI initiative becomes increasingly problematic.

Cyber theft of the know-how and advanced technologies of foreign companies is molded into Chinese economic practices. Chinese hackers stole the plans for Lockheed Martin's F-35 stealth fighter.[88] Its carbon copy based on stolen plans saved billions in research and development costs. It is commonplace for Chinese firms to steal the intellectual property of Western firms. Those operating in China are also obliged to transfer technology to cooperating Chinese firms only to discover that Chinese firms rely on these transfers to compete against these firms. Skepticism also surrounds the independence of Chinese private firms, like Huawei, a leader in providing for 5G equipment. In light of state-directed economic policies, there is concern that Beijing may compromise the foreign national security interests of other countries, which rely on Huawei or other Chinese corporations, particularly with respect to dual-use technologies, adaptive to civil and military purposes.

President Xi and Party officials are acutely aware that foreign trading partners are increasingly resistant to China's selective and partial self-adaptation to market protocols and its sustained efforts to twist a free-exchange, rule-based global market to favor Party interests. As early as November 2012, at the time of his assumption of power, the Third Plenum of the Communist Party pronounced that "the focus of the restructuring of the economic system … is to allow the market [forces] to play a 'decisive role' in the allocation of resources."[89] Five years later at the Davos World Economic Forum, President Xi reiterated China's commitment to rely on market reforms to support globalization:

> Whether you like it or not, the global economy is the big ocean you cannot escape from. Any attempt to cut off the flow of capital, technologies, products, industries and people between economies, and channel the waters in the ocean back into isolated lakes and creeks is simply not possible, Indeed, it runs counter to the historical trend.[90]

This full-throated vote of confidence in a free-exchange system is belied by Chinese policies and behavior. Xi's determination to squash all opposition and dissent in China, to attack any foreign criticisms of CCP rule,[91] and to control communications between Chinese citizens and the outside world diminish the attractiveness of the Chinese model's response to the Imperative of Welfare. Much of Xi's version of the Chinese Welfare model depends, ironically, on undermining the very market system on which China's economic miracle was made possible and on which its prowess depends.

Even if there were no pressure from China's Western economic partners to reform its errant ways, it is problematic whether full throttle market reforms would necessarily succeed in meeting the mounting challenges confronting the Chinese economy and the very survival of Xi's presidency and the Party. At the outset of the reforms of the late 1980s, the Party faced one overwhelming goal: economic growth. It now confronts a tangled nexus of issues beyond those of a simple goal. Aside from the daunting problems already noted, these deepen the Chinese crisis. While a leader in green technology, public expectations and demands for increased growth dictate large-scale reliance on fossil fuels, especially coal, for energy. China is the largest polluter on the globe. It will continue to occupy this dubious distinction in the foreseeable future despite its verbal commitment to the Paris accord on climate change.[92]

The Party must also expose State-Owned Enterprises to market competition to lighten their drag on the Chinese economy. That objective runs counter to President Xi's insistence that SOEs remain privileged wards of the state. Further diminishing the likelihood of their reform, Xi expects the Party to actively participate in SOE management. Market-driven reforms would require that the Chinese economy be open to unfettered foreign businesses. As arms of the state, neither the Party nor the SOEs are prepared to have that happen. The centralization of power in the Party and, specifically, in President Xi also hinders decision-making. It is either too slow to adapt to market dynamics or too fast before sufficient vetting is accomplished to determine the viability of a project. Several BRI initiatives suffer from the latter shortcoming. The dilemma faces Xi's reliance on the SOEs is captured in the critique by a defecting former high Party official: "China's long-standing problems of corruption, excessive debt, and unprofitable state enterprises are rooted in party officials' power to meddle in economic decisions without public supervision. Trying to liberalize the economy while tightening political control was a contradiction."[93]

There is a deep flaw in CCP welfare policies that proclaims support for China's economy to be open to the world and the vast unmatched efforts of the Xi regime to oversee the detailed doings, friendships, social media postings, and private conversations of all Chinese and to control their contracts with the outside world. Market reform and continued Chinese economic growth require that the Chinese population and all globally directed segments of the economy have unimpeded access to the Internet and transborder exchanges between firms, universities, research entities, professionals, and individuals. President Xi's denigration of Western ideas runs counter to Deng's insistence on these exchanges as indispensable for the development of the Chinese economy and popular well-being.

Why then is there a profound and seemingly intractable contradiction between Chinese pronouncement favoring market-driven reforms and the current resistance of the Xi regime to surmount its self-imposed dilemma. Occam's Razor – the simplest solution is likely the best – would appear apt to explain the disconnect. There are powerful negative incentives to reform. For Chinese leadership to abandon its flawed model and to embark fully on market-driven reform would weaken and conceivably destroy the Party as Russian economic reforms undid the Soviet Communist Party. Since its ascendancy in capturing the Chinese state and control of the Chinese people, the CCP has never wavered in choosing survival as the paramount objective.

The CCP's obsession to control the Chinese people and foreign criticism of its rule and the damaging effects of some of its security and economic policies directly contradict the claim that it is transparent and accountable in its response to global issues. Beijing praises its timely response to check the spread of the coronavirus as "a global emblem of superior governance" of CCP rule.[94] To fix that certainty into the minds of Chinese citizens and to convince foreign governments and public audiences that its handling of the epidemic was a model, the CCP launched a multipronged campaign to put the best face on its handling of the epidemic.

Domestic criticism of the CCP's handling of the pandemic has been quickly and decisively squashed. Li Wenliang, the ophthalmologist who initially reported the virus in Wuhan and later died of the virus, was arrested along with seven other physicians for allegedly spreading lies.[95] A journalist and former lawyer, Zhang Zhan, was sentenced to four years in prison for documenting the first days of the spread of the virus and the failure and cover up on the government's response.[96] Documents released by Chinese backers to the *New York Times* and *Propublica*, which translated the materials, revealed that more than 3,200 directives and 1,800 memos and other Party and governmental files directed social media sites and governmental agencies to delete references to the Wuhan crisis and "monitor internet discussion and manage armies of online commenters" to whitewash the shortcomings of the government's first responses to check the virus.[97] The Cyberspace Administration, created by Xi Jinping, orchestrated this massive suppression campaign to silence any domestic sources that might otherwise portray China as culpable in managing the COVID-19 epidemic.

The second element of the propaganda campaign was to deflect attention from China as the source of the virus. Trolls were mobilized to claim through social media and other outlets that the virus was sparked elsewhere. Italy and the United States military as well as other countries were cited as the initial source of the virus.[98] Another CCP-inspired ploy suggested that the coronavirus arrived in frozen foods imported by China. A fallback position was to assert that the virus was to be found around the world, but only first detected in Wuhan.[99]

Simultaneous with these initiatives, Beijing hindered both WHO and US virus experts from visiting China to determine the source of the virus. Eventually, it agreed to a WHO investigation,[100] but only on the condition that half of the search team be composed of Chinese scientists.[101] Foreign governments, which charged China as the source of the virus and called for an international investigation, were attacked and intimidated. Australia was singled out for insisting on an independent investigation. China banned key imports from Australia, like coal, and ships with Australian cargo were refused entry into Chinese ports. To chastise Australia for having benefited from Chinese imports of Australian products, a spokesman for the Chinese Ministry of Foreign Affairs warned: "Never allow eating the Communist Party's food and then smashing the Communist Party's cooking pots."[102]

Chinese efforts, some successful, to shape the rules and norms of the global market system and those that apply to global health with Chinese characteristics suggest that the CCP will use whatever leverage and power at its disposal to puts its stamp on the Welfare Imperative of global government. Barring another Tiananmen Square crisis or some unforeseen upheaval, the CCP will continue to have a powerful say about how the global society will be governed. There is little or no likelihood that the Chinese economy will collapse, much like the Soviet Union. Much less does the Chinese economy, freighted with inequality and corruption, portend that Party will implode anytime soon. It is bracing to remember that the Party retained power despite the Great Famine and the Cultural Revolution directed at the Party's anti-Maoist leadership.

What China has shown is that an authoritarian regime can successfully sustain economic growth, albeit with the extensive cooperation of its Western competitors. Xi's post-Maoist regime also has the coercive tools and demonstrated the will to suppress opposition and dissent.[103] The CCP propaganda machine, drawing on strong nationalistic sentiment, has been resourceful in creating narratives, however flawed, incoherent, or bereft of fact, to support CCP rule. The CCP is never wrong and its policies are always right. Dissenters are brought quickly under control. Foreign critics are attacked and are compelled to kowtow out of self-interest to CCP preferences. That the slowing economic performance and rising unmet challenges will overwhelm the Party is a possibility, but not a high probability at this time. As the data presented in this chapter suggests, the conclusion of the *Economist*'s evaluation of China's economic future under CCP rule is difficult to resist: "China's leaders believe they have a way to marry autocracy with technology, opacity with openness, and brutality with commercial predictability."[104]

Continued Chinese authoritarian rule and its spread to other countries are profoundly threatening to Western democratic values and interests. No less troubling, conversely, is the dependence of the world on China's economic success. Its success is, paradoxically, a global liability. The world economy has now made a full turn since China's opening ensured economic globalization. China's drift and progressive departure from market discipline, resistance to play on a level playing field, and preference to choose national economic interests over collective state cooperation to maintain a global market system beneficial to all participants expose both the Chinese and the global economy to chronic upheaval.[105] The Trump administration's tariff war on China and its Western allies deepen these crises. Chinese and US contempt for a rule-based economic system to which all are expected to comply for the sake of collective economic growth marks a break from the commitment of the democratic states to free trade after World War II. Imitation may be the highest form of flattery, but when the world's most important economic powers, led by the United States and China, practice mutually destructive delinquency, can large-scale national losses, parallel to those of preceding the depression of the 1930s – or even disaster for all participants – be far behind?

Notes

1 The most authoritative Chinese account of the famine of the Great Leap Forward, now banned in China, is Jisheng (2013). See also Dikotter (2016).

2 See Jisheng (2020) for a Chinese account of the Cultural Revolution, which is also banned by the CCP. For other, non-Chinese accounts, see Dikotter (2016); MacFarquhar and Schoenhals (2006).

3 Vogel (2011) is the most comprehensive treatment of Deng's impact on the Chinese government and economy. See also Deng's full presentation to a Party conference on December 13, 1978, which rejected Mao's personalized rule and substituted Party rule by a consensus of Party elders, who retained top-down control of the Chinese people. Affirmed was the Leninist principle of democratic centralism. It carried no notion of sharing power with the Chinese people. See Speech of Deng Xiaoping, December 13, 1978. digitalarchive.wilsoncenter.org/document/121690.pdf?v...
See also Schell and Delury (2013, pp. 259–325) for a description of Deng's leadership in creating a coalition supporting his reform efforts.

4 Overholt (2016, p. 1). Overholt credits China and the Communist Party with having successfully challenged the widely held view that economic development depended on adopting a liberal democratic system of government. He also argues that in the long run the CCP will be compelled to develop some form of liberalization of the Chinese economy and government if the Party is to ensure continued economic growth and technological innovation and keep its promise to increase the material welfare of its population (Overholt, 2018). This view is shared by other scholars of the Chinese economy. See, for example, Pei (2006, 2016, 2018, 2020a, 2020b).

5 *The New York Times*, May 23, 2019, p. A22.

6 Campbell and Ratner (2018). This article traces the expectation held by American policymakers that China would eventually liberalize its regime. That optimistic expectation prevailed for much of the first decade of the 21st century despite Hu Jintao's breakup of the Rights Defense Movement and the incarceration of Liu Xiaobo in 2008, a leading architect of Charter 08, a blueprint for a democratic society. The frustration of that expectation has prompted a hardening of US–Chinese relations.

7 Naughton (2018, 2019); Lin Yifu (2012).

8 Xi was elected CCP Party Secretary in 2012 and President of China the following year.

9 Kroeber (2016, p. 34). See also Brandt and Rawski (2008a) For a detailed overview of China's embrace of marketization and globalization, see the edited volume by Brant and Rawski (2008b). For an update of the current state of the Chinese political economy, consult Zeng (2019).

10 United Nations Industrial Development Organization. Cited in the *New York Times*, April 6, 2019, p. A6.

11 *New York Times*, April 6, 2019, p. A6.

12 Overholt (2016).

13 Ibid.

14 There is a rich literature recounting from different perspectives the evolution of the post-Mao Zedong years. See Brandt and Rawski (2008a, 2008b); Branstetter and Lardy (2008); Lardy (2014); Naughton (2018); Schell and Delury (2013); Shambough (2013). For an up-to-date evaluation of the key dimensions of the Chinese political economy, consult Zeng (2019).

15 Chinese decision-making in domestic and foreign policy is widely dispersed through governmental agencies but ultimately under Party control when push comes to shove. See Jacobson (2016).

16 Baldwin (2016).

17 Ibid. Baldwin cites five other states, which also gained from the "unbundling": South Korea, Poland, Indonesia, Thailand, and India; pp. 2–3.

18 One prominent example of the Western search for markets is the Opium Wars visited on the Qing dynasty to offload excessive production of opium in India on China. See Beeching (1975).

19 Overholt (2016, p. 103).

20 Huang (2008, p. 31).

21 Overholt (2016, pp. 113–114).

22 Ibid., pp. 58–59.

23 Huang (2008) MIT Professor Yasheng Huang makes this point. He is critical of the return to centralization of economic and political power, which began, with the second phase of reform in 1992. He contends that economic growth and the distribution of income and wealth then favored urban over rural areas.

24 Overholt (2016, p. 23). Bell (2015) goes further and argues that the Chinese economic model is based on merit and performance.

25 Kroeber (2016, pp14ff).

26 Rongji (2015) Zhu Rongji's memoir describes this development.

27 Schell and Delury (2013, p. 334). For Chinese state corporation rent-seeking under the Xi regime, consult Pei (2016).

28 Kroeber (2016, pp. 114–118).

29 Schell and Delury (2013, p. 341).

30 Kroeber (2016, pp. 99ff); Overholt (2018, pp. 72–73); Schell and Delury (2013, pp. 341–343).

31 Huang (2008); Rongji (2015).

32 Manion (2004); Pei (2016); Wedeman (2012).

33 Bell (2015).

34 Lardy (2014).

35 Piketty et al. (2017, p. 3). See Figure 1 also.

36 Huang (2014, p. 2).

37 Kroeber (2016); Naughton (2015); Overholt (2016, 2018).

38 *Economist*, November 2–8, 2019, pp. 64–65.

39 Pei (2006, 2016).

40 Molero-Simarro (2017) discusses inequality in China from the perspective of the technical difficulties of estimating China's Gini Coefficient from 1978 to 2015.

41 Piketty et al. (2017). Figure 10.

42 Overholt (2018, p. 129).

43 See Alvaredo (2018) for a comparison of Gini Coefficients of most countries. See also the magisterial volume of Thomas Piketty, whose work is foundational for understanding the economic, political, and social implications of growing inequality among the major economies of the world (Piketty, 2014).

44 Piketty et al. (2017), Figures 7c and 7e.

45 Ibid., Figure 20.

46 Ibid.

47 Ibid., Figure 14.

48 See Farzana et al., (2015); Wang (2004) describe the Hukou system which restricts the movement of Chinese, often violated more in the breach than in the observance,

but to the disadvantage of the rural poor moving to urban areas for work. Urban dwellers particularly profited from accession to the right to buy and sell housing properties while rural dwellers were not accorded the same rights, what Arthur Kroeber characterizes as "one of the starkest cases of urban bias in Chinese policy-making, and a major contributor to China's yawning inequality chasm." (Kroeber, 2016; p. 78). An additional negative feature of this system is the failure to increase sufficient numbers of younger Chinese to care for the increasing aging of the Chinese population. *Economist*, November 2–8, 2019, pp. 64–65.

49 Huang (2008) provides a lengthy discussion of the costs to the countryside of Chinese industrial policies.

50 Dickson (2016, pp. 112ff) makes a persuasive case, resting on recent Chinese public opinion polls and CCP tolerance of NGOs, that the Communist Party is firmly in control and enjoys considerable public support, particularly from a middle class (by Chinese standards) which has significantly improved its income and wealth as a consequence of economic reforms. For additional data, consult (Dickson, 2021).

51 Piketty et al. (2017, p. 31).

52 Shi et al. (2013). This edited volume covers 12 different areas of inequality, ranging from housing and education to gender wage gaps. It provides a rich tapestry of the pervasiveness of inequality under Communist Party rule.

53 Jinping (2014), *passim.*

54 Ibid., p. 434.

55 Quoted by Yuen, referring to a *Bloomberg News* article, "China's Xi Amassing Most Power Since Deng Raises Reform Risk," December 31, 2013 (Yuen, 2014, p. 41).

56 There is a veritable cottage industry of China specialists who follow the course of Chinese corruption. See, for example, (Manion, 2004; Pei, 2006, 2016; Wedeman, 2012).

57 Zuniga (2018, p. 2).

58 Ibid., p. 3.

59 Ibid.

60 Jinping (2014, p. 429).

61 Yuen (2014, p. 3). Graph 1.

62 Pei (2016, p. 265).

63 Horsley (2018). See Jamie Horsley, *The Diplomat*, May 30, 2018, p. 1, for a description of the CCDI's responsibilities. www.brookings.edu › opinions › whats-so-controversial-about-chin...

64 Yuen (2014, p. 3).

65 Ibid.

66 Andrew Wedeman's research is most cogent in explaining the paradox (Wedeman, 2012).

67 Economy (2018, pp. 91–120). Kroeber (2016, pp. 87–110).

68 These are among the central themes of Elizabeth's Economy's timely volume which views Xi Jinping as leading a third revolution in Chinese politics, government, and economic development (Economy, 2018).

69 See Pei (2016) for a more pessimistic assment of the insidious effects of corruption on Party control. On one hand, Xi appears adamant that corruption must be attacked to ensure Party support and control (Jinping, 2014), but, as Wedeman suggests (Wedeman, 2012) in assessing the experience of previous anti-corruption campaigns, Party leadership acts much as a governor on a car, preventing the level of corruption to go beyond a point which would threaten the survival of the Party.

70 Quoted in (Wedeman, 2012, p. 6), who affirms Gong's institutional characterization of Chinese corruption. See Gong (1997, 2002, 2006) for the full presentation of the collective and cooperative composition of Chinese corruption.

71 Pei (2016, p. 8). Pei builds on the notion of Chinese crony capitalism initially presented in his 2006 volume (Pei, 2006). Pei believes that corruption and crony

capitalism are fatal flaws of CCP rule unless broad economic and political reforms are implemented.

72 In light of the Tiananmen Square catastrophe, when Party leaders, notably Deng Xiaoping, chose to use force to maintain CCP power, it would appear that the Party's rule can tolerate high levels of corruption and still survive if its internal security system, resting on tight control of the military and police, remains intact.
73 Economy (2018, p. 108).
74 Quoted by Economy, (Economy, 2018, pp. 115–116).
75 Overholt (2018, p. 128), makes this key point. Daniel Bell also insists that the principle of political and economic meritocracy lies as the foundation of the staying power of the Chinese Communist Party. He also would have us believe that the Communist Party permits democracy with Chinese characteristics to animate local governance where officials, including party leaders, are alleged to be chosen by qualified consent of the citizenry (Bell, 2015).
76 Yuen (2014). See http://journals.openedition.org/chinaperspectives/6542
77 Pei (2016, p. 254).
78 Ibid. The principal argument of Simon Yuen's evaluation of the Xi anti-corruption campaign is that it was largely a Xi move to gain control of the Party and to squelch opposition. Desmond Shum, who was both an observer and participant of the corruption at all livels of government, including the president and party leaders in 1990s provides evidence to support the view that Xi's corruption campaign was designed to eliminate his opponents (Shum, 2021).
79 *The Economist*, November 21, 2020, p. 20.
80 Ibid., pp. 19–20.
81 See Friedman (2006). Xi's CCP prefers a "lumpy" market system defined by Chinese characteristics.
82 Allison (2017).
83 Overholt (2018, p. 78).
84 Ibid.
85 Gunther (2017, pp. 1–2).
86 See Gunther (2017), especially p. 13 for these statistics. The *Economist,* September 3, 2021, pp. 11–12, notes that the debt overhanding has not apprecieably changed since 2017.
87 Edna Curran, China's Debt Bomb," Bloomberg News, September 17, 2018.
88 Cited by Thomas Friedman, *New York Times*, May 21, 2019.
89 See "Party's Third Plenum Pledges 'decisive role' for markets in China's economy."www.scmp.com › News › China
90 For the full text of President Xi's presentation to the Davos World Economic Forum, January 17, 2017. https://america.cgtn.com/2017/.../17/full-text-of-xi-jin-ping-keynote-at-the-world-econ...
91 Chapter 6 develops this trope.
92 The BRI pushes the construction of coal-burning power stations in its contracts with other states.
93 Xia (2021, p. 93).
94 Evaluation of the CCPs to present a positive narrative of its handling of the COVID-19 epidemic, beneficial not only to the Chinese people but also to the world's population. See Vivian Wang, "As China's Propaganda Push Continues, Wuhan Emerges as a Star," *New York Times*, November 6, 2020.
95 *Washington Post*, November 14, 2020.
96 Ibid., December 29, 2020. See also Global Voices, August 7, 2020 https://globalvoices.org/2020/08/07
97 *New York Times*, December 19, 2020.
98 Ibid., December 6, 2020.
99 Ibid.
100 *Washington Post*, January 6, 2021.

101 *New York Times*, November 14, 2020. This concession to allow WHO scientists to inspect suspect sites in China had yet to be implemented by February 2021.
102 Ibid., December 3, 2020. China followed up its criticism of Australia by issuing 14 grievances against Australia, which were alleged to be damaging to China's core interests.
103 This point is further discussed in the next chapter.
104 *Economist*, March 20–26, 2021, p. 10.
105 Both Elizabeth Economy and William Overholt make this point about the present state of the Chinese economy. I extend their insight, suggested by Overholt's earlier point at the beginning of this chapter, that China was indispensable in leading the World's economy across the threshold to a global economy. It stands to reason that China's crisis also spells a global crisis in governance, the principal concern of this volume (Allison, 2017; Economy, 2019; Overholt, 2018).

6

CHINA AND THE IMPERATIVE OF LEGITIMACY

To understand and evaluate China's conception of legitimacy and citizenship some context is needed to properly appreciate the importance and potency of these issues. As stressed throughout this volume, global governance reverts by default to the anarchy of the nation-state system into which the world's populations are unequally dispersed and profoundly divided. Among the central issues of governance confronting the world's populations is evaluating the claims of legitimacy on which regimes in control of a state's authority and its monopoly of power are founded. The central question for this century is whether the Westphalian nation-state system will be governed with liberal democratic or authoritarian characteristics.

It is difficult to overestimate the saliency of assessing legitimacy claims. Whereas until the modern period the issue of legitimate rule was restricted to essentially isolated communities by geography and by limited means of transportation and communication between political communities, it is no longer a localized concern. Before the global expansion of the European states, beginning at the end of the 15th century, Europeans, Incas, Aztecs, Chinese, Indians, Japanese, American Indians, African empires and tribes, and Australian Aborigines constituted isolated political communities, each with its own unique solution to the Imperative of Legitimacy.

That has all now changed forever. The connectedness and interdependence of a global society exposes every regime to scrutiny by its own population and to criticism or emulation by other peoples and states. Each national population, if free, can weigh the worth of its regime's legitimacy against the example and experience of others. Legitimacy then becomes a crucial interest of contending regimes as a determining factor of whether they will survive and thrive. The issue of legitimacy is now deeply embedded in the politics of the global society and in the struggle for power of nation-states. How peoples and

DOI: 10.4324/9781003246572-6

states respond to the Imperative of Legitimacy looms larger than ever before in evaluating competing solutions for global governance. The power of the Imperative of Legitimacy holds its own in its struggle with the Imperatives of Order and Welfare for ascendancy in defining how the world's population will be governed.

To understand the role of legitimacy in governing 1.4 billion Chinese, a sharp distinction must be made between the Chinese Communist Party (CCP), on the one hand, and the Chinese state and civil society, on the other. Since the inception of the Party a century ago, the CCP and its leaders have shared the same understanding of legitimacy *as* power. A self-exiled former professor of the school to indoctrinate CCP officials succinctly portrays the mentality of CCP leaders: "The CCP, having come to power in 1949 through violence, was deeply wedded to the idea that it had earned a permanent monopoly on political power."[1]

The CCP's fusion of legitimacy and power, a distinction without a difference, is built on two principles, articulated by Mao Zedong early in the Party's formation: that "political power grows out of the barrel of a gun" and that "the Party commands the gun, and the gun must never be allowed to command the Party."[2] Survival is the CCP's overriding priority. The People's Liberation Army (PLA) and a vast array of internal security forces are the CCP's "guns." These coercive instruments are the handmaidens of its survival and, *ipso facto*, the foundation of its self-proclaimed legitimacy.

In basing its rule on power the CCP confronts a dilemma. Hobbes first raised the dilemma in posing the need for a Leviathan with overwhelming power to provide order for any given society. Since power defined legitimacy the Leviathan or whatever regime is invested or acquired a monopoly of coercive power would be ever confronted by being overturned by the countervailing power of opponents. That condition of conflating order and legitimacy creates a never-ending cycle of instability as one regime supplants another by exercising greater material power than its opponents.

Rousseau rebuked Hobbes for his impoverished presentation of what constituted legitimate rule. In the opening paragraphs of the *Social Contract*,[3] Rousseau raises the question of why a master's ability to force others to obey him – say a Leviathan – can be considered legitimate. "If I were to consider only force and the effect it produces," Rousseau observes, "I would say that as long as a people is constrained to obey and does so, it does well."[4] Rousseau qualifies that minimal concession to Hobbes. Rather, he salutes a people if they can

> shake off the yoke and does so, it does even better. For in recovering its freedom by means of the same right used to steal it, either the people is justified in taking it back, or those who took it away were not justified in doing so. But the social order is a *sacred right* that serves as a basis for all the others [italics added].[5]

That sacred order is defined as the creation of a social contract. Only a free people who enter into a social contract to define how they will be ruled qualifies as a domain where the authority to rule is legitimate and, simultaneously, those who have freely entered that contract rule themselves and are obliged to obey the laws flowing from the contract.

Rousseau joins the CCP's dilemma from which it is impossible to extricate itself as long as it adheres to Hobbes' solution of order in which the Leviathan possesses a monopoly of violence parading as legitimate rule. For the CCP its monopoly of violence is legitimate. Rousseau might well ask the question: How can the CCP claim to rule legitimately solely on the basis of its monopoly of power (a self-constructed Leviathan) when the social contract that confers upon it unconditional authority to rule is a social contract with itself? However successful the Party has been in fostering the interests of the Chinese people – certainly raising tens of millions out of poverty counts – the dilemma remains that the Party's self-appropriation of authority as power pits it fundamentally and permanently against the Chinese people. They have no say in the contract. Whatever freedoms or material well-being they may enjoy are only those that are accorded them by the Party. This deep flaw in the CCP's governance of China can be managed by continued exercise of its monopoly of violence. Rousseau acknowledges that "as long as a people is constrained to obey and does so, it does well." What is better is when the ruled rule themselves.

Marxist–Leninist ideology confers legitimacy on the CCP

Marxist–Leninist ideology plays a defining role in the CC's rationale for its unconditional control of the Chinese people.[6] Marxist–Leninism collapses the Imperative of Legitimacy into the Hobbesian black hole of Order. The successive and contradictory interpretations of Marxist doctrine by CCP leaders since the CCP's capture of the Chinese mainland provide them an invaluable, flexible tool to address their changing personal power needs and those of the Party. It is an all-purpose instrument – an ideological Swiss army knife – to suppress internal dissent, mobilize popular support, and blunt foreign criticism and pressures to reform. Marxism validates the CCP's survival behind the veil of its validation of CCP's unqualified power in the service of history as a Marxist prediction of the eventual victory of the global socialist revolution, the consequence of CCP leadership as the vanguard of this epic struggle.

Marxism of the moment, that is, the changing interpretations stamped on Marxism by successive CCP leaders also provides CCP leadership a vehicle to command Party loyalty and to expect Party members to accede to the CCP's latest falsification of legitimacy by the exercise of power. The Party would be destroyed if Party members rejected the CCP lie of legitimacy as power. The obsession with total control of Party members and the Chinese people exposes, ironically, the permanent crisis of legitimacy at the root of CCP rule. It confronts Vaclav Havel's metaphorical grocer who one day no longer believes in the Communist regime. It is at the moment that "the Power of the Powerless" expresses itself.[7]

The fear that the CCP might suffer the same fate as the Soviet Communist Party punctuates Party pronouncements of its invincibility, bolstered by the impressive array of suppressive measures at its disposal to forestall its demise. The Party must demand unequivocal acceptance of the lie underlying its claim to legitimacy to maintain its monopoly of power. Experienced in Party-speak and skilled in exercising power, Mao Zedong, Deng Xiaoping, and Xi Jinping, the leaders of three successive revolutions in the history of internal Party governance,[8] rely on the centrality of their particular interpretation of Marxist ideology as an indispensable, malleable weapon to sustain their personal power and CCP's ascendancy – Marxist–Leninism with Chinese characteristics.

The following discussion is divided into two parts. The first traces and delineates the central importance of ideology in underwriting the CCP's conception of legitimacy as power over three revolutions. Marxism is not an artifact of CCP power. It is embedded in the CCP's elusive pursuit of legitimacy. In confronting China under CCP rule, it is important to keep foremost in mind that the Party has survived three radical transformations of its internal governance. It has arisen from the first two crises stronger than ever. It remains to be seen whether it will also emerge stronger in the Xi Jinping era.

However contrasting and contradictory are the ideological strategies adopted by Mao Zedong, Deng Xiaoping, and Xi Jinping to strengthen the Party and their personal rule, they have never wavered in deploying the vision of the eventual historic triumph of socialism to justify their shared resolve to ensure the Party's monopoly of power and, *ipso facto*, their personal authority. They know full well that their power derives from the Party.[9] What is at issue is whose Party will it be – The Party of Mao, Deng, or Xi – or whoever else might assume the leadership of the CCP?

The second part focuses specifically on the Xi Jinping regime. His contribution to the CCP's ceaseless attempts to bridge Hobbes and Rousseau – a bridge too far – revolves around his fusion of his predecessors' incompatible presentations of Marxist doctrine to his conception of the Chinese Dream, which Xi insists that he alone and the CCP can realize. That Dream warrants his pursuit of what Hannah Arendt would characterize as totalitarian rule over approximately 90 million members of the Communist Party, over every branch of the state and military, and over the Chinese population and civil society. There is a relentless effort to submit these sectors to his personal authority and to extend the scope and depth of the Party's monopoly of power to unprecedented levels of control.

Mao Zedong's revision of Marxism

Early in the formation of the CCP, Mao recognized that

> the great strength of Marxism-Leninism lies precisely in its integration with the concrete revolutionary practice of all countries. For the

Chinese Communist Party, it is a matter of learning to apply the theory of Marxism-Leninism to the specific circumstances of China. ... [A]ny talk about Marxism in isolation from China's characteristics is merely Marxism in the abstract, Marxism in a vacuum.[10]

Marxism for Mao and for his successors is what the Party and the leadership say it is to address the changing internal and external threats to CCP power.

Successive revisions of Marxist ideology prepared the ground for fundamental shifts in the CCP's responses to OWL imperatives to sustain and increase its power. As Li Cheng observes, the Party has displayed remarkable recuperative power:

China's leadership has survived and thrived over the past three decades because it has continually sought new mechanisms, institutional regulations, policy measures, and political norms to resolve its inherent deficiencies and inadequacies. ... By keeping abreast of changes — especially those resulting from the development of new, dynamic forces in Chinese society — and adapting, accordingly, the CCP has maintained its grip on one-party rule.[11]

One could go back further in time to the Party's formation in the 1920s and its unexpected victory over a larger Kuomintang army a generation later to see these elastic and pliant Party qualities at work, guided by successive, pragmatic reformulations of Marxist doctrine.[12]

Mao turned classical Marxism upside down to explain the CCP's victory in 1949 and its elimination of all foreign occupation of China. Mao's China bore no resemblance to Marx's portrayal of the eventual, historically determined triumph of the working class. Mao held little brief for Marx's prediction of the eventual victory of a self-conscious cohesive global proletariat over a corrupt capitalistic system. He opted for his own, personal design to build Communism in China.[13] Whereas Stalin and the Soviets trusted, at least rhetorically, to an imagined global proletariat to topple capitalism, Mao relied on peasants and soldiers, not workers, to engineer the Communist Revolution with Chinese characteristics.

Mao focused primarily on building the CCP in his image and on extending its unquestioned rule across the mainland. In his effort to disengage from the West, he imposed what proved to be a disastrous autarchic economic system on the Chinese population. Despite the millions who perished in the Great Leap Forward (1958–1962) and millions more who were impaired and weakened by malnutrition, Mao and the Party prevailed. When the Party apparatus threatened to undermine his control of the Party, he launched the Cultural Revolution against the Party bureaucracy in 1966, prevailing as the head of the CCP until his death a decade later. Tens of thousands again died, were imprisoned, or sent to work in peasant communities for so-called re-education in Mao's brand of Marxism.[14] A global revolutionary ideology was domesticated to serve Mao's power needs.

While Mao was primarily concerned with his power at home, he was acutely aware of foreign threats to the CCP and his leadership. The Korean War and the prospect that American arms would reintegrate the two Koreas prompted Mao to send the PLA, the CCP's "gun," to prevent the loss or the collapse of North Korea as a buffer to Western influence. The stationing of American troops at the Chinese border would have opened the way to reintroduce foreign influence into China, conceivably leading to the overthrow of the CCP, less than two years since the CCP had seized control of the Chinese mainland.[15]

Mao's revision of Marxist doctrine as it was applied to Chinese rural circumstances also spoke to developing nations, recently emerging from Western colonialism in Africa, Asia, and Latin America. According to a recent scholarly account, China's success in ridding foreign interference in its domestic affairs inspired many in the developing world to follow its example, notably in "Peru, Indonesia, Southeast Asia, and Nepal."[16] In an effort to avoid being dragged into the Cold War, China also joined the Non-Aligned Movement (1961–1972) as an observer.[17] Mao also provided air and defense support to Hanoi in the Vietnam War. For different reasons, Mao also joined the United States in opposing the Khmer Rouge takeover of Cambodia. Beijing sought to punish North Vietnam as a consequence of its border war with Hanoi; the United States was still smarting from its defeat by Hanoi. Mao's decision to align with the United States against the Soviet Union in the 1970s marginalized Taiwan as a would-be independent state and prepared the way for Beijing's replacement of Taiwan in the United Nations, moves that strengthened China's weak geopolitical hand as well as Mao's Cultural Revolution to cow the CCP at home.

Deng Xiaoping's revision of Marxism

Mao's design for Party government collapsed with his death in 1976. His legacy of maintaining the Party's monopoly of power survived. Deng Xiaoping concluded that Mao's solution to preserve the Party's monopoly of power had outgrown him. By the 1970s, the CCP was incapable in its Maoist form to address new challenges to the Party's ascendant position – stagnant and regressive economic growth, widespread and entrenched poverty, pervasive corruption, Party factionalism, and China's geopolitical weakness. The Party had to remake itself again to address these threats to its rule. To facilitate the transformation, Marxism also had to be revised to rationalize and justify a fundamental shift in CCP strategies and policies. The feat of ideological legerdemain fell to Deng to reinvent Marxism to strengthen his hand in the struggle for power within the CCP after Mao's death in 1976. He reemerged to lead the Party over Mao's dead body after having been stripped of his status in the Cultural Revolution and sent to the countryside for rehabilitation and re-education in Maoist Marxism.

For Mao's revolutionary classes, Deng substituted and promoted "advanced productive forces (a euphemism for private entrepreneurs and high-tech specialists), advanced culture, and the 'fundamental interests of the overwhelming majority of the people of China."[18] Class struggle disappeared in the focused, even obsessed, pursuit of economic growth, technological modernization, and personal wealth – presumably elements of advanced culture. Making money was good. Deng instructed the 12th National Congress of the CCP that "In carrying out our modernization programme we must proceed from Chinese realities. …We must integrate the universal truth of Marxism with the concrete realities of China, blaze a path of our own and build a socialism with Chinese characteristics."[19] While both Marx and Mao were sacrificed on the altar of "Chinese realities," Deng still invoked both to justify his ideological *volte-face*, an ingenious psychological manipulation of Marxist doctrine to curry Party support to foster economic growth. Mao's body was placed on permanent display for the masses to revere as a patron saint of the CCP, while his brand of Marxism was interred with his remains.

Deng and his partisans decentralized economic decision-making to the local and regional levels. These units were expected to promote economic growth through their own ingenuity, resourcefulness, and entrepreneurship. Henceforward the performance of Party functionaries would be evaluated as a function of their success or failure in reaching CCP targeted economic growth levels rather than simply as loyal Party members.[20] The return to family farming spurred food production several times over. Freeing peasants from collectivization permitted them to retain whatever profits they could earn after meeting central Party targets. Locales were also encouraged to enter into agreements with foreign investors to accelerate economic and technological development. Aside from raising millions out of poverty, these radical anti-Marxist moves also launched an unprecedented building program of roads, bridges, air and ground transportation, communication networks, and electrical grids across China to provide the infrastructure for sustained economic growth.

In retrospect, as the previous chapter recounted, the key to Deng's reforms was the ability of CCP leadership to enlist the West to welcome China into its global market system. That proved indispensable for China's rapid economic development and for strengthening of the CCP's grip over the nation – the latter an unintended Western expectation. Foreign investment and the implanting of Western corporations in China, along with their advanced technology, drove the accelerating growth of China's exports and its centrality in the development of global supply chains. To foster these moves, the economic footprint of State-Owned Enterprises (SOEs) was temporarily reduced to favor private domestic and foreign enterprises. The creation of foreign economic zones, reminiscent to some degree of the imperial territorial enclaves accorded imperial powers by a weakened Qing dynasty in the 19th century, facilitated this massive movement of foreign capital and know-how. Unlike Qing's experience with the imperial West, China prospered and CCP power grew.

If greater freedoms were accorded to the Chinese people in the Deng era to bring China into the Western world, that allowance was never intended to undermine the Party's absolute monopoly of power. Marxist–Leninist theory is an adaptable tool. Deng radically transformed the theory not only to justify and legitimate a capitalist version of Chinese socialism but also to affirm, paradoxically, the CCP's monopoly of power as a Leninist regime. From the perspective of the CCP, when Party power and policy interests are at stake, there could not be any contradiction in rebranding Marxist ideology to rationalize what was needed to drive economic growth, to submit the Chinese people to the Party, and, accordingly, to tighten the Party's hold on power.[21] Any thought that Deng was prepared to share the Party's monopoly of power with the Chinese people or their elected representatives was decisively shattered when Deng ordered loyal elements of the Peoples Liberation Army to crush protesting students and workers in Tiananmen Square in 1989.

China quickly overcame its temporary isolation in the wake of the Tiananmen Square massacre. Deng's economic reforms resumed shortly thereafter. In his celebrated 1992 southern tour of China, Deng praised private enterprise and the personal acquisition of wealth. His defeat of Party opponents, still steeped in Mao's brand of Marxism, assured China's integration into the Western market system.[22] The culmination of these efforts was China's entry into the World Trade Organization in 2001.

Throughout this period, Western thinking, both in academic and official governmental circles, was largely shaped for a generation by the optimistic assumption that Chinese economic growth would create a large middle class and that this social change would purportedly result in the adoption of liberal practices.[23] Overlooked or dismissed was Deng's insistence that China would follow its own "Road both in Revolution and in Economic Development."[24] The West preferred to believe in the inevitability of political reform as a consequence of economic liberalization, an expectation frustrated by the CCP's unflagging embrace of authoritarian rule.[25] Deng turned Western developmental theory on its head.

During this period, stretching roughly into the first decade of the 21st century, Deng's successors progressively imposed tighter political controls over Chinese civil society. Many of the liberal reformers who signed the Charter 08 Manifesto, calling for greater political freedom, were arrested.[26] Others died in prison, including the 2010 Nobel Peace Prize Laureate Lui Xiaobo. Deng's strategy to foster China's rise as a global power was adopted: that China "cope with affairs calmly, hide our capacities and bide our time, be good at maintaining a low profile, and never claim leadership."[27] China kept a low exterior political profile during Hu Jintao's tenure as Party Secretary (2002–2012). His term focused on economic growth without raising alarms in Western capitals about China's geopolitical aspirations.

The CCP did indeed create a large and growing middle class, but this unprecedented socioeconomic transformation has not resulted in a movement toward democracy.[28] Under Xi Jinping the reverse has transpired. China now has a middle class, but in defiance of the expectations of modernization theory, China's mass middle class supports the Party's oppressive rule. The Faustian bargain between the CCP and the newly enriched elements of the Chinese public comprised its unquestioned submission to the Party in return for the provision of material benefits. A massive middle class has prospered under Party rule. The middle class hews the Party's mass line.[29] Dissidents do not appear to enjoy widespread public support in no small part due to the CCP's tight control of Chinese civil society. The CCP's success to date to reconcile economic growth with unswerving control of Party members, state and private corporations, and the Chinese population significantly qualify widely held Western notions of economic and political development. The CCP experiment suggests that there is more than one path to sustained scientific discovery, technological development, and economic growth than the Western model.[30]

Both the liberal democratic and Chinese responses to the imperatives of Order and Welfare may be viable, however flawed the CCP's response to the Imperative of Legitimacy may be.

Xi Jinping revision of Marxism as the Chinese Dream

The election of Xi Jinping as Party Secretary in 2012 ushered in what Elizabeth Economy characterizes as the "Third Revolution."[31] It is a hybrid of the former two revolutions. Xi has turned toward a brand of authoritarian rule that is more reminiscent of Mao than Deng. Conversely, like Deng, Xi trumpets economic globalization and foreign investment. Departing from both, he is also aggressively pursuing his Chinese Dream on a global scale. Xi has embarked on a daunting course whose paths run counter to each other: to create a closed Chinese society, insulated from foreign influence under tight Party control while continuing to open China to the world.[32]

Rather than pursue strategies that relax, if not surmount, this profound dilemma, President Xi is, instead, doubling down to achieve both incompatible aims. He is keen to define a major role for China in all important global affairs that touch on CCP concerns. Unlike Deng or Mao, Xi's China no longer walks softly but relishes carrying two big sticks: the second-largest economy, comprising the most dense network of global supply chains in the market system, and a growing military, spending for which is outmatched only by the United States. A strong PLA, progressively capable and technologically sophisticated, and a strong economy now undergird Chinese increasingly unapologetic warrior diplomacy. All branches of the Chinese military support Xi's aggressive moves in the South China Sea to advance China's sovereign claims; the Belt and Road Initiative (BRI) complements the expansion of Chinese influence around the globe.

At this juncture in Xi's presidency, the economic club is principally relied upon to pursue Xi's dream for China. That may change when the project of complete military modernization is achieved sometime in the next decade. Xi's China uses its economic muscle to muzzle foreign criticism of its dismal human rights record. The Party-state tirelessly promotes Chinese private and state-owned enterprises as national champions. The state supports these entities through subsidies, regulations restricting foreign competition, and forced transfer of foreign technology, to strengthen their competitive positions in global markets on Chinese terms. The soft power of Confucius centers around the globe and the promotion of Chinese culture, entertainment, and sport sponsorships, notably the Olympic Games in 2008 and scheduled Winter Olympics in 2022, provide additional influential arrows for China's power quiver.[33]

Xi's skilled seizure of the Party and control of its members are keys to his ability to enlarge and amplify the scope of his power. His command of the Party heights has also permitted him to create and deploy a host of new technological tools to dominate every important aspect of Chinese society and to unabashedly pursue Chinese interests abroad, breaking with the caution exhibited by Deng and Mao. Xi's design appears to be driven by the expectation that increasing China's power abroad in the service of Chinese national interests strengthens the Party's (and his) power at home, contributing implicitly to the Party's legitimation as power. Xi's dream for China is cast as a virtuous circle in which oppression at home is progressively strengthened by aggressive and self-asserted Chinese behavior abroad.

How, specifically, has he been able to assume so much power? Among the remarkable features of CCP governance is the small number of officials who actually possess authority over tens of millions of Party members, estimated at approximately 92 million in 2020 or seven percent of the Chinese population.[34] Since 1949, the size of Party membership has increased in each decade of the 20th century for which data have been published. Interest in joining the Party remains strong and brisk. In 2011, for example, 3.1 million new members were admitted to the CCP out of an application pool of 21.5 million.[35]

The National Party Congress, which meets every five years, elects the Party Leadership. The Congress also decides who will be elevated to the Central Committee, composed of approximately 376 members, divided approximately between 205 full members and 171 alternates. The Central Committee in turn elects the 25 members of the Politburo. The seven members of the Politburo Standing Committee (PSC), the CCP's most powerful governmental unit, are drawn from the Politburo. While technically voting at all levels would appear to be down up, the actual process of who is chosen for these three committees is top-down. Leninist Democratic Centralism and the leadership of the PSC determine who is in and who is out.[36]

Given the secrecy of CCP deliberations, there exists no definitive explanation of how and why Xi Jinping was chosen over his competitors, notably Premier Li Keqiang.[37] The historical circumstances surrounding Xi's choice as Party Secretary, President, and Chair of the Central Military Committee evidence his rapid rise to power. Hu Jintao, Xi's immediate predecessor as Party Secretary (2002–2012), would appear to have exhausted the utility of collective leadership to maintain the Party's monopoly of power, to placate Party factions, and to continue China's economic and technological development to keep pace with rising popular expectations of Party performance.

Hu's leadership style was to be an equal among equals.[38] One result was a marked slowdown in economic development, what William Overholt refers to as a lost decade.[39] There were also the issues of

> poor policy coordination, rampant corruption, splits in leadership, and the delegation of CCP authority to government agencies. Policy decision-making and implementation were divided at Party and at governmental levels. Party elites gained privileged access to segmented elements of economic and foreign policy, with Hu presiding rather than controlling these fractured groups to ensure overall Party and Chinese interests.[40]

There were also the disquieting reminders, seared into the memory of Party elites, of unexpected episodes challenging Party authoritarian rule. Foremost was the Tiananmen crisis – a proxy for popular uprisings not only in Beijing but also in over a hundred other Chinese cities in 1989 (the 200th anniversary of the French Revolution). There was also the implosion of the Soviet Union two years later and the subsequent collapse of Communist rule in Eastern Europe. The popular "color" revolutions in the first decade of the 21st century, notably in Ukraine, Georgia, and the Middle East, reinforced CCP concerns for its own survival.[41] Party leadership was reminded that any relaxation of the Party's monopoly of power and its control of the army and domestic security forces threatened the CCP's existence.

In light of the opaque decision-making within the CCP, contrary to Xi's claims of transparency and accountability at the Davos Economic Forum, it is very difficult to know definitively what factors figured into Xi's choice as Party Secretary General. The generalized fear coursing through member circles that the CCP might confront a color revolution may have worked to Xi's advantage. He pledged himself to continued Leninist centralized Party rule, guided by Marxist–Leninist ideology. His background as a princeling and his solid record as a successful regional leader and as mayor of Shanghai evidenced his ability to assume the post of Party Secretary. Whatever were the factors and circumstances bearing on his elevation, it is clear that Party leaders had sufficient confidence in his leadership to entrust the office of Party Secretary General to Xi in 2012. By early 2013 he assumed in quick order the Presidency and the Chair of Central Military Commission. To these key posts, he also appointed himself to head nine other leading policy groups.[42] Among these, he is chair of the Leading Group on Overall Reform, the newly established National Security Commission, and Foreign Affairs and Taiwan.[43]

These institutional sources of power positioned Xi to be invested as the "core" of the Party's leadership. Capping these tributes, "Xi Jinping Thought on Socialism with Chinese Characteristics for the New Era" was subsequently incorporated into the Chinese Constitution.[44] Xi's dutifully praised the Marxist contributions of his predecessors, an implicit bow to rival factions and their heroes. In his presentation to the 19th National Congress of the CCP, Xi reaffirmed the Party's Marxist ideological patchworks, however much these serial Marxist revisions contradicted each other: "Our Party has been guided by Marxism-Leninism, Mao Zedong Thought, Deng Xiaoping Theory, the Theory of Three Represents,[45] and the Scientific Outlook on Development."[46] Xi incorporated these contending Party doctrines into his vision of a Chinese Dream – an amalgam of objectives keyed to continued economic growth and China's national rejuvenation as a global power under strict Party control and leadership.

It might appear that cognitive dissonance is a requirement of CCP leadership. That would be misleading. Overnight changes and contradictions in ideological beliefs of Marxist–Leninist thought are not simply bold pronouncements by CCP leaders. They are heralded and embraced *as truth*. What the Party and its leaders dictate as reality *is* reality. Dissonance and contradictions have nothing to do with the Party's power to create reality to underwrite its monopoly of power and ensure its survival.

While it is important for partisans of liberal democracy to expose these logical discrepancies and psychological lapses, it is equally important to recognize that the revelation of these shifts in Party ideology has little or no effect on Party policies or membership loyalties once they are pronounced as Party doctrine by the Party General Secretary.[47] Dissidents, like Lui Xiaobo and the other signers of Charter 08, are indispensable in exposing the illegitimacy of the CCP, all the more significant because their actions have been at the cost of their professional and personal lives. What their sacrifice also implicitly indicates is that the CCP and its leadership only value power and survival under the pretense of presenting themselves as validating and promoting the interests of the Chinese people as their foremost concerns.

As George Orwell warned long ago:

> A totalitarian state is in effect a theocracy, and its ruling caste, in order to keep its position, has to be thought of as infallible. But since, in practice, no one is infallible, it is frequently necessary to rearrange past events in order to show that this or that mistake was not made, or that this or that imaginary triumph actually happened. Then again, every major change in policy demands a corresponding change of doctrine and a revelation of prominent historical figures.[48]

Xi is the latest in a series of the CCP's luminaries to proclaim his own ideological brand of Marxism to suit his needs and times. Orwell anticipated that totalitarian rulers would practice new truth-telling as a survival strategy even before the CCP's takeover of China:

> What is new in totalitarianism is that its doctrines are not only unchallengeable but also unstable. They have to be accepted on pain of damnation, but on the other hand they are always liable to be altered on a moment's notice.[49]

The tenuous lives of ideological transformations may explain why Xi has gone further than his predecessor in enshrining his new "truth" in the Chinese Constitution, what Stephen Colbert describes as "truthiness."

Xi's quandary: a closed China open to the world

How does the Chinese Communist Party, an authoritarian regime, rule without public consensual legitimacy conferred through free and unfettered elections? How can such a regime govern effectively in the absence both of transparency regarding its decisions and policies and of accountability for their implementation?

While the CCP remains vulnerable to the critique and constraints implied by these two questions, it has survived – and thrived quite well despite profound challenges to its rule. It has surmounted the elimination of millions of land-lords and opponents as well as the armies of the Kuomintang in gaining control of the Chinese mainland; of millions of more deaths to starvations produced by Mao's ill-conceived Great Leap Forward (1958–1962); and tens of thousands more deaths in the political upheaval of the Cultural Revolution to ensure Mao's continued rule of the CCP. The CCP's record of survival and that of its lead-ership merits close study as a substitute for freely conferred legitimacy by the Chinese people.

The ever-present fear of experiencing the fate of the Soviet Communist Party informs the CCP's survival strategies. That fear is prominently displayed in President Xi's determined efforts to squash dissent within the Party and within all segments of Chinese civil society as well as criticism from any foreign quarter, whether from states, corporations, journalists, or academics. The CCP's increas-ingly totalitarian rule poses a global problem. Absent fundamental political and moral reform, an unlikely prospect in the foreseeable future, the CCP poses a great risk today to the global society and, ironically, to its own survival. The principal source of the danger it poses is its reliance and promotion of an anarchic nation-state system with Chinese characteristics. Like Putin's Russia, the CCP prefers to deploy China's power and influence within this chaotic state-system rather than cooperate in constructing a rule-based international system. As a former Indian ambassador to Beijing observes, "China Doesn't Want a New World Order. It Wants This One."[50] Perversely, the CCP wants a democratic Westphalian system with Chinese characteristics as the nation-state system pop-ulated by a majority of autocratic states which not only adopt the Chinese model of autocratic rule but also favor Chinese reformulation of the Imperatives of Order, Welfare, and Legitimacy as principles of global governance.

What Ambassador Vijay Gokhale is getting at is that the CCP is confident in China's increasing economic, military, and political power – even its cultural reach. There is a widespread consensus that China has the wherewithal now, and even more in the future, to navigate effectively within a factious state system that will allow China to induce other states and non-state actors to kowtow to China's imperial posturing. As Gokhale observes,

China is the biggest beneficiary of globalization. It has systematically used Western-led multilateral institutions, such as the World Trade Organization, to advance its interests and influence. Though still fighting for greater control of the World Bank and the International Monetary Fund, it has determinedly captured the leadership of four key United Nations agencies that set international rules and standards.[51]

The Trump administration's decision to withdraw the United States from the World Health Organization (WHO) over its alleged mishandling of the COVID-19 pandemic played directly to Chinese interests to increasing its influence in all international organizations. Like Putin's Russia, Xi's China champions international organizations, especially the United Nations, viewed as a collection of states, not peoples. President Xi sees no contradiction between his support of democracy, transparency, and accountability and his rejection of the liberal democratic governments as incapable of effective rule and hypocrisy in defense of human rights. When Xi and the CCP leadership promote democracy, while denying liberal democratic practices and values, they are referring to China's support for the progressive enlargement in the number of nation-states, a growing majority, which is keen to adopt the CCP's model of oppressive rule, its brand of human rights defined by CCP law, and support of Chinese policies and leadership.

The second aspect of China's reliance on a nation-state system with Chinese characteristics is the distinct possibility that the CCP will overplay its power ploys and plays. China runs risks on two fronts. First China's aggressive behavior in the South China Sea to cow its neighbors and to deter US forces, deployed to keep the South China Sea open to international access and to support China's neighbors, has led Chinese strategists to discount the possibility of a nuclear exchange and war with the United States over its aggressive posture in the area. As an in-depth evaluation of Chinese nuclear strategy finds, China may well be "overconfident" that its nuclear deterrent will prevent such an outcome.[52] Chinese strategists appear to place too much weight on mutual nuclear deterrence to prevent a nuclear exchange or war, discounting the possibilities of misunderstanding and miscalculation in tensions with the United States or other nuclear powers, like India.[53] Second, there are also significant risks in the decision of the Xi regime to use its economic power as well as its military and political muscle abroad to strengthen its monopoly of power at home. In trading on Chinese sensitivities of over a century of humiliation from foreign powers and growing national sentiment, stoked by the Party, to promote Chinese sovereignty and interests, the CCP may lose control of its own strategy.

Rather than give up trying to reconcile the contradictory and incompatible aspirations of a closed China and an actively engaged global China, President Xi and the CCP have doubled their efforts not just to relax their dilemma but also to surmount it. Achievement of that elusive aspiration hinges on China's emergence as a model for other states to emulate and their repudiation of the liberal democratic alternative. If successful, legitimacy, which the CCP tirelessly seeks from abroad to bolster its power at home, would be indirectly conferred on the CCP by the recognition of other states of its authority and suppression of the Chinese people. Ambassador Gokhale joins the issue of the choices confronting the world's population in the challenge raised by President Xi and the CCP:

> The Beijing model ... may look attractive to some. But it cannot be widely emulated. Dependent on China's unique culture and history, the method can work only there. Democracy, by contrast, is based on universal principles that can be followed everywhere, by everyone.[54]

President Xi and the CCP have chosen to take up the challenge of reconciling a closed China under what amounts to increasingly totalitarian rule and a China open to the world and as a model for other states to emulate.

Two points must be kept uppermost in mind as the discussion proceeds. First, the Party rests on violence and coercion. Mao made that clear and unequivocal. His successors have fully endorsed that first principle. Those who falter, like Party Secretary Zhao Ziyang, are expelled from the Party and imprisoned for failing to crack down on student protesters in Tiananmen Square in 1989. Force is the indispensable component of the Party's unswerving commitment to preserve its monopoly of power. Have no illusions that the CCP's reverence for might makes right is wavering.

The second point for reference is that President Xi's power is fused to the power of the CCP. One cannot be understood in the absence of the other. Kerry Brown puts the matter squarely:

> To understand him without understanding the Party would be like trying to comprehend music while being tone-deaf. Xi and the Party are inextricable. Its power is his power, and his power is solely derived from it ... It is audacious for Xi's Party, with its roots in terror, illegality and revolution, to present itself as the bastion of stability and justice six decades after coming to power by force of arms, insurrection and war.[55]

Xi has enlisted his interpretation of Marxist ideology in the service of his Chinese Dream. He melds the vision of a closed society internally with a China actively engaged outwardly for the realization of his dream of a wealthy and powerful China. Xi's speech before the 19th National Congress of CCP in 2017 outlined his Chinese Dream for the Party faithful:

> The theme of the Congress is: *Remain true to our original aspirations and keep our mission firmly in mind, hold high the banner of socialism with Chinese characteristics, secure a decisive victory in building a moderately prosperous society*

in all respects. . . and work tirelessly to realize the Chinese Dream of national rejuvenation.[56]

The realization of Xi's dream will depend on his ability in command of the CCP to surmount the dilemma of his and the CCP's own creation. Both logic and, more significantly, inevitable political pushback from within and, especially, from outside against the Party's efforts to surmount this dilemma renders the quest problematic. It's a high-risk strategy at war with itself.

To advance his dream, Xi set out quickly to eliminate powerful opponents within the CCP and to impose strict discipline on Party members. His vigorous anti-corruption campaign had two useful aims. The announced goal was to root out the rampant corruption pervading the presidency of Hu Jintao.[57] That campaign earned Xi public support. The second and implicit objective of the campaign was to rid Xi's real or perceived rivals and strike fear into Party members if they deviated from the Xi Party line. Real or perceived rivals, as noted earlier, Politburo member Bo Xilai and the security czar Zhou Yongkang were convicted of corruption and imprisoned. More than a hundred generals and admirals were also swept up in the anti-corruption campaign. By the time of the 19th National Congress, the Discipline Commission, which Xi chairs, initiated the investigation and punishment of 1.4 million Party members for various infractions.

Punishment of Party members extended well beyond crimes and corruption to the failure of Party officials at local and regional levels to meet central CCP targets for economic and technological development and for environmental standards. To these internal controls, Xi called on CCP members to pledge unconditional loyalty to the Party and, *ipso facto*, to him personally. They were also instructed to criticize their failures and those of other Party members. Compliance with this expectation effectively exposes would-be opponents and frustrates their efforts to organize against the Xi regime.[58] Institutionalized is whistleblowing on a national scale. Party members have to be wary of each other. Fear of being denounced works to the advantage of Xi's control of the Party. This tactic of denouncing deviations from the Xi and CCP mass-line levels all Party members. As Hannah Arendt reminds us, a totalitarian regime lowers and levels all heads in obedience to the leader and the party. Equality crowds out freedom.[59]

Party members are induced to be wary and fearful of each other. The psychology of Xi-inspired whistleblowing places Party members in a permanent predicament. If they do not denounce their peers and corruption is exposed, they face loss of Party status and even punishment for their silence and implied complicity. If they denounce their faults, however petty, they risk exposing themselves to censure, not praise. Remember Mao's 1957 campaign to let a hundred flowers bloom: "Letting a hundred flowers blossom and a hundred schools of thought contend is the policy for promoting progress in the arts and the sciences and a flourishing socialist culture in our land."[60] When Party members and intellectuals critical of Mao's CCP rose to the bait, they exposed themselves as enemies of the regime and were punished for their candor, some even executed.

Xi's next step was to gain control of the state's military and internal security forces. Xi exceeds even Mao's control of the military. Unlike Mao, who shared power with revolutionary-era marshals,[61] Xi reports to himself. Besides chairing the Central Military Commission, Xi has also assumed the rank of Commander in Chief of the PLA Joint Operations Command Center. At his choosing, he can reach deeply into the operations of the PLA. A top Xi priority is to rapidly develop a modern military possessed of the latest technologically advanced weapons. Xi presided over the parade of these capabilities in the celebration of the Party's 70th anniversary of its rule. He is keen to claim that the CCP is developing a fighting PLA. Aggressive Chinese moves in the South and East China Sea to assert Chinese sovereignty also plays to nationalist sentiment, a trope appealing to many Chinese and a move calculated to strengthen the CCP's hold over Chinese consciousness.

Besides heading the Military Commission, Xi's control of security forces also extends to the units dedicated to suppressing civil unrest. Since 2011 spending on internal police and security forces actually exceeded that of the military.[62] The first priority of these two security forces is to protect the Party and President Xi's "core" leadership position. When all other non-coercive means to control the state and civil society fail, the PLA and internal security forces ensure the Party's survival and interests. National security interests and Party survival are different sides of the same coin. What is good for the CCP is always good for China and the Chinese people, but not necessarily vice versa.

The CCP will not tolerate dissent. Critics and reformist activists are quickly harassed, silenced, or imprisoned. Some perish at the hands of security units. Lui Xiaobo, a liberal critic of the Party, died in prison although he had been awarded the Nobel Peace Prize in 2010. President Xi also brooks no opposition. Xu Zhiyong, a distinguished civil rights law professor and lecturer at Beijing University, was imprisoned in 2020 for the publication of a lengthy critique of Xi Jinping's policy failures and for his call for greater freedom and political reform.[63] Hong Kong booksellers who published materials viewed as critical of Beijing were jailed, including a Hong Kong resident holding Swedish citizenship. Ren Zhiqiang, a billionaire businessman on charges of alleged bribery and corruption, was sentenced to 18 years in prison after criticizing President Xi and the CCP's handling of the coronavirus epidemic.[64] Human rights advocates and activists pressing for greater regime liberalization have suffered the same fate of imprisonment.

Religious objections to CCP rule are especially targeted for suppression in Tibet and among the Muslim Uighurs. An estimated 124 concentration camps incarcerate approximately one million Muslims in western China, notably in Xinjiang province.[65] Files leaked by a Chinese official to *the New York Times* describe President Xi's direct involvement in creating these euphemistically described "vocational skills and education and training centers."[66] The ultimate solution to the Uighur resistance is a program to limit Uighur births, a slow-moving genocide. Women are force-fed birth control pills, surreptitiously sterilized, or forced to undergo abortion. Between 2015 and 2018, birth rates in some Uighur areas fell by 60 percent. In 2019, China's national birth rate declined by 4.2 percent, while falling by 24 percent in Xinjiang.[67] CCP strategy toward Tibet is to facilitate Han immigration to flood the indigenous population and swamp its culture and religion.[68]

Freedom House reports China as among the least free states of the world. On a scale of 1 to 7, with 7 scoring least free, China scored 6.5/7 for freedom, 7/7 for political rights, and 6/7 for civil liberties. China's aggregate score was 14/100, zero signifying least free.[69] What these ratings overlook, however, is the Party's decision to allow a measured degree of relatively free personal and group behavior as long as the Party is not criticized or its power weakened and undermined. NGO activities cover a vast set of areas – health, education, sports, business, finance, etc. Over a half-million NGOs are registered in China. Their existence evidence what would on the surface appear to be a densely rich, if politically contained, civil society. That optimistic gloss obscures a more sinister motivation behind Party tolerance of NGOs.

All NGOs must register and their activities are carefully scrutinized. Foreign NGOs have especially come under Party oversight. Their number has progressively diminished as the Xi regime has severely restricted the contact of Chinese citizens with these groups. From President Xi's perspective, controlling China's NGOs is designed not as a way to permit greater freedom for Chinese citizens but as a key strategy to widen and deepen Party penetration of civil society, NGOs are enlisted as Party mechanisms to direct Chinese social life.[70]

CCP tolerance of these NGOs, even their encouragement when their activities support policy objectives, applies Mao Zedong's mass-line strategy. Party engagement with these NGOs is in President Xi's estimation a mechanism to widen and deepen the Party's penetration of civil society.[71] Party members are assigned to track the work of targeted NGOs to ensure conformity with Party rules, narratives, and expectations. Party consultation with groups within civil society occurs over a host of policy issues, affecting health, education, transportation, and environmental issues. These consultations in no way limit or weaken the Party's power, nor do they hold out the prospect that they might mutate into regularized patterns of power-sharing and become institutionalized as adjuncts to governmental processes. This mechanism of Party control is termed "consultative authoritarianism,"[72] defined as "a system that includes consultation in a selective manner, but remains distinctly authoritarian without direct accountability of the state (or Party) to society."[73]

Tracking NGOs and selective consultations with Chinese citizens and organizations are elements of a greater Party campaign to place every Chinese citizen and enterprise under continuous Party surveillance. China is the leading user of surveillance cameras. By 2017 the Chinese surveillance network comprised 176 million cameras. Plans are to increase this number to 626 million. Tied to this surveillance network is the Chinese development of facial recognition tech-nology. If fully perfected to cover the Chinese population, the Party would then be able to identify every Chinese citizen personally anywhere in the country. The possible use of these technologies is limitless.

The introduction of the Social Credit System (SCS) is designed to deepen state control to the level of the individual citizen. Digital technology affords the CCP the capacity to develop a nationwide Social Credit System to cover the entire population. More than 30 bureaucratic agencies collect data about the habits and activities of Chinese citizens who fall within their orbits. In 2015 the govern-ment directed private enterprises, like Alibaba, China's Amazon, to develop a social-credit platform for governmental use.

Data from these state and private sources refer to such varied matters as taxes paid, traffic violations, personal finances, shopping habits, online social media commentary, and Chinese Facebook contacts with friends and the like. These reports are synthesized for each person and are scored. Individual scores deter-mine whether a person can get personal loans, a job, use high-speed trains or book an airline ticket. Added to these data are DNA markers and fingerprints to fill out the personal profile of each citizen. Security officials are also collecting blood samples from men and boys from across the nation to build a genetic map of China's roughly 700 million males, giving the authorities a powerful means of surveillance of the population.[74] The availability of big data technology makes it possible to integrate these surveillance mechanisms in one giant system to con-trol the Chinese peoples generally and each Chinese citizen individually.

Whatever the official explanation for the CCP's surveillance system, such as a means to catch criminals, the political result of these vast and relentless amassings of personal information is both to progressively narrow the private space of every Chinese citizen and to have readily available to Party and governmental authori-ties a running, detailed, up-to-date profile of the doings and thinking of each Chinese citizen. That information is valuable to proactively blunt opposition or criticism of the government and Party. The data also provides guidance about how to tailor messages to the diversity of Chinese citizens and organizations to control the public narrative of Party policies and thereby enhance Party control. Once the SCS is fully up and running, the system will provide the CCP with new tools to control the Chinese population at the ground, personal level.[75] Big Data outdoes Orwell's Big Brother.

The surveillance system works in tandem with the almost total Party-state control of information reaching the population. The CCP has erected a "Great Firewall." It blocks Chinese access to messages and information damaging to the CCP or its policies over the internet. The Party has hired two million paid inves-tigators to report violating websites. Chinese websites under private ownership are enlisted in this massive censorship program. Instead of Google, Facebook, and Twitter, which are denied access to Chinese websites, the Chinese have created, respectively, Baida, Renren, and Sina to monitor internet and social media.[76]

In May 2013, the CCP's Document 9 provided a template of forbidden subjects to be discussed whether online or in classrooms. Included in these prohibitions were discussions of "universal values, civil rights, civil society, press freedoms, judicial independence, past mistakes of the communist party, and the newly wealthy and politically connected capitalist class."[77] Complementing the "Great Firewall" is the CCP's control of all forms of print, broadcast journalism, and TV. The Party's *Peoples Daily* is the largest newspaper group in China with a readership of three million. China Central Television is the predominant state TV system with a network of 50 channels and is accessible to a billion viewers. Most Chinese receive their information and knowledge of the outside world from these sources.

This elaborate control system has two intertwined objectives. On the one hand, a pall of censorship and self-censorship shrouds all information coming into Chinese homes. On the other, media control in all of its forms provides the CCP with the means of fabricating an unblemished, errorless record of the CCP's history and its contributions to the security and welfare of the Chinese people. Media control is also a powerful mobilization tool to galvanize public support for CCP domestic and foreign policies. The Party is effectively employing all forms of media at its disposal to instill pride in the Chinese people about how far China has come in so short a time to become a world power as a consequence of CCP rule.

In President Xi's celebration of the 70th anniversary of CCP's conquest of China, he spoke in glowing terms of the seemingly seamless progress of China's wealth and power as the result of the Party's leadership. Loudly silent were references to the disasters of the Great Leap Forward, the Cultural Revolution, or the uprisings against Party rule in Tiananmen Square and, contemporaneously, in 130 other Chinese cities.[78] History was being rewritten to eliminate conscious knowledge of these anti-Party uprisings. Document 9 forbids media or classroom discussion of these vastly costly Party-initiated disasters. All that has happened to China since the rise of the Chinese Communist Party is presented as having benefited China and the Chinese people. Those engaged in preserving this sordid history in violation of the Party's revisionism are, like other critics, harassed, suppressed, incarcerated, and even put to death. History is not so much at an end as it is outlawed to sustain Party rule. Even history is cast into the dustbin of history.

These instruments of thought control at the disposal of the Party play a critical role in its claim to "performance legitimacy." The CCP insists incessantly that it alone is responsible for ending China's humiliation; for defining and defending China's borders with 14 of its neighbors; for extending China's sovereignty over the East and South China Sea; for lifting tens of millions of Chinese from poverty; for creating a modern, technologically advanced military, increasingly on a par with Western adversaries; for creating a nuclear capability to deter aggression against China; for leading the world in green technologies and the campaign against greenhouse gases; and for advancing President Xi's Chinese dream.

These instruments of thought control provide the CCP a mechanism to relent-lessly proclaim its legitimacy as a derivative of its economic success and China's rise as a global power. "Performance legitimacy" substitutes for the consent of the governed. It provides evidence of the Party's historic existential role as the vanguard of a global socialist revolution.[79]

The Party actively promotes its indispensability. Illustrative is the Party's cam-paign to stimulate Chinese patriotism (and implicit support of the Party) through films, like "My People, My Country." Douban, a Chinese film review site, gave the film a high score, 8.1 out of 10. The film sold 200 million tickets in five days. 73 million Chinese visited the soundtrack on Tencent video, a private social media platform under Party oversight and supervision.[80] Films, like this, are also being used in school classrooms to foster pride in students as Chinese citizens. Inspiring national pride and loyalty to the Party translates as increased power for the Party under the guise of its claim to inherent legitimacy as a Marxist–Leninist Party.[81] The CCP is also attentive to censoring forms of entertainment reaching the Chinese public which might cast a negative light on the Party. As *The Economist* notes,

> The party no longer monopolises entertainment. But it still writes the rules. Closed off from the world by firewalls and import controls, China's internet and cultural industries have become cartels, rewarding the loyal and the biddable. That gives censors all the power they need.[82]

Whither the CCP?

What may be difficult to fathom for partisans of liberal democracy is the fact that, through carrots, sticks, and effective propaganda, it would appear that a significant portion of the Chinese population supports the CCP. As the CCP's assumption of rule over Hong Kong reveals, the CCP can mobilize the Chinese population to accept its narrative that the city's incorporation into Chinese law was necessary to preclude its secession. The rising income of tens of millions of Chinese to middle-class standards as well as the unprecedented lifting of millions more out of abject poverty furnishes the Party with widespread support. There appears to be no groundswell within Chinese civil society to reform the Party to adopt liberal democratic practices. Even if there were latent pressure for reform, the CCP's ability to suppress dissent, even modest criticism, remains formidable in its depth and national sweep. What is noteworthy is that the Party's develop-ment of an impressive array of mechanisms, notably its extensive use of digital, big data, and media instruments to manufacture the support it seeks, largely preempts the need to use force to quell opponents.[83]

CCP leadership from Mao through Deng Xiaoping, Jiang Zemin, Hu Jintao, and now to Xi Jinping have uniformly insisted on building socialism with Chinese characteristics. Applying that ideological commitment has radically varied from one leadership cadre to the other. Despite fundamental changes in inner-Party governance, the Party has been able to sustain its monopoly of power – and violence. The Chinese today, whether intimidated or reconciled to authoritarian rule, exhibit no inclination to press for Party reform. Indeed, public sentiment in China sided with the CCP in imposing its will on Hong Kong to stop protests against Beijing interference in how Hong Kong is governed. No less than its predecessors, the Xi Jinping regime is adamantly opposed to sharing power with the Chinese people or with their elected representatives.

The currently deep political, economic, and social divisions within Western states – notably the United States and Great Britain – bolster the CCP's claim that allowing splits within Chinese civil society would visit untold harm on the Chinese people, reversing the progress that the Party proclaims without respite it has afforded them. Better then for many to accede to the CCP's version of Leninist democratic centralism. In a 2016 publication, Bruce Dickson furnishes data that many Chinese actually believe that the nation is actually becoming more open, free, and democratic.[84] In a succeeding volume he offered public opinion data to support the proposition that, given the CCP's economic performance as well as increased increase upward mobility and access to education, health, a clean environment, etc., most Chinese appear willing to support the regime. Issues, like human rights and personal freedom, competitive elections, the rule of law, and other principles of liberal democracy, do not command widespread interest or support.[85] Note how the CCP ably marshaled public opinion to support its crackdown on Hong Kong's resistance to CCP rule by framing Hong Kong demonstrations as incipient efforts to declare its independence. In any event, the Party has been successful until now in precluding an alternative to its rule arising from civil society. It would appear that the silent (and silenced) Chinese majority submits to the CCP's conviction of its indispensability, a trope tirelessly repeated by President Xi. As Qinglian He observes: "In the CCP's view, the death of the Party would mean nothing less than the death of China itself."[86]

The global financial breakdown of 2008, which the Chinese weathered better than many of the Western states, further strengthens resistance to Western-like economic or political reform. Party drumbeat on the breakdown of the Western economic model results by default to further popular acquiescence in CCP rule. At this juncture in the evolution of CCP governance of China, it is clear that for the foreseeable future China will continue to be ruled by an authoritarian regime, increasingly moving under the Xi regime to the totalitarian model described in Hannah Arendt's *Sources of Totalitarianism*.[87] The endgame is to level all of the Chinese people. All will be equal and equally dependent on the Party. All will be beholden to President Xi and the CCP. What is disquieting is the realization that the CCP possesses surveillance and coercive instruments far exceeding those available to the Nazi and Stalinists regimes to which Arendt was referring. Party members and ordinary citizens are also expected to read and absorb President Xi Jinping's "Little Red Book," reminiscent of Mao Tse-tung's Little Red Book. Xi's primer collects together his speeches, thoughts, and dream for China. Over a billion copies have been published.[88] All of the CCP's 3.6 million grassroots organizations are expected to distribute copies of the book. Where coercion may be unable to extract support for the Xi regime, indoctrination may otherwise produce the same and more lasting result.

Prudence dictates that it is important to identify structural flaws in CCP rule and, especially, weaknesses in Xi Jinping's control of the Party. Otherwise, the admittedly formidable power of the CCP can be exaggerated, warping balanced evaluation, and prompting potentially counterproductive responses to influence CCP policies and behavior in productive ways. Recall that many in the West also believed that the Soviet Union would survive in perpetuity; that the bipolar, US–Soviet world was stable;[89] that Moscow's hold over Eastern Europe was permanent; that the two Germanys would never unite; or that the Western democracies would never emerge as the dominant coalition in international relations in the wake of the implosion of the Soviet Union. These unanticipated disruptions caution against the resigned expectation that unquestioned CCP power and China's rise as the dominant power in the world inexorably portend the future.

CCP rule reveals two principal flaws. The first is existential and insurmountable for a regime resting ultimately on sheer power and violence.[90] It can never claim legitimacy, defined as the free consent of the Chinese people. This is not a trivial point. It can rule for an indeterminate period of time, relying on its coercive and economic power. Or it can assuage a population through transactional bargains, their exchange of freedom for welfare gains, to elicit their acquiescence. But the survival of the regime itself, independent of these pragmatic contractual arrangements, remains fundamentally problematic. The unpredictable and punctuated uprising of the Chinese people populations against foreign or domestic oppression since the start of industrialization and modernization testify to the fragility of authoritarian rule in China. Nor should the CCP's sustained abuse of civil liberties and human rights and the pervasive suppression of dissent be discounted in assessing its prospects for continuing to rule with an iron hand.

The second flaw, which we will get to in a moment, can be remedied through economic and political reform, as William Overholt suggests.[91] While *China's Crisis of Success* invites new thinking about how to address the impasse, the Xi regime prefers to rely on the CCP's power to ride out the crisis rather than address the shortcomings of the Chinese economy. Leninist centralized rule places Party and its ruling clique over the interests of the Chinese people.

Since the Party must rule by power, in its many coercive and non-coercive forms, fear that the Party or its leaders will be overthrown underlies the thinking and behavior of successive Chinese Communist leaders, stretching from Mao to Xi. How else to explain the preoccupation of the leadership with retaining control over the Party (Mao) or the Chinese people (Deng and Tiananmen). Xi's reversion to a Maoist solution to rule over a billion Chinese manifests that fear and the insecurity it generates in the Xi regime's pervasive surveillance of the Chinese peoples and suppression of all dissent on the Chinese mainland. It also explains the decision of the National Party Congress to pass legislation that provides for Beijing's direct rule over Hong Kong.[92] The CCP hypocritically invoked the formula of "One Country Two Systems" as its justification to prevent Hong Kong from proclaiming its independence from Beijing and CCP rule.

The CCP's illegitimacy remains a persistent threat to its monopoly of power and to its very existence. For the CCP, Tiananmen, as Glenn Tiffert observes, is

> the source of an inner trauma that has been triggered repeatedly by the fall of European communism, the Arab Spring, and successive color revolutions. It brings those distant events home, makes them concrete, and imbues them with vicarious, unnerving significance. Tiananmen is also the subtext that sustains the Party's singular fixation on the demise and disintegration of the Soviet Union.[93]

The CCP's crackdown in the spring of 2020 to curb mass demonstrations in Hong Kong and incarcerate opponents illustrates how fearful the CCP and Xi are of losing control. The sedition law is written so broadly that there are no defined criteria to determine the seditious behavior of Hong Kong citizens. The law even extends to foreigner critics who are vulnerable to imprisonment if they appear in Hong Kong. Sedition is what the CCP says it is.

The continued autonomy of Taiwan, the remaining fragment of the "One Country Two Systems" policy threatens Party rule. Taiwan provides what the CCP cannot: an example of a freely elected representative democracy as well as expanded civil liberties and human rights, protected by an independent judiciary who apply the rule of law, and not law as a tool of rule. The Taiwan regime, like South Korea and Japan, is also a model of effective government. South Korea and Japan, in alliance with the United States, provide for the security and economic welfare of their populations and protect personal and group freedoms. The existence of these regimes in China's backyard undermines the CCP's claim that only a government, modeled on the CCP, can provide these imperatives of government. The CCP is not prepared to take its chances on an electoral test of its public support.

The transition to democracy, if the American and French revolutions are any guide, is a long-term process. There is also no fixed endpoint to the process, no End of History,[94] even in the highly unlikely event that all regimes became democratic. Each generation develops its own conception of democracy. Note the long and bloody evolution of the struggle to achieve human rights in the United States, notably the four centuries of efforts to end racism. All of the Western democratic states continue to experience the inherent process of renewal of the social contract between their populations and the state. When Choi En-lai was allegedly asked his opinion about the end of the uprising against the De Gaulle regime in France in 1968, he is alleged to have said, "It's too early to tell."[95] The possibility of the CCP's demise or at least its weakening cannot be ruled out in light of the upheavals dogging its history and the uprisings against oppression that now punctuate all continents and regions of the world, a trend also offset and attenuated simultaneously by the erosion of liberal democracy.[96] Free government is not a free good. It's too early to tell which regime – democratic or authoritarian – will prevail in the long run to govern globalization.

The extreme measures instituted by the CCP, subsequently expanded upon by President Xi, to repress dissent and to systemically violate human rights reflect the fears shared by successive CCP leaders that their rule by fiat does not ensure their monopoly of power. It is remarkable that Chinese human rights and democracy advocates choose imprisonment and the prospect of death when incarcerated.[97] Some close China watchers observe that interest in opening China to greater freedom is still much abroad among Chinese citizens, however much its expression is repressed.[98] Elizabeth Economy sees cracks in Xi's crackdown on opposition. Her research finds that "the political values and spirit of collective action embodied in the 1989 democracy movement have endured and even thrived."[99] The #MeToo movement has reached China. A reported 31 million Chinese discussed sexual harassment on WeChat in just one month. Chinese workers have also joined in demanding that their grievances be heard. In 2018 more than 1,700 labor protests were recorded. Other segments of Chinese society are restive – intellectuals, workers losing jobs to technology, and various groups opposed to Xi's cult of personality, his dismissal of succession procedures, and his anti-corruption campaign to eliminate rivals.

These disruptions suggest that there exists an underlying resistance to the totalitarian state that Xi is imposing on 1.4 billion Chinese. The majority may well be mostly Han in racial and ethnic identity, but they are more diverse and differentiated by locale, region, language, age groups, social and economic status, occupation, and intellectual, ideological, and religious thinking than the Party's portrayal of a Chinese monolith marching in lockstep to CCP's drum. That very complexity provides avenues for open spaces to frustrate the regime's efforts to homogenize the population.

The sensitivity of the Xi regime to criticism, even over what would appear to be trivial incidents, is illustrated in its swift reaction to the Tweet of Houston Rockets General Manager, Daryl Morey. His "Fight for Freedom. Stand with Hong Kong" Tweet prompted the immediate cancellation of National Basketball Association games in China and the withdrawal of Chinese commercial television sponsorship of NBA games. Calls were issued from Beijing to fire Morey.[100] Using its control of print, television, and social media, Xi depicted the Hong Kong protests as a movement for independence. Framed as a threat to China's sovereignty rather than as a demand for freedom, Xi and the CCP galvanized Chinese nationalism and patriotism to garner support for the eventual elimination of Hong Kong's autonomy.

Foreign corporations are also required to tow the CCP line or face economic penalties. Apple was pressured to withdraw its HKmap.live app, aiding Hong Kong protesters to track police. It had previously been compelled to withdraw another app, providing access to Quartz, a news organization that ran afoul of Chinese censors. Apple's $44 billion in profits in China was a strong incentive to cooperate with Beijing.[101] Four American airlines – American, United, Hawaiian, and Delta – eliminated mention of Taiwan at Beijing's insistence. Censorship and proactive appeasement also work. An animated movie, "Abominable," released by Dreamworks, used a map of China that encompassed the entire South China Sea. Marriott fired a social media manager who Tweeted support for Tibetan independence.[102] The Xi government is not content to silence criticism at home. Using the buying power of the Chinese economy, it relentlessly seeks to still foreign attacks, too.[103] Conversely, the CCP defends its oppressive rule by attacking the West and the United States for human rights violations greater than those that have been lodged against the CCP.[104]

Whether China's multiple and accumulating problems will prove fatal to the CCP regime and Xi's rule (the two should be distinguished), remains problematic. The instruments of control available to the CCP work in tandem to frustrate domestic reforms, which might afford citizens more space for the exercise of their freedoms. There are also no visible countervailing pressures arising within the Party, the military, or Chinese society to constrain the totalitarian bent and expansive foreign ambitions of the CCP under President Xi's direction. Xi can rely on the pride of the Chinese people in China's rise as a global power.

There are growing signs that the Xi regime will rely increasingly on a narrative that China was principally responsible for the victory over Japan.[105] The apparent aim of this shift from a victimized China to an image of a militarily strong China and its victory in the global war against Fascism is to imbue the CCP with moral legitimacy, which economic performance and consumerism cannot achieve. China (and the CCP) can now be depicted as having been not only among the architects of the postwar world but also an upholder of the existing international order, which it seeks to displace. No less than the liberal democracies and the Soviet Union, the CCP portrays China as "at the creation" – or, in this interpretation of what Professor Rana Mitter calls *China's Good War*,[106] China's CCP is at the "re-creation." The United Nations Charter, which rests on state sovereignty and, initially, on non-interference in the domestic politics of member states, suits the CCP's model of a Westphalian system with Chinese characteristics.

Professor Ian Johnson observes that "[f]or the Chinese Communist Party, history is legitimacy."[107] To rely on history to justify its rule, the CPP must, paradoxically, suppress history to use it. The CCP not only fought Japanese forces in World War II, it also concentrated much of its forces in a civil war against Chiang Kai-shek's nationalists. The nationalists, not the CCP, did most of the fighting against Japan. They signed the UN Charter, not the CCP. There is also the CCP's responsibility for the Great Leap Forward, the Cultural Revolution, and continuing and increasingly egregious violations of human rights. These unfortunate episodes must be interned into a black hole, reminiscent of George Orwell's *1984* portrayal of the end of history. Attacking history has to be perpetual and resolute. Efforts to remember the Tiananmen massacre of June 4, 1989, must be annually suppressed.[108]

In light of the CCP's capacity to twist Marxism ideology to justify fundamental shifts in regime OWL strategies, it is likely that the CCP and President Xi will have little difficulty with this latest iteration of hypocrisy to serve the CCP's power needs.

As the product both of an effective propaganda machine and extensive national school programs, many Chinese acknowledge the CCP's claim that China's rise as a global power is solely, or largely, due to the Party. In a nutshell, the CCP message is clear and unequivocal: no CCP, no China, and no China as a global power,

What leverage the Western states can effectively exert on China to accede to liberalize its rule is tenuous. The CCP has considerable resources at its disposal to confront Western pushback. China possesses the largest financial reserves of any state. These reserves provide the CCP and President Xi with large margins of error to work with. China can tolerate considerable waste, inefficiency, and corruption and still compete with the economies of the United States and the West, the pushbacks of the democracies notwithstanding.[109]

This evaluation of the CCP's relentless, but flawed and failed, pursuit of power under the guise of legitimacy, understood as free consent to rule, leads to the disquieting conclusion that its success in holding and enlarging its power as a substitute for authentic legitimacy has been successful so far. As more than one scholar has observed, authoritarian, certainly totalitarian, regimes like China, Vietnam, Cuba, and Venezuela (and the former Soviet Union), can govern, seemingly indefinitely, without consent.[110] The stability of CCP rule and, notably, its increased assertiveness and influence abroad under Xi's dictation means that China is now a formidable and credible adversary in determining how the Imperatives of Order, Welfare, and Legitimacy will define global governance. Specifically, China's unwavering authoritarian rule, whether in its softer or harder versions between Mao and Xi, joins the issue of whether repressive regimes can sustain continued economic growth without having to liberalize CCP rule.

Xi's China offers itself as a loadstar for other authoritarian regimes or wannabes. In promoting a Westphalian system with Chinese characteristics, Xi and the CCP actively support authoritarian regimes, ranging from Sudan, Russia, to Venezuela. It has already demonstrated an unsettling capacity to quash democratic and human rights criticism of its oppressive rule at home and abroad through an impressive array of soft and hard power. How can the Western democracies meet the Chinese challenge of determining the governance of the global society? Before I turn to that question in the concluding chapter, the Russian solution to global governance requires our attention.

Notes

1 Xia (2021). Brown (2017a, 2017b) agrees.
2 See Mao Zedong, *Problems of War and Strategy* M Zedong – Selected Works of Mao Zedong, 1938.
   www.dia.mil › China_Military_Power_FINAL_5MB_20190103.
   See p. 16.

3 Rousseau (1978). Given the current corruption of the term "contract" by the admin-istration of President Donald J. Trump, in which all political relations were reduced to contingent personal relations or to economic transactions, I prefer to interpret Rousseau's conception of the social *contract* as a social *compact*. The latter implies contemporaneously a deeper and more profound relation between ruler and ruled and a communal bond among the ruled than the translator's choice of contract. So when I use the translator's "contract," I really mean compact since it appears closer to Rousseau's meaning as the basis for legitimacy contra Hobbes.

4 Ibid., p. 46.

5 Ibid., pp. 46–47. (Italics added to underscore the privileged position assigned by Rousseau to legitimacy over material power.)

6 For purposes of simplicity I will refer throughout to Marxism rather than to Marxist–Leninist doctrine. I mean both since the CCP is a Leninist Party in the service of Marxist doctrine.

7 Havel (1978).

8 I owe this insight to Elizabeth Economy: Economy (2018).

9 Overholt (2016) makes this compelling point, predicting that Xi Jinping's tenure will depend on whether he can deliver on his promise to strengthen the Party. Brown (2017a and b) makes a similar point, but emphasizes the Party's monopoly of violence and coercive power to deter opposition to its rule.

10 Mao (1967, p. 126).

11 Li (2016, p. 7–8). Li's observation of the Party's pliant and pragmatic ability to reform itself for purposes of survival is echoed earlier by China experts in the form of "authoritarian resilience." See, for example, Nathan (2003). Li actually takes issue with the Party's ability to continue to adapt to new circumstances both in the volume cited here and in an earlier article (Li, 2012). Note that the volume cites the author as Cheng Li, but the article is cited as Li, Cheng. I have cited sources as they appear in book or article form.

12 See Hsu (2012); Kampen (2000); MacFarquhar and Schoenhals (2006).

13 Dikotter (2016); MacFarquhar and Schoenhals (2006).

14 Ibid. See also two indispensable works covering both crises by the Chinese histo-rian, Yang Jisheng (Jisheng, 2013, 2020).

15 Beeching (1975).

16 The quote is drawn from a review of Julia Lovell's *Maoism: A Global History, New York Review of Books*, September 15, 2019, p. 17. For a full account, consult Lovell (2019).

17 Lüthi (2016).

18 Quoted in Dickson (2016, p. 249). I have relied heavily on Dickson's stress on the Party's priority of survival. As a friendly amendment to his comprehensive review of the multiple ways in which the CCP has maintained its monopoly of power, I prefer to view its conception of legitimacy in instrumental terms. What Dickson and the CCP view as the legitimation of its rule – e.g., tolerating NGOs – I view as support mechanisms of Party power and influence. Absent the free and unfettered consent of the Chinese people to authorize their governance, China remains an authoritar-ian Party-state. From a liberal democratic perspective it is illegitimate. Moreover, it forfeits the power conveyed by the consent of the citizens it rules. The Party is totally bereft of moral authority to govern its own population, its claims otherwise notwithstanding. The democracies and their free populations will be unable to resist the power of China and other authoritarian regimes unless they fully grasp the chal-lenge confronting them for the remainder of this century: to prevail in the endless struggle between freedom and tyranny. See Hannah Arendt (1963).

19 Xiaoping (1985, p. 3).

20 Bell (2015); Overholt (2018) affirm this meritocratic element of Party rule despite the pervasive corruption throughout the system at all levels of government.

21 Vogel (2011). Vogel's biography of Deng Xiaoping makes clear Deng's devotion to the Party on which his power and that of all Chinese Communist leaders depend.

22 Zhao (1993) describes the power struggle within the CCP over Deng's reforms.

23 Kurt Campbell and Ely Ratner trace the gradual disillusionment in official Western policy circles with China as a reliable partner in developing a rule-based global system of governance (Campbell and Ratner, 2018). *The Economist* devoted the lead story of its March 3–9, 2018 issue, "How the West Got China Wrong," to the same issue. There were early dissenters from the consensus about China's eventual democratization. See Mann (2007); McGregor (2010). Bruce Dickson's critique of modernization theory's projection of the expected movement of authoritarian systems toward open societies as a consequence of economic and technological progress is of particular interest. See Dickson (2016; pp. 234–242). For a survey of modernization theory, consult Inglehart (2005, 2018).

24 Xiaoping (1985, pp. 65–66).

25 Campbell and Ratner (2018).

26 https://foreignpolicy.com › 2010/10/08 › charter-08

27 Quoted in the Chinese state newspaper, *Global Times*, June 15, 2011. www.globaltimes.cn/content/661734.shtml.

28 Jie (2013).

29 Dickson (2016), Consult especially Chapters 5 and 6 on Party support, pp. 114–300,

30 See, for example, Bell (2015); Inglehart (2005); Overholt (2018).

31 Economy (2018).

32 McGregor (2019) describes the pushback against Chinese expansion. Overholt's perceptive critique of Xi's strategic moves highlights the contradiction between insularity at home and globalization abroad. See Overholt (2018).

33 Relevant is the CSIS report on Chinese use of soft power. See McGiffert (2009). For a broader discussion of politics and culture, consult Roberts (2016). In 2016 China supported 439 Confucius Centers in 114 states (Heath et al., 2016, p. 5).

34 Cited by Ian Johnson, "A Most Adaptable Party," *New York Review of Books*, July 1, 2021, p. 36.

35 Dikotter (2016; pp. 42–43).

36 Saich (2015) provides an extensive description of the Chinese government at all levels.

37 A brief but pointed discussion of Xi's rise to power is found in Brown (2017b). Also useful is Economy (2018), Chapter 2, pp. 20–54, and Dikotter (2016, pp. 1–77).

38 Li (2016). This work is useful in reviewing the post-Deng period of collective leadership up to the election of Xi Jinping as Party Secretary. Cheng Li's exhaustive evaluation of collective leadership has since been overtaken by Xi's centralized control of the Party and the personalization of his rule, reminiscent of Mao Zedong.

39 Overholt (2018).

40 Shirk (2018) develops these points.

41 The color associated with the revolutions, respectively, in Ukraine, Georgia, and Tunisia were orange, rose, and jasmine.

42 Dikotter (2016, pp. 12–13) lists these posts.

43 Brown (2017) develops the sources of Party's institutional, ideological, and personal power in more detail than can be attempted here.

44 Shirk (2018, p. 26). In his speech commemorating the anniversary of the CCP's victory in 1949, Xi repeated his gratitude to the thought of his predecessors and, implicitly, that his new thinking, as his addition to this Pantheon, squares with theirs as the "core" of the CCP's leadership of the Chinese people. www.fmprc.gov.cn › mfa_eng › topics_66567

45 The "Three Represents" refers to Jiang Zemin's program to recruit entrepreneurs and other socioeconomic players in the CCP. See Dikotter (2016, p. 25). See also

Xia (2021) for a description of the "Three Represents and its importance in the evolution of CCP doctrine from Mao to Xi."

46 President Xi Jinping's address to the 19th National Congress of the CCP, November 3, 2017. www.xinhuanet.com/english/special/2017-11/03/c_136725942.htm, p. 15.

47 Kerry Brown describes the development of Xi's personality as a source of power, including a spouse who is a celebrated Chinese singer. See Brown, Chapter 2, "Xi the Man," pp. 49–105 (Brown, 2017b). (Shirk, 2018) shares this view. Xi's writings are also pertinent in framing him a cult figure (Xi, 2014), see also Google Images of President Xi Jinping, which visually reinforce his personal power.
www.gettyimages.com/photos/president-xi-jinping

48 See Orwell's essay, "The Prevention of Literature" published by permission of the Orwell Foundation. www.orwell.ru/library/essays/prevention/english/e_plit
Kerry Brown is close to Orwell on this point in comparing the CCP to the Catholic Church's Curia and to the Pope's infallibility (Brown, 2017a). Notes Brown:

> Again, the model of the Catholic Church becomes useful. If Party members are like religious believers, and the Central Committee is like the convocation of cardinals, the topmost Party leaders are like the Secretariat of the Vatican, and the general secretary, armed with doctrinal infallibility, like the Pope, is a rule-giver, spiritual nurturer and voice of doctrinal purity and correctness. p. 26.

Note the comparison of the CCP's and Xi's infallibility and George Kennan's long cable from Moscow about the sources of Soviet behavior, noted in Chapter 2. Perry Link makes the same point in a recent essay: Perry Link, "The CCP's Culture of Fear," New York Review of Books, October 21, 2021, pp. 23–25.

49 Ibid.
50 Quoted in an op-ed to the *New York Times*, June 4, 2020.
51 Ibid.
52 Cunningham and Fravel (2019).
53 This point is discussed at length in Chapter 4.
54 *New York Times*, June 4, 2020.
55 Brown (2017a; pp. 19–20). See also n. 1.
56 www.xinhuanet.com/english/2017-10/18/c_136687920.htm
Italics in the original. One might speculate about the origins of Xi's vision of a Chinese Dream. He is vulnerable to the criticism of plagiarism either in borrowing from Martin Luther King's "I Have a Dream" or, more generally, from the American cultural artifact of the "American Dream." See Adams (1931) for the source of the American Dream.
57 Pei (2016); Wedeman (2012).
58 Shirk (2018, p. 5).
59 This is a central theme of Hannah Arendt's *The Origins of Totalitarianism*. (Hannah Arendt, 1951).
60 www.phrases.org.uk/meanings/226950.html
61 Li (2016, p. 12).
62 Dickson (2016; p. 43).
63 For Professor Xu's profound critique of the CCP's rule and his call for reform, see his "Viral Alarm: When Fury Overcomes Fear," www.chinafile.com/reporting-opinion/viewpoint/viral-alarm-when-fury-overcomes-fear
64 www.gettyimages.com/photos/president-xi-jinping
65 https://freebeacon.com › national-security › network-of-chinese-concentrat.
66 *New York Times*, November 24, 2019. The leaked files are printed in a separate file in Chinese with English headline summaries in *New York Times*, November 16, 2019. A *The New York Times* report of September 23, 2020, notes that "China Is Building Vast New Detention Centers for Muslims in Xinjiang."

67 Report of *Washington Post*, June 29, 2020.
68 *New York Times*, September 24, 2020.
69 https://freedomhouse.org › report › freedom-world › 2018 › china
70 See President Xi's presentation of this use of NGOs and Party consultations with members of Chinese civil society in his remarks before the 19th National Congress of the Communist Party in 2017. www.xinhuanet.com/english/special/2017-11/03 /c_136725942.htm
71 Ibid.
72 Dickson (2016) makes a good case for the existence of a vigorous civil society within the limits set and enforced by the CCP. See Chapter 3, pp. 96–163.
73 Ibid., p. 103. See also (Teets, 2014).
74 *New York Times*, June 17, 2020.
75 Ibid., p. 60. This article provides an overview of the digitalization of Chinese totalitarian rule. See also Brown (2017a and b); Economy (2018).
76 Sina Weibo summarizes key Chinese social media platforms. See *New York Times*, November 19, 2018.
77 Dickson (2016, p. 45.
78 www.fmprc.gov.cn › mfa_eng › topics_66567
79 One is reminded of the Calvinist theological position that external wealth and high social status manifested God's chosen.
80 The success of these Party media efforts to instill patriotism in Chinese viewers and in classroom patriotic sessions is reviewed in *New York Times*, October 5, 2019, pp. B1 and B4.
81 Johnston (2016) offers data-based measures of Chinese nationalism. His data suggest less Party use of nationalism as a legitimating instrument than the literature he covers. Conversely, there is an informed body of scholarly work that traces the rise of nationalism in China well before the accession of Xi Jinping as Party Secretary. In lecturing at Beijing University and Shanghai University in the first decade of this century, I was struck that students, among the best and brightest in China, still viewed China as a victim despite the end of imperial control of China. They were also very proud that China had become a global power.
82 *Economist*, March 13, 2021, p. 39. The *Economist* also reports the issuance of a new series of textbooks to all students in Chinese schools, colleges, and universities to explain Xi Jinping's Thought on Socialism with Chinese characterisitcs. *Economist,* September 4, 2021, p. 34.
83 Dickson (2016) makes this point a central feature of his assessment of the CCP's power.
84 Dickson (2016; p. 16) and *passim*. Notes Dickson: "Most importantly, Chapter 6 will show that most Chinese believe the regime has become increasingly democratic throughout the post-Mao period and expect it to become more so in the near future." For an earlier view, doubling in brass on Dickson's findings, see Nathan (2003).
85 Dickson(2021), *passim*.
86 He (2003).
87 Hannah Arendt (1951).
88 www.bbc.com/news/blogs-china-blog-47236902.
89 Waltz (1981).
90 This theme of violence and CCP growth as a movement and its continued resort to force to survive and thrive is woven throughout Kerry Brown's evaluation of the regime (Brown, 2017a and b). Brown's view of the centrality of violence to Party rule is supported by the valuable work of Chinese historian, Hua Gao, who details the CCP's successful suppression of its critics, notably the Chinese intelligentsia, in Hua (2019).
91 Overholt (2018).
92 Yi-Zheng Lian, a former chief editor of the *Hong Kong Economic Journal*, outlines the oppressive measures imposed on Hong Kong in violation of its treaty obligations

with the United Kingdom in the transfer of Hong Kong to China in 1997. *New York Times*, July 1, 2020.
93 Tiffert (2019; pp. 38–39).
94 Fukuyama (1992).
95 It appears that Cho En-lai was referring to the uprising in France in 1968, not the French Revolution. See
www.scmp.com › article › not-letting-facts-ruin-good-story
96 Diamond (2019); Kurlantzick (2013); Levitsky and Ziblatt (2018); MacLean (2017); Przeworski (1986).
97 https://foreignpolicy.com › 2010/10/08 › charter-08
98 Economy (2019).
99 Ibid., p. 56.
100 https://twitter.com/dmorey
101 *New York Times*, October 11, 2019.
102 See the review by the *New York Times* of CCP efforts to discipline American corporations operating in China to adhere to Chinese censorship. *New York Times*, October 20, 2019, p. 8.
103 Simon Denyer recounts CCP efforts to control foreign companies through internal Communist Party cells that exercise influence over decision-making. See *Washington Post*, January 28, 2018.
104 See the Human Rights report of the Chinese Foreign Ministry
www.xinhuanet.com/english/2021-03/24/c_139832301.htm
105 Mitter (2020).
106 Ibid. There is a fundamental contradiction between the CCP's history of itself and China's history in World War II. The CCP's history begins with its formation in 1921 and culminates in its capture of the Chinese mainland in 1949. Which history has priority: war with Japan, beginning in the 1930s and ending in 1945 or 1921–1949? The two histories are not reconcilable.
107 Ian Johnson, "A Most Adaptable Party," *New York Review of Books*, July 1, 2021, p. 36.
108 Note *The New York Times* report of June 4, 2021, "Subdued but Not Silenced, Hong Kong Tried to Remember Tiananmen Massacre."
109 Economy (2018) makes this point that China can afford a great deal of waste and maintain growth. "China's deep pockets combined with its ability to limit foreign competition mean that it has the wherewithal to forge ahead despite the waste, inefficiency, and seeming weaknesses in innovative capacity." p. 133. Lee Ann, a business consultant with extensive first-hand knowledge of the Chinese economy, is optimistic about China's ability to address its weaknesses and to continue to be an attractive magnet for investment (Lee, 2018). David Bell, a longtime observer and commentator about Chinese politics and the economy is also bullish about China. He places great weight on the CCP's reliance on professional experts to run the economy, creating a meritocracy to counter corruption at home and strengthening Chinese competition abroad (Bell, 2015). Overholt strikes a middle position. He identifies a list of significant weaknesses in Chinese economic policy and practice. He believes they can be corrected, but the political will for reform currently remains problematic under Xi's authoritarian rule (Overholt, 2018).
110 Przeworski (1986). See also O'Donnell and Schmitter (1986).

7

THE RUSSIAN OWL SOLUTION FOR GLOBAL GOVERNANCE

Russian President Vladimir Putin's solution for global governance challenges the liberal democratic project across the entire spectrum of OWL imperatives. For Order, Putin champions a self-help global system of autonomous nation-states. He rejects enduring security alliances as threats to state sovereignty and independence. A state's material power, principally its military might, would determine the hierarchical order of a multipolar system. Alignments would be fluid and temporary, dictated by the changing convergences of state preferences and vital interests. Revived would be a Westphalian system with Russian characteristics.

For the Imperative of Welfare, Putin's Russia free rides on the public goods provided by a Western global market system to sustain its economic growth, while Putin's Kleptocracy, dominated and directed by state-controlled and subsidized private and public corporations under the control of Putin-appointed oligarchs, undermines a global rule-based free exchange system.

For the Imperative of Legitimacy, Putin proposes Russia's illiberal, populist, authoritarian regime as a model for other states. His understanding of democracy within a Westphalian system consists in investing legitimacy in a proliferation of faux elected presidents and prime ministers. These populist regimes would progressively populate the state system to comprise a majority. The Kantian ideal of a coalition of liberal democratic states, based on free and fair elections, as the basis for the legitimacy of global governance, would ultimately be subordinated to these multiplying authoritarian regimes. A nation-state system of a majority of nondemocratic regimes constitutes Putin's perverse notion of democracy.

Given that Putin conceives international politics as a zero-sum game of winners and losers, Western intervention in the affairs of other states, justified to protect civil liberties and extend universal human rights, is portrayed as a threat to the Russian state and to Putin's regime. These intrusions are also

DOI: 10.4324/9781003246572-7

condemned for destabilizing the domestic tranquility of states, for undermining their regimes, and for disrupting regional and global peace. Putin's world would purportedly create a virtuous circle of autocratic states within a multipolar system to contain what both Xi's China and Putin's Russia condemn as an unstable, war-prone Western system. A galaxy of illiberal democratic states – Turkey, Hungary, Poland, Venezuela, Egypt, Philippines, etc. – complemented by outright autocratic states, like Cuba, North Korea, and China – which do not hold elections – would frustrate the West's promotion of pluralist regimes, fractious liberal democratic politics, and ineffective rule, while ostensibly advancing peace among anti-democractic states in the bargain.

Universal human rights have no place in Putin's scheme. Putin prefers to open Pandora's box in which each state's specific history, culture, and values would determine a regime's legitimacy to underwrite its authoritarian rule. No matter that multiple forms of legitimacy would be pitted against each other. Putin's anarchic solution to the Imperative of Order complements his conflict-generating solution to the Imperative of Legitimacy. Putin's populist rule over a centralized Russian state is expected to navigate in this *sauve qui peut* global environment more adroitly and effectively than a liberal democracy. The endgame would be the reemergence of Russia as a global power.

Putin Russia's responses to OWL Imperatives[1]

The Imperative of Order

The United Nations Charter is the cornerstone of Putin's self-help, multipolar system. Under Article 2 all states in the General Assembly are accorded sovereign equality regardless of territorial size, population, endowments, or power. Each is also granted treaty protection against intervention in its domestic affairs.[2] For Putin, international law arises solely from interstate accords on rules, protocols, and processes. Putin insists that Russians enjoy human rights in scope and measure equal to and even superior to what prevails in the West. Turning Edmund Burke on his head,[3] Russian human rights are invested with Russian history, culture, values, and laws.

The UN Charter is relied upon in yet another way to support the Putin/Russian solution for global governance. According to Putin, the Charter assigns great powers, notably Russia, the United States, and China, primary responsibility for global security as Permanent Members of the Security Council. They enjoy a privileged status, not accorded other states, in a multipolar world. The practical result of this design is that the few will dominate the many. The assignation of big power status to the Soviet Union carries over to the Russian Federation. That transfer partially compensates for the implosion of the Soviet state, its Cold War loss, the subsequent diminution of Russian territory, military power, and the control of the multiple national peoples and states under previous Soviet imperial rule.

In an address to the Russian Parliament in 2005, Putin, a former Soviet KGB officer,[4] characterized the collapse of the Soviet Union as the greatest political disaster of the 20th century, a catastrophe of systemic proportions for international order as well as for the Russian state and people.[5] The overriding determinant of Putin's foreign policy is to increase Russia's hard and soft power to match its legal[6] and global status as a great power.

In this quest, Putin has seized on the UN Security Council's responsibility for security to assert Russia's right to be a party to any issue that it deems to be of substantial global or regional importance. Political arrangements between and among states are not fully binding and legitimate absent Russia's participation in their formulation and its approval of their realization. To this end Putin has defined security, the segway for UN Security Council intervention, in the broadest terms, well beyond a narrow and traditional notion of security focused largely on the use of force.[7] On February 12, 2007, at the Munich Conference on Security Policy, Putin observed, "It is well known that international security comprises much more than issues relating to military and political stability. It involves the stability of the global economy, overcoming poverty, economic security and developing a dialogue between civilizations."[8] Putin's ambitions for a renewal of Russia's big power role extends then to Moscow's potential intervention in any global issue of interest to Moscow on the strength of its privileged status in the UN Security Council. Putin's big power claims for Russia justified Moscow's armed intervention in Syria, Ukraine, Moldova, and Georgia and its meddling in democratic elections in the United States, Europe, and Africa.[9] As a self-proclaimed global power, answerable only to itself, its Security Council responsibilities merge with the pursuit of its national interests.

Putin insists that under his leadership Russia's return to great power status rests not only on the restoration of its economic and military power but also on its historic contributions to global peace and to the defeat of would-be hegemonic states. Putin reminds his detractors that, as a central member of the Westphalian system, Russia defeated Napoleon's attempt to impose French imperial rule over Europe. It also played, according to Putin's view, a central role in the post-Napoleonic Concert of Europe. The Concert preserved big power peace for a century until a fragile balance of power collapsed into World War I.[10] The Soviet Union's victory over Nazi Germany in World War II further establishes in Putin's mind that Russia is essential to maintain a global balance of power to ensure the independence and autonomy of all nation-states.

Borrowing from liberal democratic theorists,[11] Putin's Russia, not the United States, is presented as an indispensable member of what it projects as the need for a renewed trilateral Concert of the United States, China, and Russia to keep the peace. Such a Concert is Putin's friendly amendment to Hedley Bull's portrayal of the nation-state system as a society of states in which nation-state independence and domestic autonomy are the foundations of international law and global peace. The responsibility of the Concert to maintain a balance of power between each other and among the states of the system would ensure against any state dominating the system as a whole.[12]

Putin's Concert, if achieved, would position Russia to command the heights of global power from which it could weaken and unravel the Western system imposed on other states as its solution to the Imperative of Order. Conversely, a decentralized multipolar order would afford Moscow, as the purported key member of a tripolar Concert, the opportunity to arbitrate conflicts around the world – in Europe, the Balkans, the Middle East, and increasingly in Africa – even those between the three great powers. Russia's legal status and its purportedly increasing material power would anchor a revived, classical Westphalian system.[13] In a speech at the Valdai Club Conference in 2013, President Putin reminded the audience "that the Congress of Vienna in 1815 and the agreements made at Yalta in 1945, taken with Russia's very active participation, secured a lasting peace."

From global to regional power: Putin's Monroe Doctrine

Traditional Russian national interests define and qualify the scope of Russia's provision of global public goods to protect the sovereign equality and independence of nation-states around the world. These reassert Russia's regional hegemony in Eastern Europe. From Moscow's perspective there is no contradiction in these assertions of special status since big powers are the principal determiners of international law. Russia's neighbors are bound then to submit to Russia's will when its vital interests are at stake. Putin's version of Russia's Monroe Doctrine, as sanctioned by Moscow's version of international law, has two mutually supportive elements.[14]

The first is the preservation of the "Russian World" under Russian leadership in the aftermath of the demise of the Soviet Union. Soviet Marxist-Leninist ideology failed to hold the Russian World together. It was not up to the challenge of integrating the ethnic, national, cultural, and religious divisions within Russian society and those of the republics of the Soviet Union. Putin proposes to return Russia to the millennial ties of Russians everywhere, those who share Russia's unique history and language as well as its cultural, religious, and civilizing values. On the basis of this historically determined moral foundation, the Russian world would be restored and its reach extended and assured.

Russia's historically sanctified values and interests are incompatible with liberal Western principles of democratic rule and human rights. Putin contends that Western intervention into the domestic politics of the Russian Federation to install these principles forestalls the resurrection of a socially complex Russian World and impedes Russian regional hegemony. Putin, like Xi Jinping,[15] portrays Western claims of universal human rights as instruments of Western hegemonic domination.

Putin also stipulates Russia's unconditional right and obligation to protect Russians of the near abroad from discrimination and oppression by their host states.[16] Crimea's forceful integration into the Russian Federation in 2014, approved by the Russian Parliament and a national referendum, was in keeping with Putin's vision of a transnational "Russian World." That visionary ideal justified the absorption of new territories into the Russian Federation as well as Russia's interventions in the internal affairs of neighboring states to protect their minority Russian populations.

The creation of a Russian World bolsters Putin's notion of a Russian Monroe Doctrine in yet another way. It rationalizes Russian hegemony over its non-Russian neighbors. They are expected to submit to Russian geopolitical and economic interests as Moscow defines them. They are specifically constrained from entering into geopolitical or economic relations with the West, that is, the United States, NATO, or the European Union. These perceived threats to Russian regional hegemony largely explain Russian military intervention in Moldova, Georgia, and Ukraine during Putin's tenure as head of the Russian Federation. Russian troops, stationed in Transnistria, frustrate Moldova's efforts to pursue independent foreign and security policies. The Moldovan government, pro-Western and pro-European, is a clear challenge to Moscow's control over Moldovan foreign policy and to its irredentist aims in the wake of the collapse of the Soviet Union.

Russian forces also defeated a Western-leaning Georgia in 2008 to preclude any formal economic relation with the European Union or any likelihood that Georgia might join NATO. Russia recognized the Georgian enclaves of South Ossetia and Abkhazia as independent states, a move followed by six other authoritarian states, including the former Georgian enclaves.[17] These entities, along with Transnistria, are effectively satellites of Moscow and extensions of the Russian World. Russian troops in these enclaves are tripwires against any attempt by Georgia or Moldova to reclaim sovereignty over them.

Putin's twin drives to restore the Russian World as well as Russia's hegemony over its neighbors converge in his covert military intervention into Ukraine. From a historical perspective, this episode is nothing new. Russia's control or periodic absorption of Ukraine began as early as the 17th century. Intermittent periods of integration between the two states then followed.[18] The reemergence of an independent Ukraine in the wake of the collapse of the Soviet state sets the stage for Putin's determination to reestablish Russia's hegemony over Ukraine. A web of factors – geopolitical, cultural, religious, and economic – fuels Putin Russia's aim to ensure that Ukraine remains within Russia's sphere of influence along with Moldova, Georgia, Belarus, and the states of Central Asia and the South Caucasus.

At the Valdai Forum in September 2013, President Putin dated the entangling ties between Ukraine and Russia with the emergence of the Kievan Rus' a millennium ago, what Putin understood as the nucleus of the Russian state and, simultaneously, the Russian empire. In his mind, the Russian state and empire, including Ukraine, were fused from the start. That beginning destined Ukraine to be an integral member of the Russian World. Its independence today is hostage to that history. Putin acknowledges the current reality of an independent Ukraine, but it is not clear how long it will remain so:

> Ukraine, without a doubt is an independent state. That is how history has unfolded. But let's not forget that today's Russian statehood has roots in the Dnieper; as we say, we have a common Dnieper [baptism]. Kievan Rus' started out as the foundation of the enormous future Russian state. We have a common tradition, a common mentality, a common history and a common culture. We have very similar languages. In that respect, I want to repeat again, we are one people.[19]

For Putin, one people make one state. Only current, presumably transient, circumstances create a pause in the reintegration of the Russian and Ukrainian peoples into the Russian state. In Putin's interpretation of Ukrainian-Russian history, Russia is a multi-ethnic, -lingual, -cultural, and -religious nation-state. Ukraine may be an independent state today, but its people are an integral member of the Russian World. It is still subject to Moscow's tutelage, pending its eventual reintegration into mother Russia.

The Ukrainian uprising in 2014, resulting in over a hundred dead, precipitated the Russian military intervention in Ukraine. Western-oriented Ukrainians took to the streets to protest the decision of President Victor Yanokovich to reject an Association and Free Trade Agreement with the European Union. That would have precluded Ukraine from joining the Russian-led Eurasian Economic Union. The rapprochement with the EU, more widely, would have precipitated Ukraine's escape from Putin's Russian World and Moscow's sphere of influence. It would be only a matter of time before Ukraine would be positioned to join NATO.

Yanokovich's ouster in February 2014 and his exile in Russia forced Putin's hand. Russian separatists in eastern and southern Ukraine proclaimed their independence from Ukraine. As in Moldova and Georgia, they were abetted by Moscow's provision of economic and military assistance. Unmarked Russian troops, including alleged volunteers in support of the rebellion, ensured the viability of the separatist movement.[20] Moscow aims in reasserting its historic hegemony over Ukraine were not only to forestall Ukraine's Western economic and geopolitical drift but also to retain permanent leverage over Ukrainian domestic politics and government. Consistent with these objectives, and shortly after the military intervention in Ukraine, Putin annexed Crimea from Ukraine further expanding the Russian World. By force of arms, Putin's imagined virtual Russian World was enlarged territorially and materially as a reality on the ground.

It is important to recognize that Russian military interventions in Moldova, Georgia, and Ukraine were prompted by three mutually reinforcing factors: to foster Putin's conception of the Russian World; to bolster the legitimacy of the Putin regime in pursuit of its big power aims and regional interests; and to staunch the threat of regime change if Russia did not forcefully control political events in its sphere of influence. Putin's concerns about the drift of these states toward the West and the prospect of their escape from Russian control merge with his determination to regain as much of the sphere of influence of the Soviet Union as possible and to assert his personal rule over these domains.

Putin rekindled Russian fears of Western expansion as a threat to Russian national security and of Western promotion of regime change on assuming the presidency in 2000. Scholarly opinion confirms that, cumulatively over a decade, a series of popular uprisings in the Russian World and elsewhere contributed to Putin's decision to intervene directly in Ukraine in an effort to reestablish Russian hegemony, lost in the implosion of the Soviet Union.[21] Reinforcing Putin's fears of regime change in Russia were the memory of the collapse of the Soviet Union, widespread demonstrations across Russia protesting rigged parliamentary elections in 2010–2011, and again, in a renewed popular Ukrainian uprising against a Putin puppet in February 2014. The short-lived Arab Spring in the Middle East and American interventions in Afghanistan and Syria reinforced his concerns for the survival of his illiberal populist regime.

These foreign and domestic uprisings undermine the legitimacy of the Putin regime and opened the possibility of its overthrow. Russian interventions abroad can be understood as a key element of Putin's unrelenting pursuit of self-legitimacy to disguise his pursuit of power as legitimacy. A contrived legitimacy through manipulated elections is also indispensable to insulate the Kleptocracy, which Putin and his oligarchs have constructed in response to the Imperative of Welfare, from criticism and to counter moves to weaken or overthrow the regime.

Putin appears convinced that elements in the West and, specifically, in the United States, seek his demise and the overthrow of his regime. This concern was expressed in his denunciation of NATO's bombing of Serbia in the Balkan wars that eventually resulted in the creation of the state of Kosovo. Regime change and the destruction of states opposed by the West were also on Putin's mind in the Western destruction of the Kaddafi regime and the Libyan state. These events – internal revolutions inspired by the West, new state creations, and regime change – reinforced Putin's realist conception of international relations as a zero-sum game. For Putin only a militarily strong Russia could prevent regional, state, and regime disruptions from being visited on Russia, too. Only a militarily strong Russia, able to project its power regionally and abroad, could contest Western expansion and ensure against his overthrow.

It is important to recognize that Russian military power has its limits, even in controlling Russian citizens. Russia's successful interventions in annexing Crimea, destabilizing Ukraine, and dividing Moldova and Georgia mask his tenuous hold over Chechnya, a potential Achilles heel of the regime. Putin's concessions to Ramzan Kadyrov's iron rule over Chechnya, largely freeing him from Moscow's oversight or intervention, exposes a festering weakness in his otherwise commanding rule over Russia. It undermines his claim to legitimacy as a charismatic leader who alone can ensure a powerful Russian state capable of providing for domestic order.[22] That claim would include presumably the Russian state's capacity to bend Chechnya to Moscow's will. Anna Politkovskaya, a celebrated journalist and Putin critic, who was later assassinated for her opposition to the Putin regime, captured the submissiveness of Moscow to Kadyrov's rule. "It is an old story," she wrote, "repeated many times in our history: The Kremlin fosters a baby dragon, which it then has to keep feeding to stop from setting everything on fire."[23]

Politkovskaya was referring to Putin's policy of "Chechnization." In contrast to other threats to his regime from abroad, political rivals, or oligarchs, Putin compromised Russian sovereignty by entering into a Faustian bargain with Ramzan Kadyrov. The rule of law in Chechnya is not Russian law, but Kadyrov's. It is a melding of Kadyrov's conception of Shari'a and customary Chechen law. "Under Putin, power in Russia has retreated to the shadows, with most high-ranking officials wary of publicity or attention; Kadyrov, by contrast, seeks it [to assert his authority]."[24] To keep his part of the bargain, Moscow furnishes Kadyrov's Chechnya 85 percent of its budget with minimal oversight of the outlay. Russian military and security forces are forbidden to intervene in Chechnya, Moscow's "baby dragon."[25]

The diplomatic, military, and hybrid warfare strategies of Russia's pursuit of a multipolar world[26]

The West and, notably, the United States are the principal obstacles to Putin's design for global governance. Putin's attack on the liberal solution to OWL imperatives serves, as suggested above, several mutually contingent objectives: the fostering of traditional Russian geopolitical and economic interests; the advance of Russian power as a derivative of a weakened West; the solidification of Russia's hegemony over regional neighbors; the enlargement of the Russian World; and, less discernible, but no less significant, the bolstering of the Putin regime and its unbroken rule during the course of his time in office. Power trumps legitimacy.

Putin attacks the West for what he avers was its deliberate decision to keep Russia weak and to submit it to Western dicta. The West did little or nothing to assist Russia in transitioning from a state-controlled economy to the rigors and discipline of a market system. Instead, it was complicit in the catastrophic destabilization of the Russian economy after the collapse of the Soviet state. Russia's perceived Western-induced weakness justified Moscow's refusal to integrate Russia into the Western system. Putin bristled at the West's dismissal of Russia simply as a regional power, too weak in military and economic resources to play a big power global role. Membership in the G-7, until its ouster over Crimea in 2014, subjugated Moscow, in Putin's estimate, to Western leadership, an intolerable subordinate status. On his reelection in 2018 Putin, declaring Russia a superpower,[27] demanded an equal voice for Moscow (and himself) with the West and China in determining the norms and rules for global order and economic development.

A continuing theme of Putin's critique of the Western system is that the United States, in collusion with the European Union, deliberately exploited Russia's weakness. For its part, the European Union incorporated several of the Soviet Union's former satellites into the EU. Its expansion undermined the Russian project for a Eurasian Economic Union (EEU) led by Moscow.[28] NATO expansion also absorbed the former states of the Warsaw Pact. NATO troops were stationed on Russia's borders, depriving it of a security buffer, in violation of promises made by the West after the implosion of the Soviet Union. Both were accused of undermining Russia's historically legitimated sphere of influence in Eastern Europe and in the Central Caucasus.[29] The US deployment of anti-missile systems in Europe, perceived by Moscow as aimed at Russia's nuclear deterrent, further deepened Putin Russia's sense of insecurity. These moves were cited in justifying Russia's violation of the Intermediate-Range Nuclear Forces Treaty signed by Presidents Mikhail Gorbachev and Ronald Reagan in 1987.[30]

Putin identified what he characterized as the unilateralist drive of the United States for global hegemony as the principal moral and material flaw of the liberal model for global governance. There is some merit in the charge. In President Bush's address to the graduating class at West Point in 2002, he proclaimed that the balance of power among states had decisively shifted to the United States. Other states, given overwhelming American military power, ostensibly had little option other than to bandwagon on the United States, if they wished to live in peace. This global public good was freely available to all states if they submitted themselves to American hegemony and leadership.[31]

Putin's Russia has no intention of being absorbed into American or Western European orbits. Like China, he is certain that authoritarian rule is the wave of the future, not liberal democracy. History is purportedly on Putin's side: "We have no doubt," President Putin observed at the 2016 meeting of the Valdai Forum,

> that sovereignty is the central notion of the entire system of international relations. Respect for it and its consolidation will help underwrite peace and stability both at the national and international levels. There are many countries that can rely on a history stretching back a thousand years, like Russia, and we have come to appreciate our identity, freedom, and independence.[32]

Populations were expected to follow Russia's lead in affirming their national identities, their independence, and state sovereignty as the guarantor of their security and welfare. No less were they expected to accept authoritarian, populist rule as preferable to secular, pluralist, liberal democratic government.

Putin contends further that American and Western usurpation of the principle of nation-state sovereignty has set in train global crises at several parallel and reinforcing levels. At a global level, the West is portrayed as imposing its preferred rules for global order, welfare, and regime legitimacy on other states to suit its interests. Other states are marginalized or precluded from participating in their development to protect and advance their values and interests. Putin characterizes this system as coercive and, ironically, as anti-democratic. It favors a minority of Western states against the many states and peoples comprising Putin's conception of the Westphalian system.[33] Putin's form of elected democratic centralism, his response to the Imperative of Legitimacy, ostensibly resolves widespread popular discontent and malaise by freeing the self-determination of populations. Global and regional peace is purportedly fostered once distinct ethnic, national, cultural, and religious identities are respected and freed from the Western yoke.

Western military power, spurred by its alleged animating hegemonic aims, has also led to armed interventions in Iraq, Syria, Libya, and Serbia in violation of state sovereignty. Except for the Libyan case, none of these actions was authorized by the Security Council of the United Nations. In Libya, the United States and its British and French allies went beyond the limits of the UN mandate to destroy both the Kaddafi regime and the Libyan state. When other states refuse to conform to Western rules, they are sanctioned (Russia, Iran, North Korea). Conversely, Russian military assistance to the Assad regime in Syria, justified by Moscow to stop what it termed as a terrorist attempt to seize the Syrian state, is condemned by the West as a violation of international law and human rights.

From Moscow's perspective, the West's military interventions in the domestic affairs of other states expose its hypocrisy as well as the futility of these efforts. Viewed from the Kremlin, the West's use of force cannot ultimately compel other states and resistant populations to do its bidding. No state or even a group of Western states have either sufficient power or legitimacy to impose their form of government. Putin predicts that Western power, hard and soft, is waning as a consequence of the moral degeneration of Western society. He also contends that the self-serving economic policies of the United States are accelerating the eventual dissolution of the Western system – chronic debt, trade imbalances, a weakening dollar as an international currency, US-spurred financial instability marked by the 2008 global financial meltdown, and excessive military expansion. The center of global power, with Russian assistance, is projected to be gradually moving eastward toward Russia and China. Beijing shares Moscow's commitment to a multipolar world and the diminution and eventual demise of the Western system. History, as back to the future, is moving inexorably away from a centralized Western-imposed global system to a resurrected decentralized Westphalian system where the powerful hold sway over the weak.

According to Putin, Western military interventions have also given rise to terrorist organizations around the globe. In weakening or in destroying the states that have been attacked, a power vacuum was created that terrorists, like the Islamic State of Iraq and Syria (ISIS), quickly filled. Had the West respected the independence and autonomy of other states and, *ipso facto*, the international rule of law, defined by state sovereignty, terrorism in its various transmutations – ISIS, the Taliban, warring factions in Libya, Africa, and the Middle East as well as other anti-state movements – would have been staunched or significantly arrested. There existed no terrorist organizations until the states of Iraq and Libya were destroyed and the Syrian state was severely weakened. Russian military assistance to the Assad regime in Syria is justified as a fight against unwitting Western-spawned terrorist organizations.

The global crises unleashed by the leaders of the Western states have, thoughtlessly, had another profound destabilizing impact on global order. According to Putin, these unwarranted and costly interventions have engendered a growing rift between Western political elites in power and the populations, who they serve and to whom they are responsible. These fissures are purportedly deep and insurmountable under the current Western system. National, populist movements in Poland, Hungary, Venezuela, Turkey, Egypt, and the Philippines, in tandem with Russian resistance, are challenging the liberal democratic states. These illiberal regimes, paradoxically, are credited with having elicited popular support. Putin contends that they represent the future of global governance.[34]

Putin's philippic against the Western system is not simply rhetorical. His regime has developed elaborate strategies to undermine the Western model and to install a multipolar Westphalian system. Putin's strategy can be characterized as low cost and low risk in challenging the West. The aim is to push back against the West short of military hostilities, where Russia today is at a disadvantage. As the discussion of the Welfare imperative below makes plain, Russia lacks the economic, technological, and military resources to fully engage Western military forces. What it can effectively do is weaken the system by pursuing a shrewd strategy that relies more on Western vulnerabilities, notably deep divisions in democratic societies, than on the material capacity of Russia to advance its interests and its model for global governance.

The increasing interdependence of the peoples and states of the world across all areas of human concern – national and international security, sustainable economic development, environmental and ecological well-being, the validation of discrete personal, national, cultural, and religious identities – poses a dilemma for Russian diplomacy. Putin's design for a multipolar state system to overwhelm the West must necessarily still pass through the power grid of the current Western ascendant multilateralist, rule-based systems to address these issues. Western-created international organizations entangle Russia in constraints running counter to the Putin regime's preference for domestic autonomy and a free hand in security and foreign affairs.

It is not surprising then that Putin prizes the BRICS – Brazil, Russia, India, China, and South Africa. While the divergences of this grouping are ill-suited to solve global issues, BRICS does provide a forum to voice Russian criticisms of the West and to advance its interests. While clearly not a substitute for membership in the UN Security Council, BRICS usefully highlight issues of interest to Moscow and provide the long-term prospect of "a new model of global relations."[35] BRICS act as something of a default mode, after the Group of Seven terminated Russia's membership to punish Moscow for annexing Crimea.

BRICS also has the advantage that neither the United States nor the European states are members. Moscow does not risk being overshadowed by these rivals. China, as a key BRICS member, shares Putin's multipolar model.[36] Besides BRICS, Russia also plays a discernible leadership role in the Eurasian Economic Union, the Collective Security Treaty Organization, and the Shanghai Cooperation Organization. These non-Western organizations are favored as potential long-range counterweights to the Western-led global International Monetary Fund, the World Bank, and the World Trade Organization.

Putin's military strategy to advance the emergence of a multipolar system

Since Russia's preferred multilateral organizations lack the capacity to overthrow the Western global order, Putin's Russia has assigned priority to the reform of the Russian military as a way forward to creating the conditions for a multipolar system. After the collapse of the Soviet Union, the Russian army rapidly decomposed along with its intelligence services and secret police. According to one estimate, Moscow's armed forces shrank from five to one million between 1988 and 1994. Military expenditures also dramatically declined from US$246 billion in 1988 to US$14 billion in 1994.[37]

The challenge confronting the Putin regime was to totally reconstruct Russian strategic doctrine and geopolitical practices within the constraints of limited economic growth and technological development. The difficulty experienced by the Russian military in suppressing the Chechnyan revolt in 2000 and its equally disappointing performance in defeating a militarily weaker Georgia in 2008 dramatized Putin's problem. While the remnants of the Soviet military were able to prevail in both crises, their shortcomings as a fighting force were also clearly revealed. Equipment and weaponry were outdated, malfunctioning, or simply unavailable; breakdowns punctuated combined armed force cooperation; and communications were at times so precarious that commanders had to rely on commercial cell phones to direct troops in the field. The reform of the military and a fundamental shift in Russian strategy can be roughly dated with the unfortunate experience of the Georgian intervention.

Reform assumed four interlocked dimensions. First, nuclear forces remain central to deter what is perceived as the principal threat to the Russian Federation. American conventional and nuclear forces, the NATO alliance, and NATO's deployment of anti-missile systems in Europe are perceived as threats to Russia's security and its nuclear deterrent forces. Moscow is estimated to have a stockpile of 4,300 nuclear warheads assigned to strategic and tactical missile launchers and bombers. Of this total, roughly 1,950 strategic warheads are deployed on ballistic missiles and bombers.

While the nuclear stockpile is scheduled to be reduced, its effective reach and destructive power will increase with the deployment of MIRVed warheads and the modernization of its ground ICBMs, deployed on mobile platforms.[38] Newer systems will replace aging SS-18s. These include the SS-27 and SS-30 ICBMs.

Russia's principal nuclear striking force is six Delta class submarines, each equipped with 16 Submarine-Launched-Ballistic-Missiles (SLBMs). These are scheduled to be replaced eventually by eight Borei class submarines, each supplied with 16 SLBMs and armed with 6 MIRVed warheads. At his inauguration as president in March 2018, Putin announced the development of a submarine equipped with nuclear torpedoes purportedly capable of frustrating Western naval nuclear forces.[39]

All of the military services will also be armed with tactical nuclear weapons. Russian strategists attach importance to these non-strategic air, ground, and sea nuclear forces. These systems are armed with approximately 1,850 tactical nuclear weapons. These forces are relied upon to offset the superiority of NATO conventional forces. These systems are also implicitly aimed to balance large Chinese conventional capabilities. Added to these forces are what appear to be two cruise missiles: a new ground-launched cruise missile in violation of the 1987 Intermediate-Range Nuclear Forces Treaty[40] and the development of a Zircon Hypersonic cruise missile capable of precision targeting at speeds exceeding 6,000 miles per hour.[41]

Putin's violation of the Intermediate-Range Ballistics Missile Treaty (INF), prompting the Trump administration to renounce the treaty, does not fully exclude Moscow's interest in arms control accords if they enhance Russia's military posture and security strategy. Unlike the Trump administration, it supports the agreement with Iran – the Joint Comprehensive Plan of Action (JCPOA) – to preclude its development of nuclear weapons. It has expressed interest in another round of negotiations of the START treaty to limit the number of deployed strategic nuclear weapons with the United States. It is also scheduled to withdraw from the Open Skies Treaty in the wake of the Trump administration's rejection of the treaty. The treaty permits over flights on a rival's airspace to detect the possible preparations to resort to the use of its armed forces.

What is particularly striking about the modernization of Russian military forces is the progress made since 2008 in developing professionally led and well-equipped conventional forces. This is the second element of Putin's modernization program. In contrast to the poor showing of the military in the Chechen and Georgian wars, Russian forces, principally its special forces, disguised as "little green men," acquitted themselves well in the forceful reintegration of Crimea into the Russian Federal Republic.[42]

More broadly, Russian conventional forces have been especially effective in Russia's Syrian intervention in 2015. Thousands of air sorties were flown to support the Assad regime against ISIS and regime opponents, notably those supported by the United States. These strikes included long-range cruise missiles launched from bombers in Russia and surface vessels in the Caspian Sea and from submarines in the Mediterranean. Russian strike forces also participated in the final defeat of rebellious forces.

As one security analyst noted: "In Putin's terms, Russia has conducted a comprehensive application of force ... allowing [Russia] qualitatively to change the situation in Syria."[43] One indication of the Russian impact on the Syrian conflict is the accord reached by Israel and Russia to keep Iranian troops in Syria 25 miles away from Israel and eventually to clear Iranian forces and their Hezbollah surrogates from Syrian soil.[44] Conspicuous is the diminishing presence of the United States, as Israel's closest ally, in resolving the Syrian crisis.

The weakest link of Russia's military buildup is the development of a blue ocean fleet, the third and lagging component of modernization. The priority assigned to the submarine force underscores the deficiencies of the Russian surface fleet. The Russian Navy suffers as a legacy of the Soviet period. The heavy capital expenditures required to build and maintain a surface fleet currently exceed Russian economic capabilities. Its sole aircraft carrier, the Admiral Kuznetsov, is unable to sustain long deployments without breakdowns. The ship's aircraft, which flew multiple sorties in the Syrian conflict, had to be transferred to a Syrian air base because of Kuznetsov's unreliability.[45]

Within the framework of the Russian nuclear and conventional arms buildup, the Putin regime has also perfected the art of hybrid warfare, the fourth component of its strategy to challenge Western military superiority. This approach to conflict management with adversaries has, arguably, been the regime's most effective strategic instrument in controlling its neighbors, in destabilizing the Western alliance, and in degrading the integrity of the domestic politics and governing institutions of the United States and the democratic states of the European Union. Hybrid warfare refers to Moscow's use of a broad range of subversive instruments to further Russian national interests.

General Valery Gerasimov, Chief of the General Staff of the Russian Federation, outlined some of the principal nonmilitary features of hybrid warfare in a military journal.[46] Gerasimov argued that the rules of war have fundamentally changed. Increasingly, nonmilitary forms of power were gaining ascendancy over direct use of force in "achieving political and strategic goals."[47] The distinction between war and peace between adversaries has progressively been blurred as the duration of a conflict endures. "The focus of applied methods of conflict," observed Gerasimov, "has altered in the direction of the broad use of political, economic, informational, humanitarian, and other nonmilitary measures — applied in coordination with the protest potential of the population."[48] Manipulating an opponent's population to advance Moscow's interests and global objectives is a key target of hybrid warfare.

Crimea's absorption into the Russian Federation and Moscow's intervention in Ukraine illustrate the rich mix of military and especially of nonmilitary forms of power to accomplish President Putin's strategic aims. In Crimea Moscow relied on so-called "little green men," specially trained Russian forces, to bloodlessly invest the territory and to mobilize its Russian supporters to legitimate the takeover. More military force and "little green men" were needed to assist breakaway Russian elements in western Ukraine. The result has been to freeze Ukrainian foreign policy in an armed stalemate with Moscow and its proxies to preclude any move by Kiev to move toward the West. The stationing of Russian troops in Moldova and Georgia is also designed to limit economic and security ties between these states and the West.

Notable achievements in Crimean and Ukraine pale before the success of Russia's penetration of the domestic politics of the democratic states of Europe and the United States. Russia's hybrid strategy is the key component of Putin's strategy to undermine the West and advance his design for global order. Russian state-fueled money flows to populist parties in Europe. Moscow's support for the National Front in France is a prominent example of its efforts to strengthen nationalist parties opposed to close ties with the European Union or NATO. Moscow has sown fear and disunion through public and social media. By playing on sensitive issues, like Muslim immigration into Europe and the United States. Nationalist, right-wing governments in Poland, Hungary, Slovenia, and Italy have come to power on the wave of public concerns about perceived increases in crime, sexual depredations, and the dilution of national cohesion as a result of unregulated immigration from the developing world and, specifically, of Muslims from the Middle East and Africa.

The indictment of 13 Russian operatives by the Special Counsel, Robert Mueller, investigating Russian intervention in American elections, notably the presidential election of 2016, is a textbook of Russian initiatives to disrupt the integrity of the electoral process in the United States and to elect Donald Trump as president.[49] Agents were sent to the United States to gather intelligence about domestic political vulnerabilities, which might be attacked. Moscow created a unit, the Internet Research Agency, to house hackers and operatives to penetrate online services in the West. Multiple false identity accounts were registered with Facebook, Instagram, and Twitter. Identities were stolen, including Social Security numbers, home addresses, and birth dates to hide the identities of Russian perpetrators. One Russian Twitter account, "TEN_GOP," attracted 100,000 followers.

Minorities were targeted either not to vote for Hillary Clinton or to vote for a third-party candidate, moves calculated to aid the Trump campaign. Rallies in New York and Florida, a purple state, were organized under false pretenses. Fake personas were used to recruit and cover the expenses of Trump supporters to mount rallies for their candidate. Using stolen identities, Russian operatives opened multiple Pay Pal accounts to support their activities. Using these accounts, defendants paid for political advertisements favoring Trump and covered expenses for Trump rallies.

The sinister reach of these extensive interventions into the US electoral process is captured in Russian use of a Facebook account in the name of a fabricated US persona, "Matt Skriber." From this account "Skriber" sent a private message to a real Facebook account, "Florida for Trump." The Russian communication elicited the support of Trump followers to do Moscow's bidding:

> Hi there! I'm a member of Being Patriotic online community. Listen, we've got an idea. Florida is still a purple state and we need to paint it red. If we lose Florida, we lose America. We can't let it happen. right? What about organizing a YUGE [sic] pro-Trump flash mob in every Florida town? We are currently reaching out to local activists and we've got the folks who are okay to be in charge of organizing their events almost everywhere in FL. However we still need your support. What do you think about that? Are you in?[50]

There is no doubt that, with limited resources, the Russian government of President Putin mounted an impressive campaign to undermine the Western model of global governance and to advance his vision of a return to the Westphalian multipolar system. In such a decentralized order, a system of billiard balls vs. global web-like networks, Russia would expect to play a role equal to that of the United States, the Western democracies, and China. For Putin's Russia this would also be a congenial world of increasing numbers of illiberal democracies and authoritarian regimes.

The Imperative of Welfare: Kleptocracy

Putin is a free rider on the Western economic system. He has no vision of how it might be revised or reformed to benefit all states. While the Putin regime relies on the global market system's trading and financial mechanisms to support Russian economic growth, Putin's Kleptocracy,[51] resting on his centralized direction and exploitation of large state and private corporations, undermines the basic principles of a free and unfettered exchange system.

As used here, Kleptocracy is a wide-ranging, inclusive term. It refers to all forms of personal, corporate, and political behavior as well as economic exchanges that fall short of a market test. A market test would require, *inter alia*, that prices determine economic priorities and investment, a clear, reliable, and enforceable definition of private property rights, and the freedom of individuals and corporations to invest their material assets in the pursuit of economic gains absent governmental controls. The touchstone of whether an economic exchange falls within Putin's Kleptocratic control, however difficult to define, is whether political power rather than the incentives of a free market directs the outcomes of economic exchanges.

Putin's Kleptocracy covers widespread rent-seeking both in public and private exchanges, subsidies to inefficient and otherwise bankrupt enterprises, sweet-heart loans to privileged insiders, state control of labor, corruption of all kinds at all levels of nontransparent interfaces between public officials and the citizenry, and outright illegal behavior involving state officials and criminal elements. Political power deploys public assets for private gains at the expense of the Russian people.

This is a more inclusive conception of Kleptocracy than is typically understood. It implicates the Russian president and his closest associates, the oligarchs who control the Russian economy, and encompasses lower governmental officials throughout the states of the Russian Federation. The pervasive corruption throughout Russia's officialdom extends to Russian civil society between private actors in their relations with each other, say, in securing a bank loan, access to public health facilities, or placing a child in a favored school.

It is important to acknowledge that, perversely, Putin's Kleptocracy works. Across a number of leading economic indicators, it can claim to have made discernable economic progress, however much it falls short of the measures of an efficiently and effectively run corrupt-free market system. Putin's Kleptocracy is self-sustaining since there is no effective opposition to the system. It has continued to grow since the election of President Putin in 2000. Its tentacles reach throughout Russian society. The monopoly of political power in Putin's hands and his control of suborned oligarchs keeps the Kleptocracy going as an economically enfeebled enterprise, highly profitable for them, sizably much less so for the public's well-being.

Its shortcomings notwithstanding, economists largely agree that Russia has instituted a market economy.[52] In the Soviet era, the state owned most property as well as the means of production, industrial and agricultural. That is no longer the case. Individuals and corporations can hold vast amounts of private property. They can dispose of these assets in a global market system, though always under the threat that their property may be subject to state appropriation. The rule of law in Russia to protect private property is still hostage to the arbitrary whims and needs of the Russian president and his oligarchical associates. As opponents of President Putin have discovered, rule by law is always present below the surface of economic transactions.

The shift from state to private wealth holdings is striking in the period from 1990 to 2014. In the last year of the Soviet Union, new national wealth was 425 percent of national income of which public and private wealth was 300 and 125 percent, respectively. In 2014 these percentages were reversed. While national wealth grew marginally at 450 percent of national income, private wealth soared, with much of it held abroad by Russian elites. Thomas Pikkety and associates estimate private wealth in 2014 at 370 percent of national income; public wealth, at 80 percent.[53] Correspondingly, the state owned slightly more than 75 percent of national property in 1980 and only 20 percent in 2015.[54]

The privatization of Russia's large corporations was rapidly instituted in the 1990s. Gazprom, Russia's largest corporation, in which the state owns a controlling share, is traded on global stock markets. Russian corporations are sufficiently independent of the state in legal status to qualify Moscow's entry into the World Trade Organization in 2011. Its transformation to a market system was also recognized in its membership in the Group of Seven of leading Western economies, until Russia's expulsion in 2014.

During Putin's rule since 2000, Russia's GDP has progressively grown. In the period 2000–2008, GDP growth grew annually at a rate on the average of 7–8 percent. Disposal income rose by 160%, which in dollar terms amounted to a seven-fold increase. Per capita income rose from a low of 22,000 Euros in 1995 to 34,000 in 2016. In tandem, unemployment also declined over this period.[55] Over Putin's tenure balance of payments annually remained positive. Through much of this period, Russia's public debt was also low relative to national income in contrast to many Western capitalist states. The United States is a notable outlier. After large tax cuts in 2017, it faces trillions of dollars in new debt, enlarged by substantial stimulus spending to sustain the economy in response to the COVID-19 pandemic. Despite the Kleptocracy's positive economic results, it still lags behind other East European states freed from the Soviet command economy.[56]

Putin's Kleptocratic economy, partially inherited from the Soviet and Yeltsin Kleptocracies, differed from them in several ways. The foundation of the Putin Kleptocracy is embedded in the enormous oil, gas, and mineral reserves of the Russian Federation. Gas reserves are estimated at US$75 trillion dollars. Russia is the largest exporter of natural gas and second in petroleum exports. Oil and gas account for approximately 16 percent of Russian GDP, half of the state's revenues, and 70 percent of its exports.[57] Other sectors, notably arms sales, contribute to exports, but they are dwarfed by energy exports.[58]

The dependency on energy exports creates the challenge of a Resource Management System (RMS). In market theory, an RMS presents no problem if revenues are derived at global market prices and if costs of production, distribution, and sales are market efficient. The Putin Kleptocracy ensures that these tests will not be applied.

Putin installed his vertical control of the Russian state and economy through four principal moves. The first was his gradual submission of the oligarchs who had acquired major control of the Russian economy during the "market shock treatment" of the 1990s.[59] Oligarchs who opposed him lost access to the president's power, personal status, and much, if not all, of their wealth. In the extreme, a resistant oligarch was stripped of his position, jailed, or exiled.

The case of Mikhayl Khodorkovskiy, owner of Yukov, illustrates Putin's ability to use the court system to destroy those who oppose him. Khodorkovskiy was convicted on charges of fraud and tax evasion in 2003. He was jailed until his pardon a decade later. Putin's associates assumed control of Yukov. Its most profitable sectors were sold below market value to Rosneft, controlled by Putin's appointees. Other prominent recalcitrant oligarchs also suffered Khodorkovskiy's fate. Boris Berezovsky and Vladimir Gusinsky were forced into exile by a "host of lawsuits and the Kremlin's persistent scrutiny of their business interests."[60] These examples served as a warning to other oligarchs to submit to Putin's rule or be dispatched in short order.

Putin introduced new rules of the game. Putin's Kleptocracy is short of being thoroughly lawless yet far less than the rule of law. As Karen Dawisha observes, "(R)ule number one would be that the law would be applied only to someone who had broken the Kremlin's internal rules — the guarantee of impunity before the law was the primary benefit of maintaining loyalty."[61] Early on in his presidency, Putin declared before the Russian Duma that the state would abide by the rule of law:

> This is why we insist on a single dictatorship — the dictatorship of the Law. Although I know that many people do not like this expression. That I why it is so important to indicate the limits of the area where the state is the full and only owner.[62]

Since Putin and the Russian state are indistinguishable, the limits of state power are what Putin determines is the scope of the rule of law. In practice, it is rule by law. Putin revived the sobriquet of Oscar R. Benavides, president of Peru from 1933 to 1939, "For my friends everything, for my enemies the law."[63]

Putin's second challenge was breaking the power of the federated states, which siphoned off revenue that would otherwise have gone to the Russian state. This was a widely used practice during the Yeltsin years when the Russian state was weak. Putin gained control of what he called these "little islands of power." These islands referred to governors in Russia's then 89 regions. Shortly after entering office, Putin established seven federal districts headed by his appointees to oversee the governors of the federated system. That reorganization ensured his control over tax collections and state revenues. As Rudra Sil and Cheng Chen conclude, "Together with the moves against the oligarchs, these efforts at reining in the regions point to a recentralization of political authority that is very much at the core of Putin's 'dictatorship of the law.'"[64]

The third and fourth challenges refer to Putin's control over the Russian Duma, the legislative branch of the government, and his manipulation of successive elections to submit the Russian population to this rule. How he installed an illiberal democracy is developed below under Putin's response to the Imperative of Legitimacy.

An economy centered on the exploitation of energy and mineral resources is in theory a rent-seeking system.[65] As Gaddy and Ickes note,

> the simple definition of *rent* is revenue received from the sale of the resource minus the cost of producing it. By this definition, rent is equal to the economic profit, that is, revenues minus economic, or opportunity costs (including depreciation of fixed assets and a "normal" return on capital.[66]

A Resource Management System (RMS) that complies with these constraints avoids any taint of corruption. The Putin RMS clearly violates these requirements.

Russian state control of the RMS generates powerful incentives to depart from market protocols in multiple ways.[67] Resources can be sold below current prices; costs of production can be fraudulently stated; or revenues and profits can be directed to political insiders. The state's RMS is transformed into a smoothly running rent-seeking machine for the benefit of President Putin and his oligarchs. These funneled funds support the President's domestic and foreign policy goals or the preferences of insiders. Billions that might otherwise go to shareholders or toward social welfare are directed to swell the personal and public accounts of the president and privileged elites.

The corruption at the top of the system filters down to lower levels of the economy and government. Every level of civil society is infected. At the top, the state promotes the inefficiencies, bribes, and rents of state and state-directed corporations as the costs of doing business. These depredations are politically insulated from market punishment. State employees are also implicitly encouraged to seek bribes from citizens before they provide government services, like seeking a driver's license or a visa. Corruption extends perniciously to access to health, education, police protection, and other services.[68] These bribes also cover a wide range of crimes (avoiding taxes or traffic tickets, money laundering, embezzlement, colluding with crime syndicates, etc.).

Karen Dawisha, who has published a detailed description of how Putin's Kleptocracy works, notes that

> instead of cracking down on corruption, the state uses bribes both to feed the venality of the elites and as a way to supplement the insufficient salaries of low-paid workers. Instead of paying them from state coffers, the state allows low-level civil servants to supplement their meager incomes with petty bribes. This constitutes an additional tax on the population and a drag on the economy's overall efficiency. Over the long run this "corruption effect." [is] equivalent to $2,000 per Russian and equal to the size of the Russian budget.[69]

The International Monetary Fund estimates the worldwide cost of bribes annually at between US$1.5 and US$2.0 trillion (roughly two percent of Global Domestic Product).[70] Russia contributes substantially to this fraught total. In 2017, Transparency International's corruption index on which the World Bank relies ranks Russia 135th out of 180 countries in corruption, a fall of 16 points since 2015. Upward of half of the Russian economy is tributary to bribes and corruption. Russia's low score of 29 out of 100 has held steady for over a decade. Russia is grouped with developing states in which, like Putin's Kleptocracy, the rule of law is captive of state power.

Putin's Kleptocracy results in a wide array of negative economic outcomes. There is a growing disparity of income and wealth in Russia since the fall of the Soviet Union. In 1995 there were no billionaires and only a handful at the start of the Putin regime in 2000.[71] Since then, their number and their acquisition of national wealth have been spectacular. In 2017, Forbes listed 96 Russian billionaires. They held approximately 30 percent of national income.

In 2016 the top 10 percent of Russians earned 45 percent of national income versus 24 percent in 1990. The gap was appreciably less between the top 10 and the lower 90 percent during the Soviet era. From 1935 to 1995 the top ten never rose above 25, reaching a low of 21 percent in 1980. In 2016 the income share of the top 1 percent was slightly more than 20 percent.[72]

While the income of the top 10 percent in 2016 was 45 percent of national income, the middle population of 40 percent was 38 percent and the bottom 50 percent held only 17 percent of national income.[73] Russia's Gini coefficient, which measures country income differences, doubled between 1980 and 2016 from .27 to .54 – among the largest increases of all states.[74]

The accumulation of wealth in Russia is also increasingly concentrated. The top 10 percent possess 71 percent of national wealth; the middle 40 percent, 25 percent; and the bottom 50 percent, 4 percent.[75] What is particularly striking about this disparity is the amount of national wealth held outside of Russia. Pikkety and associates estimate that

> offshore wealth is about three times larger than official net foreign reserves (about 75 % vs. around 25 %) and is comparable in magnitude to total onshore household financial assets. There is as much financial wealth held by rich Russians abroad — in the United Kingdom, Switzerland, Cyprus, and other offshore centers — as there is held by the entire Russian population in Russia itself.[76]

As Pikkety and his associates suggest, inequality in Russia and the concentration of rent-based resources "are unlikely to be the best recipes for sustainable development and growth."[77] Russia's GDP fell approximately 8 percent in the wake of the 2008 global financial crisis after a nine-year string of positive growth, averaging about 7.6 percent. It has not been able to regain that level of growth since. Growth slowed sharply below the 7.6 level, falling below 2 percent in 2013 and 2014 and falling into negative growth in the following two years. World Bank estimates project a growth of slightly less than 2 percent for 2018.[78] Russia's economy at market value is ranked twelfth, well below California's economy, which is ranked fifth and is twice as large as that of the Russian Federation.

Besides wealth concentration and inequality, several other factors account for Russia's slow growth. The elites controlling Russia's rent-seeking RMS economy have little incentive to invest in other promising growth sectors. The large profits derived from energy and minerals discourage risk-taking and efforts to seek gains from other economic sectors. This is one of the effects of the "Dutch disease" wherein a prized commodity dominates economic activity. This set of negative incentives for investments, on the one hand, and strong positive incentives for short-term gains, on the other, explains the flight of capital and the wealth held outside Russia by rich Russians, including President Putin.

These negative initiatives help explain the inability of the Russian state to accumulate large foreign assets despite positive balance of payments surpluses between 1990 and 2015. Those surpluses have largely been converted into capital flight. Conversely, Norway, which roughly enjoys comparable trade balances during this period, has accumulated large foreign assets. These stood at 210 percent of national income in 2015.[79]

Sanctions levied by the United States and the Europeans, targeted primarily at President Putin, his captive oligarchs, and state-directed hackers compromising US elections as well as corporate and military data have added impediments to economic growth and technological development. They include the so-called Magnitsky sanctions of 2012 to punish those responsible for the death of Sergei Magnitsky, a Russian whistleblower accountant who charged widespread corruption. Additional US-EU sanctions were imposed as a consequence of Russia's annexation of Crimea and its intervention in Ukraine. Still Congress passed others in 2017 and 2018 to penalize Russian state interference in US elections and military engagements in Ukraine and Syria. Yet the Kleptocracy survives.

In sum, Putin's Kleptocracy, its evident flaws and its contravention of free-market rules, is still advanced as a model for other illiberal and authoritarian states to follow and for their regimes to install to ensure their continued rule and elite control of their economies for the private gain of a privileged few.

The Imperative of Legitimacy

No less paradoxical than President Putin's solution to global welfare – a corrupt and crime-ridden Kleptocracy, scaled to global proportions, that continues to function, however impaired – is Putin's retention of power despite his failure to build the legitimacy of the Russian state, his regime, and his personal rule. In their respective spheres they survive despite a permanent crisis of legitimacy across this governmental trilogy. In tracing below the strategies pursued by President Putin to orchestrate a public consensus on legitimacy, it becomes clear, as Lilia Shevtsova observes, that there is an "absence of any coherent ideology and principles."[80] Rather, President Putin has adopted "circumstance-based 'pragmatism' that often conceals the incompatible ideas and principles [on which his regime rests]."[81] The Kleptocracy has been self-sustaining. The state, regime, and Putin's personal rule have been no less self-replicating despite the absence of a national consensus about the legitimacy of these governing elements.[82] Putin's relentless pursuit of an elusive legitimacy devolves into a complex of strategies to sustain and enlarge his personal power and that of his regime.

Since there exists no widely shared, morally coherent validation of authoritative rule among the Russian population and elites, the seeming stability of Putin's rule obscures the precariousness of a Russian polity without the undergirding of a shared legitimacy among the Russian population. Post-Soviet leaders and Putin over a generation of rule have not been able "to arrive at any consensual notion of Russia's national identity around which ordinary forms of legitimate domination might be constructed."[83] This view is also shared by Vladimir Gel'man, a close observer of Russian politics: "[O]ver the last twenty years Russia moved from one (consolidated but illegitimate) authoritarian regime to another not yet fully consolidated and not yet legitimate) despite legitimacy crises."[84] The Russian people and their self-appointed governing elites are reduced to a Rousseaunian state of nature.[85] They persist but without clear guidelines or widespread accord about how to fashion a new social contract. Building legitimacy and thrust in the Russian state, Putin's regime, and in Putin's personal rule remains a work in progress with apparently no end game – Putin as Sisyphus writ large.

Public opinion polls conducted at the time of the Soviet Union's implosion reveal a confused, demoralized, and cross-pressured population. There was no majority sentiment for a return to the Soviet model built on force and fear. Polls taken during the Yeltsin years registered that only 36 percent of the population were willing to restore the Soviet Union.[86] Putin was also realistic that there was no turning back: "He who does not regret the break-up of the Soviet Union has no heart; he who wants to revive it in its previous form has no head."[87] Nor were Russians ready, then or now, to adopt a Western liberal democratic model.[88]

Throughout their long history under Czars or Commissars, Russians were never given the opportunity of self-rule.[89] Nor have they demonstrated much sentiment to create a liberal democracy. While polls showed that a majority of Russians preferred "democracy" in the abstract, they also revealed little support for the constraining principles and disciplining protocols of a Western democracy. Nor did most of the Russian population show much interest in assuming the heavy responsibilities of civic engagement. The flawed elections of the Yeltsin decade, launched before the Russian state had been re-created, provided no assurance that adoption of a foreign system of government would advance the security or material welfare of the Russian people. Most Russians share a deeply held resistance to a liberal democratic solution to their Rousseauian dilemma. A mix of factors conspired to reject this option – history, culture, religion, habitual submission over centuries to elite authority, and the experience of widespread impoverishment during the 1990s, when elections were organized by the Yeltsin government to hold onto power.

The Russian people are still mired in the politics of a parlous polity, weakened by their distrust of all levels of sociopolitical government and by widely shared doubts about their capacity for self-government. Russians are frustrated in their search for a way out of illegitimate rule. Jean-Paul Satre's depressing *No Exit* joins Rousseau's *Social Compact*, requiring legitimacy to be based on consent. Russians largely submit to being ruled, while withholding their trust and their investment of legitimacy in their government.

Between 2000 and 2014, public opinion polls record chronic distrust of formal governmental institutions and criticism of state constraints on civil society. Only President Putin and the Russian Orthodox Church enjoyed a level of trust above 50 percent of respondents. Trust in President Putin fell briefly in 2011–12 during an economic downturn, magnified by demonstrations across Russian cities,

protesting rigged elections for the Parliament and the Presidency. Having surmounted that *"accident parcour,"* Putin's popularity, if not his legitimacy, continues
to be high, measured by the large majority voting for him in 2012 (76.7%). Six
years later, he garnered 71 percent of the vote. With no serious opposition to his
control of Russian media, and not to overlook his willing reliance on coercion to
neutralize his detractors, it is difficult to measure the level of real popular support
that Putin enjoys if the public were able to freely express itself.

Deep public distrust extends to the Army, State TV, Courts, Government,
Trade Unions, Private Enterprise, Police, Regional Government, Parliament,
and Political Parties. Between 2000 and 2014, (except briefly for the Army in
2000), public opinion fell below 50 percent in the trust accorded by Russians
to these institutions. Trust in the Duma, Russia's Parliament, never rose above
21 percent. Parties fell as low as 9 and 10 percent, respectively, in 2000 and
2004 and never rose above 20 percent. This is scarcely fertile soil on which to
cultivate a liberal democracy.

As one important study of trust and legitimacy noted:

> Putin's approval ratings have not translated into increased government
> legitimacy. ... Public opinion polls show mass dissatisfaction with politi-
> cal institutions and politically relevant actors. ... [W]hile the differential
> between Putin's approval and disapproval ratings stood at +56% [in 2003]
> the differential between approval and disapproval ratios for the Duma
> stood at −30% and that for the government as a whole at −23%.[90]

Based on these bleak results, Russian Sociologist, Lev Gudkov observed that
"those institutions meant to ensure social stability — the courts, and public prosecutor's office, the police, labor unions, etc. — were regarded beyond
redemption."[91] The corruption and crime riven through Russia's sociopolitical
institutions, as discussed earlier, lend credence to these findings of the low trust
and legitimacy of the government held by a majority of Russians.

President Putin continues to consider legitimacy critical to his rule. It is central to his strategy to retain power. His relentless efforts to build legitimacy
in himself, his regime, and the Russian state underline the importance that he
attaches to this source of power.[92] At different times Putin not only employed
Max Weber's catalog of legitimacy strategies – traditional, charismatic, and legal-
rational – but he mixed them to suit their relevance to his interests. He also
expanded on Weber's tripartite prescriptions to fashion his own reformulations
to meet the demands of a modern state. As Lillia Shevtsova and others have suggested,[93] Putin acted pragmatically with no fixed understanding of legitimacy.
The aim was power under the guise of legitimacy. Since the former has always
been his loadstar, all roads to legitimacy were open for exploitation.

In serially recounting Putin's use of strategies to gain legitimacy, it should
be kept in mind that they were not deployed in chronological order. Different
mixes are relied upon to suit the challenges to his power of the moment. Begin

with tradition. Appeals to tradition run throughout Putin's tenure in office. His rationale for constructing a Russian World, described earlier, also served domestic purposes. Putin stipulates that Russia's millennial history, culture, religion, and language are the glue, binding the Russian peoples together. In dedicating his rule to the preservation of what Putin conceives is the unique identity of the Russian peoples, Putin claims to rule legitimately and authoritatively.

Putin's reliance on tradition for legitimacy dictates his close alignment with the Russian Orthodox Church, previously suppressed by the Bolshevik regime. They enjoy a symbiotic, complementary relationship. Both Putin and the Orthodox Church favor a strong and centralized Russian state and a global role for Russia: Russia to enhance its power at home and abroad, the Church to expand its influence within and beyond Russia's borders.[94] Church advocacy of state authority and its insistence that laws and customs be observed bolster Putin's power, if not his legitimacy.

The converse of seeking legitimacy through Putin's affirmation of Russia's unique identity and its cultural and religious values is Putin's belief that the West is irredeemably corrupt and in a permanent moral crisis. His indictment of the West and his rejection of the export "of [its] model all over the world" bears repeating:[95]

> We can see how many of the Euro-Atlantic countries are actually reject-ing their roots, including the Christian values that constitute the basis of Western civilization. They are denying moral principles and all traditional identities: national, cultural, religious and even sexual. They are imple-menting policies that equate… belief in God with the belief in Satan. … People in many European countries are embarrassed or afraid to talk about their religious affiliations. Holidays are abolished … their essence is hid-den away, as is their moral foundation. …I am convinced that this opens a direct path to degradation and primitivism, resulting in a profound demo-graphic and moral crisis.[96]

The complexity of Putin's appeal to tradition is most clearly displayed in his sub-tle and nuanced reliance on Russian nationalism. This move goes well beyond Weber's three categories. It is specifically directed to the complex social com-position of the Russian population and the strain that its complexity poses for unity and order. Rather than downplay or diminish the multicultural, multi-religious, and multiethnic composition of the Russian population, Putin insists that Russia's diversity is, paradoxically, the source of Russian nationalism and its identification with a strong Russian state.

> Russia was formed specifically as a multi-ethnic and multi-confessional country from its very inception. Nationalists must remember that by call-ing into question our multi-ethnic character, and exploiting the issue of Russian, Tatar, Caucasian, Siberian or any other nationalism or separatism,

means that we are starting to destroy our genetic code. In effect, we will begin to destroy ourselves.[97]

Nation and state are one.

Putin embraces an authoritarian form of democracy to overcome the problem of "nationalities."[98] The Soviet Union failed to integrate the diversity of the Russian population into a one size fits all Soviet person. Putin has no illusions about the formidable dimensions of this challenge. In 2012, Putin acknowledged that one of his principal priorities was "creating the country's unity [and the] establishment of sovereignty of the Russian people, rather than the supremacy of individuals and groups, across the entire territory."[99] He fuses his illiberal version of democracy with the vision of a united Russian nation, a strong Russian state, ruled by "vertical power" centered in the Russian President. For Putin, democracy, understood as a will of the Russian people, was embodied in the Russian President through periodic elections. His brand of electoral democracy validated a strong President and powerful state as well as "Russia's sovereignty, independence, and territorial integrity."[100]

Putin invokes popular sovereignty and its expression in the elections of the Parliament and the President as a version of Weber's legal-rational category of legitimacy.[101] For domestic order and stability to be created and maintained and for Putin to realize his aim of restoring Russia's role as a great power – a goal shared by many Russians – the modern state requires the engagement of the population into its rule, however achieved.[102] "Colleagues, Russia has made its choice," he informed the audience at the Valdai Forum in 2014. "Our priorities are further improving our democratic and open economy institutions, accelerated internal development, taking into account all the positive modern trends in the world, and consolidating society based on traditional values and patriotism."[103]

As a prop for legitimacy, Putin places much stock in strict adherence to the Russian Constitution. Taking no chances that free and fair elections might divide an already fractured elite and population, plunging them into internecine conflict and the state into disrepair, Putin has been solicitous to ensure that his successive elections as President and that of stand-in, Dmitri Medvedev, in 2008, would be consistent with the requirements of the Russian Constitution.[104] When the Constitution blocked his election to more than two terms, it was amended to permit him to be reelected for more than two terms. The Constitution is now Putin's Constitution, replacing Yeltsin's Constitutions of 1993. The Constitution is designed to maintain the dominance of United Russia, Putin's party in the Duma. In 2018 it controlled 343 of the 450-seat Parliament. Candidates for local elections are named by the Kremlin to complete the organization of a tightly regulated electoral system to protect Putin's power and position. Opponents who might run against the President are restricted in their access to the media, precluded from running by Putin-controlled courts, or are simply incarcerated. Alexei Navalny, head of the Progress Party, was jailed for organizing demonstrations against President Putin and was denied by court order from running against the President in the 2018 election.[105] He was later poisoned in 2020, while on an organizing mission against the Putin regime in Siberia, but later survived.[106] He now languishes in a Russian prison on trumped up charges.

From this vantage point, the Kremlin dictates the narrative lauding uncritically governmental policies and actions. Alternative viewpoints or criticisms are blocked from reaching the public. Journalists are intimidated to toe the government's line. Self-censorship is pervasive. Those who dare to attack state policies or Putin face prosecution and harassment. Those who are especially resourceful in revealing the corruption and crime at the center of the Kremlin face prison or assassination. The fate of Anna Polikovskaya in 2006 is a case in point.[107] A steady stream of murders of journalists has been recorded until the present. In 2017 Dimitriy Popkov and Nikolay Andrushchenko, journalists working on governmental corruption and crime, were murdered.[108] Those who betrayed Putin and Russia, like Russian General Sergei Skripal, a double intelligence agent who defected to England, are especially targeted for assassination wherever they might be.[109]

Besides the media, other elements of civil society fall under the Kremlin's thumb. Non-governmental organizations are under persistent and pervasive state surveillance. Those receiving funds from outside sources, notably Western civil liberties and human rights organizations, must register as "foreign agents." This is tantamount to identifying them as spies. Freedom of assembly is closely regulated. Freedom House reports "overwhelming police responses, the use of force, routine arrests, and harsh fines and prison sentences have discouraged unsanctioned protests."[110] Labor unions are under state supervision. The court system is not independent but under the executive branch. Career advancement depends on governmental discretion. The rule of law is subject to governmental dicta as Putin opponents, Mikhail Khodorkovsky and Alexei Navalny, have discovered.

It is instructive to read President Putin's address to the Russian Duma in April, 2000, at which he declared Russia a democracy. The media and press as well as civil society were guaranteed to be free from state interference and control. "In the establishment of civil society, the media plays an exclusive role. … (W)ithout a truly free media, Russian democracy cannot survive, and a civil society cannot be created. … Censorship and interference with media activity is prohibited by law."[111] On these scores, Putin was prophetic, Russian democracy as well as a free media and civil society have yet to be created. Censorship is prohibited by law, but law is defined by the Putin regime as rule by law.

President Putin has also appropriated Weber's characterization of charismatic leadership as a source of legitimacy. This is an especially vexing challenge since Putin does not possess the physical attributes of his predecessor, Boris Yeltsin. As one scholar observed, "Yeltsin had the advantages of a charismatic personality and a commanding physical presence. Putin has neither."[112] To compensate for his slight build, Putin presents himself as ultra-manly. A *Politico* profile of Putin celebrates him as the "King of All Sports."[113] In a series of photos, he is depicted as winning at arm wrestling with a seemingly stronger man, riding shirtless on horseback, swimming the butterfly stroke, leading a scientific expedition at sea to study grey whales, defeating an opponent at judo, hunting with a long-range rifle, scuba diving for lost treasure, playing hockey, and skiing. To amplify his athletic prowess, Putin actively promotes Russian sports. He succeeded in winning Sochi for the Winter Olympics in 2014.[114] He is already bidding for the Summer Olympics in 2032 since Tokyo, Paris, and Los Angeles have already been chosen for the intervening games.

These staged sporting events have not added up to the kind of charismatic leadership associated with other authoritarian leaders like Hitler, Castro, or Mao. Their principal utility is a metaphor for his uncontested political power. In any event, as Weber suggested, charisma as a source of legitimacy is necessarily temporal and fleeting. It attaches to the leader. There is no way to institutionalize the charisma of a leader to sustain the legitimacy of a regime beyond the time of his political life. Putin's displays of personal prowess and athleticism and the priority he attaches to Russia's participation and success in international athletic competitions, even to cheat to win at the Sochi Winter Games in 2014, serve to reveal their significance for his hold on power.[115] They do not constitute a coherent and validating ideology to substantiate the authority of his rule or that of the Oligarchical and Kleptomatic rule of his regime.

So what explains Putin's survival and the popularity he enjoys since entering into office? Putin's authoritarian regime and the coercion it is prepared to use to stifle dissent, intimidate opponents, control all forms of media, and squelch organized protests provide some explanation for his popularity based partially on rigged elections. There is some evidence to suggest that he would have won these elections without recourse to manipulating the vote, that is, he might well have prevailed in a free and fair election.

Polling suggests that Putin's power depends primarily on his government's delivery of domestic order, palpable if limited economic prosperity, and the public perception of Russia's return as a big power.[116] That there does not exist a coherent and widely shared public consensus on legitimacy is apparently of less importance to most Russian citizens than the priority they attach to these policy outcomes. Democratic processes and institutions resonate weakly in the general public except for elements of the intelligentsia and a minority of Russian citizens. Putin provides assurances to Russians that the disruptions and uncertainties – indeed the sheer miseries visited on the Russian public during the 1990s – will not be repeated. The Kleptocracy's trickle down wealth and welfare policies, while exploiting most Russians, still compares favorably with the experience of the transition from the Soviet Union to the Russian Federation. The bar of public expectations of increasingly larger personal welfare remains low.

There is also the public's deeply held value, consistent with its history, that Russia reassume big power status.[117] On this score, Putin and most Russians are joined at the hip. Walter Laquer reports a respected 2014 Levada Center poll that "70 percent expressed satisfaction that Russia has again become a great power,"[118] its actual status to the contrary notwithstanding. Fifty-six percent also opted for

Russia as a great power over increased personal material wealth.[119] Russian youth were particularly enthusiastic about a future in which Russia would be a big power rather than one in which they would profit more materially but in which Russia's status as a power would recede.[120]

A final and persuasive reason for Putin's power is the "resigned acceptance" of the Russian population to his rule and regime. Russians do not have an alternative to either. Using Albert Hirshman's concepts of *Exit, Voice, and Loyalty*, Vladimir Gel'man traces the public responses to Putin's authoritarianism over the first decade of his rule. Data show that most Russians unquestionably favor *Exit over Voice*, that is, they prefer withdrawal and resignation to engagement in public affairs to reform the state or to topple the Putin regime.[121] There is little evidence to contradict this conclusion in light of President Putin's string of electoral successes since 2000, topped by his decisive victory in 2018.

Public opinion data from a study conducted by the Swiss Academy of Development in 2009 echo this paradoxical conclusion: the consent of the public to authoritarian rule in which they have little or no say:

> According to the great majority, there was a national leader deciding all important political issues concerning the present and future of their country; the rest of the people have no influence on this; and there was no reason to change this state of affairs. Active participation in politics was not an issue, nor were any reforms of the system needed.[122]

Critique of the Putin OWL

President Putin's responses to the Imperatives of Order, Welfare, and Legitimacy are profoundly flawed as solutions to global governance. For Order, Putin would have the world return to the failed Westphalian system. The Congress of Vienna, as Paul Schroeder has exhaustively shown,[123] was able to prevent a global conflagration for a century. The big powers shared a collective interest to prevent a global conflagration or to engage in uncontrolled arms races in efforts to impose their will on the other imperial powers. As long as the major states sought what Schroeder terms "equilibrium," war between them was avoided. Multiple local wars did erupt in Europe's colonies, but a struggle for world dominance was not joined. Rampant and uncompromising nationalism swept through Europe at the turn of the century. The diplomacy of "equilibrium" gave way to uncontrolled arms races and a return to a precarious balance of power struggle and zero-sum politics. The result of these unmanageable forces was the catastrophe of World War I. The self-destructive mentality of the pre-World War I era extended into the interwar period and the inexorable outbreak of World War II.

Putin's solution to the Imperative of Order is designed to increase, not decrease, conflict among the states, notably among the major powers. In stark contrast, the alliances of the Western democratic states were created to surmount the incentives of a self-help system. In practice, until the election of President

Trump, they actually moved beyond the "equilibrium" strategies of the major powers after the Congress of Vienna that kept global peace for a century. They collectivized their discrete national security interests. Article V of the North Atlantic Treaty pledged alliance partners to come to the assistance of any member under attack. An attack on one state was an attack on all. Witness the invocation of European support under Article Five for the United States in the aftermath of the 9/11 crisis.[124] The success of these security decisions is evidenced in their mutual cooperation to preserve and promote open societies and the victory of the democracies in the Cold War. Unprecedented in history was the advance of the Kantian ideal of a coalition of democracies at peace with each other. This experience strengthened the proposition still to be fully demonstrated that democracies don't fight each other.[125]

An increasingly divided interstate system divided against itself, including Putin's sowing of discord among the democratic coalition, bolsters Russian power. Reminiscent is the advice of Beaumarchais, minister to Louis XVI, who favored assistance to American rebels to offset British power. "Security is in the division of our enemies," he counseled.[126] France's military assistance to the American Revolution divided the British from their colony. By the same token simply by diminishing the collective power of the Western Alliance and pitting allies against each other, Russia's power to advance its self-interested security and foreign policy aims is enhanced. Incentives for Russian aggression are increased in a *sauve qui peut* global security system, whether by using armed forces to expand Moscow's notion of a Russian World under its tutelage or to undermine the integrity of democratic politics and institutions through cyber attacks. Western sanctions on Moscow have not dissuaded the Putin regime from continuing its aggressions against the democracies, notably three successive federal elections in 2016, 2018, and 2020.

Putin's return of Russia to a big power role in global politics, moves supported by the Russian population, is principally defined by the negative effects Putin's Russia has had on undermining regional and global security. It is hard to see how that serves Russian interests in the long run. Arms races, particularly the expansion of the nuclear capabilities of the major states, are inflamed. The probability of armed conflict among states is increased. It would appear that Putin is playing a short game of enhancing his personal status and Russia's reputation as a security threat rather than the long game of promoting durable global security for the Russian people – and the world.

It is ironic that Putin relies on the United Nations Charter to base international security on state sovereignty and non-interference in the domestic affairs of states, yet Putin's Russia intervenes militarily with impunity in Moldova, Georgia, and Ukraine. Russian troops undermine the independence and sovereignty of these states. Thousands of Ukrainians have been killed in the Russian-provoked Ukrainian civil war. Moscow also denies that it has compromised the electoral processes of the United States, the European democracies, and targeted African states. The contradictions between Putin's vision of global order and his destabilizing interventionist security and foreign policies are blithely ignored in his determination to resurrect a mini-Russian empire. From a position of material and military weakness, Putin's Russia is induced to adopt a strategy to violate the very principles of global order and legitimacy that Putin contends are the basis for global peace. The logic of power overwhelms logic.

The Putin Kleptocracy is no less a spoiler of global economic stability and growth. Its principal contribution to the material development of the world's populations is to undermine the Western-created solution to the Imperative of Welfare. Russia free rides on the global market system, while undermining its rule-based protocols and procedures for resolving disputes. Putin's Moscow exploits its energy resources rather than utilizes them in ways that not only increase Russia's material welfare but also provide public goods for other states. It also uses the dependency of Western states as well as those within Russia's World on Russia's energy resources for political leverage.[127]

The Western market system and its governing institutions (the WTO, IMF, and World Bank) are public goods. The United States also supported the creation of what later evolved into the European Union although it was a closed trading system, putting American economic interests at a disadvantage. It also launched the Marshall Plan to restore Europe's economy and create the conditions for open societies to rise again in Europe. The aim was to end four centuries of civil war in Europe. Long-term peace was more important than temporary economic gain or short-term political advantage. Putin's Russia has neither the interest much less resources to underpin a global Welfare system. The widening income inequality of his Kleptocracy, animated by wholesale corruption and pervasive crime, scarcely qualifies as a solution to the Imperative of Welfare. Its emulation by other authoritarian states further disrupts global economic growth and technological development. The proliferation of states in which autocrats and oligarchs steal from the many for the benefit of the few results in increasing inequality, a prescription for class warfare and interstate conflict.

Putin's Russia scores poorly on measures used by Freedom House to determine whether a regime is democratic or not. Freedom House, which cites Russia as Not Free, ranks Russia 180 out of 199 countries for press freedom behind Iraq and Sudan.[128] On a 7-point scale, with 7 as least free, Russia ranked 6.5 for Freedom, 7 for political rights, and 6 for civil liberties.[129] Freedom House also ranked Russia 190 of 210 states on this aggregate scale. Except for some private media outlets, which are allowed to functions under close state supervision and duress, all important segments of Russian media are under tight state control. Freedom House notes that the "government controls, directly or through state-owned companies and friendly business magnates, all of the national television networks and many radio and print outlets, as well as most of the media advertising market."[130]

A regime that fails to build legitimacy at home is scarcely positioned to provide a solution to the Imperative of Legitimacy globally. Putin's solution to this imperative is to promote an increase in the number of illiberal democracies and authoritarian regimes around the globe. Bereft of a coherent conception of legitimacy, acknowledged by the Russian people, Putin's power depends partially, but significantly, on multiplying these repressive regimes. The rise of populist regimes in which majorities vote for authoritarian rule in Poland, Hungary, Turkey, and Venezuela strengthen Putin's power and reach. The erosion of liberal democratic rule strengthens authoritarian states to impose their power over their populations. In a global society, where the governing form of domestic regimes is the reciprocal of the governance of an interdependent world of mutually engaged peoples, a Putin world requires as a prerequisite of its sustainability the growth of Putin-like states. As the power of nondemocratic states increases, that of the liberal democratic states necessarily decreases in their capacity to preserve and extend open societies. At stake is the universal principle that all humans are free and equal; that they have a natural right to determine how they will be governed.

Putin's Russia offers no solution to the governance of the interdependent states and peoples composing a global society. Putin's design to enlarge Russian power is really a strategy to abandon the search for solutions to OWL imperatives. It treats the Imperatives of Order, Welfare, and Legitimacy as opportunities for the pursuit of the Russian president's personal benefit and Russian state power. Emulation of the Putin model ushers in a dystopian future for the world's populations.

Notes

1 Works relied upon for this section include the following: Kotkin (2016); Lukyanov (2016); Monaghan (2015–16); Nygren (2008); Oliker (2015); Russian Federation (2013); Trenin (2016); Wagnsson (2009) For general accounts of Putin's security and foreign policies, consult (Bobo Lo, 2015; Hill and Gaddy, 2015; Kanet, 2018b; Laquer, 2015; Mendras, 2012). For a recent comprehensive review of the security strategies and policies of the Russian Federation, see Kanet (2019).

2 President Putin relies on a traditional conception of state sovereignty, which has since been revised by the United Nations itself. In 2001 the United Nations and Secretary-General Kofi Annan were awarded the Nobel Prize for peace. The Nobel citation saluted the UN Secretary General for his support of human rights: "In an organization that can hardly become more than its members permit, He has made clear that sovereignty can not be a shield behind which member states conceal their violations." www.nobelprize.org/prizes/peace/2001/annan/lecture/

3 Burke (2019, p. 21). Burke defended the British rule and civil liberties against the excesses of the French Revolution, whose partisans proclaimed the universality of human rights. While Putin may appear to align with Burke in the latter's rejection of the French Revolution's proclamation of universal rights, he scarcely shares Burke's commitment to civil liberties and human freedom.

4 Hill and Gaddy (2015) develops the importance of Putin's early career as a KGB intelligence officer to explain his eventual rise to power from a middle-level post in a failed state to become what would appear to be the permanent president of the Russian Federation until his passing or the unlikelihood of his overthrow.

5 President Putin's speech to the Russian Federal Assembly, 2005, quoted in Roger Kanet, "Russia's Challenge to the Existing Global Order," European Union Center Paper Series, University of Illinois, vol. 1, Special Issue, p. 3.

6 Russian Federation (2013). See also President Putin's speeches to the Valdai Club in 2013 and 2014 and especially his address to the Munich Security Conference in 2007, n. 8 below. Valdai presentations can be found at russialist.org › transcript-puti n-at-meeting-of-the-valdai-international-discu… and https://thesaker.is›putins-spe ech-at-the-valdai-club-full-transcript

7 For a critique of the realist theory and its flawed explanation of the implosion of the Soviet Union and end of the Cold War, see Lebow (1994); Lebow and Stein (1994). See also Kolodziej (2005), pp. 77–126.

8 Putin's address to the Munich Conference on Security Policy, February 12, 2007. https://en.wikipedia.org/wiki/Munich_speech_of_Vladimir_Putin
Also consult (Russian Federation, 2013), which parallels Putin's boundless and borderless conception of security.

9 *New York Times*, November 11, 2019, reports that Russia has hacked into the democratic electoral processes of Madagascar.

10 See Paul Schroeder, Preface, n. 3 and Schroeder (1989, 1994) for an illuminating exposition of how the modification of the Westphalian system through a process of "equilibrium" by the principal imperial powers to preserve world peace after 1815. The big powers compromised their conflicting interests in the developing world to avoid a global conflagration until their aggressive expansionist policies and unlimited arms races, fueled by rampant nationalism, plunged them again into an unstable, war-prone balance of power system that imploded in World War I.

11 See, for example, the works of G. John Ikenberry (2011, 2020).

12 Bull (1977).

13 Bogdanov (2017).

14 The notion of a Russian "Monroe Doctrine" is developed in Karagiannis (2014); Skak (2011).

15 See Chapter 6, China and the Imperative of Legitimacy.

16 Bogdanov (2017); Skak (2011).

17 Nicaragua, Venezuela, Syria, and Nauru. These four states also recognize Transnistria as a state.

18 Recall that I stated earlier that I would first present the case for global governance from the perspective of Russia and China. Ukrainian scholars and political leaders reject President Putin's conception of Ukraine, as an integral part of the Russian World and of imperial Russia. They insist on a unique Ukrainian history and Ukraine as an independent state. For an overview of Ukraine-Russia relations, consult Andres Kappeler. He presents a balanced discussion of the widely held Ukrainian view of Ukraine's history with Russia that contrasts with Putin's version (Kappeler, 2014). For a complex discussion of this centuries-old fraught relation, consult (Pikulicka-Wilczewka and Sakwa, 2016).

19 Putin's remarks to the Valdai Forum in September 2013. See n. 6 for citation.

20 Galeiotti (2015) describes Russia's use of "Hybrid Warfare" to plunge Ukraine into a civil war that facilitates Moscow's control of Kiev's foreign and economic policies, blocking its ability to join either the European Union or NATO.

21 Consult (Bobo Lo, 2015; Hill and Gaddy, 2015; Mendras, 2012; Stent, 2014).

22 Legitimacy based on charismatic leadership is discussed below under Putin's response to the Legitimacy imperative.

23 Yaffe (2016b).

24 Yaffe (2016a).

25 Yaffe (2016b).

26 Works relied upon for this section include the following: Kanet (2018a); Kotkin (2016); Lukyanov (2016); Monaghan (2015–16); Nygren (2008); Oliker (2015); Russian Federation (2013); Trenin (2016); Wagnsson (2009).

27 Speech of President Putin on his election in March, 2018. *New York Times*, March 2, 2018.

28 Sergi (2018) The members of the EEU, including Russia, Belarus, Kazakhstan, Armenia, and Kyrgyzstan, would appear to be impressive economic powers. In 2015 they had a collective GDP of US$1.59 trillion, an industrial production of US$1.3 trillion in 2014, and a population of almost 200 million. Russia accounts for most of the GDP. The GDP of the European Union in 2017 of US$17.3 trillion dwarfs the EEU. Nor does the EEU operate with anything that approaches the EU in coordinating the economic cooperation of its member states (including the United Kingdom). See https://tradingeconomics.com/european-union/gdp.

29 There is no one document or presentation by President Putin or by the Russian foreign office that fully develops the critique of the West's global leadership or that presents a comprehensive explanation of the Putin solution to global governance. This volume's presentation is a distillation of Putin's initiatives in security and foreign policy as well as his speeches, notably those before the Valdai Forum, organized annually under the sponsorship of the Russian state. It also draws on extensive scholarly analyses and evaluations, noted throughout, of Russian foreign and economic policies and his dominance of the Russian state. Putin's speech to the Munich Security conference in 2007 (n. 8) and his presentation at the Valdai Forum in 2016 are particularly helpful in cobbling together a coherent understanding of his challenge to the liberal model for global governance. In reviewing the Valdai Forum materials, readers are urged to read through the long and discursive question and answer record of each meeting. These exchanges contain in piecemeal fashion much of Putin's case against the Western system and his championing of the Russian solution to global governance. For the 2016 address to the Valdai Club, see https://larouchepac.com›20161028›putin-valdai-club-calls-new-world-.

30 Woolf (2018).

31 Review Chapter 3 for the discussion of President Bush's West Point speech.

32 Responses of President Putin in the question and answer portion of the Valdai Forum in 2016. See https://justice4poland.com/2016/11/24/putins-2016-speech-at-valdai-discussion-club.

33 Ibid. Putin makes this anti-democratic charge in his remarks to the Valdai Forum in 2016.

34 Some scholars of Russian public opinion argue that nondemocratic regimes can rule legitimately. While this view has some plausibility, I prefer a higher standard for legitimacy than simply the capacity of the state's power to rule or to provide for the material welfare of its subjects. What is required is public consent in the form of free and fair elections. Also relevant are toleration of minority rights, an open civil society, and the protection of free speech for individuals, groups, and all forms of public and private media, the right of petition and assembly, and unfettered formation of political parties. These are indispensable tests in evaluating whether a regime is truly a liberal democracy and legitimate in the sense understood by Rousseau. Non-democratic and even partially democratic states do not meet these more demanding standards. See Dahl (1989) and Chapters 1 and 2 for more detailed discussion of the requirements of a democratic regime. That many authoritarian regimes, like Putin's Russia, have survived for almost a generation is more a testimony to their coercive and economic power and their ability to manipulate a majority in managed elections than to their commitment to seek consensual legitimacy to their rule. Rose and his associates offer this bleak prediction: "Since most regimes in the world are undemocratic or only partially democratic, the Russian system may today be more typical of how the world's peoples are governed than are Anglo-American democracies." See Rose et al. (2011, p. 6). See also Hanson (2014) who addresses this issue, pp. 175ff. With India under Bharatiya Janata Party increasingly falling into the populist camp, a vast majority of the world's population are now under undemocratic rule. That grim unbalance dramatizes the challenge of survival confronting the liberal democratic states.

35 Quoted in Bobo Lo (2015, p. 78).

36 Ibid. and Hanson (2014),
37 See the comprehensive 2017 report on Russian military capabilities of the Defense Intelligence Agency from which data for this section is largely drawn. www.dia.mil›documents›news›militarypowerpublications›russ...
See also Facon (2017); Oliker (2015); Trenin (2016).
38 MIRVs refer to Multiple-Independently Targeted-Reentry Vehicles, while ICBMs refer to Intercontinental Ballistic Missiles.
39 *New York Times,* March, 2017.
40 See Woolf (2018).
41 www.thedrive.com/the-war-zone/36945/russia-says-this-is-our-first-glimpse-of...
42 President Putin's continued reliance on these special forces is noted in Vladimir Voronov, "Krym i Kreml': ot plana 'A' k planu 'B,'" March 15, 2015, *svoboda.org* (Radio Liberty), https://www.svoboda.org/a/26899899.html].
43 Quoted in (Monaghan, 2015–16), p, 69.
44 Report in *New York Times,* June 10, 2018, p. 1ff.
45 Business Insider, April 17, 2018, and No Author, "Nazvany glavnye problems voenno-morskogo flota Rossii," December 26, 2017, *pravda.ru,* www.pravda.ru/news/politics/military/26-12-2017/1363532-sea-0/].
46 Valery Gerasimov, "The Value of Science Is in Foresight: New Challenges Demand Rethinking the Forms and Methods of Carrying out Combat Operations," *Voyenno-Promyshlennyy Kurier,* February 26, 2013.
47 See the translation of the Russian journal article by Robert Coalson, June 12, 2014, at "Russian Military Doctrine Article by General Valery Gerasimov" www.facebook.com›notes›robert-coalson›russian-military-doct...
48 For the full presentation of the 37-page indictment, consult https://www.nytimes.com › russians-indicted-mueller-election-interference
49 Ibid.
50 Ibid., p. 26. Consult the full Mueller Report describing Russian interference in the 2016 presidential election (Mueller, 2019).
51 Dawisha (2015).
52 Alexeev and Weber (2013). This is the shared view of the 51 economists comprising this edited volume on the Russian economy.
53 Novokmet et al. (2017).
54 Ibid., Figures 7c.
55 Ibid., Figure 2.
56 Aslund (2013a, 2013b); Ericson (2013).
57 Gaddy and Ickes (2013); Kryukov and Moe (2013a, 2013b).
58 Rosefielde (2013).
59 Besides the volumes cited earlier which cover these acquisitions, see also the brief explanation offered by Pikkety and associates. (Novokmet et al., 2017), p. 38.
60 Sil and Cheng (2004, p. 360).
61 Dawisha (2015, p. 305).
62 http://en.kremlin.ru/events/president/transcripts/21480
63 See www.quora.com›Who-originally-said-To-my-friends-everything-t...
64 Sil and Cheng (2004, p. 360).
65 Gaddy and Ickes (2013, p. 311).
66 Ibid.
67 Aslund (2007) develops this point throughout.
68 See Transparency International for a long list of corrupt activities that are tracked convering most states, including Russia.
www.transparency.org
See also Dawisha (2015); Levitsky and Ziblatt (2018) See also Holmes (2008).
69 Dawisha (2015), p. 322. Confirming Dawisha's findings are two studies, which elaborate on her findings. See Belton (2020); Pomerantsev (2014).
70 https://www.imf.org/external/pubs/ft/issues6/index.htm

71 Novokmet et al. (2017), Figure 2.
72 Ibid., Figure 8b.
73 Ibid., Figure 8c.
74 Ibid., Figure 10c.
75 Ibid., Figure 12a.
76 Ibid., p. 5. Shortly before this volume went to press, the International Consortium of Investigative Journalists (ICIJ) revealed that 330 high public officers from 90 countries laundered trillions of dollars of their personal wealth. The ICIJ identified hundreds of offshore companies used by 4,400 Russians, including 46 Russian oligarchs, to secure their assets, looted from public coffers or profits subject to taxation. The ICIJ's Pandora Papers provides additional evidence of the Putin Kleptocracy. See *New York Times*, October 4, 2021.
77 Ibid., p. 38.
78 https://www.imf.org/external/pubs/ft/issues6/index.htm
79 Novokmet et al. (2017), Figure 7f.
80 Shevtsova (2012, p. 210).
81 Ibid.
82 The paradox of a Russian government lacking trust and legitimacy but still existing short of the totalitarian rule of the Soviet era has prompted a number of academic and public policy analysts to explain this seeming paradox. The results of this debate remain mixed and inconclusive. Yet the puzzle of the Putin regime persists. See, for example, Cannady (2013); Colton (2003); Fish (2005); Gel'man (2010); Gel'man (2012); Hanson (2011); Holmes (2010); Rose (2011); Rose (2002); Rose (2004); Shevtsova (2012); Sil (2004).
83 S. E. Hanson (2011, p. 32).
84 Gel'man (2010, pp. 56–57).
85 Rousseau (1978).
86 Gel'man (2010). See also Gel'man (2012).
87 Quoted in Cannady and Kubicek (2013, p. 2).
88 See Dahl (1989) and Chapter 2.
89 Pipes (1974, 1995).
90 Sil and Cheng (2004, p. 350). Indispensable also are the studies of Russian public opinion by Richard Rose, William Mishler, and Neil Munro: Rose et al. (2011); Rose and Munro (2002); Rose et al. (2004). These more detailed works generally support Sil's findings.
91 Ibid.
92 See Coicaud (2002); Reus-Smit (2007) for the view that legitimacy is a source of political power as significant as coercion or economic resources in governing. See also Kolodziej (2016), especially pp. 227–272.
93 Shevtsova (2012).
94 Richters (2013); Cannady and Kubicek (2013) confirm Richters findings. See also Bobo Lo (2015, pp. 34–35).
95 Presentation of President Putin at the Valdai Forum in 2013. n. 6.
96 Ibid.
97 Ibid.
98 Carrère d'Encausse (1993). The Soviet Union, as Carrère d'Encausse suggests, was never able to suppress the many, complex, contrasting and clashing social identities of the Russian population, divisions that ultimately contributed to its collapse.
99 Cannady and Kubicek (2013).
100 Presentation of President Putin at the Valdai Forum in 2013. n. 6.
101 See Beetham (1991), who exposes the limitations of Weber's notion of legal-rational, resting on a narrow juridical base rather than on a substantive and normative foundation associated with religion, a secular ideology like the creation of the Soviet man, or democratic popular sovereignty where legitimacy can only be granted through free elections.

102 It is instructive to note that Charles de Gaulle, as president of France, insisted on a referendum to legitimate the Fifth Republic and his rule as prerequisites for ending the Algerian war and for regaining a global role for France, at least in leading France into what would become the European Union. See Jackson (2018); Kolodziej (1974) where this point is developed.

103 Concluding remarks of President Putin at the Valdai Form in 2014. See n. 6.

104 For many scholars it remains a paradox that majorities will vote to be ruled by an authoritarian regime. Putin contends that his popular election, however flawed, demonstrates that the Russian Federation is a democracy. For scholars wrestling with this paradox and efforts to relax this dilemma, see, particularly, Gel'man (2010); Gel'man (2012); Rose (2002, 2004, 2011).

105 Gessen (2016).

106 https://nypost.com/2020/10/07/alexei-navalny-says-near-death-poisoning-felt-like-the-end

107 Lipman (2016).

108 Ibid., p. 111. The award of the Nobel Peace Prize to Dmitry Muratov in 2021 for courageously fighting for free expression in Russia underscores the grave threats facing journalists who struggle for transparency and accountability in Putin's Kleptocracy. https://www.nobelprize.org/prizes/peace/2021/muratov/facts

109 *New York Times*, June 20, 2019. Both Navalny and Skripal were poisoned with a Russian, military-developed toxin, Novichok. See also Blake (2019) for a discussion of Putin's assassination program.

110 Freedom House, *Freedom in the World 2018: Russia*.
     https://freedomhouse.org › report › freedom-world › 2018 › russia

111 http://en.kremlin.ru/events/president/transcripts/21480

112 Tempest (2013), p. 11.

113 Elizabeth Ralph, Vladimir Putin, King of All Sports, *Politico*, February 7, 2014.

114 Whatever prestige may have been accrued by Putin and Russia in sponsoring the 2014 Winter Olympic Games was negated by the scandal of state-sponsored doping of Russian athletes and Russia's elimination as a nation in the 2018 games. Russian athletes who passed a doping test competed as individuals. See Duval (2017).

115 *The Washington Post*, January 9, 2015.

116 See n. 104.

117 Laquer (2015)

118 Ibid., p. 228.

119 Ibid.

120 Daflon (2009).

121 Gel'man (2010, 2012) See also Hirschman (1970)

122 Quoted in Laquer (2015, p. 228).

123 See n. 10.

124 *Le Monde,* September 12, 2001, p. 1.

125 Russett (1993).

126 Corwin (1916) Corwin develops this point in this landmark volume.

127 Balmaceda (2007); Baran (2010).

128 Freedom House, *Freedom in the World 2018: Russia*.
     https://freedomhouse.org › report › freedom-world › 2018 › russia

129 Ibid.

130 Ibid.

8

A MODEST WAY FORWARD

We are at the end of the beginning of this discussion. This volume has attempted to establish six propositions:

First, that all humans are members of a global society for the first time in the evolution of the species.

Second, no human society can survive and thrive absent an effective and legitimate government.

Third, the primordial challenge confronting the world's populations is to address the challenge of global governance.

Fourth, the diversity and division of the peoples of the world society preclude the creation of a government universally acknowledged as effective and legitimate.

Fifth, within a profoundly flawed, war-prone nation-state system, the pursuit of global governance resolves itself into a struggle between two contending and incompatible visions to govern the world's resistant populations: a Westphalian system populated either by liberal democratic or authoritarian regimes.

Sixth, the liberal democratic alliance can regain its currently receding ascendancy if it returns, with appropriate institutional and governmental reforms to fit the times, to the solutions to OWL imperatives adopted by the liberal democracies after World War II. Absent the reaffirmation and the strengthening of that OWL power structure, sketched in Chapter 2, the liberal democracies will increasingly cede the spaces occupied by global governance to the Chinese and Russian authoritarian regimes.

What can the liberal democracies do to regain the initiative to meet the challenges posed by authoritarian regimes? Specifically, what should they do to meet the Chinese and Russian solutions to global governance?

DOI: 10.4324/9781003246572-8

A full response to these questions goes well beyond any singular attempt to provide comprehensive and meaningful answers. The issues facing the liberal democracies are too complex and range over far too many interdependent policy domains to be submitted to cursory summary. In this concluding chapter, I will restrict myself to recommendations to promote collective decision-making and cooperation among the liberal democracies in their response to OWL imperatives. The aim is to adapt and strengthen the governmental responses of the liberal democracies to the stresses imposed on these regimes by the dynamic and damaging forces operating throughout an increasingly connected and interdependent nation-state system and global society.

Some doable reforms

There is an urgent need to ensure that the liberal democracies construct a united OWL front to address the challenges of China and Russia in league with other authoritarian states. Each democratic state should create a new global OWL post at the cabinet level. The Assistant Secretary of State for OWL Imperatives of each democracy would have two principal missions. The first would be to evaluate and certify whether the policies and initiatives issuing from the various branches of the government complement and are consistent with those of other liberal democratic states in response to OWL imperatives.

The second mission is to propose changes in a state's policies to align with those of other democracies. The decision of the United States, Great Britain, Canada, and the European Union to sanction China for human rights violations of more than a million Uighurs is precisely the kind of united front not only to support human rights but also to affirm the principles of legitimacy underlying liberal democratic rule.[1]

Going beyond certification and policy revisions there is the added requirement that new initiatives be proposed to meet new conditions. The proposal of the Biden administration for a global minimum tax rate on multinational corporations illustrates a solution to the global problem arising from the mutually harmful practice of states competing for foreign investment. The result is a race to the bottom in which all of the states are losers. If a common tax policy can be achieved across the democracies, it would shift the priority from enhancing corporate profits at the expense of state revenues to the interests of workers who have been left behind by globalization.[2] Other welfare needs can also be addressed – education, health, environmental protection, and the care of the old and young, etc.

The Assistant Secretaries of State for OWL imperatives across democratic regimes would be in constant contact. They would meet regularly in person or through interactive internet and social media-assisted exchanges. They would be charged to advance recommendations to improve the negotiating and bargaining position of the liberal democracies in the struggle to hold and capture the spaces bearing on global governance for the benefit of the liberal democracies and their populations. Central to their work would be the annual issuance of a global trends report of dynamic forces impacting negatively on liberal democratic governmental institutions. These reports would be patterned after the quadrennial report of the US *National Intelligence Council's Global Trends: 2040.*[3]

In its 2021 report, the Council identified several disruptive trends confounding democratic rule. First, global challenges will likely increase in number and intensity over climate change, disease, financial crises, and rapidly diffusing technological innovations, disruptive of social cohesion. Second, communities, states, and the international system will be increasingly fragmented in their capacity to address these issues. Third, a yawning rift is predicted to develop between populations demanding that their governmental institutions deliver solutions to these challenges and the progressive inability of these institutions to respond effectively. Fourth, this imbalance between demands and delivery will foster greater conflict within and between states. The report concluded that

> politics within states are likely to grow more volatile and contentious, and no region, ideology, or governance system seems immune or to have the answers. At the international level, the geopolitical environment will be more competitive — shaped by China's challenge to the United States and the Western-led international system.[4]

It is important for this national report to be scaled to the democratic alliance as a whole. The annual high-level intelligence findings of the joint workings of the Assistant Secretaries for OWL imperatives would be expected to permeate OWL thinking through all policy circles. The empirically grounded trend projections of the report should also inform the legislative branch of each democratic regime. Each state legislature would be expected to create an OWL committee to continually review and evaluate the effectiveness of each state's OWL positions and those of its allies to determine their contemporary and long-term effectiveness. These committees would also be charged to propose legislation to bolster the power of the democratic alliance to promote a Westphalian system with democratic characteristics throughout what is likely to be a century-long struggle with authoritarian systems.

As for the Imperative of Order, two initiatives are uppermost. First, Article 5 of the Atlantic Alliance must be re-affirmed: "that an armed attack against one or more of ... [member states] in Europe or North America shall be considered an attack against them all."[5] The Trump administration's reduction of the Atlantic Alliance to national, self-interested transactional exchanges seriously undermined the trust underlying Alliance commitments. The Atlantic Alliance relaxed the Hobbesian dilemma between allies and pooled their military and technological power. These remarkable and unprecedented achievements contributed significantly to the ascendancy of the democracies in the Cold War. Conversely, President Trump's self-defeating response to the Imperative of Order strengthened the Chinese and Russian solutions to global governance.

The upshot of these mindless moves pushed the Westphalian state system closer to its anarchical endgame, stripped of the constraints of democratic values.

What held the democracies together in the Cold War was not only the pooling of their material resources and power to deter Soviet aggression but also their shared commitment to the promise and rigors of liberal democratic rule. President Trump's praise for authoritarian regimes and his support of Russian strategic objectives undermined the collective power of the democracies to deter Russian aggression in Europe and beyond. Russia's expansionist objectives manifested themselves in Putin's seizure of Crimea, Russian military intervention in Ukraine, Georgia, and Moldova, support for the Assad regime in Syria, and mischief making in Afghanistan and Africa. These aggressive moves testify to Putin's corrupt, warped, and backward-looking vision of a return to a truncated Russian empire as partial compensation for what he has lamented was the catastrophe of the Soviet Union's implosion and the demise of its empire.

Trump's welcoming of Russia's disruptive intervention in the presidential elections of 2016 and 2020 to elect him as president served further to divide both the American public and the Western alliance. His relentless assault on allies and his politics of fear, rage, racism, anti-Semitism, and immigrant threats were, in retrospective evaluation, deliberately designed to polarize the American public. Divide and rule were the building blocks of his 2016 electoral victory and his anti-democratic, populist administration. Sapped was the unity of purpose and public support required for America's resumption of its leadership role. The principal benefits of converging Trump and Putin political objectives were the aggrandizement of Putin's personal power and support for his efforts to "Make Russia Great Again" at the price of the collective security and freedoms of the liberal democracies.

Returning the United States to its leadership role will not be easy or quick. A simple reaffirmation of Article 5 will not be sufficient to restore allied confidence in American reliability. What one administration can do, another can nullify, much as the Trump administration demonstrated in undoing in a stroke 75 years of confidence building among the allies.

The most daunting obstacle to restoring alliance cohesion is overcoming the polarization of the American public. The Trump administration exacerbated that division rather than created it. His electoral defeat will not automatically galvanize public opinion to de-politicize foreign policy and alliance commitments. A distracted and deeply divided public is scarcely the foundation for an expanded US role in addressing the issues besetting the democracies and the rest of the world's populations.

A large segment of the American people believes that what happens beyond the shores of the United States is not their concern. Seventy-two million Americans voted in 2020 to retain the Trump presidency, more votes cast for a presidential candidate in American history, although short of the 81 million votes for President Biden. Implicitly, if unwittingly, voters were consenting to Trump's policies, his violation of the American Constitution, and his relentless assault on the public norms safeguarding American democracy. Absent the restoration of public support for the projection of US power to foster, simultaneously, its security and economic interests and those of the democracies, the Chinese and Russian models will gain in power and attractiveness.

As a start toward re-earning allied confidence in the United States, there should be a return to renewed and active allied engagement in joint strategic policymaking in NATO. Repair must also extend to frequent and strengthened consultations on strategic policy, joint military operations, and debate within the alliance over what stance the alliance should take toward anti-liberal regimes, especially China and Russia, and how the military resources of the democracies should be raised, financed, and employed to counter Russian and rising Chinese military power on the way to parity with the United States. Free-riding, hiding, or shame blaming won't do.

A common stance is also necessary to hold to account defectors from liberal democracy rule and norms within the democratic alliance. The Polish and Hungarian regimes should be boycotted from alliance meetings and strategic negotiations until they again revert to liberal democratic rule. The European Union's unanimity rule hampers its ability to impose sanctions on Warsaw and Budapest. The same implicit rule hinders NATO Alliance moves to induce both states as well as illiberal Turkey to return to liberal democratic practices.

Individual members are not precluded from proposing that these illiberal democracies receive no further assistance from the EU and that they be excluded from NATO strategic planning as well as military exercises. These errant states should be confronted with choices to lose significant economic aid from the EU. They should also be put on notice that the NATO pledge to come to their aid if threatened is qualified by their adherence to democratic rule. Sustained criticism by individual EU and NATO states of Polish, Hungarian, and Turkish populist rule could conceivably gradually qualify the unanimity rule by exposing populist regimes as threats to the liberal democracies in their confrontation with authoritarian states. The Polish and Hungarian apostate regimes are especially vulnerable. They should be pressed to choose between their economic interests and the loss of EU assistance; no less would they be forced to choose between their national security and populist rule. They have more to fear from Putin's Russia than from their allies. As a general principle, illiberal democracies should be marginalized in the EU and NATO to ensure the democratic integrity of these multilateral organizations.

This brings me to the second and even more problematic response to the Imperative of Order. Somehow the security threats to Japan, South Korea, and Taiwan have to be incorporated into NATO strategic thinking – and vice versa. It may appear to be a bridge too far to globalize the Western alliance to include democracies around the world, notably those in Asia who confront Chinese aggression and subservience. Currently, the national populations of the democracies in the West and Asia are scarcely prepared for such a bold move. Anne Applebaum reports, for example, that the Spanish populist Vox party expresses no interest in supporting East European security interests,[6] failed memory of the Spanish Civil War as the prelude to World War II notwithstanding. How much less likely can one expect Western populations to be keen to be drawn into Asian conflicts or Asian democracies to be willing to assist the containment of Russian aggression in Europe.

It is telling to recall that the entry of the United States into World War II and its invasion of Europe in June 1944 began with the Japanese attack on Pearl Harbor. The Asian and European theaters then formed one seamless battle-ground in the battle against Nazi and Japanese imperialism. The nuclear threat posed by North Korea, which is aimed at Japan, Korea, and the United States, necessarily fuses European and Asian security interests. The growth of Chinese military capabilities, increasingly matching and in some areas surpassing US mil-itary power, is also an existential threat to the European states if war should break out between the United States and China over Chinese aggression either in the South China Sea or its invasion of Taiwan. Both scenarios are highly probable. The European states cannot insulate themselves from a US–Chinese military confrontation and the threat that one or both will use nuclear weapons to avert defeat. There is also the shared economic interest of all trading states to preserve free passage through the South China Sea. The economic interests of the EU and United States depend on the unimpeded movement of trade, commerce, and peoples through this vast area.

If the populations of the democracies could be informed that their mutually contingent interests and values are at stake around the globe, it is not unrealis-tic to believe that a global alliance of democracies in the struggle to determine global governance could be progressively forged. While the fact and logic of stra-tegic interdependence is clear and urgent, moving to widespread popular knowl-edge and acknowledgment of this inescapable condition will not be achieved overnight. Democratic leaders have an obligation to link national domestic and foreign objectives to their nation's alliance with other democracies to shape a world that sustains free and open regimes. They did just that after World War II. The experience of global warming and pandemics, now increasingly understood by democratic populations as national security threats, should be seized upon to convince them to support and extend collective action across all policy domains of concern to preserve and expand democratic rule over the world society. What John Donne enjoined four centuries ago as the dependency of humans on each other extends now to the inter-penetrated peoples of the world society. This condition entwines the free peoples of the democracies in a shared destiny: No people are islands, entire of themselves, every social community is a piece of the continent, a part of the main.

Rather than expect an alliance of Western and East Asian states anytime soon, it is prudent and pragmatic to initially begin joint strategic discussions among these states at an informal level. These meetings could lead to a Forum for regularly scheduled meetings, organized by the Assistant Secretaries for OWL imperatives. In reaching this level of confidence, the stage would be set to institutionalize strategic discussions at an OWL level of policymaking. These would cover specific threats to each member and how the other democracies might help a vulnerable ally. They could also be used to pool the resources of the democracies to deter Chinese or Russian aggression in Asia, Europe, and elsewhere where Western interests are at risk. The containment of China and Russia depends on the cooperation and military engagement of all of the democracies.

The Trump administration took the right step but in the wrong direction in acting unilaterally to confront China's state capitalism, its favoritism of Chinese corporations, widespread corruption, the digital theft of property rights and of corporate commercial and technological data and production plans. The obvious strategy is to organize a common democratic-state position to confront China. Working together the democracies have more negotiating and bargaining leverage over Beijing. No one state can push back with sufficient power to discipline a self-interested China to preserve a free-market system dedicated to the benefit of all participants. The Chinese state-centered economic approach to global welfare enhances its economic interests at the expense of other states. Beggar-thy-neighbor policies foster conflict, not peaceful commercial exchange.

The currently moribund World Trade Organization also has to be revived and reformed to provide an institutional mechanism and arbitration process to return to a rule-based system supportive of free exchange. It is an appropriate multilateral agency to confront Chinese power seeking to impose its preferred rules on economic exchange. The BRI can be viewed as an end run around a rule-based trading system. The United States and European Union, which share similar grievances against China, should insist that China modify its autarchic response to the Imperative of Welfare to ensure a level playing field. The record of the postwar period of sustained economic growth and technological development should be the loadstars of trading states to foster their mutual interests rather than skew the system to favor the individual interests of its most powerful partners.

A return to *status quo ante* will still not be enough. Too many people are left out of the benefits of a global market system. These refer not only to those at the poverty line or below in developed countries, but also to the disadvantaged hundreds of millions in the developing countries. There is also the growing inequality of incomes as a product of market operations favoring capital over labor across most states. Countervailing policies to cope with poverty, inequality, and the massive loss of remunerative jobs to globalization must be initiated to preserve public support for a liberal market system.

The Western alliance must also develop joint policies and strategies to respond to the economic and environmental issues confronting the developing world. China has launched an ambitious Belt and Road Initiative to address poverty, equality, and environmental issues in the developing world. That much of the thrust of this initiative is driven by Chinese interests should not obscure recognition of the material and technological benefits, which (at this writing) 139 states currently enjoy from BRI, notwithstanding the many drawbacks to BRI for these states outlined in Chapter 4.

The current disarray in the assistance offered by the democratic states must be collectively re-thought. Greater use of the World Bank and the International Monetary Fund to fund aid to the developing world should be pursued in lieu of the current uncoordinated, piecemeal, state-by-state approach. Targeted assistance at promoting concrete programs that promise success will have three important outcomes. First, aid will likely be more efficiently and effectively distributed to needy nations. Second, there will be greater and more sustained economic and technological progress of underdeveloped economies. Finally, more expanded and effective aid will also increase incentives for populations to stay at home to build their societies rather than embark on hazardous, large-scale immigration to developed states. The latter are not capable, economically, politically, or culturally, to accommodate the millions of immigrants in incessant movement to better their lots. As of 2020 more than 270 million persons were living in a country to which they have migrated, 100 million more than 2000.[7] If the developed states share their wealth and knowledge with the disadvantaged, they are actually pursuing their own self-interests. These are moves by which the democracies can steal a march on China's BRI program.

The COVID-19 epidemic has also clearly exposed the fundamental dependence of economic growth on global health. Parallel to the strengthening of the World Trade Organization, the World Health Organization (WHO) must be reformed and its mission enlarged. It must be preserved as a global service agency and insulated as much as possible from the power struggles of participating members. Warring COVID-19 diplomacy between China and the United States, each claiming that its system has been more effective than that of its opponent, damages collective WHO efforts to organize a united effort of all states against a common enemy. Pandemic viruses are impervious to state boundaries. If one reviews real and threatened epidemics of the last half-century, a pattern emerges that suggests that these eruptions are not isolated instances, but elements of a grim trend in global health. In the brief compass of a half-century, populations around the globe have been attacked by HIV, SARs, Swine Flu, and Ebola. And now COVID-19.

On reflection this pattern should come as no surprise. Outbreaks arise from the connectedness and interdependence of the world's over seven billion people – and counting. Whereas Jules Verne could imagine going around the world in 80 days as an extraordinary feat, one now can get to any point in the world in less than 24 hours.[8] That means infections can travel around the world faster than ever before as one infected population infects another. No state can isolate and insulate itself from these global pandemic threats. That is a futile enterprise. Unless attacked globally, all states and their populations will suffer economic losses. Each state will confront new, formidable threats to its national security and health interests within a global society at risk.

A final word refers to what the democracies can do collectively to defend themselves and to expand the promise of democratic rule. The overriding aim is for liberal democratic regimes to live up to their promise. The lure of illiberal, illegitimate rule must be contained and averted. Chapter 3 briefly outlines what has to be done. Specifically, Trumpian populism must be confronted and defeated if the United States is to regain its role as leader of the liberal democratic coalition.

Authoritarian regimes should also be under ceaseless scrutiny for their abuse of civil liberties and human rights. The democracies should orchestrate their criticisms to magnify their voices and to provide encouragement to opponents of authoritarian regimes. The beleaguered partisans of democratic governance need help whether through sustained and collective democratic state criticism or through ceaseless petitions before international organizations and tribunals to expose authoritarian oppression.

Clearly, violence to impose liberal democratic rule should be eschewed. Note the grim record of Vietnam, the second Iraqi invasion, and the collapse of Libyan state in the aftermath of the violent overthrow of the Kaddafi regime. No less poignant and painful is the abject failure of the United States and its allies to erect a liberal democracy in Afghanistan after 20 years of war. It is a fool's errand to force a people whose national, cultural, and religious identities as well as history and social habits are alien to the norms and values of a liberal democracy. It can only end, as these flawed military interventions evidence, in needless tens of thousands of casualties and loss of lives. And for no honor, merit, or purpose.

Recognizing the limits of military force is not an invitation to disarmament as a response to Chinese or Russian aggression or the suppression of their populations. Maintaining allied military forces to deter Chinese or Russian aggression is a collective responsibility of the democracies. Hanging over authoritarian and democratic states – all of humanity – is the specter of nuclear war. Deterrence is still, *faute de mieux*, the only feasible, if dangerously unstable, strategy to avoid nuclear war and preserve, however disquietly, the preservation of democratic rule and a fragile and vulnerable global society.

The states of the Westphalian system, a mix today of democratic and authoritarian regimes, are trapped in a Shakespearean tragedy of their own making. There is no easy exit from this drama, no *deus ex machina* on the horizon to save the world's states and peoples who are both spectators and players. Distasteful compromises will be necessary between the two systems and their partisans to live in continuing conflict, but short of nuclear confrontation as the struggle between free and authoritarian rule plays out over this century.

As Hannah Arendt reminds us, the struggle between the liberal democratic, Chinese, and Russian solutions for governing globalization is not new. It is the latest iteration of an endless drama, deeply and profoundly embedded in the psyche, clashing interests and intractable values animating humans ever at sixes and sevens: "No cause is left but the most ancient of all, the one, in fact, that from the beginning of our history has determined the very existence of politics, the cause of freedom versus tyranny."[9]

It is what it is.

Notes

1 See the Associated Press report of March 23, 2021:
  https://abcnews.go.com/International/wireStory/eu-slaps-sanctions-chinese-officials
2 See *Financial Times*, April 5, 2021:
  www.ft.com/content/79023ff2-c629-429c-8a34-16bf68b4ea15
  For German backing of the Biden proposal, see
  www.businessinsider.com.au›janet-yellen-globa...
3 www.dni.gov›index.php›global-trends-home (Italics in the title)
4 See "Key Themes." https://dni.gov/index.php/gt2040-home/keythemes.
5 www.nato.int/cps/en/natolive/official_texts_17120.htm
6 Applebaum (2020, p. 129).
7 See n. 4, above.
8 See the BBC special program "COVID19: The History of Pandemics": Bryan Walsh, March 25, 2020.
  https://bbc.com/future/article/20200325-covid-19-the-history-of-pandemics
9 Arendt (1963, p. 11).

BIBLIOGRAPHY

Abramowitz, Alan. (2018). *The Great Alignment*. New Haven, CT: Yale University Press.

Acemoglu, Daron. (2021). *Redesigning AI: Work, Democracy, and Justice in the Age of Automation*. Boston: Boston Review Forum.

Acheson, Dean. (1969). *Present at the Creation*. New York: Norton.

Adams, James Truslow. (1931). *The Epic of America*. New York: Little, Brown.

Akerlof, George A., & Shiller, Robert J. (2009). *Animal Spirits: How Psychology Drives the Economy and Why It Matters for Global Capitalism*. Princeton, NJ: Princeton University Press.

Alden, Edward. (2017). *Failure to Adjust: How Americans Got Left Behind in the Global Economy*. New York: Rowman & Littlefield.

Alexeev, Michael, & Weber, Shlomo (Eds.) (2013). *Oxford Handbook of the Russian Economy*. Oxford: Oxford University Press.

Allison, Graham T. (2017). *Destined for War: Can America and China Escape Thucydides's Trap?* New York: Houghton Mifflin Harcourt.

Allison, Graham T. (February 2020). *The U.S.-China Strategic Competition: Clues from History*. Aspen, CO: Paper presented at the Aspen Institute.

Allison, Roy. (2013). *Russia, the West, and Military Intervention*. Oxford: Oxford University Press.

Alvaredo, Fecundo, et al. (2018). *World Inequality Report 2018*. Cambridge, MA: Harvard University Press.

Ang, Yuen Yuen. (2020). *China's Golden Age: The Paradox of Economic Boom and Vast Corruption*. Cambridge: Cambridge University Press.

Angell, Norman. (1909). *The Great Illusion*. London: Heinemann.

Anonymous. (2014). *Military Doctrine of the Russian Federation*. Moscow: Ministry of Foreign Affairs.

Applebaum, Anne. (2020). *Twilight of Democracy: The Seductive Lure of Authoritarianism*. New York: Doubleday.

Arendt, Hannah. (1951). *The Origins of Totalitarianism*. New York: Harcourt, Brace.

Arendt, Hannah. (1963). *On Revolution*. New York: Penguin.

Asland, Anders. (1995). *How Russia Became a Market Economy.* Washington, DC: Brookings Institution.

Aslund, Anders. (2007). *Russia's Capitalist Revolution: Why Market Reform Succeeded and Democracy Failed.* Washington, DC: Peterson Institute for International Economics.

Aslund, Anders. (2013a). *How Capitalism Was Built: The Transformation of Central and Eastern Europe, Russia, the Caucasus, and Central Asia* (2nd ed.). Cambridge: Cambridge University Press.

Aslund, Anders. (2013b). Russia's Economic Transformation. In Michael Alexeev & Schlomo Weber (Eds.), *The Oxford Handbook of the Russian Economy* (pp. 86–101). Oxford: Oxford University Press.

Atkinson, Rick. (2019). *The British Are Coming: The War for America, Lexington to Princeton, 1775–1777.* New York: Henry Holt.

Autor, David H., et al. (2008). Trends in U.S. Wage Inequality: Revising the Revisionists. *American Economic Journal: Papers & Proceedings, 90*(2), 300–323.

Autor, David H., et al. (2016). The China Shock: Learning from Labor-Market Adjustment to Large Changes in Trade. *Annual Review of Economics, 8*(1), 205–240.

Ba, Alice D. (2011). Staking Claims and Making Waves in the South China Sea: How Troubled Are the Waters? *Contemporary Southeast China, 33*(3), 269–291.

Bailyn, Bernard. (2017). *The Ideological Origins of the American Revolution: Fiftieth Anniversary Edition.* Cambridge, MA: Harvard University Press.

Bair, Sheila. (2012). *Bull by the Horns: Fighting to Save Main Street from Wall Street and Wall Street from Itself.* New York: Free Press.

Baldwin, Richard. (2016). *The Great Convergence: Information, Technology, and the New Globalization.* Cambridge, MA: Harvard University Press.

Baldwin, Richard. (2019). *The Robotics Upheaval; Globalization, Robotics, and the Future of Work.* Oxford: Oxford University Press.

Balmaceda, Margarita M. (2007). *Energy Dependency, Politics, and Corruption in the Former Soviet Union.* London: Routledge.

Baran, Zeyno. (2010). EU Energy Security: Time to End Russian Leverage. *Washington Quarterly 30*(4), 131–144.

Bartels, Larry. (2016). *Unequal Democracy: The Political Economy of the New Gilded Age.* New York: Russell Sage Foundation.

Bautista, Lowell, & Schofield, Clive. (2013). Philippine-China Border Relations: Cautious Engagement Amid Tensions. In Bruce A. Ellman, Stephen Kotkin, & Clive Schofield (Eds.), *Beijing's Power and China's Borders: Twenty Neighbors in Asia* (pp. 235–249). London: M.E. Sharpe.

Beck, Ulrich. (2007). *World at Risk.* Cambridge: Polity.

Beeching, Jack. (1975). *The Chinese Opium Wars.* New York: Harcourt Brace Jovanovich.

Beetham, David. (1991). Max Weber and the Legitimacy of the Modern State. *Analyse & Kritik, 13,* 34–45.

Beetham, David. (2013). *The Legitimation of Power.* Houndmills, United Kingdom: Palgrave.

Beissinger, Mark R., & Kotkin, Stephen (Eds.) (2014). *Historical Legacies of Communism in Russia and Eastern Europe.* Princeton, NJ: Princeton University Press.

Bell, Daniel A. (2015). *The China Model: Political Meritocracy and the Limits of Democracy.* Princeton, NJ: Princeton University Press.

Belton, Catherine. (2020). *Putin's People: How the KGB Took Back Russia and Then Took on the West.* New York: Farrar, Straus, and Giroux.

Bianchi, Robert R. (2019). *China and the Islamic World: How the New Silk Road Is Transforming Global Politics.* Oxford: Oxford University Press.

Blainey, Geoffrey. (1976). *Triumph of the Nomads: A History of Aboriginal Australia.* Woodstock: Overlook Press.

Blake, Heidi. (2019). *From Russia with Blood: The Kremlin's Ruthless Assassination Program and Vladimir Putin's Secret War on the West.* Los Angeles, CA: Mulholland.

Blanton, Shannon Lindsey. (2005). Foreign Policy in Transition? Human Rights, Democracy, and U.S. Arms Exports. *International Studies Quarterly, 49*(4), 447–467.

Bloch, Marc. (1961). *Feudal Society* (L. A. Manyon, Trans.). Chicago: University of Chicago Press.

Bobbio, Norberto. (1987). *The Future of Democracy: A Defence of the Rules of the Game* (Roger Griffin, Trans. Richard Bellamy Ed.). Minneapolis, MN: University of Minnesota Press.

Bobo Lo, Sydney. (2015). *Russia and the New World Disorder.* Washington, DC: Brookings Institution.

Bogdanov, Alexey. (2017). Preserving Peace among the Great Powers: Russia's Foreign Policy and Normative Changes to the International Order. In Roger E. Kanet (Ed.), *The Russian Challenge to the European Security Environment* (pp. 37–60). Houndmills, United Kingdom: Palgrave.

Bolton, John. (2020). *The Room Where It Happened.* New York: Simon and Schuster.

Brady, Rose. (1999). *Kapitalizm: Russia's Struggle to Free Its Economy.* New Haven, CT: Yale University Press.

Brandt, Loren, & Rawski, Thomas G. (Eds.) (2008a). *China's Great Economic Transformation.* Cambridge: Cambridge University Press.

Brandt, Loren, & Rawski, Thomas G. (2008b). China's Great Economic Transformation. In Loren Brandt & Thomas G. Rawski (Eds.), *China's Great Economic Transformation* (pp. 1–26). Cambridge: Cambridge University Press.

Branstetter, Lee, & Lardy, Nicholas R. (2008). China's Embrace of Globalization. In Loren Brandt & Thomas G. Rawski (Eds.), *China's Great Economic Transformation* (pp. 633–682). Cambridge: Cambridge University Press.

Brautigam, Deborah. (2009). *The Dragon's Grip: The Real Story of China and Africa.* New Haven, CT: Yale University Press.

Brown, Kerry. (2017a). *China's World.* London: I.B. Tauris.

Brown, Kerry. (2017b). *GEO, China: The Rise of Xi Jinping.* London: I.B. Tauris.

Brown, Michael, et al. (Eds.) (1995). *Debating the Democratic Peace.* Cambridge: MIT Press.

Bruusgaard, Kristin Ven. (2016). Russian Strategic Deterrence. *Survival, 58*(4), 7–26.

Bull, Hedley. (1977). *The Anarchical Society: A Study of Order in World Politics.* London: Macmillan.

Burke, Edmund. (2019). *Reflections on the French Revolution.* Monee, IL: Kakapo Books.

Burke, Edmund J., et al. (2019). *China's Military Activities in the East China Sea: Implications for Japan's Air Self-Defense Force.* Santa Monica, CA: RAND Corporation.

Campbell, Kurt M., & Ratner, Ely. (2018). The China Reckoning: How Beijng Defied American Expectations. *Foreign Affairs, 97*(2), 60–70.

Cambell, Kurt M., & Sullivan, Jake. (2019). Competition with Catastrophe: How America Can Both Challenge and Coexist with China. *Foreign Affairs, 98*(5), 96.

Cannady, Sean, & Kubicek, Paul. (2013). Nationalism and Legitimation for Authoritarianism: A Comparison of Nicholas I and Vladimir Putin. *Journal of Eurasian Studies, 5*(1), 1–9.

Capaccio, George. (2018). *The Marshall Plan and the Truman Doctrine.* New York: Cavendish Square Publishing.

Carrai, Naria Adele. (2018). It Is Not the End of History: The Financing Institutions of the Belt and Road Initiative and the Bretton Woods System. In Julien Chaisse

& Jedrzej Gorski (Eds.), *The Belt and Road Initiative: Law, Economics, and Politics* (pp. 107–145). Leiden: Brill Nijhoff.

Carrère d'Encausse, Hélène. (1993). *The End of the Soviet Empire: The Triumph of the Nations* (Franklin Philip, Trans.). New York: BasicBooks.

Cassidy, John. (2009). *How Markets Fail: The Logic of Economic Calamities.* New York: Farrar, Strauss, and Giroux.

Cerny, Philip G. (2010). *Rethinking World Politics: A Theory of Transnational Pluralism.* Oxford: Oxford University Press.

Chabris, Christopher F., & Simons, Daniel J. (2010). *The Invisible Gorrilla: and Other Ways Our Intuitions Deceive Us.* New York: Crown.

Chaisse, Julien, & Gorski, Jedrzej (Eds.) (2018). *The Belt and Road Initiative: Law, Economics, and Politics.* Leiden: Brill Nijhoff.

Chajda, Tymoteusz. (2018). BRI Initiative: A New Model of Development Aid? In Julien Chaisse & Jedrzej Gorski (Eds.), *The Belt and Road Initiative: Law, Economics, and Politics* (pp. 416–424). Leiden: Brill Nijhoff.

Charap, Samuel, Drennan, John, & Noel, Pierre. (2017). Russia and China: A New Model of Great-Power Relations. *Survival, 59*(1), 25–42.

Chohan, Usman W. (2018). The Political Economy of OBOR and the Global Economic Center of Gravity. In Julien Chaisse & Jedrzej Gorski (Eds.), *The Belt and Road Initiative: Law, Economics, and Politics* (pp. 59–82). Leiden: Brill Nijhoff.

Coalson, Robert. (2013). *Russian Military Doctrine: Article by General Valery Gerasimov.*

Cohen, Stephen F. (2000). *Failed Crusade: America and the Tragedy of Post-Communist Russia.* New York: W. W. Norton.

Cohen, Stephen F. (2009). *Soviet Fates and Lost Alternatives: From Stalinism to the New Cold War.* New York: Columbia University Press.

Coicaud, Jean-Marc. (2002). *Legitimacy and Politics.* Cambridge: Cambridge University Press.

Cole, Bernard D. (2016). *China's Quest for Great Power: Ships, Oil, and Foreign Policy.* Annapolis, MD: Naval Institute Press.

Colley, Linda. (2021). *The Gun, the Ship, and the Pen: Warfare, Constitutions, and the Making of the Modern World.* New York: Liveright.

Colton, Timothy J., & McFaul, Michael. (2003). *Popular Choice and Managed Democracy: The Russian Elections of 1999 and 2000.* Washington, DC: Brookings Institution.

Cooper, Richard. (1968). *The Economics of Interdependence: Economic Policy in the Atlantic Community.* New York: McGraw-Hill.

Copper, John F. (2016). *China's Foreign Aid and Investment Diplomacy* (Vol. 1). New York: Palgrave.

Cordesman, Anthony H. (September 2018). China and the New Nuclear Arms Race: The Forces Driving the Creation of Nuclear Delivery Systems, Nuclear Weapons, and Strategy. Washington, DC: Strategic and International Studies.

Cordesman, Anthony H. (2019). *China's New 2019 Defense White Paper: An Open Strategic Challenge to the United States But One Which Does Not Have to Lead to Conflict.* Washington, DC: Center for Strategic and International Studies.

Corwin, Edward S. (1916). *French Policy and the American Alliance of 1778.* Princeton, NJ: Princeton University Press.

Craig, Paul, Jungerman, John, & Krass, Allan. (1986). *Nuclear Arms Race: Technology and Society.* New York: McGraw-Hill.

Cunningham, Fiona S., & Fravel, M. Taylor. (2015). Assuring Assured Retaliation. *International Security, 40*(2), 7–50.

Cunningham, Fiona S., & Fravel, M. Taylor. (2019). Dangerous Confidence? Chinese Views on Nuclear Escalation. *International Security, 44*(2), 61–109.

Daflon, Denia. (2009). Youth in Russia: Portrait of a Generation in Transition. Biel/Binne, Switzerland: Swiss Academy of Development.

Dahl, Robert A. (1971). *Poliarchy, Participation, and Opposition.* New Haven, CT: Yale University Press.

Dahl, Robert A. (1989). *Democracy and Its Critics.* New Haven, CT: Yale University Press.

Davis, Steven J., & Haltiwanger, John. (2014). *Labor Market Fluidity and Economic Performance.* Cambridge, MA: National Bureau of Economic Research.

Dawisha, Karen. (2015). *Putin's Kleptocracy.* New York: Simon & Schuster.

De Tocqueville, Alexis. (1945). *Democracy in America* (Henry Reeve & Francis Bowen, Trans.). New York: Knopf.

Defense Intelligence Agency. (2017). *Russia Military Power: Building a Military to Support Great Power Aspirations.* Washington, DC.

Defense Intelligence Agency. (2019). *China Military Power 2019: Modernizing A Force to Fight and Win.* Washington, DC.

Demick, Barbara. (2020). Uncovering the Cultural Revolution's Awful Truths. *Atlantic* (January/February), 1–23.

Deng, Xiaoping. (1985). *Building Socialism with Chinese Characteristics* Beijing: Foreign Languages Press.

Deng, Yong, & Moore, Thomas G. (2004). China Views Globalization: Toward A New Great-Power Politics? *Washington Quarterly, 27*(3), 117–136.

Denoon, David B. H. (Ed.) (2017). *China, the United States, and the Future of Southeast Asia.* New York: New York University Press.

Department of Defense. (1971). *Pentagon Papers: The Defense Department History of United States Decisionmaking on Vietnam.* Boston, MA: Beacon Press.

Department of Defense. (2019). *Annual Report to Congress: Military and Security Developments Involving the Peoples Republic of China 2019.* Washington, DC.

Derlugguian, Georgi M. (2005). *Bourdieu's Secret Admirer in the Caucasus: A World-System Biography.* Chicago: University of Chicago Press.

Diamond, Jared. (1992). *The Third Chimpanzee: The Evolution and Future of the Human Animal.* New York: HarperPerennial.

Diamond, Jared. (1997). *Guns, Germs, and Steel: The Fates of Human Societies.* New York: W. W. Norton.

Diamond, Jared. (2005). *Collapse: How Societies Choose to Fail or Succeed.* New York: Viking.

Diamond, Larry (2019). *Ill Winds: Saving Democracy from Russian Rage, Chinese Ambition, and American Complacency.* New York: Penguin.

Dickson, Bruce J. (2016). *The Dictator's Dilemma.* Oxford: Oxford University Press.

Dickson, Bruce J. (2021). *The Party and the People: Chinese Politics in the 21st Century.* Princeton, NJ: Princeton University Press.

Dikotter, Frank. (2016). *The Cultural Revolution: A People's History, 1962–1976.* New York: Bloomsbury Publishing.

Dinan, Desmond. (2010). *Ever Closer Union: An Introduction to European Integration* (4th ed.). Boulder: Lynne Rienner.

Diokno, Maria Serena I., Hsiao, Hsin-Juang Michael, & Yang, Alan H. (Eds.) (2019). *China's Footprints in Southeast Asia.* Singapore: NUS Press.

Dittmer, Lowell. (2018). *China's Asia: Triangular Dynamics Since the Cold War.* New York: Rowman & Littlefield.

Dittmer, Lowell & Bing, Ngeow Chow (Eds.) (2017). *Southeast Asia and China: A Contest in Mutual Socialization.* New Jersey: World Scientific.

Dutton, Peter. (2011). Three Disputes and Three Objectives: China and the South China Sea. *Naval War College Review, 64*(4), 42–67.

Duval, Antoine. (2017). The Russian Doping Scandal at the Court of Arbitration for Sport: Lessons for the World Anti-Doping System. *International Law Sport Journal, 16*(3–4), 177–197.

Ebtov, Revold M., & Lugovoy, Oleg V. (2013). Growth Trends in Russia after 1998. In Michael Alexeev & Shlomo Weber (Eds.), *Oxford Handbook of the Russian Economy* (pp. 132–160). Oxford: Oxford University Press.

Economy, Elizabeth C. (2018a). *The Third Revolution: Xi Jinping and the New Chinese State*. Oxford: Oxford University Press.

Economy, Elizabeth C. (2018b). Author's Response: The Third Revolution Is Real. *Asia Policy, 25*(4), 162–165.

Economy, Elizabeth C. (2019a). 30 Years After Tiananmen: Dissent Is Not Dead. *Journal of Democracy, 30*(2), 57–63.

Economy, Elizabeth C. (December 11, 2019b). *Yes, Virginia, China Is Exporting Its Model*. New York: New York Council on Foreign Relations.

Elliott, John E. (1981). *Marx and Engels on Economics, Politics, and Society*. Santa Monica: Goodyear.

Elsby, Michael W. L., Hobbijn, Bart, & Sahin, Aysegul. (2013). *The Decline of the U.S. Labor Share*. Washington, DC: Brookings Institution.

Elster, Jon. (1985). *Making Sense of Marx*. Cambridge: Cambridge University Press.

Erickson, Andrew S. (Ed.) (2016). *Chinese Naval Shipbuilding: An Ambitious and Uncertain Course*. Annapolis, MD: Naval Institute Press.

Ericson, Richard E. (2013). Command Economy and Its Legacy. In Michael Alexeev & Shlomo Weber (Eds.), *Oxford Handbook of the Russian Economy* (pp. 51–85). Oxford: Oxford University Press.

Facon, Isabelle. (2017). *Russia's National Security Strategy and Military Doctrine and Their Implications for the EU*. Brussels, Belgium: EU, Directorate-General for External Policies.

Fanell, James E. (2018). China's Maritime Sovereignty Campaign: Scarborough Shoal, the "New Spratly Islands," and Beyond. In Anders Corr (Ed.), *Great Powers, Grand Strategies* (pp. 106–120). Annapolis, MD: Naval Institute Press.

Farzana, Afridi, Xin Li, Sherry, & Ren, Yufei. (2015). Social Identity and Inequality: the Impact of China's Hukou System. *Journal of Public Economics, 123*(March), 17–29.

Federalist. (n.d.). Garden City: Modern Library.

Fewsmith, Joseph. (2016). The Challenge of Stability and Legitimacy. In Robert S. Ross & Jo Inge Bakkevold (Eds.), *China in the Era of Xi Jinping* (pp. 82–116). Washington, DC: Georgetown University Press.

Finchelstein, Federico. (2019). *From Fascism to Populism in History*. Oakland, CA: University of California Press.

Finer, Samuel E. (1999). *The History of Government*. Oxford: Oxford University Press.

Fish, Steven M. (2001). When More is Less: Superexecutive Power and Political Underdevelopment in Russia. In George W. Breslauer & Victoria E. Bonnell (Eds.), *Russia in the New Century: Stability or Disorder*. Boulder, CO: Westview Press.

Fish, Steven M. (2005). *Democracy Derailed in Russia*. Cambridge: Cambridge University Press.

Fishman, Brian H. (2016). *The Master Plan: ISIS, al-Qaeda, and the Jihadi Strategy for Final Victory*. New Haven, CT: Yale University Press.

FitzGerald, Frances. (1973). *Fire in the Lake: The Vietnamese and Americans in Vietnam*. New York: Simon and Schuster.

Freedman, Lawrence. (1989). *The Evolution of Nuclear Strategy* (2nd ed.). London: Macmillan.

French, Howard W. (2014). *China's Second Continent: How a Million Migrants Are Building a New Empire in Africa.* New York: Knopf.

Friedman, Thomas L. (2006). *The World Is Flat: A Brief History of the Twenty-First Century.* New York: Farrar, Straus, and Giroux.

Fritzsche, Peter. (2020). *Hitler's First Hundred Days: When Germans Embraced the Third Reich.* New York: Basic Books.

Fukuyama, Francis. (1992). *The End of History and the Last Man.* New York: Free Press.

Fukuyama, Francis. (2011). *From Prehumantimes to the French Revolution.* New York: Farrar, Straus, Giroux.

Gaddy, Clifford G., & Ickes, Barry W. (2013). Russia's Dependence on Resources. In Michael Alexeev & Shlomo Weber (Eds.), *Oxford Handbook of the Russian Economy* (pp. 309–340). Oxford: Oxford University Press.

Galeiotti, Mark. (2015). "Hybrid War" and "Little Green Men": How It Works and How It Doesn't. In Agnieszka Pikulicka-Wilczewska & Richard Sakwa (Eds.), *Ukraine and Russia: People, Politics, Propaganda, and Perspectives* (pp. 156–164). Bristol, UK: E-International Relations.

Gel'man, Vladimir. (2010). Regime Changes Despite Legitimacy Crises: Exit, Voice, and Loyalty in Post-Communist Russia. *Journal of Eurasian Studies, 1*(1), 54–63.

Gel'man, Vladimir. (2012). Subversive Institutions, Informal Governance, and Contemporary Russia Politics. *Communist and Post-Communist Studies, 45*(3–4), 295–303.

Gerth, H., & Mills, C. Wright (Eds.) (1958). *From Max Weber: Essays in Sociology.* New York: Oxford University Press.

Gessen, Masha. (2016). Alexey Navalny's Very Strange Form of Freedom. *The New Yorker* (January 15, 2016).

Ghemawat, Pankaj. (2016). *The Laws of Globalization and Business Applications.* Cambridge: Cambridge University Press.

Ghiasy, Richard. (2017). *China's Belt and Road Initiative: Security Implications.* Stockholm: SIPRI.

Ghiasy, Richard, Su, Fei, & Saalman, Lora. (2018). *The 21st Century Maritime Silk Road: Security Implications.* Stockholm: SIPRI.

Giddens, Anthony. (1984). *The Constitution of Society.* Berkeley: University of California Press.

Giddens, Anthony. (2002). *Runaway World: How Globalization Is Shaping Our Lives.* London: Profile Books.

Glaser, Bonnie S., & Medeiros, Evan. (2007). The Changing Ecology of Foreign Policy-Making in China. *China Quarterly, 190,* 291–310.

Glaser, Bonnie S., & Murphy, Melissa E. (2009). Soft Power with Chinese Characteristics. In Carola McGiffert (Ed.), *Chinese Soft Power and Its Implications for the United States: Competition and Cooperation in the Developing World* (pp. 10–26). Washington, DC: Center for Strategic and International Studies.

Goldin, Claudia, & Katz, Lawrence F. (2010). *The Race between Education and Technology.* Cambridge, MA: Harvard University Press.

Golding, William. (1954). *Lord of the Flies.* London: Faber and Faber.

Gong, Ting. (1997). Forms and Characteristics of China's Corruption in the 1990s: Change with Continuity. *Communist and Post-Communist Studies, 30*(3), 277–288.

Gong, Ting. (2002). Dangerous Collusion: Corruption As a Collective Venture in Contemporary China. *Communist and Post-Communist Studies, 35*(1), 85–103.

Gong, Ting. (2006). Corruption and Local Government: The Double Identity of Chinese Local Government in Market Reform. *Pacific Review, 19*(1), 85–192.

Gong, Xue. (2018). The Role of Chinese Corporate Players in China's South China Sea Policy. *Contemporary Southeast Asia, 40*(2), 301–326.

Gordon, David F., Tong, Haoyu, & Anderson, Tabatha. (2020). *Beyond the Myths — Towards a Realistic Assessment of China's Belt and Road Initiative: The Development-Finance Dimension.* London: International Institute of Strategic Studies.

Gorski, Jedrzej. (2018). Central and Eastern Europe, Group 16 + 1 and One Belt and One Road: The Case of 2016 Sino-Polish Comprehensive Strategic Partnership. In Julien Chaisse & Jedrzej Gorski (Eds.), *The Belt and Road Initiative: Law, Economics, and Politics* (pp. 557–606). Leiden: Brill Nijhoff.

Gowing, Margaret. (1974). *Independence and Deterrence: Britain and Atomic Energy* (Vol. 1 & 2). London: Macmillan.

Gunther, Frank. (2017). Corruption, Costs, and Family: Chinese Capital Flight, 1984–2014. *China Economic Review, 43*(April), 105–117.

Halberstam, David. (1972). *The Best and the Brightest.* New York: Random House.

Halberstam, David. (1989). *The Reckoning.* New York: Morrow.

Hannum, Emily, et al. (2008). Education in the Reform Era. In Loren Brandt & Thomas G. Rawski (Eds.), *China's Great Economic Transformation* (pp. 215–249). Cambridge: Cambridge University Press.

Hanson, Philip. (2014). Russia As a Developing Economy. In Robert E. Looney (Ed.), *Handbook of Emerging Economies* (pp. 46–60). New York: Routledge.

Hanson, Stephen E. (2010). *Post-Imperial Democracies.* Cambridge: Cambridge University Press.

Hanson, Stephen E. (2011). Plebiscitarian Patrimonialism in Putin's Russia: Legitimating Authoritarianism in a Postideological Era. *American Academy of Political and Social Science, 636*(July), 32–48.

Haskel, Jonathan, et al. (2012). Globalization and U.S. Wages: Modifying Classical Theory to Explain Recent Facts. *Journal of Economic Perspectives, 26*(2), 119–140.

Hassner, Pierre. (1997). Rousseau and the Theory and Practice of International Relations. In Orwin Clifford & Nathan Tarvoc (Eds.), *The Legacy of Rousseau* (pp. 200–219). Chicago: University of Chicago Press.

Havel, Vaclav. (1978). *The Power of the Powerless* (Paul Wilson, Trans.). New York: Vintage.

Hayek, Friedrich von. (1988). *The Fatal Conceit: The Errors of Socialism.* London: Routledge.

Hayton, Bill. (2014). *The South China Sea: The Struggle for Power in Asia.* New Haven, CT: Yale University Press.

He, Qinglian. (2003). A Volcanic Stability. *Journal of Democracy, 14*(1), 66–72.

Heath, Timothy R., Gunness, Kristen, & Cooper, Cortez A. (2016). *The PLA and China's Rejuvenation: National Security and Military Strategies, Deterrence Concepts, and Combat Capabilities.* Santa Monica, CA: National Defense Research Institute.

Heberle, Rudolf. (1945). *From Democracy to Nazism: A Regional Case Study on Political Parties in Germany.* Baton Rouge: Louisiana State University Press.

Heginbotham, Eric, et al. (2015). *U.S.-China Military Scorecard: Forces, Geography, and the Evolving Balance of Power, 1996–2017.* Santa Monica: Rand Corporation. Political Trust, and Governing Crisis. Chicago: University of Chicago Press.

Hibbard, Scott. (2010). *Religious Politics and Secular States.* New York: Columbia University Press.

Hill, Fiona, & Gaddy, Clifford. (2015). *Mr. Putin: Operative in the Kremlin.* Washington, DC: Brookings Institution.

Hirschman, Albert O. (1970). *Exit, Voice, and Loyalty*. Cambridge, MA: Harvard University Press.

Hobbes, Thomas. (1997). *Leviathan*. New York: W. W. Norton.

Hobsbawn, Eric J. (1989). *The Age of Empire 1875–1914*. New York: Vintage Books.

Hochschild, Adam. (1998). *King Leopold's Ghost*. New York: Houghton Mifflin.

Hoffman, David E. (2002). *The Oligarchs: Wealth and Power in the New Russia*. New York: Public Affairs.

Hoffmann, Stanley, & Fidler, David (Eds.) (1991). *Rousseau on International Relations*. Oxford: Oxford University Press.

Holmes, Leslie. (2008). Corruption and Organized Crime in Putin's Russia. *Europe-Asia*, *40*(6), 1017–1037.

Holmes, Leslie. (2010). Legitimation and Legitimacy in Russia Revisited. In Stephen Fontescue (Ed.), *Russian Politics from Lenin to Putin* (pp. 101–126). Houndmills: Palgrave.

Hong, Nong. (December 2016). The South China Sea Arbitral Tribunal Award: Political and Legal Implications for China. *Contemporary Southeast Asia*, *38*(3), 356–361.

Hopkins, Jonathan. (2020). *Anti-Systems Politics: The Crisis of Market Liberalism in Rich Democracies*. Oxford: Oxford University Press.

Horsley, Jamie. (2018). What's So Controversial about China's New Anti-Corruption Body? *The Diplomat*.

Horwitz, Morton J. (1966). Tocqueville and the Tyranny of the Majority. *Review of Politics*, *28*(3), 293–307.

Howell, William G., & Moe, Terry M. (2020). *Presidents, Populism*. Chicago: University of Chicago Press.

Hsu, Wilbur. (2012). *Survival through Adaptation: The Chinese Red Army and the Extermination Campaigns, 1927–1936 (e book)* Fort Leavenworth, Kansas: Combat Studies Institute Press.

Hua, Gao. (2019). *How the Red Sun Rose: The Origin and Development of the Yan'an Rectification Movement: 1930–45* (Stacy Mosher & Guo Jian, Trans.). Hong Kong: Chinese University Press.

Huang, Yasheng. (2008). *Capitalism with Chinese Characteristics: Entrepreneurship and the State*. Cambridge: Cambridge University Press.

Huang, Yasheng. (2014). *What's Next for the Chinese Economy?* Cambridge: MIT Sloan Management Review.

Huntington, Samuel P., Jr. (1991). *The Third Wave: Democratization in the Late Twentieth Century*. Norman, OK: Oklahoma University Press.

Huq, Aziz, & Ginsburg, Tom. (2018). How to Lose a Constitutional Democracy. *UCLA Law Review*, *78*, 80–169.

Hurley, John, et al. (2016). Examining the Debt Implications of the Belt and Road Initiative from a Policy Perspective. Washington, DC: Center for Global Development.

Ikenberry, G. John. (2011). *Liberal Leviathan: The Origins Crisis, and Transformation of the American World Order*. Princeton, NJ: Princeton University Press.

Ikenberry, G. John. (2020). *A World Safe for Democracy: Liberal Internationalism and the Crises of Global Order*. New Haven, CT: Yale University Press.

Inglehart, Ronald. (2005). *Modernization, Cultural Change, and Democracy: The Human Development Sequence*. Cambridge: Cambridge University Press.

Inglehart, Ronald. (2018). *Cultural Evolution: People's Motivations Are Changing, and Reshaping the World*. Cambridge: Cambridge University Press.

International Monetary Fund. (2009). *Global Financial Stability Report*. Washington, DC: International Monetary Fund.

International Transparency. (2017). Corruption Perception Index 2017: Global. Berlin Germany: International Transparency.

Jackson, Julian. (2018). *De Gaulle*. Cambridge: Belknap Press.

Jacobson, Linda. (2016). Domestic Actors and the Fragmentation of China's Foreign Policy. In Robert S. Ross & Jo Inge Bakkevold (Eds.), *China in the Era of Xi Jinping* (pp. 137–164). Washington, DC: Georgetown University Press.

Jentleson, Adam. (2021). *Kill Switch: The Rise of the Modern Senate*. New York: W. W. Norton.

Jie, Chen. (2013). *A Middle Class without Democracy: Economic Growth and the Prospects for Democratization in China*. New York: Oxford University Press.

Jisheng, Yang. (2013). *Tombstone: The Great Chinese Famine, 1958–1962*. New York: Farrar, Straus, and Giroux.

Jisheng, Yang. (2020). *The World Turned Upside Down: A History of the Chinese Cultural Revolution* (Stacy & Guo Jian Mosher, Trans.). New York: Farrar, Straus, and Giroux.

Johnston, Alastair Ian. (2016). Is Chinese Nationalism Rising? *International Security, 41*(3 Winter), 6–43.

Jones, Bruce D., & Talbott, Strobe (Eds.) (2017). *The Marshall Plan and the Shaping of American Strategy*. Washington, DC: Brookings Institution.

Jones, Eric Lionel. (1987). *The European Miracle: Environments, Economies, and Geopolitics in the History of Europe and Asia* (2nd ed.). New York: Cambridge University Press.

Jones, Eric Lionel. (1988). *Recurring Growth*. Oxford: Oxford University Press.

Jones, Robert P. (2017). *The End of White Christian America*. New York: Simon and Schuster.

Jones, Robert P. (2020). *White too Long: The Legacy of White Supremacy in American Christianity*. New York: Simon and Schuster.

Juergensmeyer, Mark. (2003). *Terror in the Mind of God: The Global Rise of Religious Violence*. Berkeley, CA: University of California Press.

Juergensmeyer, Mark (Ed.) (2005). *Religion in Global Civil Society*. Oxford: Oxford University Press.

Juergensmeyer, Mark. (2008). *Global Rebellion: Religious Challenges to the Secular State, from Christian Militias to Al Qaeda*. Berkeley, CA: University of California Press.

Kagan, Robert. (2003). *Of Paradise and Power: America and Europe in the New World Order*. New York: Knopf.

Kahneman, Daniel. (2011). *Thinking Fast and Slow*. New York: Farrar, Straus, and Giroux.

Kampen, Thomas. (2000). *Mao Zedong , Zhou Enlai and the Evolution of the Chinese Communist Leadership (e-Book)*. Denmark: NIAS Publisher.

Kanet, Roger E. (2018a). Russia and Global Governance. *International Politics, 55*(2), 177–188.

Kanet, Roger E. (2018b). Russia and Global Governance: The Challenge to the Existing Liberal Order. *International Politics, 55*(2), 177–188.

Kanet, Roger E. (Ed.) (2019). *The Routledge Handbook of Russian Security*. London: Routledge.

Kant, Immanuel. (1991). *Kant: Political Writings* (H. D. Nisbet, Trans. 2nd ed.). Cambridge: Cambridge University Press.

Kaplan, Fred. (1983). *The Wizards of Armageddon*. New York: Simon and Schuster.

Kaplan, Fred. (2020). *The Bomb: Presidents, Generals, and the Secret History of Nuclear War*. New York: Simon and Schuster.

Kappeler, Andreas. (2014). Ukraine and Russia: Legacies of the Imperial Past and Competing Memories. *Journal of Eurasian Studies, 5*(2 July 2014), 107–115.

Karabarbounis, Loukas, & Neiman, Brent. (2014). The Global Decline of the Labor Share. *Quarterly Journal of Economics*, *129*(1), 61–103.

Karagiannis, Emmanuel. (2014). The Russian Interventions in South Ossetia and Crimea Compared: Military Performance, Legitimacy, and Goals. *Contemporary Security Policy*, *35*(3), 400–420.

Kashmeri, Sarwar A. (2019). *China's Grand Strategy: Weaving a New Silk Road to Global Primacy*. Santa Barbara, CA: Praeger.

Kennan, George ('X'). (1947). The Sources of Soviet Conduct. *Foreign Affairs*, *25*(4), 466–482.

Keohane, Robert O. (Ed.) (1986). *Neorealism and Its Critics*. New York: Columbia University Press.

Keohane, Robert O., & Joseph S. Nye. (1989). *Power and Interdependence* (2nd ed.). Glenview: Scott, Foresman.

Key, V. O. (1949). *Southern Politics in State and Nation*. New York: Knopf.

Keylor, William R. (2001). *The Twentieth-Century World: An International History* (4th ed.). New York: Oxford University Press.

Khanna, Parag. (2016). *Connectography: Mapping the Future of Global Civilization*. New York: Random House.

Kirby, E. Stuart. (1954). *Introduction to the Economic History of China*. London: Allen & Irwin.

Klein, Ezra. (2020). *Why We're Polarized*. New York: Simon and Schuster.

Kolodziej, Edward A. (1966). *Congress and the Uncommon Defense*. Columbus, OH: Ohio State University Press.

Kolodziej, Edward A. (1970). France and the Atlantic Alliance. *Polity*, *II*(2), 241–266.

Kolodziej, Edward A. (1972). France Ensnared: French Strategic Policy and Bloc Politics after 1968. *Orbis*, *XV*(4), 1085–1108.

Kolodziej, Edward A. (1974). *French International Policy under De Gaulle and Pompidou: The Politics of Grandeur*. Ithaca: Cornell University Press.

Kolodziej, Edward A. (1987). *Making and Marketing of Arms: The French Experience and Its Implications for the International System*. Princeton, NJ: Princeton University Press.

Kolodziej, Edward A. (Ed.) (2003). *A Force Profonde: The Power, Promise, of Human Rights*. Philadelphia, PA: University of Pennsylvania Press.

Kolodziej, Edward A. (2005). *Security and International Relations*. Cambridge: Cambridge University Press.

Kolodziej, Edward A. (2016). *Governing Globalization: Challenges for Democracy and the Global Society*. New York: Rowman and Littlefield.

Kolodziej, Edward A., & Kanet, Roger E. (Eds.) (2008). *From Superpower to Besieged Global Power: Restoring World Order after the Failure of the Bush Doctrine*. Athens, GA: University of Georgia Press.

Kornai, János. (1992). *The Socialist System: The Political Economy of Communism*. Princeton, NJ: Princeton University Press.

Kotkin, Stephen. (2016). Russia's Perpetual Geopolitics: Putin Returns to the Historical Pattern. *Foreign Affairs*, *95*(3), 2–9.

Kristensen, Hans M., & Korda, Matt. (2019). Chinese Nuclear Forces, 2019. *Bulletin of the Atomic Scientists*, *75*(4), 171–178.

Kristensen, Hans M., & Norris, Robert S. (June 2019). *Status of World Nuclear Force*. Washington, DC: Federation of American Scientists.

Kroeber, Arthur R. (2016). *China's Economy: What Everyone Needs to Know*. Oxford: Oxford University Press.

Kryukov, Valery, & Moe, Arild. (2013). The Russian Oil Sector. In Michael Alexeev & Shlomo Weber (Eds.), *Oxford Handbook of the Russian Economy* (pp. 341–362). Oxford: Oxford University Press.

Kryukov, Valery, & Moe, Arild. (2013). The Russian Natural Gas Sector. In Michael Alexeev & Shlomo Weber (Eds.), *Oxford Handbook of the Russian Economy* (pp. 363–382). Oxford: Oxford University Press.

Kurlantzick, Joshua. (2007). *Charm Offensive—How China's Soft Power Is Transforming the World*. New Haven, CT: Yale University Press.

Kurlantzick, Joshua. (2013). *Democracy in Retreat: The Revolt of the Middle Class and the Worldwide Decline of Representative Government*. New Haven, CT: Yale University Press.

Laquer, Walter. (2015). *Putinism: Russia and Its Future with the West*. New York: St. Martin's Press.

Lardy, Nicholas R. (2014). *Markets and Mao: The Rise of Private Business in China*. Washington, DC: Peterson Institute for International Economics.

Leandro, Francisco Jose. (2018). The OBOR Global Geopolitical Drive; The Chinese Access Security Strategy. In Julien Chaisse & Jedrzej Gorski (Eds.), *The Belt and Road Initiative: Law, Economics, and Politics* (pp. 83–106). Leiden: Brill Nijhoff.

Lebow, Richard Ned. (1994). The Long Peace, The End of the Cold War, and the Failure of Realism. *International Organization*, *48*(2, Spring), 249–278.

Lebow, Richard Ned. (2009). *A Cultural Theory of International Relations*. Cambridge: Cambridge University Press.

Lebow, Richard Ned, & Thomas Risse-Kappen (Eds.) (1995). *International Relations Theory and the End of the Cold War*. New York: Columbia University Press.

Lee, Ann. (2018). *2017*. Cambridge: Polity.

Lenin, V. (1977). *Imperialism*. New York: International Publishers.

Levin, Dov H. (2016). When the Great Power Gets a Vote: The Effects of Great Power Interventions on Election Results. *International Studies Quarterly*, *60*(2), 189–202.

Levitsky, Steven, & Ziblatt, Daniel. (2018). *How Democracies Die*. New York: Crown.

Lew, Jacob J., & Roughhead, Gary. (2021). *China's Belt and Road*. New York: Council on Foreign Relations.

Lewis, Donald J., & Moise, Diana. (2018). One Belt One Road (OBOR) Roadmaps: The Legal and Policy Frameworks. In Julien Chaisse & Jedrzej Gorski (Eds.), *The Belt and Road Initiative: Law, Economics, and Politics* (pp. 17–58). Leiden: Brill Nijhoff.

Li, Cheng. (2012). The End of the CCP's Resilient Authoritarianism? A Tripartite Assessment of Shifting Power in China. *China Quarterly*, 211(September), 595–623.

Li, Cheng. (2016). *Chinese Politics in the Xi Jinping Era: Reassessing Collective Leadership*. Washington, DC: Brookings Institution.

Lian, Sophia. (2018). *China and Russia; Collaborators and Competitors?* New York: New York Council on Foreign Relations.

Lin, Justin Yifu. (2012). *Demystifying the Chinese Economy*. Cambridge: Cambridge University Press.

Lipman, Maria. (2016). How Putin Silences Dissent: Inside the Kremlin Crackdown. *Foreign Affairs*, 95(May–June), 38–47.

Lippmann, Walter. (1947). *The Cold War*. New York: Harpers.

Loftus, Suzanne, & Kanet, Roger E. (2019). The Russian Challenge to the Liberal World Order. In Roger E. Kanet (Ed.), *Routledge Handbook of Russian Security* (pp. 55–71). London: Routledge.

Lovell, Julia. (2019). *Maoism: A Global History*. New York: Alfred A. Knopf.

Lucas, Edward. (2014). *The New Cold War: Putin's Threat to Russia and the Wests*. New York: Palgrave.

Lukyanov, Fyodor. (2016). Putin's Foreign Policy: The Quest to Restore Russia's Rightful Place. *Foreign Affairs, 95*(3, May–June), 30–37.

Lüthi, Lorenz M. (2016). The Non-Aligned Movement and the Cold War, 1961–1972. *Journal of Cold War Studies, 18*(2, Fall), 98–147.

Lybeck, Johan A. (2011). *A Global History of the Financial Crash of 2007–2010.* Cambridge: Cambridge University Press.

Maçães, Bruno. (2018). *Belt and Road: A Chinese World Order.* London: Hurst & Company.

MacFarquhar, Roderick, & Schoenhals, Michael. (2006). *Mao's Last Revolution.* Cambridge, MA: Harvard University Press.

MacGregor, Richard. (2019). *Xi Jinping: The Backlash, e-Book.* New York: Penguin.

MacLean, Nancy. (2017). *Democracy in Chains: The Deep History of the Radical Right's Stealth Plan for America.* New York: Viking.

Maizland, Lindsay. (2020). *China's Modernizing Military.* New York: Council on Foreign Relations.

Manion, Melanie. (2004). *Corruption by Design: Building Clean Government in Mainland China and Hong Kong.* Cambridge, MA: Harvard University Press.

Mann, James. (2007). *The China Fantasy.* New York: Penguin Books.

Mann, Michael. (1986). *The Sources of Social Power: A History of Power from the Beginning to A.D. 1760* (Vol. 1). Cambridge: Cambridge University Press.

Mann, Michael (Ed.) (1990). *The Rise and Decline of the Nation State.* Oxford: Blackwell.

Mann, Michael. (1993). *The Sources of Social Power: The Rise of Classes and Nation-States, 1760–1914* (Vol. 2). New York: Cambridge University Press.

Mann, Thomas, & Ornstein, Norman. (2012). *It's Even Worse Than It Looks: How the American Constitutional System Collided with the New Politics of Extremism.* New York: Basic Books.

Mao, Tse-Tung. (1967). *Selected Readings from the Works of Mao Tse-Tung.* Peking: Foreign Language Press.

Marx, Karl. (1970). *A Contribution to the Critique of Political Economy* (S. W. Ryazanskaya, Trans.). Moscow: Progress.

Maryanski, Alexandra. (1992). *The Social Cage: Human Nature and the Evolution of Society.* Stanford: Stanford University Press.

McFate, Katherine, et al. (1995). *Poverty, Inequality, and the Future of Social Policy in the New World Order.* New York: Russell Sage.

McGiffert, Carola. (2009). *Chinese Soft Power and Its Implications for the United States.* Washington, DC: Center for Strategic and International Studies.

McGregor, Richard. (2010). *The Party: The Secret World of China's Communist Rulers.* New York: HarperCollins.

McGregor, Richard. (2019). Xi Jinping: *The Backlash, e-Book.* New York: Penguin.

Mearsheimer, John J. (2001). *The Tragedy of Great Power Politics.* New York: W. W. Norton.

Mendras, Marie. (2012). *Russian Politics: The Paradox of the Weak State.* New York: Columbia University Press.

Miller, Tom. (2018). *China's Asian Dream: Empire Building Along the New Silk Road.* London: Zed Book.

Milosz, Czeslaw. (1953). *The Captive Mind.* New York: Knopf.

Mitter, Rana. (2020). *China's Good War: How World War II Is Shaping a New Nationalism.* Cambridge: Belknap Press.

Molero-Simarro, Ricardo. (2017). Inequality in China Revisited: The Effect of Functional Distribution of Income on Urban Top Incomes, The Urban-Rural Gap and the Gini Index, 1978–2015. *China Economic Review, 42*(February), 101–117.

Monaghan, Andrew. (2015–16). The 'War' in Russia's 'Hybrid Warfare'. *Parameters, 45*(3), 65–74.

Morgenthau, Hans J. (1985). *Politics among Nations: The Struggle for Power and Peace* (6th ed.). New York: Alfred A. Knopf.

Mounk, Yasha. (2021). Democracy on the Defense: Turning Back the Authoritarian Tide. *Foreign Affairs, 100*(2), 163–173.

Mueller, Robert S. III. (2019). *The Mueller Report: Final Report of the Special Counsel into Donald Trump, Russia, and Collusion.* Washington, DC: Department of Justice of the United States.

Mukherjeee, Siddhartha (2016). *The Gene: An Intimate History.* New York: Scribner.

Müller, Jan-Werner. (2016). *What Is Populism?* Philadelphia, PA: University of Pennsylvania Press.

Müller, Jan-Werner. (2021). *Democracy Rules.* New York: Farrar, Straus, and Giroux.

Nathan, Andrew J. (2003). Authoritarian Resilience. *Journal of Democracy, 14*(1, January), 6–17.

Nathan, Andrew J. (2016). China's Rise and International Regimes: Does China Seek to Overthrow Global Norms? In Robert S. Ross & Jo Inge Bekkevold (Eds.), *China in the Era of Xi Jinping* (pp. 165–195). Washington, DC: Georgetown University Press.

Naughton, Barry. (2010). China's Distinctive System: Can It Be a Model for Others? *Journal of Contemporary China, 19*(165, June), 437–460.

Naughton, Barry. (2015). The Transformation of the State Sector: SASAC, The Market Economy, and the New National Champions. In Barry Naughton & Kellee S. Tsai (Eds.), *State Capitalism, Institutional Adaptation, and the Chinese Miracle* (pp. 46–74). Cambridge: Cambridge University Press.

Naughton, Barry. (2018). *The Chinese Economy: Adaptation and Growth* (2nd ed.). Cambridge, MA: MIT Press.

Naughton, Barry. (2019). China's International Political Economy — the Changing Economic Context. In Ka Zeng (Ed.), *Handbook on the International Political Economy of China* (pp. 20-41). Cheltenham, UK: Edward Elgar.

Neil, Sheehan. (1988). *A Bright Shining Lie: John Paul Vann and America in Vietnam.* New York: Random House.

Norris, Robert, & Kistensen, Hans M. (2010). Global Nuclear Weapons Inventories 1945–2010. *Bulletin of the Atomic Scientists, 66*(July 1), 77–93.

Novokmet, Filip, Pikkety, Thomas, & Zucman, Gabriel. (2017). *From Soviets to Oligarchs: Inequality and Property in Russia: 1990–2015.* Cambridge, MA: National Bureau of Economic Research.

Nygren, Bertil. (2008). *The Rebuilding of Greater Russia: Putin's Foreign Policy towards the CIS States.* New York: Routledge.

O'Donnell, Guillermo, & Schmitter, Philippe C. (1986). *Transitions from Authoritarian Rule: Tentative Conclusions about Uncertain Democracies.* Baltimore, MD: Johns Hopkins University Press.

OECD. *Growing Unequal? Income Distribution and Poverty in OECD Countries.* Paris: OECD, 2008.

OECD. *Divided We Stand: Why Inequality Keeps Rising.* Paris: OECD, 2011.

OECD. *In It Together: Why Less Inequality Benefits All.* Paris: OECD, 2015.

Oliker, Olga, et al. (2015). *Russian Foreign Policy in Historical and Current Context.* Santa Monica, CA: Rand Corporation.

Oliker, Olga. (2017). Is Putanism a Thing? *Survival, 50*(1, February–March), 7–24.

Osgood, Robert E. (1962). *NATO: The Entangling Alliance.* Chicago: University of Chicago Press.

Osgood, Robert E. (1968). *Alliances and American Foreign Policy.* Baltimore, MD: Johns Hopkins University Press.

Overholt, William H. (2016). China and the Evolution of the World Economy. *China Economic Review, 40*(September), 267–271.

Overholt, William H. (2018). *China's Crisis of Success*. Cambridge: Cambridge University Press.

Pei, Minxin. (2006). *China's Trapped Transition: The Limits of Developmental Autocracy*. Cambridge, MA: Harvard University Press.

Pei, Minxin. (2016). *China's Crony Capitalism*. Cambridge, MA: Harvard University Press.

Pei, Minxin. (2018). China in Xi's "New Era". *Journal of Democracy*, *29*(2), 36–50.

Pei, Minxin. (2020a). China: From Tiananmen to Neo-Stalinism. *Journal of Democracy*, *31*(1, January), 148–157.

Pei, Minxin. (2020b). China's Coming Upheaval: Competition, the Coronavirus, and the Weakness of Xi Jinping. *Foreign Affairs*, *99*(May/June), 82–96.

Piketty, Thomas. (2014). *Capital in the Twenty-First Century* (Arthur Goldhammer, Trans.). Cambridge: Belknap Press.

Piketty, Thomas, Li, Yang, & Zucman, Gabriel. (2017). *Capital Accumulation, Private Property, and Rising Inequality in China, 1978–2015*. Cambridge, MA: National Bureau of Economic Research.

Pikulicka-Wilczewka, Agnieszka, & Sakwa, Richard (Eds.) (2016). *Ukraine and Russia: People, Politics, Propaganda, and Perspectives*. Bristol, England: E-International Relations Publishing.

Pillsbury, Michael. (2015). *The Hundred-Year Marathon: China's Secret Strategy to Replace America as the Global Superpower*. New York: Henry Holt.

Pipes, Richard. (1974). *Russia under the Old Regime*. New York: Scribner.

Pipes, Richard. (1995). *Russia under the Bolshevik Regime*. New York: Vintage Books.

Pippa, Norris, & Inglehart, Ronald. (2019). *Cultural Backlash: Trump, Brexit, and Authoritarian Populism*. Cambridge: Cambridge University Press.

Plato. (2004). *The Laws* (Trevor J. Saunders, Trans.). London: Penguin.

Polanyi, Karl. (1944). *The Great Transformation*. Boston, MA: Beacon Press.

Pomerantsev, Peter. (2014). *Nothing Is True and Everything Is Possible: The Surreal Heart of the New Russia*. New York: Public Affairs.

Przeworski, Adam. (1986). Some Problems in the Transition to Democracy. In Guillermo O'Donnell, Philippe C. Schmitter, & Laurence Whitehead (Eds.), *Transitions from Authoritarian: Comparative Perspectives* (Vol. 3, pp. 47–63). Baltimore, MD: Johns Hopkins University Press.

Przeworski, Adam. (2019). *Crises of Democracy*. Cambridge: Cambridge University Press.

Qiang, Xiao. (2019). The Road to Digital Unfreedom: President Xi's Surveillance. *Journal of Democracy*, *30*(1, January), 53–67.

Reich, Robert B. (2020). *The System: Who Rigged It How We Fix It*. New York: Knopf.

Repnikova, Marie. (2017). *Media Politics in China: Improvising Power under Authoritarianism*. Cambridge: Cambridge University Press.

Reus-Smit, Christian. (2007). International Crises of Legitimacy. *International Politics*, *44*(2–3, March/May), 157–174.

Richters, Katja. (2013). *The Post-Soviet Russian Orthodox Church: Politics, Culture and Greater Russia*. London: Routledge.

Rigby, T. H. (1982). Introduction: Political Legitimacy, Weber and Communist Mono-organisational Systems. In T. H. Rigby & Ferenc Ferer (Eds.), *Political Legitimacy in Communist States* (pp. 1–26). London: Macmillan.

Roberts, Priscilla Mary. (2016). *The Power of Culture: Encounters between China and the United States*. Newcastle upon Tyne: Cambridge Scholars.

Robertson, Charles L. (1997). *International Politics Since World War II: A Short History*. Armonk, NY: M.E. Sharpe.

Rodrik, Dani. (1998). Globalisation, Social Conflict and Economic Growth. *The World Economy*, *21*(4), 143–158.

Rodrik, Dani. (2012). *The Paradox of Globalization: Democracy and the Future of the World Economy*. New York: W.W. Norton.

Rongji, Zhu. (2015). *Zhu Rongji on the Record: The Road to Reform: 1998–2003*. Washington, DC: Brookings Institution.

Rose, Richard, Mishler, William, & Munro, Neil. (2011). *Popular Support for an Undemocratic Regime: The Changing Views of Russians*. Cambridge: Cambridge University Press.

Rose, Richard, & Munro, Neil. (2002). *Elections without Order: Russia's Challenge to Vladimir Putin*. Cambridge: Cambridge University Press.

Rose, Richard, Munro, Neil, & Mishler, William. (2004). Resigned Acceptance of an Incomplete Democracy: Russia's Political Equilibrium. *Post-Soviet Affairs, 20*, 195–218.

Rosefielde, Steven. (2013). Economics of the Military-Industrial Complex. In Michael Alexeev & Shlomo Weber (Eds.), *Oxford Handbook of the Russian Economy* (pp. 453–467). Oxford: Oxford University Press.

Rousseau, Jean-Jacques. (1978). *On the Social Contract* (Judith R. Masters, Trans.). New York: St. Martin's.

Roy, Denny. (2013). *Return of the Dragon: Rising China and Regional Security*. New York: Columbia University Press.

Roy, Nalanda. (2016). *The South China Sea Disputes: Past, Present, and Future*. New York: Lexington Books.

Rozelle, Scott, & Hell, Natalie. (2020). *Invisible China: How the Urban-Rural Divide Threatens China's Rise*. Chicago: University of Chicago Press.

Rucker, Philip, & Leonnig, Carol. (2020). *A Very Stable Genius*. New York: Penguin Press.

Russett, Bruce. (1993). *Grasping the Democratic Peace: Principles for a Post-Cold War World*. Princeton, NJ: Princeton University Press.

Russett, Bruce, & Starr, Harvey. (2000). From Democratic Peace to Kantian Peace: Democracy and Conflict in International Relations. In Manus I. Midlarsky (Ed.), *Handbook of War Studies II* (pp. 93–128). Ann Arbor, MI: University of Michigan Press.

Russian Federation, Ministry of Foreign Affairs. (2013). *Concept of the Foreign Policy of the Russian Federation*. See en.kremlin.ru/supplement/4116

Saez, Emmanuel, & Zucman, Gabriel. (2019). *The Triumph of Injustice: How the Rich Dodge Taxes and How to Make Them Pay*. New York: W. W. Norton.

Saich, Tony. (2015). *Governance and Politics in China*. London: Palgrave.

Saich, Tony. (2021). *From Rebel to Ruler: One Hundred Years of the Chinese Communist Party*. Cambridge: Belknap Press.

Saich, Tony, & Hu, Biliang. (2012). *Chinese Village, Global Market: New Collectives and Rural Development*. New York: Palgrave.

Sandel, Michael J. (2012). *What Money Can't Buy: The Moral Limits of Markets*. New York: Farrar, Straus, and Giroux.

Schell, Orville, & Delury, John. (2013). *Wealth and Power: China's Long March to the Twenty-First Century*. New York: Random House.

Schofield, Clive. (December 2016). A Landmark Decision in the South China Sea: The Scope and Implications of the Arbitral Tribunal's Award. *Contemporary Southeast China, 38*(3), 339–348.

Schroeder, Paul W. (1989). The Nineteenth Century System: Balance of Power or Political Equilibrium? *Review of International Studies, 15*, 135–153.

Schroeder, Paul W. (1992). Did the Vienna System Rest upon a Balance of Power? *American Historical Review, 97*, 683–706.

Schroeder, Paul W. (1994a). *The Transformation of European Politics: 1763–1848*. Oxford: Oxford University Press.

Schroeder, Paul W. (1994b). Historical Reality vs. Neo-Realist Theory. *International Security*, *19*(1, Summer), 108–148.

Schulman, Daniel. (2014). Sons of Wichita. New York: Grand Central.

Schumpeter, Joseph. (1955). *Imperialism*. New York: Meridian.

Sergi, Bruno S. (2018). Putin's and Russian-Led Eurasian Economic Union: A Hybrid Half-Economics and Half-Political "Janus Bifrons". *Journal of Eurasian Studies*, *9*(1, January), 52–60.

Shambaugh, David (Ed.) (2013). *Tangled Titans: The United States and China*. New York: Rowman and Littlefield.

Shambaugh, David. (2016). *China's Future*. Cambridge: Polity.

Shambaugh, Jay, et al. (2017). *Thirteen Facts about Wage Growth*. Washington, DC: Brookings Institution.

Shambough, David. (2013). *China Goes Global*. Oxford: Oxford University Press.

Sheehan, Neil (1988). *A Bright Shining Lie: John Paul Vann and America in Vietnam*. New York: Random House.

Shevtsova, Lilia (2012). Russia under Putin: Titanic Looking for Its Iceberg? *Communist and Post-Communist Studies*, *45*(3–4, September–December), 209–216.

Shi, Li, Sato, Hiroshi, & Sicular,Terry (Eds.) (2013). *Rising Inequality in China: Challenges to a Harmonious Society*. Cambridge: Cambridge University Press.

Shirk, Susan L. (2018). China in Xi's "New Era". *Journal of Democracy*, *29*(2), 21–31.

Shum, Desmond. (2021). *Red Roulette: An Insider's Story of Wealth, Power, Corruption, and Vengeance in Today's China*. New York: Simon and Schuster.

Sides, John, et al. (2018). *Identity Crisis: The 2016 Presidential Election Campaign and the Battle for the Meaning of America*. Princeton, NJ: Princeton University Press.

Sil, Rudra, & Cheng, Chen. (2004). State Legitimacy and the (In)significance of Democracy in Post-Communist Russia. *Europe-Asia*, *56*(3), 347–368.

Singer, Peter. (2002). *One World: The Ethics of Globalization*. New Haven, CT: Yale University Press.

Singer, Peter. (2011). *The Expanding Circle: Ethics, Evolution, and Moral Progress*. Princeton, NJ: Princeton University Press.

Skak, Mette. (2011). Russia's New 'Monroe Doctrine'. In Roger E. Kanet (Ed.), *Russian Foreign Policy in the 21st Century* (pp. 138–150). Houndmills, UK: Palgrave.

Small, Andrew. (2015). *The China-Pakistan-Axis: Asia's New Geopolitics*. Oxford: Oxford University Press.

Smith, Adam. (1937). *An Inquiry in the Nature and Causes of the Wealth of Nations*. New York: Modern Library.

Spitzer, Robert J. (2018). *The Politics of Gun Control*. New York: Routledge.

Staff. (May 2016). *Corruption: Costs and Strategies*. Washington, DC: International Monetary Fund.

Stell, Ben. (2018). *The Marshall Plan: Dawn of the Cold War*. Oxford: Oxford University Press.

Stent, Angela E. (2014). *The Limits of Partnership: U.S.-Russian Relations in the Twenty-First Century*. Princeton, NJ: Princeton University Press.

Stiglitz, Joseph E. (2006). *Making Globalization Work*. New York: W. W. Norton.

Strauss, Leo. (1953). *Natural Right and History*. Chicago: University of Chicago Press.

Strauss, Leo. (1963). *The Political Philosophy of Hobbes: Its Basis and Its Genesis* (Elsa M. Sinclair, Trans.). Chicago: University of Chicago Press.

Strauss, Leo. (1979). *What Is Political Philosophy?* New York: Free Press.

Sun, Irene Yuan. (2017). *The Next Factory of the World: How Chinese Investment Is Reshaping Africa*. Boston, MA: Harvard Business Review Press.

Talbott, Strobe. (1979). *Endgame; The Inside Story of SALT II*. New York: Harper.

Talbott, Strobe. (1984). *Deadly Gambits*. New York: Vintage.

Taleb, Nissim Nicholas. (2007). *The Black Swan: The Impact of the Highly Improbable*. New York: Random House.

Taylor, Brendan. (2018a). *The Four Flashpoints: How Asia Goes to War*. Melbourne: La Trobe University Press.

Taylor, Brendan. (2018b). Bitter Enmity: The East China Sea. In *The Four Flash Points* (pp. 65–96). Melbourne: La Trobe University Press.

Teets, Jessica C. (2014). *Civil Society under Authoritarianism: The China Model*. Washington, DC: Brookings Institution.

Tempest, Richard V. (2013). Yeltsin and Putin: A Study in Comparative Mythopoetics. In Kostas Gouliamos, et al. (Ed.), *Political Marketing: Strategic 'Campaign Culture'*. New York: Routledge.

Tiffert, Glenn. (2019). 30 Years after Tiananmen: Memory in the Era of Xi Jinping. *Journal of Democracy, 30*(2, April), 38–49.

Tönnies, Ferdinand. (1957). *Community and Society* (Charles P. Loomis, Trans.). New York: Harper.

Torre, Carlos de la (Ed.) (2019). *Routledge Handbook of Global Populism*. New York: Routledge.

Trenin, Dmitri. (2016). The Revival of the Russian Military. *Foreign Affairs, 95*(May–June 2016), 23–29.

Trump, Mary L. (2020). *Too Much and Never Enough: How My Family Created the World's Most Dangerous Man*. New York: Simon and Schuster.

Urbinati, Nadia. (2013). The Populist Phenomenon. *Raisons Politiques, 51*(3), 17–54.

Urbinati, Nadia. (2014). *Democracy Disfigured: Opinion, Truth, and the People*. Cambridge, MA: Harvard University Press.

Vines, David. (2016). Chinese Leadership of Macroeconomic Policymaking in a Multipolar World. *China Economic Review, 40*(September), 286–296.

Vitug, Marites Danguilan. (2018). *Rock Solid: How the Philippines Won Its Maritime Case against China*. Quezon City: Manila University Press.

Vogel, Ezra F. (2011). *Deng Xiaoping and the Transformation of China*. Cambridge, MA: Harvard University Press.

Wagnsson, Charlotte, et al. (Ed.) (2009). *European Security Governance: The European Union in a Westphalian World*. London: Routledge.

Wallison, Peter, J. (2011). Housing Initiatives and Other Policy Factors. In Jeffrey Friedman (Ed.), *What Caused the Financial Crisis* (pp. 172–182). Philadelphia, PA: Pennsylvania University Press.

Walt, Stephen. (1987). *The Origins of Alliances*. Ithaca: Cornell University Press.

Waltz, Kenneth. (1979). *Theory of International Politics*. Reading: Addison-Wesley.

Waltz, Kenneth N. (1959). *Man, the State and War*. New York: Columbia University Press.

Waltz, Kenneth N. (1964). The Stability of the Bipolar World. *Daedalus, 93*(Summer), 881–909.

Waltz, Kenneth N. (1981). The Spread of Nuclear Weapons: More May Be Better (Adelphi Paper No. 171). London: International Institute for Strategic Studies.

Waltz, Kenneth N. (1986). Reflections on a Theory of International Politics: A Response to My Critics. In Robert O. Keohane (Ed.), *Neorealism and Its Critics* (pp. 322–345). New York: Columbia University Press.

Wang, Fei-Ling. (2004). Reformed Migration Control and New Targeted People: China's Hukou System in the 2000s. *The China Quarterly, 177*(March), 115–132.

Weber, Max. (1958). Politics As a Vocation. In H. H. Gerth & C. Wright Mills (Eds.), *From Max Weber: Essays in Sociology* (pp. 77–128). London: Routledge.

Wedeman, Andrew. (2012). *Double Paradox: Rapid Growth and Rising Corruption in China.* Ithaca: Cornell University Press.

Wendt, Alexander E. (2003). Why a World State Is Inevitable. *European Journal of International Relations, 9*(4), 491–542.

Wessel, David. (2009). *In Fed We Trust.* New York: Crown Business.

Wilkerson, Isabel. (2020). *Caste: The Origins of Our Discontents.* New York: Random House.

Williams, Daniel K. (2010). *The Making of the Christian Right.* Oxford: Oxford University Press.

Wilson, Julius Wilson. (1999). *When Work Disappears: The World of the New Urban Poor.* New York: Random House.

Wohlforth, William. (1994). Realism and the End of the Cold War. *International Security, 19*(Winter), 91–129.

Wohlstetter, Albert. (1959). The Delicate Balance of Terror. *Foreign Affairs, 37*(2), 211–235.

Woodward, Bob. (2018). *Fear.* New York: Simon and Schuster.

Woodward, Bob. (2020). *Rage.* New York: Simon and Schuster.

Woolf, Amy F. (2018). *Russian Compliance with the Intermediate Range Nuclear Forces (INF) Treaty.* Washington, DC: Congressional Research Service.

World Bank. (2002). *Transition the First Ten Years: Analysis and Lessons from Eastern Europe and the Former Soviet Union.* Washington, DC: World Bank.

World Bank. (2013). *China 2030.* Washington, DC: World Bank.

World Bank. (2014). *Urban China.* Washington, DC: World Bank.

Wright, Thomas J. (2017). *All Measures Short of War: The Contest for the 21st Century and the Future of American Power.* New Haven, CT: Yale University Press.

Xi, Jinping. (2014). *The Governance of China.* Beijing: Foreign Languages Press.

Xia, Cai. (2021). The Party That Failed: An Insider Breaks with Beijing. *Foreign Affairs, 100*(1), 78–97.

Yaffe, Joschua. (2016a). Putin's Dragon. *The New Yorker* (February 8–15).

Yaffe, Joschua. (2016b). The Putin of Chechnya's Flair for Instagram. *New Yorker* (February 4).

Yuen, Samson. (2014). Disciplining the Party: Xi Jinping's Anti-Corruption Campaign and Its Limits. *China Perspectives 3*(3), 41–47.

Zakaria, Fareed. (1997). The Rise of Illiberal Democracies *Foreign Affairs, 76*(6), 22–43.

Zakaria, Fareed. (2020). The New China Scare. *Foreign Affairs, 99*(1), 52–69.

Zeng, Ka. (2019). *Handbook on the International Political Economy of China.* Cheltenham, UK: Edward Elgar.

Zhang, Ketian. (2019). Cautious Bully: Reputation, Resolve, and Beijing's Use of Coercion in the South China Sea. *International Security, 44*(1, Summer), 117–159.

Zhao, Suisheng. (1993). Deng Xiaoping's Southern Tour: Elite Politics in Post-Tiananmen China. *Asian Survey, 33*(August), 739–756.

Zuniga, Nieves. (2018). *China: Overview of Corruption and Anti-Corruption.* Berlin: Transparency International Index.

INDEX

246 Index

voter suppression, forms of 63
Voting Rights Act (1965) 63

Wallace, George 61
Waltz, Kenneth N. xvin7, 13n25,
  32–33n40
Wang, Vivian 135n94
Warsaw Pact 19, 29–31
Wealth of Nations (Smith) 6, 9
Weber, Max 12n17, 192, 193, 196
Weber, Shlomo 203n52
WeChat 161
Wedeman, Andrew 124, 134nn56, 66,
  69–70
Western Pacific 32n15
West Germany 19, 24, 26
Westphalian system xi, xii, xvin3, 100,
  163, 169, 178, 208, 214; equilibrium
  and 201n10; liberal democratic solution
  and 14, 15, 39, 40, 65
white supremacy 56–58, 70n94,
  71n115
WHO *see* World Health Organization
Wilkerson, Isabel 70n93
Williams, Daniel K. 71n115
Wilson, William Julius 51
Wilson, Woodrow 16–17, 39
Wilsonian internationalism 67n11
Wisconsin 63
Wohlforth, William 32n40
Wohlstetter, Albert 21
Woodward, Bob 67n19, 71n111
World Bank 121, 127, 188, 213; Control
  of Corruption Index 122
World Health Organization (WHO) 213
World Trade Organization (WTO) 109,
  116, 125, 185, 212
Wright, Thomas J. 101n3
WTO *see* World Trade Organization
  (WTO)

Xi Jinping 42–44, 48, 68n51; anti-
  corruption campaign of 121, 122,
  124–125, 135n78, 152; CCP and 144,
  146; and Deng Xiaoping compared

117; dream, for China 87, 88, 104n60,
  105n66, 119, 140, 145–149, 151–152,
  166n56; on Hong Kong protests
  161; Imperative of Legitimacy and
  158–159, 162, 167n70; Imperative of
  Order and 87, 94, 97, 99, 101nn4, 12;
  Imperative of Welfare and 109, 110,
  115, 126, 134nn68–169; leadership
  of 147, 152–153; on market system
  128–129; personality, as source
  of power 166n47; presentation to
  Conference on Interaction and
  Confidence Building Measures (2014)
  76; presentation to World Economic
  Forum (2017) 108n120, 128, 135n90,
  147; presentation to World Economic
  Forum (2021) 47; quandary of 149–157;
  reforms of 117; revision of Marxism
  145–149; on state-owned enterprises
  (SOEs) 124, 129; *see also* Trump,
  Donald J.
Xin Zhang 105n71
Xu Zhangrun 97, 166n63
Xu Zhiyong 153

Yang Jisheng 132nn1–2
Yanokovich, Victor 174
Yasheng Huang 117, 133n23, 134n49
Yeltsin, Boris 66n2, 191, 195
Yi-Zheng Lian 167n92
Yuen, Samson 134n55
Yuen, Simon 135n78
Yukov 186
Yulin Naval Base (Hainan Island)
  (China) 84

Zakaria, Fareed 102n20
Zhang Zhan 130
Zhao Ziyang 101n11, 151
Zhou Bo 102n22
Zhou Yongkang 122, 152
Zhu Rongji 115–116, 133n26
Ziblatt, Daniel 28, 203n68
Zircon Hypersonic cruise missile 181
Zucman, Gabriel 68nn41, 45, 69n67